"Like a trip to Bi-Rite Market, this book is super help-ful, incredibly informative, fun, and full of great ways to use all the food that's in it. Spend twenty minutes shopping at Bi-Rite Market and you're pretty much guaranteed to leave with a basketful of well-made, great tasting, sustainably produced food, a lot of informative insights about what you bought, recipe ideas for how to serve it, and a big smile. With this book, you'll experience all of that—aside from the actual food—and will likely want to start putting what you've learned about smart, sustainable shopping to work right away at your local market and then later in your kitchen."

— Ari Weinzweig, co-founder of Zingerman's Community of Businesses and author of *Zingerman's Guide to Good Eating*

"If every American heeded the words in this book, we would live in the healthiest, cleanest, and most delicious country in the world."

— Patrick Martins, co-founder of Heritage Foods USA and Heritage Radio Network, founder of Slow Food USA

"*Eat Good Food* is a lot more useful than your typical coffee-table cookbook. It's a teaching tool that's sure to change the way you shop, source, and cook good food."

— Charles Phan, James Beard Award–winning chef-owner of The Slanted Door

BI·RITE MARKET'S
EAT GOOD FOOD

A GROCER'S GUIDE
TO SHOPPING, COOKING, AND
CREATING COMMUNITY THROUGH FOOD

Sam Mogannam and Dabney Gough

Photography by France Ruffenach

TEN SPEED PRESS
BERKELEY

SINCE 1940

BI·RITE

BOUQUETS
$15.99

ROSES

HANDMADE
BAKED GOODS

ORGANIC
GROCER

CONTENTS

CREATING COMMUNITY THROUGH FOOD

TASTINGS

MARCH 31ST.
NUMA SNACKS

APRIL 2ND
ECCO COFFEE

LOCAL
FULL BELLY
RANUNCULU
$10.99

PLACERVILLE, CA.

BUY FRESH
BUY LOCAL
Organically Grown
Vegetable & Herb
Starts
6 pk → $3.99/ea
3.5 in pot → $2.99/ea
Greenhouse Grown Richmond, CA

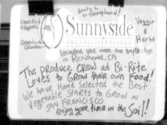

Ready to be transplanted!
Certified
Organic
Greenhouse
Grown
Sunnyside
ORGANIC SEEDLINGS
Veggies
& Herbs
Located just over the Bay Bridge
in Richmond, CA
The Produce Crew at Bi-Rite
Loves to Grow their own Food!
We have hand selected the Best
Vegetable Starts to Grow in
SAN FRANCISCO
Enjoy your time in the Soil!

1

CREATING COMMUNITY THROUGH FOOD

I NEVER WANTED TO BE A GROCERY GUY, but here I am. My dad and uncle had owned San Francisco's Bi-Rite Market since the 1960s, which for me meant a childhood spent stocking shelves, helping out, and generally serving as free labor. Starting at the young age of six, I would go home after school every day, pick up the dinner that my mom had prepared for me and my dad, and head over to the market, where I would work until the store closed at 9 p.m. The grocery business was hardly my idea of fun, and as soon as I left home I didn't look back.

I found my calling in the restaurant world. I went to culinary school, cooked in Switzerland for a year, and continued to cook once I returned to San Francisco. I loved cooking, and I didn't miss the grocery business at all. So in 1997, when my dad gave me the opportunity to take over the family grocery business, I initially said, "No way." At the very least, I was hellbent on doing something—anything—other than running a market.

Still, Dad's offer piqued my interest. Just like him, I had entrepreneurial blood running through my veins, and at the age of twenty-nine was coming off of six years of owning and operating my own restaurant. With his offer, I immediately started visualizing the store's potential as a restaurant space. I fantasized about gutting the store to put in a large kitchen and a spacious dining room. Dad nipped that in the bud, though. He knew how hard I had been working at my restaurant—the long hours, the less-than-healthy lifestyle—and he denied me flat out. "You'll never have a family if you stay in that business," he warned. (Like many fathers

of childbearing-age adults, he was pushing hard for grandchildren. Which he eventually got.)

So no restaurant. I still refused to do a grocery store, so we began to think about other ways to use the space. We entertained all kinds of ideas; someone even suggested to Dad that we open a pet food store, so we kicked that around for about a week. After much debate and no ideas that really excited me, I caved. I agreed to take over the market and continue to run it as such, but under one condition: I had to do it my way.

THE ODDS WERE AGAINST US. At that time, the neighborhood was hardly the trendy, vivacious, bursting-with-energy place it is today. The Mission has always been lively, but for a long time it was the wrong kind of liveliness. Dolores Park, just half a block from the Market, was home to junkies. Stabbings and shootings happened regularly. By the time I was twelve, I had been mugged twice on my way to and from the store.

Still, when we started our renovations in November 1997, one of the first things we did was take down the metal bars that covered the windows. What a drama that was! All these old-timers—people we hadn't seen in years—came around and asked, "What are you doing? Are you crazy?" To me, those bars made the store feel like a fortress. I wanted the store to look inviting and welcoming, so I told myself (and those questioning bystanders), "I'm taking the bars off, and I'm just going to deal with it."

The renovated store reopened on June 8, 1998. And it was crazy. My brother Raphael and I were partners in the business (he is no longer a partner but still works at the store), supported by six staff from my old restaurant and all the family members we could corral. I wore many hats in those days: I would go to the produce market in the morning, come back and cook for the deli, stock the shelves, *and* ring on the register.

IN THE BEGINNING, WE HAD NO IDEA WHAT WE WERE DOING. We made it up as we went along, running it like a restaurant, which turned out to be a huge advantage. And, it turns out, we reinvented the grocery store in the process.

I DID KNOW ONE THING FROM THE VERY BEGINNING. Coming from the restaurant world, I understood the importance of making things entertaining and treating the market as a theater of sorts. The flattering lighting, the upbeat music, the open kitchen and exuberant signage are all designed to create an energetic, fun vibe. I also knew that having friendly, informed staff would be key. So we hired former waiters for our "front of house" staff, and we expected them to know our food inside and out, just as they would at a restaurant. Even if they're stocking shelves, their main role is always to inspire customers, put them at ease, and get them excited about good food. All with the overarching goal of making grocery shopping an interactive, fun, and enjoyable experience.

THE PRODUCT SELECTION GOT A MAKEOVER, TOO. We revamped the offerings and got rid of products that my dad and uncle had carried for years—things like cigarettes and forties of malt liquor. It came as a big shock to some folks in the neighborhood. After we reopened, people would come in, take a look around, and eventually ask, "Ain't you got smokes?"

We didn't. We filled the shelves with things that I as a chef would want: pantry items like good wine vinegar and panko bread crumbs, farm-direct produce, and sustainably raised meat. Basically, it was a lot of the same ingredients I had used at my restaurant.

I PREFERRED THESE INGREDIENTS BECAUSE THEY TASTED BETTER, not just because they were organic or local. That evolution came over time and happened largely because of the people around me. These were people—mostly our own staff at first, but more and more guests as well—who wanted to make a difference in the world, and they began to push me in ways that nobody had before. Our produce buyer, Simon

Richard, had a huge impact on me. A farmer himself, he helped me see farming in a new way, and I gradually understood why organic and sustainably raised produce was so important. I owe him a lot for that.

Once I made the connection—that *where* produce is grown, *how* it's grown, and *who* is behind it are all just as important as flavor—it was easy to apply that thinking to all our products. It eventually evolved into a rigorous but informal set of criteria for everything we sold: *Would we eat this ourselves? Would we feed it to our children? How was this raised, grown, or made? What was the impact on the environment? How are the workers treated? Can we feel good about that?*

Often, the only way to answer these questions was to talk to the producers themselves. Not many grocers can say they are on a first-name basis with the people behind the products on their shelves, but we can. In addition, since we support so many local products, it's possible to visit the producer and see firsthand how the products are grown or raised. We also taste nearly every product before deciding whether to sell it. Even meat, cheese, or bread with the most pristine provenance will not get very far with us if it doesn't taste good. This process of evaluating and vetting products means everything that's here is here for a reason. The products support each other and enable cooks to achieve their vision. This alone has done a lot to establish a sense of trust between us and our guests, because they know that if we carry it, it's going to be good.

When we started making these changes, some guests grumbled about the higher prices that came with these more sustainable foods. We tried to help them understand the factors behind those price tags, including the lower yields (but higher quality) associated with organic farming. We worked hard to instill the idea that every grocery purchase affects the environment, the economy, and the well-being of the people who feed us. We talked about the true cost of food, including the hidden costs of subsidies (paid for by our taxes) and health care. In short, we *all* have the power to either contribute to the problem or be part of the solution. We all have the opportunity to make an impact every time we eat.

The old days: my dad and uncle Jack in 1965, dad with the neighbor kids in 1969, and Raph and I with mom in 2000.

BI·RITE
OUR SELECTION OF QUALITY DELI MEATS

Molinari Salami (hot or mild) ..4.95 /lb.	Coppa Veneziana ....7.95 /lb.
Molinari Mortadella.......4.95 /lb.	Hot Coppa.............7.95 /lb.
Black Forest Ham........5.95 /lb.	Prosciutto di Parma ......18.95 /lb.
Pastrami ....5.95 /lb.	
Roast Beef ....6.95 /lb.	SANDWICH CHEESES
Smoked Turkey Breast....6.95 /lb.	Hot Pepper Jack, Cheddar,
Molinari Pancetta.........7.95 /lb.	Swiss, Provolone ....5.95 /lb.

A DIFFERENT KIND OF MARKET

Walking down 18th street, you may not immediately recognize the Art Deco facade in the middle of the block as belonging to a grocery store.

There's a huge display of flowers outside, so overflowing that the blooms completely obscure the buckets and shelving that hold them. Is this a floral shop? As you enter the store, you're transported to another world altogether. A few things hit you right away: The store is fairly small—only slightly bigger than your average bodega. Not a bit of space is wasted—although there aren't traditional aisles to speak of, the shelves soar high and wrap around every corner. And as a result, there is *a lot* to look at. The produce display grabs your attention and leaves no question as to what season it is; basket after basket of apples and pears in every size, shape, and color are a vibrant reminder that it's autumn. Some varieties

are familiar, but many you haven't seen before.

"Have you tried these Gravensteins yet? They're off the hook, and they'll only be around for a little while longer." One of the produce guys pauses, grabs an apple, cuts a wedge, and offers it to you. As you nibble and marvel at the tart intense flavor, he tells you why this particular variety is so special—and fleeting. And they're from just north in Sebastopol.

You stroll the length of the deli case, which is filled with enticing, colorful dishes of prepared food and signs telling you exactly where the ingredients came from—some from Bi-Rite's own farm. Towers of sandwiches greet you at eye level, their contents carefully and artfully arranged within golden crusty rolls of bread. It's all so tempting that you consider ditching your current lunch plans just to take advantage of what's here.

Although you're not in the market for meat, you can't help but pause at the butcher counter. Most stores' meat displays are hardly what you'd call beautiful, but this one is different. It's packed with golden-skinned pasture-raised chickens, maroon lamb racks, and ready-to-roast pork spiked with sprigs of rosemary and lavender. As you scan the case, something catches your eye—is that *goat* in there? The butcher behind the counter asks if he can get you anything. You ask how much demand there is for goat in a city like San Francisco. "BN Ranch has a small but loyal following," he tells you. "We get a whole goat in every week, and it usually sells out in a couple of days." You can't resist. Before you know it, the butcher has wrapped up a couple of shoulder

chops, given you detailed instructions on how to cook them, and jotted down the key points on the brown paper bundle.

Over his shoulder, you notice a small, bustling kitchen behind him. Concealed behind a large refrigerated display case, the kitchen is easy to miss visually but impossible to ignore with your other senses. As in any busy kitchen, there's the clang of metal spoons against pots, the *whh, whh, whh* of a knife gliding through onions, and the lively (sometimes salty) banter of cooks that filters through the air. Similarly, the aromas wafting out make the kitchen's presence known. It's a mouthwatering amalgam of meatballs cooling on the speed rack, salmon cakes coming out of the fryer, and the metallic sweetness of beets being peeled.

You grab a basket and pick up a few other items to round out your goat dinner. When you finally reach the checkout, you're surprised at the sincerity of the cashier when she asks you if you found everything you needed, how your day is going, and whether you've tried that wine before (she confides that it's her favorite).

Heading out the door, you notice a table just outside the store's front window. It's set up as a tasting station featuring a local cheese you've heard of but never tried. You chat with the woman standing behind the table and slowly realize she's not a marketing person, but the cheesemaker herself.

As you head down the street, you realize you're full—not just from tastes and samples, but from all the newfound knowledge you just acquired. Which leaves you wondering: *Who knew that grocery shopping could possibly be so . . . fun?*

WE'RE ABOUT MORE THAN "SERVICE WITH A SMILE." Although we have always prioritized hiring friendly, personable staff, to me, that's just a small part of our customer service strategy. We treat customers like they're visitors in our own home; in fact, we refer to them as "guests." And rather than thinking about customer service as something limited to our frontline staff, we consider our guests in just about every decision we make. We're a *customer-directed business.*

This, again, goes back to the fact that at the beginning, we didn't know what we were doing. We knew we had reincarnated the market into the kind of place where *we'd* want to shop. But what about everyone else? For this reason, we knew it would be especially important to keep an ear to the ground—to listen and respond to guest requests, whether big or small. Otherwise, we'd have no way of knowing that there was demand for gluten-free cookies or additional bicycle parking. Constantly listening to guests, and constantly evolving in response to them, has been the number one key to our success.

THERE'S ALWAYS MORE TO LEARN. Education goes hand in hand with great guest service. That means constantly pushing ourselves to learn more and dig deeper about the products we sell. We regularly take our staff on field trips to farms, dairies, slaughterhouses, breweries, and more. The payoff is huge: not only does it give our staff a sense of how good food is produced, but also once they're back at the store they can say to guests, "This is how this is made, and I know because I saw it." That's pretty unusual in this business, and it's also a lot of fun.

Educating ourselves also means *doing* things ourselves. From day one, we've produced our own sausages, smoked salmon, and pâtés, which we sell out of the deli case. In 2003, my parents bought a farm in the former gold mining town of Placerville; from the orchard's fruit, my mom makes jams, jellies, and preserves that we sell at the market. We also started growing our own herbs on the roof of the store, and more recently we added a couple of beehives. In 2008, under Simon's leadership, we started our own mini-farm in Sonoma,

Creating Community Through Food

5

just north of San Francisco, where our staff could actually get their hands in the dirt and grow vegetables. It's fun, but also helps our staff appreciate and understand how much work goes into producing food. It's an ongoing process; the more we learn, the more there is to know.

EDUCATING GUESTS IS JUST AS IMPORTANT. All that work that we do to research and vet products is lost if we don't communicate it to our guests. Telling the story of individual products is important to us. Sometimes we do that by chatting with guests. Signage is also important; we make our signs by hand and include all the key details about that cheese you're considering: not just the kind of milk and where it's from, but also what makes it special. In other words, why are we bothering to sell it? Why did we choose it? Why will you love it?

Tasting is another form of food education and the easiest and best way for us to share our own excitement about a product. We're constantly put-

ting food into our guests' mouths, whether it's a slice of American prosciutto or a sip of a great small-batch soda. We're known for our produce samples—every day we offer precut samples of nearly every fruit we sell. It's especially popular with our guests' kids, who turn out to be some of our most discerning and loyal guests; many are so won over by our fruit that they won't let their parents buy fruit anywhere else!

WE ARE COMMUNITY. Nobody is anonymous in our store. It's a lot like the bar in *Cheers*—we're the place where everyone knows your name. We encourage our staff to build relationships with our guests— to know not just who they are, but also what they like to eat, what they're looking for, and what kinds of foods are exciting to them. This enables our staff to recommend and share new discoveries and creates an interactive, long-term dialogue.

We're serving not only our guests but also the people whose products we carry. Some of our producers, like Ginger Balakian from Balakian Family

THEY HAD IT STRAIGHT IN 1914...

food

1- buy it with thought
2- cook it with care
3- use less wheat & meat
4- buy local foods
5- serve just enough
6- use what is left

don't waste it
U.S. FOOD ADMINISTRATION

WE STILL DO.

— BI·RITE —

Farm in Reedley, California, have been providing us with their amazing stone fruits since the very beginning. Others are newer. And when we find someone who's making something that people aren't familiar with, we'll go out of our way to promote it and introduce it—passionately—to our guests. We often invite the producers to the store to give out tastes and talk about their product. This gives our guests a chance to talk to producers directly, ask questions, and put a face to where their food comes from. We encourage our staff and our guests to think about the connection to the producer, farmer, or rancher every time they eat; we don't take for granted the hard work and dedication those producers have committed to feeding us.

It's not just about connecting guests with producers. We have found other ways to support producers, such as our unique arrangement with Soul Food Farm. As a burgeoning farm, they had the best possible problem: they had more demand for their gorgeous eggs than they could supply. To scale up, they needed capital. So we loaned it to them, repayable through a steady supply of eggs and chickens for the next year. Sort of like a community-supported agriculture (CSA, or "farm shares") arrangement, but with bigger volume and a single customer—us! And everyone benefited from it—Soul Food Farm, our guests, and Bi-Rite.

Over the years, we realized how important it was for us to facilitate these relationships between our staff,

our vendors, and our guests—each one interdependent on the other for success. Our business was, in essence, a collaboration between these groups. We realized we couldn't imagine doing business any other way, so we eventually formalized it as our mission: Creating Community Through Food.

EVERYTHING CHANGED. Even in the early days, it was clear that we were on to something. The most obvious, easily quantified indicator was our sales. We set a first-year, admittedly ambitious goal of $1 million in revenue. We ended up exceeding that by 25 percent. By our third year, we did $3 million. After more than a decade, our business continues to grow by about $1 million a year. Our staff has grown, too—our little original crew of six has grown to well over one hundred. (First-time visitors, upon seeing the store, are often shocked to hear that we employ that many people. The store really is that busy, and we want to maintain a good work-life balance!)

The store's success has made it possible to grow the Market into a whole family of businesses. In December 2006, we opened Bi-Rite Creamery down the street to create a permanent showcase for the sugary talents of my wife, Anne Walker, and our business partner Kris Hoogerhyde. Our salted caramel ice cream—an intense blend of sweet, bitter, and salty—became an instantaneous hit; the line of guests eager for a cone wrapped around the block. In 2008, we started a

EAT GOOD FOOD

neighborhood community center called 18 Reasons, an intimate venue that brings our community together with producers, activists, and innovators in the world of food. In bringing people together, we strengthen our bonds with one another and deepen our relationship to food. 18 Reasons has gained recognition across the city and nationally for its incredibly popular classes, art exhibitions, workshops, tastings, dinners, and lectures for adults and kids. A second Market and Creamery is slated to open by summer 2012.

We continue to be part of a larger shift in the neighborhood as well. Soon after we opened the Market, Craig and Annie Stoll bought the restaurant space two doors down from us and opened Delfina, now widely recognized as one of the best restaurants in San Francisco. The neighborhood started to take on a different feel. Crime decreased. Nearby Dolores Park, previously a haven for drugs, got cleaned up and eventually became a destination for sun worshippers, picnickers, and playground-loving families from all over the city. Now the Mission, particularly the blocks surrounding the Market, is one of the most desirable neighborhoods in town.

THE FOOD LANDSCAPE HAS CHANGED, TOO. For the first few centuries of America's existence, community was inseparable from grocery shopping. Large open-air markets, both urban and rural, were hubs for socializing and interaction just as much as they were for commerce and food. Even as supermarkets came onto the scene in the twentieth century, corner markets and bodegas continued to thrive and, because they served the residents of the immediate surroundings, still provided a means for people

to bump into their neighbors on a regular basis. But as suburban sprawl took hold and we started to prioritize parking lots and one-stop shopping, large supermarkets in shopping centers gradually took over. Shopping became more anonymous. You were less likely to run into your neighbors, and the supermarket staff didn't bother to learn your name. Food started coming from farther and farther away, so we were less likely to know who was behind the food we ate. Instead of making small, frequent shopping trips, we began to shop only once a week, buying as much as our ever-larger vehicles and refrigerators could hold. Today, most Americans buy their groceries at Walmart and most of that food comes from a handful of multinational corporations.

In contrast, our Market is in the middle of a densely populated neighborhood. We have no parking lot, but the foot traffic on our block is high. Those factors have made it possible for us to be the kind of store where people want to and can shop daily and can run into their neighbors at the same time.

That's not to say that we are a lone buoy bobbing in a sea of ever-duplicating SuperCenters. The last ten or fifteen years have seen a renewed interest in local, organic, and sustainable foods. As a result, farmers' markets have thrived and proliferated, and CSAs can barely keep up with demand. Most importantly, consumers care more and more about where their food comes from. They want to know what's best for their bodies, for their local economies, and for the Earth. And, not least of all, they want it to taste good.

Opposite: produce buyer Simon Richard, in his element

THE MARKETPLACE MANUAL

The more I learn about where most food comes from, the more I want to change the system. There's room for improvement everywhere, from the way that food is grown, harvested, and processed, to how the workers are treated, to how food is marketed and distributed. But since World War II, the American food system has become heavily centralized, industrial, and cripplingly dependent on oil and monoculture crops such as corn. It has become all but impossible for small family farms to survive. This new approach to agriculture is conducted not just on factory farms but also in laboratories and on Capitol Hill. In order for us to thrive, we must learn to feed ourselves and our own communities without relying on the industrial machine.

Those of us who seek to change the status quo face some daunting goals:

- Reducing our dependence on oil and the oil-intensive monocrops: corn, soy, and the like, which are often grown from GM seeds
- Lessening our carbon footprint
- Minimizing factory farming and highly processed, laboratory-driven foods
- Reducing our exposure to chemical pesticides and fertilizers and our secondhand consumption of hormones and antibiotics
- Strengthening our local economies and communities
- Preserving unique breeds of livestock and produce
- Improving our health and reducing our dependence on medication

How can one person possibly make a difference in all these things?

TAKE HEART. Each time we go grocery shopping or sit down to a meal, we're casting a vote about the kind of food we want to see more of.

We need to reverse the trend of sucking the Earth dry and begin to restore its natural resources. **IF WE ARE TO LIVE SUSTAINABLY, WE MUST RETURN MORE THAN WE TAKE.** Being conscious of what we eat and thus making better shopping decisions is one of the most powerful ways to change the food landscape for the better.

Shopping

It's not always easy. Farmers' markets have become a popular and viable option for those of us who want to incorporate organic and local foods into our routine, but they don't offer us everything we need. It's often necessary to turn elsewhere for cooking oil, pasta, canned tuna, and other staples, and for most of us, that means going to the grocery store.

It can be a daunting task. The average grocery store now boasts more than forty-five thousand SKUs (individual products), making it easy to fall victim to the paradox of choice. It's hard to keep track of what's out there, let alone home in on what's good, especially with all the advertisements and promotions that savvy food marketers inundate us with. These distractions have conditioned us to prioritize price and brand over quality and good health.

The proliferation of choices isn't just junk food, either. Every category in the supermarket confronts us with a different array of options and dilemmas.

We have a general idea of what kinds of things we should be eating, but when we're actually standing in the aisles at the supermarket, it's hard to put theory into action. With all this knowledge about the food world today, too many of us still don't know what to put in our shopping carts.

In the chapters that follow, I'll take you aisle by aisle through the grocery store and tell you everything you need to know about buying specific products: chicken, bread, olive oil, and much more. But no matter what's on your grocery list, there are a few general guidelines that will help you be a savvier shopper.

ASK LOTS OF QUESTIONS. Most grocery stores don't put the same amount of effort into signage and education that we do at Bi-Rite, but don't let that stop you when you're trying to figure out where that pork was raised. Be proactive. Find a staff person and ask them. They may not always know the answer, and that can be frustrating in the short term. However, the simple act of asking can instigate change; it lets them know we care where our food comes from, and it's their responsibility to tell us. And if you don't like the answer you do get, you can choose not to buy the product.

EAT GOOD FOOD

ASK FOR BETTER PRODUCTS. Change doesn't always happen as quickly as we'd like, and you may have trouble finding some of the products that I describe in this book. But if enough people ask for better, more sustainable products, we'll get them. Here's just one example: In 2008, Walmart, Inc. (and its subsidiary Sam's Club) announced that its store-brand milk would no longer come from cows treated with artificial growth hormones. In the years leading up to this change, customers had become increasingly aware of and concerned about the health risks associated with milk from treated cows. Walmart (the nation's biggest grocery retailer) listened and overhauled some of their milk offerings as a result. All because the public asked for it. Remember: **GROCERY STORES WILL NOT CHANGE UNLESS WE TELL THEM WHAT WE WANT.**

WHENEVER POSSIBLE, GO LOW ON THE "RETAIL CHAIN." By that I mean supporting local farmers and producers—such as at farmers' markets—but also cooperatives, natural food stores, and local, independent grocery stores that don't rely as heavily on distributors and actually have relationships with the producers of the food they sell. It helps sustain the local economy and puts more money in the pockets of the people who actually produce our food. They're also more likely to be able to answer your questions.

LOOK FOR AND SUPPORT UNIQUE VARIETIES AND ARTISANAL TECHNIQUES. The goal of industrialized food is to produce as much food as quickly, cheaply, and profitably as possible. This homogenizes the food landscape, pushing out heirloom varieties and artisanal techniques. For example, out of the hundreds of varieties of apples in the United States, most grocery stores carry only a handful (those being the most prolific, sturdy, and profitable varieties). And nowadays most salami is made entirely with machines, rather than the old-fashioned way—by hand and under the watch of a skilled artisan. The factory-made product, although cheaper than the handmade version, is simply not as good. The best way to ensure the perpetuation of these varieties and techniques is to support those products.

ASK FOR TASTES. Any good retailer budgets a certain amount of their product for sampling out to customers. And if they're not offering tastes proac-

tively, you should always feel entitled to ask. How else are you going to know if those peaches are any good, or if that imported ham is really worth the price tag? Tasting products helps you make informed buying decisions and is also a good way to keep your palate fine-tuned. I still taste fruit, cheese, and meat on a daily basis—not just to try new things but also to see how they evolve throughout a season or from batch to batch. One of the beauties of artisanal food is that it is not always going to be exactly the same—something to be celebrated.

LOOK AT INGREDIENTS. If you can't pronounce an ingredient, think twice about putting it into your body. Beyond that, steer clear of trans fats, preservatives, high-fructose corn syrup, emulsifiers, stabilizers, artificial colors and flavors, and anything meant as a substitute for good ol' fat and sugar. The more recognizable the ingredients, the better. As author and good-food advocate Michael Pollan says, if your great grandmother wouldn't recognize it, you should avoid it.

CHOOSE ORGANIC WHEN YOU CAN. It's better for the environment, it's better for the people who grow and produce the food, and it's better for us. There are some foods for which it's especially important to buy

AVOIDING GENETICALLY MODIFIED ORGANISMS

According to many scientists, genetically modified organisms (commonly referred to as GM or GMOs) pose significant risks to our environment and to the security of our food supply. The rest of the world is far ahead of the U.S. in GMO planting restrictions and labeling requirements that protect citizens from these potentially dangerous foods. The U.S. government does not require labeling of foodstuffs containing GM ingredients, and 60 to 70 percent of packaged food in a common grocery store has at least one GM ingredient in it. So, when in doubt, assume the product has GM ingredients in it unless specifically stated otherwise.

Here are five ways to decrease your consumption of GMOs:

1. Buy Organic

Products labeled "certified organic" or "made with organic ingredients" cannot intentionally contain any GM ingredients. This is the safest way to ensure your food is free of GMOs.

2. Eat Fresh Produce and Whole Grains

Most GM ingredients are used either as primary ingredients (e.g., soybeans used in soy milk and corn in corn chips) or as components and additives in processed foods (such as high-fructose corn syrup and soy lecithin). Outside of Hawaiian papayas and a small amount of squash, fresh produce is currently immune to the GMO issue. Eating fresh produce and whole grain foods means less exposure to GMOs, a more nutritious diet, and the opportunity to slow down and cook more often.

3. Buy Locally Produced Food

Being close to the source of your food makes it possible to get more—and more accurate—information about how it's produced. Look for organic, locally grown (or made) food that you can buy directly or from a retailer who has a direct relationship with the producer.

4. Beware Risky Ingredients

Corn, soybeans, canola, cottonseed, and sugar beets are the biggest domestic sources of GMO—85 to 90 percent of the acreage of each crop is dedicated to growing GM strains. You may encounter these crops in many different forms so read labels carefully, especially when buying these ingredients:

- **Sugar** Unless a product is organic or specifically lists "pure cane sugar" then it is most likely a combination of sugar from both sugar cane and GM sugar beets.

- **Milk and other dairy products** Alfalfa hay is a main feed ingredient for dairy cattle; with the recent approval of GM alfalfa, our dairy supply is next to be contaminated.

- **Oils** Avoid canola or cottonseed oils unless they are labeled organic or non-GMO. Buy 100 percent extra-virgin olive oil, as some olive oil blends contain canola or cottonseed oil.

- **Corn** With the exception of organic varieties, cornstarch, corn oil, and corn chips are made from GM corn.

- **Soybeans** Soy is the basis for countless ingredients, vitamins, and additives: everything from oils to emulsifiers, flours, soy milk, tofu, and soy sauce. Unless labeled as non-GMO or organic, products are likely to contain GMOs.

5. Look for the Non-GMO Project Seal

Products that carry the Non-GMO Project Seal are independently verified to be in compliance with North America's only third party standard for GMO avoidance. The Non-GMO Project is a nonprofit organization committed to providing consumers with clearly labeled and independently verified non-GMO choices.

---

organic (for instance, peaches and other stone fruits, which are very heavily sprayed in conventional farming), and I highlight these throughout the book.

MAKE ROOM IN YOUR BUDGET FOR BETTER FOOD. Put simply, good food costs more. But then again, most of the food available to us is artificially cheap, thanks to government subsidies, unnaturally high yields from fertilizers and pharmaceuticals, and reliance on workers who earn sub-minimum wage pay. On the other hand, farmers and producers who take the road less traveled work harder and spend more time (and money, in the form of fair wages for their workers) to produce food that is not just better tasting and more nourishing, but is also better for workers, for the environment, and even for our economy. And because it's more flavorful, you need less of it to feel satisfied.

BUY LESS, EAT LESS, AND WASTE LESS. Food production consumes more energy and contributes more to global warming than anything else. The average household wastes 14 percent of the food they buy, by either neglecting leftovers or allowing perishables to expire before they're eaten at all. This is not just a huge waste of money; it's disrespectful of the effort and resources devoted to producing it. And as a culture, we eat more than we need to anyway. So be conscious of how much food you buy and eat. Make more frequent, smaller shopping trips, and try to buy only what you can truly consume before it goes bad. This alone can be enough to offset the higher cost of better-tasting, more sustainable ingredients. Use reusable bags, buy products with minimal packaging, and recycle and compost as much as you can.

Throughout this book I've sprinkled profiles of Bay Area farmers, ranchers, and producers whose products we carry and celebrate at the Market. With these profiles I hope to show not just the faces behind some of my favorite foods but also examples of people who are doing things "the right way." However, as I discuss individual ingredients, I've purposely avoided rattling off brands and producers to look for. For one thing, I tend to emphasize the importance of supporting small producers, and a brand of milk that's available to me in San Francisco may not be available in New York or Chicago. Similarly, you may have a great producer in your area that I don't know about. For another thing, the food landscape is constantly evolving and changing, and I'd hate to promote one brand when another great one is just about to hit the scene. So instead, I give you the tools and knowledge to identify great products and producers wherever you are.

. . . .

A NOTE ON LIMITATIONS: It's not my aim to tackle every single item in the grocery store. Rather than tediously inventorying every cookie, beverage, and breakfast cereal imaginable, I've chosen to focus primarily on *ingredients*—meat, fresh produce, pantry staples, and so on. I think it's the best all-around approach for eating: buying fresh, high-quality products and making simple, satisfying meals from them.

. . . .

Cooking

My approach to cooking was shaped by a single movie. I was in my second year in cooking school when I saw it, and my father and I had been tangling for a year and a half about my decision to be a cook. He thought that I had chosen a path to loserdom, and because I valued my dad's opinion, I was struggling internally as well. My friend Jimmy, knowing what was going on, suggested that I watch *Babette's Feast*, a movie about a famous Parisian chef (Babette) who escapes the French Revolution and becomes a housekeeper in a remote part of Denmark. She goes from a luxurious, decadent society to one where every day is a struggle. In this new environment, food is a basic need—a requirement for survival, and no more. Babette ends up winning the lottery, and she decides to spend her entire winnings on an epic meal for her village, bringing all the best ingredients from France: foie gras, giant turtles, wine, and more. She prepares an amazing dinner, and although the guests are not willing to express the pleasure they experience, she can tell that they are transformed. With this one meal, Babette instigates a change in her neighbors' perspective, which was fulfilling in itself. By the end I was in tears because I identified so much with this idea—that *the whole point of cooking* is to find fulfillment in feeding others. I realized I had found my calling in the kitchen and, in turn, my place in the world. **FOOD WOULD BE MY WAY OF BRINGING PEOPLE TOGETHER.**

Cooking is also about taking responsibility and ownership for what you put in your body. It's about sharing. It's about sustaining yourself and the people you're feeding. It's what keeps us alive and gives us energy, and we need to be conscious of it. If we can all find that pleasure in feeding others and feeding ourselves—even just a little bit—then we will make better decisions about what we eat and buy and who we support in the process.

You don't have to cook Babette's feast to make satisfying food. It can be as simple as toast with butter, but the key is to get great bread and butter, and then take the time to really enjoy it. *Cooking should be fun—and as easy and as enjoyable as you choose to make it.*

DON'T OVERPRIORITIZE QUICK COOKING.
I cringe at the sales pitch for the thirty-minute meal, because there's an underlying assumption that cooking is a chore. Some of the best, most satisfying dishes (like the Braised Beef Cheeks on page 179) take very little skill or hands-on effort but do require a bit of time. Don't shy away from these dishes—just save them for a weekend or other times when you can be more leisurely in your cooking. (And don't worry—there are plenty of weeknight-appropriate recipes in here as well.)

FOCUS ON FRESH FOODS RATHER THAN PRO-CESSED ONES. The flavor payoff is huge, and you'll also save yourself from all the preservatives, fillers, and excess packaging that come along with convenience foods. And you'll get much better value for your money.

KEEP STAPLES ON HAND. Eggs, dried pasta, good extra-virgin olive oil, onions, and garlic are just a few ingredients that have a long shelf life and make it easy to throw together an impromptu meal. The shelf-stable items I discuss are mainly those that are ingredients for cooking, rather than packaged ready-to-eat food. My hope and goal is to empower and inspire you to cook more, using fresh fruits, vegetables, and meats.

GIVE YOURSELF THE RIGHT TOOLS. Most of the recipes in this book rely on a handful of key pieces of equipment: a medium and a large skillet, a Dutch oven or an ovenproof soup pot, a large salad bowl, and a couple of rimmed baking sheets. And a sharp knife and a roomy cutting board will make things infinitely easier.

USE ALL YOUR SENSES WHEN YOU COOK. It'll bring you more closely in tune with your ingredients and will help make you cook more intuitively. So smell the oil before you drizzle it in the pan. Toss the salad with your hands. Taste the soup as it simmers and reduces. Notice how the tastes, textures, and aromas evolve and come together as you cook; it's the best way to refine and learn to cook instinctively.

BE FLEXIBLE AND RESPOND TO THE SEASONS.
Seasonality is an ever-shifting variable in cooking. What's in the market one week may be gone the next, so if something looks good, buy it even if you don't know what to do with it yet! Similarly, don't be afraid to adapt or substitute ingredients based on seasonality. If you're making the Stone Fruit Galette on page 232

and the peaches in your market aren't quite at their peak, don't be afraid to substitute apples or whatever else strikes your fancy.

FOLLOW THE RECIPE—OR NOT. This book offers plenty of simple recipes that have all been vetted and approved by our panel of testers. However, throughout the book I also include "off the cuff" ideas for how to use various ingredients—not so much formal recipes as they are descriptions of my favorite ways to enjoy each ingredient. If you're more comfortable sticking with recipes, that's great. But if you want to take off the training wheels, so to speak, give some of those non-recipes a shot. Feel free to put your own spin on them and embellish or tweak where you see fit. It's a great way to exercise your cooking instincts and have a little fun.

USE WHAT YOU'VE GOT. Don't let food go to waste—eat leftovers before they go bad, repurpose them into something new, stash them in the freezer for a future date. It's pretty easy to make a soup out of almost anything.

CONSCIOUSLY TASTE. Use your senses to look, smell, feel, and taste—not just food, but whatever you drink as well. This pays off in appreciating and enjoying food, developing your palate, and learning about your likes and dislikes. Note your experiences in a journal. This is especially helpful when tasting wine and cheese, as both evolve and change from season to season and year to year; a journal makes it possible to compare your experiences and reactions over time.

AND MOST OF ALL . . . Be spontaneous. Have fun. Share. Give thanks.

It may seem like a tall order—one that's sometimes easier said than done—but that's exactly what I'm going to help you with.

WE HAVE THE POWER TO MAKE A DIFFERENCE THREE TIMES A DAY. WHAT WE EAT CAN BE THE SOLUTION. Come on a shopping trip with me. I'll walk you through *your* grocery store. I'll tell you what to look for, what to ask, and what to do with it once you get home. Grab a shopping bag and let's go!

Opposite: The feeling in the Market in the morning, at noon, and at night

Creating Community Through Food
Bob's Red Mill
Almond Flour

BY | PACKED | $/lb
| | 7.99 | WEIGHT(lb 0.605
0.010
TOTAL PRICE
$4.83

WWW.BIRITEMARKET.COM

Creating Community Through Food
Bob's Red Mill
Almond Flour

SELL BY | PACKED | $/lb
| | 7.99 | WEIGHT(lb 0.615
0.010
TOTAL PRICE
$4.91

WWW.BIRITEMARKET.COM

Full Belly Farm
FRESH-GROUND
CORN MEAL
1.5 LB

CERTIFIED ORGANIC
By CCOF

FULL BELLY FARM

Full Belly Farm
FRESH-GROUND
CORN MEAL
1.5 LB

CERTIFIED ORGANIC
By CCOF

FULL BELLY FARM

Mill
FRIEND of the HEART
FLOUR
RINA
MILL

", is the traditional
s. It is made with
cooked and soaked
masa. Masa harina
rom dried masa.

OZ) 680g

39978 00335 5
efrigerated or frozen
0009

IL BIOLOGICO ITALIANO

alce nero

farina
di grano tenero
tipo **"00"**

*da agricoltura
biologica*

grano coltivato
in Lombardia, Veneto
Emilia Romagna e Toscana

1000g

The Best You Can Bake With
GIUSTO'S
SPECIALTY FOODS
SINCE 1940

A QUALITY PRODUCT
FOR BETTER NUTRITION

**GOURMET #1
SEMOLINA**

Net Wt. 2 lbs

CK
PARVE

FRESHLY MILLED ALL NATURAL AND ORGANIC
FLOURS, CEREALS AND GRAINS FOR ALL YOUR BAKING NEEDS
www.giustos.com

ALLERGEN ALERT: This product is manufactured, packaged, and or warehoused
in a facility that handles cereals containing gluten, i.e. wheat, rye, barley, oats,
and spelt. Milk and products thereof. Soybeans and products thereof.
GIUSTO'S SPECIALTY FOODS • 344 LITTLEFIELD AVE. • SOUTH SAN FRANCISCO, CA 94080 • (650) 873-6566

NET WT. 2 LBS. (.907 Kgs)

Creating Community Through Food
**Giustos Organic
Cake Flour**

SELL BY | PACKED | $/lb
| | 2.49 | WEIGHT(lb 1.610
0.010
TOTAL PRICE
$4.01

2 271070 004016

WWW.BIRITEMARKET.COM

Alce Nero "00" Flour
01 Grocery $3.99
8009004208490

Giusto's Semolina Flour
252680 $6.99
Ital Foods
653793452022

illed from 100% U.S.-grown wheat
employee-owned, 100% committed to quality

KING ARTHUR FLOUR
Naturally Pure and Wholesome

GOING
GREEN

CENTRAL MILLING COMPANY

Est. 1867
RAL CHOICE

Milled from 100% U.S.-grown wheat
100% employee-owned, 100% committed to quality

KING ARTHUR FLOUR
Naturally Pure and Wholesome

100% Organic

2

THE GROCERY

We have such limited shelf space here at the market that we have to be really selective about what we carry. So we taste samples before we decide whether to bring something in. And when we consider a new product, good is not good enough. It has to be exceptional.

We love supporting local artisanal producers. We recently met these guys who were producing honey in the neighborhood—it doesn't get more local than that.

Our guests are very vocal about what they'd like us to carry, and they're a great source of information as well. They keep us aware of trends and help us understand what they're looking for. Sometimes guests will bring a sample of something they want or bring an
empty package. That makes it
easier for us to research the
product. Because in the end,
convenience is critical and we
want to be a one-stop shop
for all our guests.

— Raphael Mogannam,
grocery buyer

IN THE SUPERMARKET'S DRY-GOODS section (or, as we call it in the biz, the "grocery" department), certain aisles contain a dazzling array of enticing products. The packaging alone is enough to make you want to buy them, with their exotic names printed in gold foil, wrappers sealed with wax stamps, and shapely bottles equally well suited for perfume.

It's tempting to collect them all, but it's important to actually use those pantry items. Most people's refrigerator doors are full of tiny jars of condiments and spreads, used once, then forgotten. It's more important to stock your pantry with a few items that are versatile, that work for your tastes, and that you'll actually use.

The middle aisles of the average supermarket are much more than just a collection of products. Shelf placements, or "slots," are effectively rented out by the supermarket to food conglomerates, who pay to have their products displayed in the most eye-catching spots. The coupon dispensers that jut out from the shelves and the promotional decals on the floors are also paid for by corporations. In most grocery stores, the products you see and where you see them are a reflection not of the retailer's idea of what's good, but of what will make the most money for the store itself as well as the companies that make the food. The products themselves are often overpackaged, and many are full of preservatives. Keep this in mind as you browse the aisles of the grocery store. Look beyond the prime, eye-level shelf slots. Ask questions. And choose based on taste, quality, and need rather than packaging, placement, and glitz.

Remember that statistic I mentioned about 14 percent of a household's food going to waste? Most of it is probably pantry items purchased from the center of the store, now getting old and collecting dust in your cupboard or refrigerator. This next section will give you information on the basics, the things that you'll use often and, more importantly, *use up*. Buy them as you need them; remember, you are better off saving the money than throwing it away.

BEANS

After many years of disdain by the general public, beans are finally getting their due. I count myself among the converted: until seven or eight years ago, I thought of beans as cheap peasant food—at best, an obligatory component for dishes like cassoulet, hardly worth showcasing on their own. And I figured beans were all the same. However, my perceptions changed entirely with two epiphanies, I realized how critical freshness is when cooking beans from scratch, and I discovered heirloom varieties that go way beyond your standard pinto bean. Now I know how delicious, creamy, and downright *interesting* beans can be, and I'm always looking for new ways to use them.

How to Buy

Beans are one of the easiest, most inexpensive, and most nutrient-packed foods you can make. And although I prefer the texture, flavor, and value of cooking beans myself, I also recognize the incredible convenience that canned beans offer. There's room for both types in your cupboard: use the canned variety for quick weeknight meals, the dried ones when you're able to plan ahead a bit.

IF YOU BUY CANNED BEANS, MAKE SURE THEY'RE ORGANIC, for your own health, but also for those who grow and harvest the beans. Make sure that salt and beans are the only two ingredients; avoid those that also contain preservatives.

WHETHER CANNED OR DRIED BEANS, BUY BRANDS THAT SPECIALIZE IN BEANS AND GRAINS (THEY'RE USUALLY SMALLER COMPANIES). There are many European specialty importers of beans, but there are also several notable domestic bean specialists. Pound for pound, you will pay a little more for their beans, but this is an instance where an extra buck or two gets you infinitely better quality and flavor. For dried beans especially, the portion cost will still be quite low; a single pound of beans will serve eight to ten people for only 30 or 40 cents each.

LOOK FOR HEIRLOOM OR UNUSUAL VARIETIES. There's more to the legume world than pinto beans, navy beans, and kidney beans, and some producers are

> **AT THE VERY LEAST, LOOK FOR BEANS THAT ARE:**
> - Organic canned beans, with salt and beans as the only ingredients
> - Producers that specialize in beans, both domestic and imported
> - Retailers with high turnover of dried beans
> - Dry beans that are in good shape (not many broken ones)
>
> **IDEALLY, LOOK FOR:**
> - Heirloom varieties

leading the charge to revive long-forgotten varieties. These beans offer as many nuances in flavor, texture, and color as you'd find in wine or cheese.

FRESHNESS IS CRITICAL FOR ANY KIND OF DRIED BEAN. If you've ever made beans from scratch and gotten disappointing results, old beans were probably the culprit. Dried beans do have quite a long shelf life, but it isn't infinite. After a couple of years, dried beans lose their resilience and ability to become tender. It's often difficult to tell how old beans are just by looking at the package, so the best strategy is to buy beans from places that have a lot of turnover in their product. Latino or other ethnic grocers, natural food stores, co-ops, and specialty stores are great places to start. Inspect the beans and make sure there aren't too many broken ones—a sign that they're old or have been mishandled.

How to Store

Keep dry beans in a cool, dry place, and use within six months of buying them. Mark the container with the date of purchase so you know how long you have had them.

How to Use

If you can boil water, you can cook dried beans. They take a little time, but require minimal attention as they cook, and they're a great value. First, spread the beans out on a baking sheet and remove any pebbles or other foreign objects. Transfer to a large bowl and add enough water to cover by at least an inch. Soak for at least 4 hours or overnight, changing the water at least once, but a couple of times if possible. In a large pot, sauté some onions, garlic, a bay leaf, and any spices or herbs you'd like to use. Drain the soaked beans and add them to the pot along with enough fresh water or stock to cover by about an inch. Bring to a simmer and cook gently until tender: as little as 30 minutes or so for lentils, up to several hours for larger beans. Add more water (or stock) if the liquid reduces too much.

Salt does *not* cause bean skins to toughen; the culprit is usually acid (such as in tomatoes). Still, because the liquid reduces significantly during cooking, it's wise to delay salting too heavily until the beans are almost done.

WITH CANNED BEANS, ALWAYS RINSE AND DRAIN WELL BEFORE USING to remove extra salt and get rid of the slippery packing liquid.

Beans add a boost of protein and fiber to salads and soups, and although it's less commonly seen in America, they're a classic addition to some pasta dishes. (Try the Orecchiette with White Beans and Chard on page 60.) Mixed with rice, they make a complete protein, as in the Mujadara on page 59, or the classic Southern dish of rice and beans and greens.

Pureed beans make delicious, downright sexy soups that are both warming and fortifying, like the White Bean Puree on page 57. Beans are also perfect for easy, inexpensive dips, such as the hummus on page 51. You can also substitute other beans and seasonings to make an endless array of dips and spreads.

As with so many foods, a little pig fat never hurt anything, but it works especially well to round out the earthy flavors of beans. Bacon, pancetta, or even leftover bacon drippings are all great additions.

TOFU

Once the butt of many a culinary joke, tofu has finally started to get a little respect. There seems to be no limit to the shapes and forms that soybeans can take (Tofurkey, anyone?), and more and more people are making room in their shopping carts for these items.

Just like corn and canola, soybeans are one of those U.S. monocrops that's more likely to be GMO than not. So whether you're buying soy milk for your lactose-intolerant kid or tofu for tonight's stir-fry, **make sure it's organic** and/or **made with non-GMO soybeans.**

Tofu is made using a technique very similar to cheesemaking; soy milk is mixed with a coagulant that causes curds to form, and the curds are drained and molded into blocks. **Soft or silken** tofu has had relatively little water extracted from it, and its smooth, delicate consistency makes it ideal for smoothies and dressings (it falls apart if you sauté it). **Firm or extra-firm** tofu has been pressed to extract more water. This gives it a more resilient texture that keeps its shape while cooking. It has a very mild flavor. **Pressed or baked** tofu has an even denser texture, and often has been marinated in a savory sauce, which gives it a boost of flavor. If you're just starting to explore tofu, this last category is a tasty way to start.

CHOCOLATE

Once upon a time, Hershey's, Cadbury, and Nestlé were just about the only brands of chocolate you could find in the grocery store. But artisan chocolate has exploded in the last ten or twelve years. At our market, the grocery buyers can hardly keep up with all the new artisan chocolatiers, and the variety is matched only by our customers' enthusiasm for trying them all.

We focus on chocolate used for baking and cooking, although many of the points also apply to truffles, bars, and confectionary chocolate.

How to Buy

Although the *Theobroma cacao* trees used to make chocolate grow exclusively in the tropics (typically in third world countries), the industry itself has historically been controlled by a handful of large European companies that built their businesses through domination and slave labor—some of which still exists today. Additionally, the chocolate industry consists of much more than the farmer and the chocolate company. The two entities are connected by a long chain of middlemen who not only control pricing but are also the only way for farmers to get their product to market. Many farmers never even get a chance to taste the finished product made from their cacao. Paralyzed by a system that is both complex and obscure, farmers often have no idea of the true value of their product, and they only ever see a tiny fraction of the profits. This is why RESPONSIBLE SOURCING IS ESPECIALLY CRITICAL when buying chocolate.

A growing number of chocolate producers have found ways to operate that are more beneficial to cacao farmers. These may be denoted in several different ways on the label:

- **Fair Trade** means the product has been certified to be in compliance with specific criteria that benefit farmers and the environment. This certification ensures fair pricing for farmers and guarantees against slave or child labor.
- **Farmer Owned** means that the cacao farmers share ownership in the company. This not only gives

> **AT THE VERY LEAST, LOOK FOR CHOCOLATE THAT IS:**
> - **The best quality that reasonably fits within your budget**
> - **Of a cacao percentage that is appropriate for the recipe**
> - **To your taste and liking**
>
> **IDEALLY, LOOK FOR:**
> - **Fair trade or from a farmer-owned or bean-to-bar producer**

farmers a say in how the company is run but also means more equitable distribution of profits.
- **Bean-to-Bar** chocolate makers take on the entire process of chocolate making, from raw cacao beans to finished bar. This gives the producer control over every step of the process, which in turns means more control over the quality of the finished product. Bean-to-bar implies a more artisanal approach as well as a higher degree of transparency in sourcing the raw materials. And because many of the middlemen are removed from the process, farmers get a better price for their products.

With the advent of high-quality chocolate bars, it can sometimes be difficult to tell which ones are intended for baking and which for eating. There is often no right answer. THE KIND OF CHOCOLATE YOU USE FOR BAKING SHOULD BE DICTATED BY YOUR BUDGET, THE RECIPE, AND YOUR TASTE:

- **Budget**—It's possible to spend a king's ransom on chocolate (especially when you need a whole pound of it for a recipe) but it's certainly not necessary. At minimum, the chocolate you bake with should be good enough to enjoy eating on its own, but beyond that it is up to you.
- **Recipe**—If you're using a recipe that calls for a chocolate with a specific percentage of cacao, try to get as close to that as you can with the chocolate you use—within 5 percent or so. Straying far from the author's stated percentage can produce unintended sweetness and/or texture in the final product.

- **Taste**—Chocolates from different regions, producers, and production methods display a range of flavor profiles that evolve when you cook with them. A chocolate that you love to nibble on might taste boring once baked into a cake, and a chocolate that tastes ho-hum straight might come alive in the same recipe. (Pastry chefs are often fiercely loyal to one brand or another for this very reason, even using different brands for different recipes.) Try a few different brands to discover your favorite!

In many grocery stores, the best "value" chocolate is found not in the baking aisle but in the deli or cheese section. These are the large, random-weight pieces that are cut from large blocks and individually wrapped and weighed by the grocery store.

Although incredibly diverse in their characteristics, the flavor notes of chocolates tend to fall into four basic categories: citrus, nutty, fruity, and "chocolaty." Each chocolate expresses a unique combination of these notes: one might be very citrusy and fruity, another nutty and slightly chocolaty. Try tasting a few chocolates side by side and notice how the four flavor types show up in each one.

Chocolate disks or chips offer uniformity and convenience, but you'll get better value and shelf life by buying chocolate in bigger chunks and chopping it yourself.

How to Store

Moisture and heat are chocolate's two biggest enemies, so for best results keep your chocolate wrapped airtight and in a cool place. A cool, dark cabinet is best—the refrigerator is too humid. Chocolate absorbs flavors readily, so the less surface area that's exposed, the better. Store in a sealed container, or wrapped well in plastic wrap or aluminum foil, for up to a year.

If you see a white dusty-looking substance on the surface of your chocolate, it's likely bloom, the result of cocoa powder crystallizing on the surface of the chocolate. It's harmless and in most cases does not affect the flavor or texture of the chocolate. When in doubt, close your eyes and taste a bit. If it tastes odd or bland or has an unusual texture, throw it away and buy a new stash.

How to Use

"Semisweet" and "bittersweet" are general terms used to describe the cacao percentage of a given chocolate.

COCOA POWDER

In its pure form, chocolate is made of two main components: chocolate "liquor" (it's not alcoholic) and cocoa butter. Bar chocolate is made by emulsifying pure chocolate with additional cocoa butter; cocoa powder is made by removing the cocoa butter from chocolate, leaving pure chocolate "liquor" in powdered form. Because the chocolate liquor is no longer diluted by the cocoa butter, cocoa powder gives a more intense chocolaty flavor to baked goods.

In an ideal world, organic and fair trade cocoa would be the way to go. However, in my experience, the flavor of these cocoas simply doesn't match up to the best European cocoa powders. I hope that over time these European producers will improve their sourcing and purchasing ethics to support a living wage for farmers and encourage organic methods.

Most baking recipes that use cocoa powder specify "natural" cocoa powder, which is made as I just described. **Dutch-processed** cocoa powder has been treated with an alkali to increase its pH (make it less acidic); it also makes it darker, milder in flavor, and easier to blend into liquids.

In general, I prefer natural cocoa powder for its higher quality and minimal processing. But because of their varying pH levels, "natural" and Dutch-processed cocoa powders can produce very different results in a baking recipe and are therefore not directly interchangeable. To compensate for this, I use the following formula whenever I use a recipe that calls for Dutch-processed cocoa:

3 tablespoons Dutch-processed cocoa powder = 3 tablespoons natural cocoa powder + 1/8 teaspoon baking soda

Higher percentages correspond to darker chocolate and proportionately less sugar. Producers apply the terms differently, which means that two chocolates of identical cacao percentage might be called bittersweet by one company and semisweet by another. In general, semisweet is often sweeter than bittersweet, but a chocolate labeled as bittersweet can be anywhere from 35 percent to 75 percent cacao (or higher). For the most precise comparison, refer to percentages whenever they're available.

• •

Stone-ground chocolate has a unique texture thanks to its coarse-ground cacao and crystalline sugar. It does not melt in the same way that other chocolates do, so it's best enjoyed out of hand or used in hot chocolate rather than in baked goods.

COFFEE AND TEA

Coffee and tea have a great deal in common with chocolate, and not just because they thrive in similar climates. Like the chocolate industry, the coffee and tea industries are rife with shady middlemen, under-the-table transactions, and unfair price fixing that keeps the growers impoverished and at the mercy of those higher up in the chain. The tide is turning, though, and **FAIR TRADE AND FARMER-OWNED** (or "co-op grown") coffees and teas are increasingly available at supermarkets and coffee shops.

How to Buy

Coffee and tea have also attracted both renewed connoisseurship and increasing demand for origin-specific and small-batch products. Coffee roasters in particular have proliferated accordingly, and many now pride themselves on not only the quality and freshness of their beans, but also the means used to source the beans. Rather than relying on distributors or middlemen, some roasters operate on **DIRECT TRADE**, which means they buy the beans directly from the farmers. The benefits are many. The roaster knows firsthand that the farmers are paid fairly and have good working conditions. It also creates a unique dialogue between roaster and grower and often leads to a better product, as the buyer can influence the growing and production process.

BUY ORGANIC COFFEES AND TEAS WHENEVER POSSIBLE. Conventionally grown coffee is one of the most heavily pesticide-laden crops worldwide, and considering that it's something that many of us consume daily, buying organic can make a true positive impact on the people who grow and harvest these crops and on their rivers and lakes. And speaking of the environment, buy **SHADE-GROWN OR BIRD-FRIENDLY COFFEE** when you can. In an attempt to boost production and shorten time to harvest, many producers cut down taller trees to give the coffee trees more direct sunlight. This disrupts the ecosystem and renders certain species of birds homeless. Shade-grown coffee is more environmentally friendly, and it tastes better due to the fruit's longer, more leisurely "hang time" on the tree.

BUY WHOLE BEANS. Coffee will stay fresh much longer if you buy whole beans and grind them yourself. On the package, look for a roast date (it should be no more than two weeks prior). Vacuum packs buy you a little more time.

BUY WHOLE-LEAF, LOOSE TEAS. Bagged tea is made from low-quality leaves and often tastes as dusty as the pulverized tea looks. Whole leaf, loose teas tend to be much higher quality and are a more precise reflection of the *terroir* from which they came.

LOOK FOR COFFEE AND TEA THAT ARE:

• Fair trade • Farmer owned • Direct trade

COFFEE:

• Organic and/or shade-grown and/or bird-friendly

• Whole bean

• Stamped with a roast date within the last week

TEA:

• Organic • Whole, loose leaf

EAT GOOD FOOD

How to Store and Use

Store coffee in an airtight container away from heat and light for up to two or three weeks. Grind coffee beans just before you use them, and grind them appropriately for the brew method you are using.

Store teas in an airtight container at room temperature. Steep each appropriately for its particular type; consult the package if you aren't sure.

You'll get the best results and cleanest flavor by using filtered water. The temperature of the water is also important. The ideal brewing temperature for coffee is 190°F. For herbal tea, use boiling water; for black tea, just below the boiling point—around 200°F; for green tea, around 175°F. Coffee should be steeped for 4 to 5 minutes; teas, from 1 to 5 minutes depending on the type.

FISH: ANCHOVIES, SARDINES, AND TUNA

When I was a kid, my dad bought 29-cent tins of Geisha sardines, and I couldn't stand them. So I thought that all sardines had that funky, fishy, cat-foody taste, and I steered clear of them altogether. It was only after I opened the market that I started to discover how good canned fish could be. I found some Portuguese and Spanish sardines so pure in flavor that they are almost sweet, with none of the qualities that had grossed me out as a kid. Now I can't imagine life without them!

How to Buy

Spain, Portugal, and Italy have longstanding traditions of canning fish, and these products are cornerstones of their cuisines. Canned fish is so prized that the best ones fetch unbelievably high prices—up to $200 for a one-kilo tin! Some producers have been in operation for many generations (first preserving with salt and air, and later through canning), and to this day they hand pack the fish one by one into tins. Often the processing takes place on the fishing boat itself, which helps keep the fish tasting incredibly fresh.

Still, most Americans are unfairly prejudiced against sardines, anchovies, and most other canned fish. (Canned tuna is a notable exception.) Quality makes a big difference in this department, and it's easy to find the good stuff when you know what to look for:

- **The more "whole" the fish, the better**—Whether it's whole bone-in anchovies or a single chunk of tuna loin in oil, the more intact forms of fish usually correlate with better quality.
- **The packing liquid matters**—For oil-packed fish, make sure it's in olive oil (ideally extra-virgin). Otherwise, look for fish that's packed in its own juices.
- **Responsible fishing is important**—Sardines and anchovies are generally abundant and considered sustainable. But for canned tuna, make sure it bears a third-party certification for sustainable fishing practices, such as the Marine Stewardship Council's seal of approval. "Dolphin-safe" and "pole caught" (as opposed to nets that impact other sea life) are other signs of fish being harvested in a sustainable manner.

Sardines and anchovies are abundant and have a short life cycle, which makes them some of the most sustainable fish around. They're also low on the food chain, so there's less threat of mercury or other toxins that are more commonly found in larger, older, carnivorous fishes.

Tuna labeled with "ventresca" means the meat came from the rich and fatty belly of the fish. It boasts a tender, silken consistency and is highly prized (and often priced accordingly).

> **AT THE VERY LEAST, LOOK FOR CANNED AND JARRED FISH THAT IS:**
> - In the most "whole" state available
> - Packed in salt, olive oil, or its own juices
> - Sustainably harvested

FISH, CANNED AND JARRED

This photo shows some great examples of what to look for in canned and jarred fish. Clockwise from top left:

TUNA in large chunks, packed in olive oil.

AMERICAN WILD-CAUGHT TUNA bearing the Marine Stewardship council seal.

SALT-PACKED ANCHOVIES boast a clean flavor that beats oil-packed anchovies any day, any way. This particular brand, Recca, is from Italy; *acciughe salate* means "salted anchovies." Large tins like this one tend to be a better value than the tiny ones.

MORE SALT-PACKED ANCHOVIES, this time from the Spanish producer Ortiz. *Anchoas en salazón* means, you guessed it, "anchovies in salt."

OIL-PACKED SARDINES are usually plain, like these, but are sometimes also available with hot peppers or in tomato sauce.

OIL-PACKED ANCHOVIES can be a good option, as long as they're packed in olive oil. The highest quality are packed in jars rather than tins, so the quality is visible.

OIL-PACKED TUNA in an oval tin. Here, *bonito del norte* refers to the type of tuna, and *aceite de oliva* shows it's packed in olive oil.

How to Store

Once you've opened a can or jar of fish, you don't necessarily need to use it all at once. Of course, keep it tightly sealed and refrigerated. Anything that comes in a tin should be transferred to a new container and "topped off" with more of whatever it was packed in. Try to use the rest within three months so flavor and quality are not compromised. I usually write the date on a piece of masking tape and attach it to the container.

How to Use

When it comes to **ANCHOVIES**, salt-packed is the way to go. Compared to oil-packed anchovies, salt-packed ones have a much cleaner flavor and a more pleasing, meaty texture. They do require a little prep to reduce their saltiness and make them more pliable:

> ### BI-RITE'S BASICS:
> ■ Anchovies, preferably salt-packed
> ■ Sardines in olive oil
> ■ Tuna in olive oil or its natural juices

Soak salted anchovies in warm water for 15 to 20 minutes, at which point you can remove the fillets from the skeleton. It's not difficult—a nudge of the thumbnail is all you really need. After that, one more brief soak helps remove any extra salt from the inner surfaces. Although salted whole anchovies look much larger than oil-packed fillets, they end up being about the same size once you remove the skeleton and head.

I really can't overemphasize the flavor difference you'll experience by using salted anchovies and how minimal that extra prep really is. They're so good that you might just want to eat them on their own. Try whole fillets on a Caesar salad!

Anchovies are integral to the classics Bagna Cauda (page 52) and the Lemony Kale Caesar Salad (page 97). But they're also fabulous as a secret weapon to add a savory undercurrent of *umami* to stews and braises. Also known as the fifth taste in addition to sweet, salty, bitter, and sour, *umami* is deep-flavored and savory. Found in mushrooms, salted fish, soy sauce, and Parmesan cheese, *umami* is often described as a "meaty" flavor.

- -

> Avoid anchovy paste (the kind that comes in a tube). It doesn't save you that much time, and it offers little more than a muddy, bottom-of-the-sea flavor. I've yet to find one that truly tastes like anchovies.

- -

Now that I've discovered really excellent **SARDINES**, I happily eat them right out of the tin. They're also nice with grilled bread and a smear of spicy mustard, added to an antipasti platter, piled onto crostini, or folded into salads.

You can take **TUNA** salad in a thousand different directions and overlay it with just about any of the world's cuisines. Tuna salad is also one of those amazingly flexible, "whatever's in the fridge" type of dishes that doesn't need a recipe. Try a vinaigrette dressing rather than mayonnaise.

Tuna and pasta is hardly a new combination, but the Spaghetti with Tuna, Capers, and Chile Flakes (page 62) is a far cry from the tuna noodle casserole you may have grown up with.

FLOUR

One of my favorite Bay Area farms, Full Belly, hosts a Hoes Down Festival every fall to celebrate the year's harvest. Full Belly grows their own wheat, and during the festival manual grinders are set up for folks to try their hand at milling flour. Kids especially love to watch wheat berries turn into flour, which is mixed into pizza dough and baked in a wood-fired oven for all to share.

Full Belly is just one of many small farmers across the country starting to grow their own wheat, grinding it themselves or using local millers, and selling it through farmers' markets and CSAs. This bourgeoning industry has helped revive heritage wheat varieties that were common over fifty years ago but fell out of favor among the big producers. These heritage varieties require less chemical fertilizers and insecticides to thrive than their modern counterparts, and they also offer unique tastes and textures.

How to Buy

Flour is most often sold in porous paper bags, which makes it susceptible to absorbing nearby odors and moisture in the air. This not only affects the flavor of the flour but also can affect the way the flour behaves in a recipe. So whatever type of flour you need, **BUY IT FROM A STORE THAT HAS HIGH TURNOVER OF ITS FLOUR INVENTORY.** (Your corner store, for instance, is not the ideal place to buy flour!)

LOOK FOR FLOUR THAT IS LABELED "NEVER BLEACHED" AND "NEVER BROMATED." Bleached flour undergoes a whitening process using chlorine gas. That in itself is unsavory enough, but the process also lowers the protein content of the flour, and for that reason it's not always interchangeable with unbleached flour. Potassium bromate, or simply "bromate," is a chemical that's sometimes added to flour to strengthen dough. When improperly used, it can cause illness and is a suspected carcinogen.

IT'S ALSO IMPORTANT TO BUY ORGANIC FLOUR, simply because of the impact you can have by doing so. In the United States, over fifty million acres of farmland are devoted to growing wheat—that's a lot of acreage! Buying organic flour can make a big difference in keeping watersheds and people healthy.

IF YOU CAN FIND IT, STONE-GROUND FLOUR IS VASTLY PREFERABLE to conventionally milled flour. Most flour you see on the shelves is ground using steel rollers, which causes the flour to heat up excessively; this, in turn, causes natural fats in the flour to oxidize, which destroys some of the nutrients. In contrast, grinding wheat using traditional stone mills does not cause the flour to heat up, and therefore maintains more of the wheat's innate nutrients.

How to Store

Store flour in an airtight container at cool room temperature. Use all-purpose and other "white" flours within eighteen months of purchase. Whole wheat flour contains natural oils that have a tendency to go rancid, so it has a shorter shelf life. Use it within a year or so, but always smell it before using to make sure it hasn't "turned."

How to Use

The most critical thing to know about using flour is how to measure it. Cup measures are not very accurate, because much depends on how you fill it. If you dip the cup into a bag of flour and scoop it up, you will get a lot more flour (by weight) than if you used a spoon to transfer flour into the cup. The difference can be as much as 20 percent! **THE BEST AND MOST ACCURATE WAY TO MEASURE FLOUR IS TO WEIGH IT USING A KITCHEN SCALE (IDEALLY A DIGITAL ONE).** It's a small investment, but one that will start to pay off immediately by giving you consistent measurements every time.

Using a scale is also easier. Instead of dealing with filling and leveling off measuring cups one at a time, a scale lets you pour and measure flour directly in the mixing bowl. Plus, there's less to clean up.

The kind of flour you use depends a great deal on what you're using it for. The biggest differentiator between various types of flour is the protein content. Protein is the building block for the gluten that gives bread its elastic texture. The higher the protein, the more elastic and chewy the final product will be; the lower the protein, the more delicate it will be. A flour's protein content is often described as its "hardness"; hard flour is high in protein, and soft flour is low in protein.

ALL-PURPOSE FLOUR gets its name for good reason. It has a medium protein content, which makes it suitable for most breads, cakes, cookies, and batters.

WHOLE WHEAT FLOUR is milled from wheat that still has the bran and germ attached. Most whole wheat flour has a slightly coarser texture than all-purpose flour, and it produces baked goods that are somewhat denser than those made with white flour. If you want to substitute whole wheat flour for all-purpose, it's a good idea to start by replacing only a portion of the all-purpose with whole wheat (say, half) on the first try. If that works, you can always increase the amount the next time around.

BREAD FLOUR has a high amount of protein, which makes it well suited for pizzas, bagels, breads, and other recipes where you want a good "chew."

CAKE AND PASTRY FLOURS have lower amounts of protein and are finely milled, which helps produce very tender and delicate baked goods.

SELF-RISING FLOUR is flour with leavener and a small amount of salt already mixed in. I don't usually keep self-rising flour on hand; instead, I use an easy formula to substitute:

For 1 cup (4$\frac{1}{2}$ ounces) self-rising flour, use

1 cup (4$\frac{1}{2}$ ounces) flour

+ 1 teaspoon baking powder

+ scant $\frac{1}{4}$ teaspoon baking soda

+ $\frac{1}{2}$ teaspoon salt

SEMOLINA FLOUR is made from durum wheat, which is particularly high in protein. It is the ideal flour for pasta.

00 FLOUR is ground to a very fine consistency, making it an ideal choice for supple pizza doughs. Protein-wise, it usually falls in the middle of the hardness range, but there is considerable variation from one brand to the next.

HONEY

I am a rancher of sorts, but not the kind you might assume: I have no field, my "herd" ranks at around sixty thousand, and it's located right in the middle of the city. How is that possible? I am the proud keeper of bees who live on the rooftop of the Market. We harvest about sixty pounds in the spring and again in the fall. The honey varies slightly with each harvest, but it always carries the faint flavor of the fennel and jasmine that grows wild in neighboring backyards and surrounding hills.

Honey is fascinating; all around the world, bees produce honey using the same process, yet the product of their labor is infinitely variable. Depending on what plants are available to the bees, the climate, and the time of year, honey can be viscous or runny, mildly flavored or intense. Even honey from the same hive might taste light and floral in the spring, and robust and almost spicy in the fall.

How to Buy

Honey is a super-saturated solution, which means it has a tendency to crystallize (come out of solution) and turn solid over time. Because of this, most producers filter and pasteurize their honey to prevent crystallization and create a more uniform product.

BUY RAW AND/OR UNFILTERED HONEY IF YOU CAN. For one thing, heating and filtering destroy the subtle flavors found in honey straight from the hive, so unprocessed honeys have much more personality than processed ones. Raw honey also offers more antibacterial and antioxidant benefits than processed honey. The USDA doesn't regulate the use of "raw" and "unfiltered" on honey labels, but the terms suggest that the product has been minimally processed.

Be aware that many commercial producers treat the hives themselves with pesticides to protect the bees from mites that can threaten the colony. This disrupts the bees' reproductive cycles and general health, so look for honey labeled "pesticide-free."

LOCAL (OR AT LEAST DOMESTIC) HONEY IS GENERALLY PREFERABLE TO IMPORTED, yet there are many wonderful international honey producers, especially in Italy, Australia, New Zealand, France, and Spain; the best and most reputable ones are specialists who deal only in honey. Honey that is local to where you live provides a unique taste of the landscape that surrounds you. Look for it at natural food stores, co-ops, and farmers' markets.

Honey labels often indicate a **SPECIFIC FLOWER VARIETAL** (like clover or lavender), which indicates the type of plant or plants that the bees visited most heavily. These varietals are the major influence on what the honey will look and taste like.

WE NEED BEES

Bees aren't just producers of a delicious nectar; as natural pollinators, they're also a critical part of other agricultural crops. About one-quarter of the foods we eat are pollinated by bees, even more when you consider that the feed given to livestock also depends on bees for pollination.

Bees have fallen on hard times in recent years with the advent of colony collapse disorder (CCD), which manifests in entire colonies of bees mysteriously and suddenly dying off. The phenomenon baffled scientists and farmers alike, who could not pinpoint any specific cause of CCD. In 2010, though, leaked government documents uncovered not only the cause but also a government conspiracy. It turned out that CCD was caused at least in part by the pesticide clothianidin, which is used extensively in canola, soy, and wheat farming, and whose use the EPA continued to permit even after multiple warnings from EPA scientists. It's an excellent reminder that we can't just rely on the government to decide what's safe for us, or our environment.

Our first rooftop harvest

AT THE VERY LEAST, LOOK FOR HONEY THAT IS:

- **Raw and/or unfiltered (preferably both)**
- **From the United States; if imported, from a reputable company that specializes in honey**

IDEALLY, LOOK FOR:

- **Locally produced**
- **Varietal-specific**
- **Pesticide-free**

How to Store

Because honey has natural antimicrobial properties, there's no need to refrigerate it. Just keep it tightly sealed to deter ants or other critters.

How to Use

Raw honey will eventually crystallize and turn solid; this doesn't affect the flavor but obviously affects the texture and consistency. You can reliquefy crystallized honey by heating the jar in a water bath or in the microwave on low power. But it's not absolutely necessary; crystallized honey is perfect for spreading—and wonderful slathered on a buttered baguette.

EAT GOOD FOOD

In general, **DARKER COLORED HONEYS HAVE A MORE ROBUST FLAVOR**; these are great for drizzling over yogurt or stirring into strong tea. Lighter colored honeys are milder and well suited for baked goods and other recipes featuring delicate flavors.

Honey and blue cheese (like gorgonzola) is a knock-out combination; if you've never tried it, you're in for a treat. Honey is fabulous in savory dishes, as well. I like to make my own sweet-and-sour marinade by mixing honey and vinegar together and brushing it onto chicken during the final minutes of cooking (if you do it too early, it's likely to burn).

JAMS, JELLIES, AND PRESERVES

It's no overstatement to say that June Taylor is a superstar in the culinary world, which is why I'm especially proud to say, "I knew her when . . ." We worked together at The Pasta Shop in Oakland in the late '80s and early '90s. She was a cheesemonger; I cooked. During that time, she began to miss the English marmalades she'd grown up with—the kind made in small batches from hand-cut citrus. The day she brought in some samples of her own preserves, everyone's eyes lit up in epiphany. This was not your average supermarket marmalade: it was downright intense, with ripe fruit balancing the gentle bitterness of the citrus peel. She had turned two simple ingredients—great fruit and sugar—into an extraordinary product.

June went on to become a producer herself—and inspire the artisanal jam making movement in this country. She sets the standard to which many people now aspire, using only pristine heirloom fruit harvested from single trees, cutting it all by hand, and making her own pectin from the seeds. She works in batches as small as ten to twelve jars at a time, and the labels on her jars are hand-applied. We proudly sell her jams, conserves, and marmalades in the market, and everyone who tastes her product has the same epiphany that we did twenty years ago.

Note: Strangely, there is no general term for the category of jams, jellies, butters, conserves, preserves, and marmalades, so for simplicity's sake I refer to the group as "preserves."

How to Buy

With that first taste of small-batch jam I realized how utterly *diluted* most supermarket jams and jellies are. In fact, commercial versions are made mostly of sugar and pectin rather than fruit, which is why you have to slather thick layers of it onto your toast to get any flavor.

The biggest difference between those bulked-up generic supermarket preserves and high-quality ones is the fruit used. **IN FACT, GOOD FRUIT IS THE BACKBONE OF ANY HIGH-QUALITY PRESERVE.** There are a couple of ways to suss this out when you're shopping. Look for:

- **Fruit listed as the first ingredient**, or preserves that have more fruit than they do sugar. The lower sugar is on the ingredient list, the better. Some producers state the sugar content as a percentage on the

---

PECTIN—THE PLOT THICKENS

A key objective in making preserves is taking juicy, liquidy fruit and turning it into something relatively thick and spreadable. One way to accomplish this is simply cooking the fruit until much of the moisture has evaporated, thus reducing the fruit to a jammy consistency. The other way is with pectin, a naturally occurring substance that acts as a binder to turn fruit's juice into gel. Some fruits contain no pectin of their own and so need supplemental pectin (either home-extracted or commercially produced) for thickening. But some fruits—like grapes, berries, and apples—contain enough pectin to gel on their own. There's nothing wrong with using supplemental pectin as a preserve ingredient, but there *is* something special about preserves made without extra pectin. It requires more skill, they have to be made in small batches, and it often means a more concentrated fruit flavor.

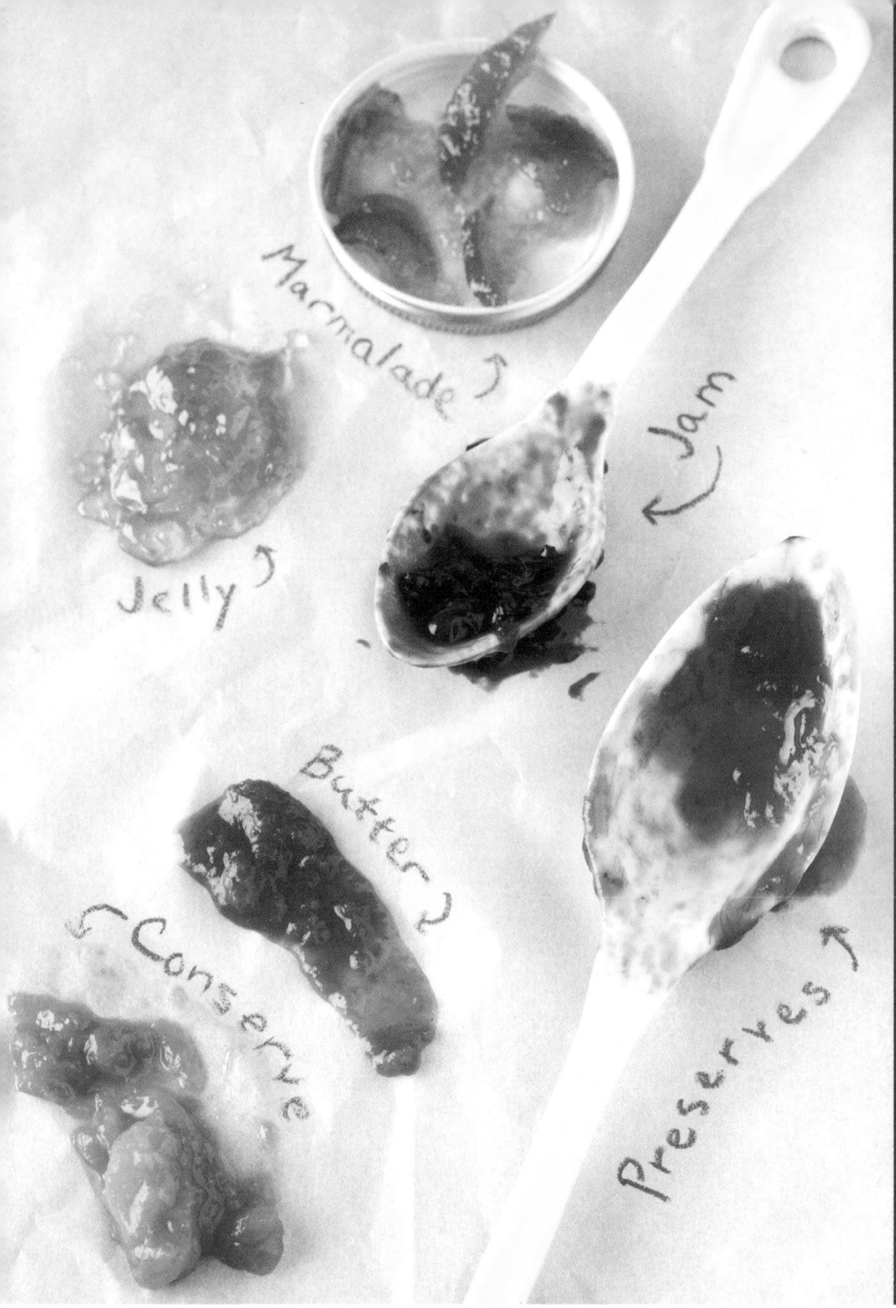

IN A REAL JAM

A selection of different types of preserves:

MARMALADE is made with the zest or rind of citrus fruit, giving it a bittersweet taste.

JAM is made from pureed or crushed fruit.

PRESERVES typically feature small chunks of fruit, creating a more interesting texture.

CONSERVE is usually made with little or no added pectin, so it has a looser consistency.

BUTTER is typically made from apples or pears but may also be made from other fruit such as peaches or nectarines. Think of it as a highly concentrated, cooked-down applesauce.

JELLY gets its jewel-like translucency from the fact that it's made from juice rather than the whole fruit.

label. In general, 30 percent sugar or less is a good range to look for. Most commercial preserves hover around 60 to 70 percent sugar.

Similarly, **AVOID PRESERVES THAT CONTAIN ANY SWEETENER OTHER THAN SUGAR OR FRUIT JUICE,** including artificial sweeteners. Note that some "sugar-free" preserves contain no sweetener whatsoever, whereas others contain artificial sweeteners. If sugar is a concern for you, read the label carefully and avoid the artificially spiked ones.

- **Organic fruit**—It's better for you and the environment and often tastes better.
- **Varietal-specific fruit**—I get excited whenever I see a label that lists Dapple Dandy pluots, Meyer lemon, Chandler strawberries, or other specialty fruits. It shows that the producer is passing up commodity fruit and choosing specific varieties for the best flavor possible.
- **Limited-edition flavors**—If you see flavors come and go within a certain brand, it probably means

they're working in smaller quantities, using what the seasons offer, rather than trying to produce year-round flavors (which likely means importing fruit from far-flung locales).

- **Farmer direct**—I love preserves that are made by the same person who grew the fruit. Supporting these value-added products gets more money back to the grower as well.

· ·

If you see "natural flavors" or "artificial flavors" in the ingredient list, beware. It's a sign that the producer is using not-so-great fruit and needs to compensate with additional flavors.

· ·

Some farmers can and preserve their own fruits and vegetables and offer them for sale alongside their fresh items. In the biz, these are called "value added" items, because they allow the farmer not just to preserve their product, but also to make use of slightly blemished produce that they might not otherwise be able to sell. These preserved items are often packed with flavor and also help provide a more sustainable cash flow for the farmer. Seek out and support farmer-made foods when you can!

· ·

Yes, high-quality preserves cost more than the mass-market versions, but it all comes back to the fruit: good preserves rely on ripe, flavorful fruit, which is by nature expensive. Additionally, good preserves take time; this is compounded by the fact that the very best producers work in small batches. Jar for jar,

---

AT THE VERY LEAST, LOOK FOR PRESERVES WITH:

- **More fruit than sugar (fruit first in the ingredient list)**
- **Organic fruit**
- **Sugar as the only sweetener (if any)**

IDEALLY, LOOK FOR:

- **Varietal-specific preserves or seasonal flavors**
- **No added pectin**
- **Less than 30 percent sugar**

---

artisan-made jams require more labor and time than factory-made ones. And a little bit of good jam goes a long way—you'll use much less of it compared to the standard kind.

How to Store

Once opened, preserves should be kept in the refrigerator. They'll last for months this way, but toss them once they become a growing medium for mold!

How to Use

Preserves can be used in many ways beyond slathering on toast. Stir it into yogurt, use as an ice cream topping, or serve it as a condiment with your favorite cheese. Try stirring a dollop of preserves into your favorite barbecue sauce; the sweet fruit will add a nice flavor dimension, as well as a glistening sheen, to whatever you use it on.

OILS

A small variety of oils is essential for any good cook. I generally keep three or four different oils on hand at a given time: two extra-virgin olive oils (one mild and one pungent), grapeseed oil for frying and sautéing at high heat or for a more neutral flavor, and a citrus-infused oil for finishing salads, pastas, or seafood. I'll talk shortly about what to look for and how to use the various oils you'll encounter in the grocery store. What's most important is to buy in small quantities and use it up quickly, rather than buying a larger bottle and taking longer to use it up. Oils become rancid very quickly and will add an unpleasant flavor to your dish. So don't hang on to that nice olive oil as though it were liquid gold—use it up and enjoy it while it's fresh!

Olive Oil

If I had to choose one fat to cook with—my "desert island" cooking fat, if you will—it would definitely be olive oil. It's an ingredient backed by (literally) millennia of tradition, and plays an important role in the cuisines and religions of many Mediterranean and Middle Eastern cultures. Even the techniques for making olive oil have withstood the test of time; many contemporary producers use virtually the same processes that were employed hundreds of years ago.

OLIVE OIL COMES IN ENDLESS PERMUTATIONS OF FLAVORS AND STYLES, which makes it infinitely interesting to use and enjoy. Where the olives are grown, the varietals used, and when the olives are picked are all variables that, in different combinations, can produce an oil that is fruity, buttery, peppery, grassy, pungent, citrusy, or even artichoke-y.

GOOD OLIVE OIL TRANSFORMS FOOD. In its most humble role as a sauté lubricant, it contributes subtle flavor to onions and other aromatics. But olive oil's true strength emerges when used in greater quantity—the flavors permeate and infuse, and the aromatics waft and tantalize. It is as much structural as it is aesthetic. I consider and use good extra-virgin olive oil more as a sauce and a condiment than as an oil.

How to Buy

AMONG OLIVE OILS, EXTRA-VIRGIN IS THE ONLY WAY TO GO. Buying extra-virgin olive oil (not "light" or "pure" varieties) guarantees that you're getting all the benefits that good olive oil has to offer:

- **Minimal processing using mechanics, not chemicals**—By definition, extra-virgin olive oil is made by grinding the fruit, centrifuging or cold-pressing the resulting paste once, and then filtering the oil. That's it! Other, more highly processed oils are often made through heat and chemical means, which results in poorer quality oil.
- **Balanced flavor**—Good olive oil will, more than anything, taste like olives, and be free of other competing flavor components. There is, of course, a wide range of qualities and styles of extra-virgin olive oil, but acidity is one easily quantifiable quality that is regulated by international standards. To be labeled "extra-virgin," the olive oil must have no more than 0.8 percent acidity; anything with less than 2 percent acidity is labeled as simply "virgin."
- **Health-boosting qualities**—All olive oil is rich in monounsaturated "heart healthy" fats, but extra-virgin olive oil also boasts a healthy dose of polyphenols. These antioxidants have anti-inflammatory properties and are associated with a lower risk of heart disease.

. . . .

A recent study found that 69 percent of imported extra-virgin olive oils tested (a sample that represented many of the most widely available supermarket brands) contained flaws and therefore did not meet the criteria for "extra-virgin." It just goes to show that a single phrase isn't enough to find a good olive oil. You have to look more closely for the criteria I outline here.

. . . .

Because olive oil is marketed as a "luxury" ingredient, its packaging has a tendency to be a bit over the top. You're likely to see uniquely shaped bottles, gold leaf lettering, fancy stamps, wax seals, and dangling tags—sometimes all on a single bottle! To a degree, the packaging does matter, but what's printed on the label is often more important. Here's a rundown of what you should look for, and why:

- **A dark glass or metal container**—This is the one instance in which the packaging really matters.

NUOVO OLIVE OIL

Called *olio nuovo* or "new oil" in northern Italy, *olio novello* in southern Italy, this is unfiltered oil made from the very first harvest of the olive season. The younger olives yield less oil than later-in-the-season harvests, but what they do produce is pungent, intensely flavorful, and highly prized. Nuovo oil is unfiltered and therefore highly volatile; its unique flavor lasts for only a few months after the bottle has been opened. It's generally shipped by air to the United States so that it gets to the consumer as fresh as possible. It's usually available until the spring, when the rest of the filtered oil arrives by container ship. It is best appreciated in the simplest of ways: poured onto a plate for dipping, or used to finish pasta, seafood, or meats. My favorite way is to drizzle it over the uberluscious cream-filled mozzarella known as burrata cheese and a loaf of crusty bread.

A selection of olive oils from around the world.

Oil will oxidize (go rancid) faster with extended exposure to light, and a dark or opaque container counteracts this tendency. Conversely, be cautious of olive oil in clear glass bottles. Good producers that use clear bottles often pack these bottles in boxes to minimize exposure to light.

- **The *real* country of origin**—Once upon a time, Italy was the only domestic source for great extra-virgin olive oil. There were plenty of other countries making high-quality oil (Greece, France, Israel, Spain, and Tunisia, to name a few), but they kept it to themselves and exported their sloppy seconds. Meanwhile, Italy eventually became synonymous with good-quality oil. Producers of lesser-quality oil began to say their product was "packed in Italy" as a way to confuse and mislead consumers. But in fact, "Packed in . . ." refers to where the oil was bottled, not necessarily where the olives were grown. There are great oils produced in these other countries, but they are often much cheaper than Italian oils. Having Italy on the bottle increases the perceived value, and these "packers" are blatantly ripping off the uninformed consumer. Be suspicious of ones that use this kind of wording. Good olive oil should proclaim its true origin loud and proud!
- **Harvest date**—Only a small fraction of olive oil producers bother to label their product with the harvest date, but if you can find it, it's an important indicator of quality. For one thing, it tells you the oil's age (harvest happens only once a year, so avoid any that are more than two years old), but it also shows that the producer cares about the freshness of their oil. The more specific the date, the more precisely the oil will reflect where and when it came from. Oils that list a span of time as the harvest date ("Fall 2011") or no date at all are usually blended to consistently match a certain flavor profile.
- **Estate bottled oil**—The key to good olive oil is to press the fruit as soon as possible after it is picked, generally the same day. With too much delay, the fruit deteriorates or even ferments; this leads to funky, musty, or otherwise defective oil. To minimize the time between picking and pressing, many producers have their own press situated on the same property as the olive trees.

**AT THE VERY LEAST,
LOOK FOR OLIVE OIL THAT IS:**

- **Extra-virgin**
- **In a dark glass or metal container**
- **Estate bottled**
- **Straightforward in its labeling of origin**
- **Less than two years old**

IDEALLY, LOOK FOR:

- **A specific harvest date, ideally from the most recent fall harvest**
- **Specific olive varietals listed on the bottle**

"Pure" olive oil, as virtuous as it sounds, is a cut-rate blend consisting of mostly low-grade chemically extracted olive oil, with at least 10 percent virgin olive oil added for flavor. It only vaguely resembles extra-virgin olive oil.

These are the most important, and also most frequently seen, indicators of quality olive oil. However, there are many other such indicators, and they often vary from one producing country to the next. A sampling is shown in the box below.

IF YOU CAN, TASTE BEFORE YOU BUY. Relatively few stores offer this service, but it's worth seeking out, especially if you're buying high-end oils. Olive oil tasting works much like wine tasting.

1. **Start by warming the tasting cup,** which helps aerate the aromatic molecules. Hold the cup in one hand and cover the cup with the other hand as you swirl the contents around. After twenty seconds or so, lift up the covering hand and take a whiff. The oil should smell like fresh-cut grass. It should not smell musty at all; if it does, it can be a symptom of a defective oil. (Or it may just mean that the sampling bottle has been open too long and the oil has become rancid. Ask a staffer to try it, and open a new sample bottle if necessary. We've had sample bottles go "off" after a couple of months and not realized until we tasted with a guest.)
2. **Take a small sip of the oil** and suck in some air along with it. This helps "open up" the oil on your palate. Swish the oil around in your mouth.

UNPACKING OLIVE OIL LABELS

Estate bottled—The producer has an olive press on site, thus shortening the time between harvest and pressing to a matter of hours, rather than days.

Harvest date—This is when the olives were picked and pressed. Afterward, the oil is transferred to large holding tanks to settle.

Bottling date—This is when the oil was transferred from the tank into this particular bottle.

Fair trade certified—This third-party certification ensures

that the people who produced the oil had good working conditions and were paid fairly.

Best before end—This gives you an idea of the oil's shelf life. Most producers give their oil eighteen to twenty-four months.

Demoninacio d'origen or DO—Guarantees that the oil came from a specific designated region whose production standards are certified and approved by the home country's government.

Acidity = 0.1 percent—A producer may note that their oil's acidity is lower than that required by international standards.

Imported from Italy—A tricky one! It doesn't necessar-

ily mean the olives were grown in Italy. The back label often tells the whole story: "Packed in Italy with selected oils from Italy, Spain, Greece, and Tunisia."

California Olive Oil Council (COOC)—This organization of intensely passionate California olive oil producers is helping to establish the culture of American-made olive oil. Its certification process ensures defect-free extra-virgin olive oil with no more than 0.5 percent acidity (lower than international standards).

McEVOY RANCH OLIVE OIL:
Shari de Joseph and Jeff Creque

"Cutting corners" is not part of McEvoy Ranch's vocabulary. When Nan McEvoy started the company in 1991, nobody else was growing Tuscan olive varietals in California. That meant there was nobody to buy the olive trees from, so she imported them from Italy. And rather than transporting her olives to a remote mill, she had one built on the property. This made it possible to press the olives within eight hours of being picked—well within the California Olive Oil Council's maximum of twenty-four hours, which, more importantly, makes for better oil. Two decades later, Nan still runs the company with the help from orchard manager Shari de Joseph and mill manager Jeff Creque. They, along with the rest of the McEvoy Ranch staff, have set the bar for olive oil in California—and the world.

3. Swallow and tune in to the flavors that unfold. You might choke a little bit—that's the peppery polyphenols showing their punch—but that's normal. Now that you've primed the pump, take another sip and let it all sink in. What do you notice? How strong or mellow does it seem? Does it have any particularly unique flavor qualities? If greasiness is the predominant quality you experience, the oil is probably "off" or not of good quality.

This technique is designed to amplify the olive oil's qualities so that they're easier to notice and identify. This can make some oils seem overwhelmingly bitter or pungent, but keep in mind that they will seem tamer and smoother when you actually use them with food.

How to Use

If you're like me and use olive oil more than any other fat in the kitchen, you'll probably want to keep a couple of different olive oils on hand. This may seem extravagant, but the truth is that one olive oil does not fit all cooking situations, and you'll get more mileage out of it, ingredient-wise, when you diversify.

FIRST, A LIGHT AND ELEGANT EXTRA-VIRGIN OLIVE OIL. This is the oil to use for delicate salad dressings, aioli, and other gently flavored dishes that would be dominated by a more assertive, bitter olive oil. The Citrus Olive Oil Cake on page 63 is a good example. The cooler coastal regions of the Mediterranean, such as Provence, Catalonia, and Liguria, as well as Chile, produce these smoother and nuttier oils. Picholine, taggiasca, and arbequina olives generally produce this type of oil.

SECOND, A PUNGENT, SOMEWHAT BITTER VERSION. You might use this for Bagna Cauda (page 52), roasting earthy root vegetables, or tossing with similarly feisty broccoli rabe. A robust oil is also good as a final flourish drizzled onto soups. This flavor profile is most classically represented in Tuscan olive oils; it can also be found in Californian and some Spanish oils. Frantoia, leccino, moraiolo, and piqual are examples of olives that produce more robust oils.

Armed with these two very different types of olive oil, you'll feel more agile in the kitchen, with more control over the end result of a dish.

> ### BI-RITE'S BASICS:
> ■ Two extra-virgin olive oils: one delicate, the other assertive
> ■ Grapeseed or other neutral, non-GMO oil

"Vegetable" Oil and Alternatives

As wonderful as extra-virgin olive oil is, sometimes you simply do not want that fruity, olivey flavor in your food. In those cases, like the Ginger-Lemongrass Chicken Skewers on page 184, a neutral-flavored oil is more appropriate.

Canola or "vegetable" oil (which is usually soybean or cottonseed oil) would be the obvious choice, but this poses a glaring and hard-to-avoid problem: GMOs. Like corn, **THE CANOLA AND SOYBEAN INDUSTRIES ARE HEAVILY DEPENDENT ON GENETICALLY MODIFIED SEEDS,** whose safety and sustainability are highly questionable. Canola in particular poses a significant threat: a small, delicate seed, easily carried by the wind, it's prone to contaminating nearby fields. Unless the label specifies otherwise or is organic, you can assume that any canola or vegetable oil in the grocery store comes from GMO seeds.

FOR A NEUTRAL OIL, GRAPESEED IS THE BEST AND MOST READILY AVAILABLE CHOICE. This oil is made as a byproduct of winemaking (the seeds are separated after the grapes are pressed into juice). Look for "cold press" grapeseed oil, which means the oil was extracted mechanically rather than by way of a chemical solvent. Other good neutral-tasting options include oil made from peanuts, rice bran, avocado, and macadamia nuts. Of these, peanut oil is the most readily available in stores; the others can be a little harder to find.

For frying or other high-heat cooking, smoke point is an important factor to consider. Smoke point is the temperature at which a particular oil starts to smoke and break down; extra-virgin olive oil has a low smoke point, which makes it unsuitable for frying. For best results (and health), use a high smoke point oil to fry (one that can withstand 400°F is a good target). Grapeseed, rice bran, peanut, almond, and avocado oil are all good choices for high-temperature cooking.

Other "Accessory" Varieties

Aside from your basic, workhorse oils like olive and grapeseed, there are other specialty oils on the market that you may want to explore. Most of these oils are highly concentrated in flavor and carry a heftier price tag, so they're best reserved for light-handed finishing and drizzling.

- **Nut oils** include hazelnut, walnut, and pecan oils. These oils go rancid very quickly, especially when exposed to light or heat, so be sure to buy from a reputable retailer with good turnover. La Tourangelle and J. Leblanc are two good brands to look for.
- **Truffle oil** is easy to overdose on; a little goes a long way, so if you use it, do so sparingly. Most truffle oil is made with a synthetic chemical, a far less expensive ingredient than actual truffles. To make sure you're getting the real deal, look for bottles that specifically list truffles in the ingredients.
- **Citrus oils** are made by crushing whole citrus fruit and olives together. The result has a unique, deep flavor that is a wonderful complement to grilled fish or salad dressings. You can even drizzle it over ice cream, like in the Sam's Sundae (page 67).

How to Store

Proper storage is the number one thing you can do to keep your oils delicious and usable. The main goal is to slow down oxidation—an inevitable process that eventually makes an oil go rancid.

KEEP IT COOL (NOT COLD) AND DARK. Heat and light accelerate oxidation, so a cool, dark place such as a cabinet is best. Avoid cabinets above the refrigerator or stove, which tend to be warmer than other parts of the kitchen. And do not store oils in the refrigerator, as the condensation that forms will have a negative impact on the flavor.

WHAT'S THAT SMELL? Although I have no data to back this up, I'd venture to say that 90 percent of the oil in American households is rancid. The reasons should be obvious: we buy oil in huge quantities, we store it in the hottest areas of the kitchen, and we're reluctant to use it. Rancid oil not only is unpleasant on the palate but also poses a variety of threats to our health. **AIM TO USE YOUR OIL WITHIN A MONTH OR TWO OF OPENING, BUT ALSO USE YOUR NOSE AS A GUIDE.** If an oil smells musky, funky, or just plain "off," don't use it—for anything. Discard it and get a new bottle.

How to Use

Recently I watched a foodie travel show featuring the cuisine of Spain. As I watched each dish being prepared, I couldn't help but notice that every single one, from the most elaborate entrée to the simplest tapa, was finished with a healthy drizzle of extra-virgin olive oil. Moreover, this trick showed up in the home kitchens as much as it did in restaurants. It's a striking contrast to us here in the States, where that final splash of oil tends to be considered a chef's trick, not something we do at home. It needn't be that way—like a squeeze of lemon, a judicious drizzle of olive oil makes just about everything more delicious—and it's an easy way to work more of those healthy fats into your diet.

USE GOOD OIL WITH RECKLESS ABANDON. It kills me to see people plonk down $20 to $30 on a bottle of gorgeous olive oil, only to treat it like their good china by stashing it away and saving it only for special occasions. Oil is meant to be used and enjoyed in its prime. (For a reference point, in my house we go through a liter of extra-virgin olive oil every two weeks.)

PASTA

There's no better convenience food than dried pasta. A one-pound box, along with some garlic, olive oil, and Parmigiano-Reggiano will have you well on your way to a twenty-minute, four-ingredient dinner. But such simple preparations do rely on excellent quality raw materials, starting with the pasta. Much like bread, pasta is made of simple ingredients: flour and water. But also like bread, the quality of the flour and the technique used to make it have a tremendous effect on the final product.

OLD-SCHOOL PASTA IS BEST. The technological advances of the last century have not been kind to dried pasta. Modern machinery speeds up the process undesirably and creates a physically different and inferior product. The best pastas are made the way they were a hundred years ago and are identifiable by several hallmark traits:

- **Better flour**—The best pastas use semolina flour, yellow-tinged and made from high-protein durum wheat. This protein (also known as gluten) gives pasta a particularly nice "chew" when cooked. For even more unique flavor, a few companies use heirloom varieties of wheat; these are worth trying.

- **Bronze dies**—Once the pasta dough is made, it's extruded through a die, very similar to the way meat comes out of a meat grinder. The material of the die actually has a major impact on the pasta. Bronze dies, although they're expensive and wear out quickly, are the choicest ones because they produce pasta with a distinctively rough texture due to the softer quality of the metal. That extra surface area acts as a magnet for sauce and makes it cling nicely to the pasta. Modern pasta machinery uses nonstick coated dies, which are cheap, last longer, and extrude the pasta more quickly and efficiently, but they create an ultra-smooth surface on the pasta, so sauce slides right off. If you look closely, you can see the visibly rough texture of bronze die–extruded pasta. See the photo on page 38 for a few examples.

- **Long drying time**—Back in the olden days, you'd make your pasta, cut it out, and let it dry in the sun or a warm kitchen over the course of a day or two. Aside from transforming the pasta into a shelf-stable product, that leisurely drying time actually improves the flavor and texture of the pasta. However, most commercial pasta producers use high-temperature heaters to dry their pastas in a matter of minutes, thus sacrificing quality for efficiency. Look for "air-dried" pastas, or ones that specify a twenty-four-hour (or longer) drying time.

AT THE VERY LEAST, LOOK FOR PASTA MADE WITH:

- Semolina flour, otherwise known as durum wheat or "hard" wheat

- A bronze die (if the label doesn't specify, you can tell just by looking at the pasta)

IDEALLY, LOOK FOR:

- Heirloom wheat / whole grains

- A long drying time—ideally twenty-four hours or longer

PASTA PROFILES

Any self-respecting Italian would probably tell you that each size and shape of dried pasta is perfectly suited for one sauce only. To me, though, all dried pastas can be grouped into one of several broad categories and are more or less interchangeable within each one:

- **LONG, TWIRLABLE PASTA** like spaghetti and linguine. These are perfectly suited to sauces with a fairly smooth, uniform texture. (Sauces with large chunks of meat or veggies can be awkward to eat with tangly shapes like these.)

- **SHORT, OFTEN TUBULAR PASTA** like penne, ziti, rigatoni, and fusili. These are fairly sturdy and hold up to chunky or thick sauces, particularly ones featuring hefty doses of meat or cream. They are also good choices for creamy sauces or using in pasta salads.

- **CUP-SHAPED PASTA** like shells, orecchiette, and the confusingly named "gnocchi" (named after their resemblance to the fluffy potato nuggets). These are similarly suited to meat- or veggie-heavy dishes, as the sauce can nestle into the cups.

- **HAND-ROLLED PASTAS** are often delicate, almost wispy in character, and work best with the same kinds of smooth sauces that you'd use on linguine or spaghetti.

- **GRAIN-SHAPED PASTAS** like orzo, ditalini, and fregola are nice additions to soups, or mixed with grains and veggies for a hearty salad.

How to Store

As long as it's in an airtight container away from moisture and in a cool, dark place, pasta will last nearly indefinitely.

How to Use

Unless I'm making filled pasta like ravioli, or a simple linguine from scratch, I rely on the dried kind for the majority of my pasta cooking needs. I love the toothy texture that dried pasta offers, and it's easy to keep on hand.

A few simple tricks will help pasta cook quickly and evenly:

- **Use lots of water**—A nearly-full soup pot is about right for a pound of pasta.

- **Salt the cooking water generously**—It should taste salty like the sea. How do you know? Dip a spoon in and taste it!

- **As soon as you add the pasta, do two things**—stir for the first few minutes, and make sure the heat is cranked all the way up. The stirring prevents the pasta from sticking together, and the high heat ensures that the water stays at a boil (or returns to it quickly) for even cooking.

FINISH IT IN THE SAUCE. Chefs always admonish home cooks to avoid overcooking pasta: to cook it just to al dente, and no further. Although this is certainly true—pasta really does lose much of its nutrition, spring, and personality when cooked to total softness—in my mind it's secondary to the "mother rule" of cooking pasta, and that is to finish cooking pasta in the sauce. This accomplishes a couple of things. One, it slows down the pace at which the pasta cooks, which makes it easier to determine when to pull the plug, so to speak. And two, it gives the pasta a chance to soak up and bind with the sauce, which creates a more cohesive dish.

To do this, scoop out and reserve a cup or so of the starch-enriched pasta cooking water, and drain the pasta a minute or two before you think it will reach al dente. (If you bite into a piece, you should still see a speck of white at the center.) Combine the pasta with the sauce and add a splash or two of the pasta water. Continue to cook over medium to low heat, stirring frequently, until the sauce has thickened and absorbed into the pasta, and the pasta is just barely al dente. If the sauce thickens before the pasta is done, add a little more pasta water to loosen it up.

Because the pasta water is salted, make sure your sauce is slightly under-salted so you don't end up with a salty dish. You can always add more salt later.

NON-WHEAT PASTAS

No longer limited to white-wheat pasta, the pasta aisle now features products made from whole wheat, corn, rice, kamut, and beyond. Aside from offering certain health benefits (such as extra dietary fiber or being gluten-free), they present an even wider variety of flavors and textures. Because these pastas often lack the gluten present in traditional pasta, they are less forgiving and become mushy if overcooked. Take care in cooking them to preserve their shape and texture.

Several of the recipes here illustrate this technique: Delfina's Spaghetti (page 61) features a classic tomato sauce, whereas the Orecchiette with White Beans and Chard (page 60) is more of a brothy pan sauce.

RICE AND GRAINS

Many so-called "specialty" items you see on grocery store shelves are there thanks to the fanaticism of restaurant chefs. The Italian grain farro is a perfect example; it started making appearances on restaurant menus in the early 2000s, about the same time we began featuring it in our deli salads. As guests became enamored with the chewy, nutty grain, more of them wanted to make it at home, so we decided to put uncooked farro on our shelves. At first, the only farro we could get was in food service–size five-kilo bags, which we then repackaged into smaller quantities. Within a year, though, the producer started to offer retail-size bags—an undeniable sign that farro had made the leap from restaurant to home.

How to Buy

Although rice and grains have fairly good holding power on the shelf, brown rice and most whole grains (those that have not been polished or "pearled") contain fats that will eventually turn rancid. If you buy your grains from the bulk section of the store (a good idea, because you can buy as little or as much as you like), be sure to sniff before you scoop. It should be free of any "off" odors, which signal rancidity.

If not buying in bulk, be sure to buy rice and grains that are in airtight packages. (Porous materials like burlap allow odors and moisture to permeate the product inside.)

These crops are typically grown with a heavy dose of pesticides, especially in rice fields, so buy organic rice and grains whenever you can. Additionally, there are now many farmers growing grains and rice across the country, especially in the Northwest, Southeast, and Western regions. You may have one or more grain or rice farmer near you, so keep an eye out for their products and support them.

LOOK FOR RICE AND GRAINS THAT ARE:

• Free of any "off" odors (if you can smell them)

• In airtight packages (if prepackaged)

• Organically and/or locally grown

How to Store

Store rice and grains in airtight containers, which ensures they don't absorb moisture or odors. Store them at cool room temperature or in the refrigerator for a few months. You may also freeze them for longer storage (up to a year). Always sniff before using, to make sure they haven't gone rancid.

How to Use

BARLEY has a pleasant chewy texture; the most common type of barley has been polished, or "pearled," to remove the exterior bran and germ. It releases some of its starch as it cooks, which gives soups a little extra body. Barley is a wonderful hearty addition to salads.

FARRO, a member of the wheat family, is traditional to certain Italian cuisines. It has a nutty, robust flavor and a decidedly chewy texture (more so than barley, for instance). Depending on how much of the bran has been removed, farro may be labeled as *perlato* or *semi-perlato,* the latter being more common and more polished. It's nice as a side dish, especially when paired with mushrooms or roasted vegetables, in soups, or slow-cooked as you would for risotto.

OATS can be used in many different ways, depending on how they're processed. Steel-cut or Irish oats are oat grains that have been cut crosswise into just two or three pieces, so they maintain their wonderful chewy texture when cooked. Rolled oats have been steamed and flattened, which allows them to absorb liquids quickly. Rolled oats are commonly used in baking recipes, as well as the meatloaf on page 191. Steel-cut oats are not interchangeable with rolled oats, unless you're just cooking a pot for breakfast. They take longer to cook than rolled oats do, but you can use a slow cooker for easy, hands-off preparation.

POLENTA (and its cousin, grits) is corn that has been dried and ground—essentially, it's cornmeal. Polenta comes in a variety of consistencies; some (especially stone-ground ones) can be very coarse, and others are quite fine, almost powdery. Experiment to find your favorite. For runny polenta, use six parts liquid to one part dry polenta; for firm, use four parts liquid to one part dry. Polenta is one of my favorite all-purpose side dishes, especially when paired with stews or braised meats. It goes especially well with cheese, butter, ricotta, and fresh herbs.

QUINOA is an ancient grain of Peru's Inca people. The pellet-like grains are a complete protein and come in white, red, or black varieties. I like the red for its color, but all are tasty. When cooked, they have a fluffy, almost couscous-like texture, which makes them particularly good in salads, but they are also nice in soups. Cook it just as you would pasta.

RICE is generally classified as long-, medium-, or short-grained; short-grained rices are short and fat, and long-grained rices are long and skinny. In general, long-grained rices such as jasmine and basmati will produce fluffy, separate grains once cooked. They're good for pilafs and salads, or just plain as a starchy side.

Short-grained rices are often labeled as "glutinous" or "sticky" rice, even though they contain no gluten, because they release a lot of starch that causes the grains to cling together. This makes them perfectly suited for risotto, paella, and similar dishes; Arborio, Bomba, and Carnaroli are some of the most widely available varieties.

The term "brown rice" refers to rice that still has the germ and bran attached, and nowadays you can find brown versions of most varieties of rice. Red and black rices are similarly unprocessed, and have honey-like flavor notes (though they are not actually sweet). These rices don't have quite the same absorbent quality that white rice does, but they are more nutritious and offer more interesting flavor and texture. Note that brown, red, and black rices take longer to cook than white rice, so they cannot always be substituted directly in a recipe.

SEASONING

Learning how to season food is something that takes practice but can immeasurably improve one's cooking.

Salt

Salt is critical not just to our very existence but also to so many culinary techniques. Without salt, we would have no lox, bacon, or salami. It is also the key in keeping bread dough in check and in turning cheese curds into aged cheese—and, of course, it makes your ice cream freeze a lot faster.

It's also one of the most basic ingredients in the kitchen, and if you remember nothing else from high school chemistry, odds are that you know NaCl is the formula for salt. It's funny, then, that salt shows up in so many "chefy" forms, especially in gourmet stores. There's smoked salt, lavender salt, and fennel salt; pink salt from the Himalayas, gray salt from France, and countless others from locations in between. Although these salts are interesting and can be fun to play with, I prefer to keep things simple and stock just a few types of salt in my kitchen.

BI-RITE'S BASICS:
- Fine sea salt, for baking recipes that call for it
- A finishing salt, for sprinkling
- Kosher salt, for everything else

How to Buy

AVOID IODIZED TABLE SALT. Although iodine is essential to our health, I find that iodized salt has an artificial, metallic flavor that is unpleasant. Besides, it seems silly to "fortify" salt when you can get iodine naturally in foods such as seaweed and seafood.

FINE SEA SALT is similar to table salt in size and shape, but has a slightly moister consistency that causes the grains to cling together (unlike table salt grains, which slide and spread easily). The smaller grains disperse and dissolve quickly, which is why it's often used in baking recipes.

Sea salts give a pleasant mineral tang to food, but for some reason it generally comes in only two grades. Although the fine version is great for baking, the coarse one is too chunky for my everyday needs.

KOSHER SALT is my number one, go-to salt. Not only do the size and shape of the grains make it easy to pick up, but the heftier grains also make it easy to sprinkle evenly over a broad surface. I prefer Diamond Crystal over all other brands. It's perfect for brines, blanching water, or pasta cooking water. Keep in mind that 1 tablespoon coarse or kosher salt equals 2 teaspoons table salt, so be sure to adjust accordingly if substituting one for another. Tasting is still the best way to ensure a great dish.

FINISHING SALTS have a delicate flavor and/or texture, and as such are generally used almost as a garnish for food. I keep two distinct varieties on hand. England's Maldon brand salt is one of my favorites; it's a pure white salt that naturally forms as distinctive hollow pyramids. It has a flakiness that lends itself to crumbling over a dish, and it adds a nice little crunch as well. I also use *sel gris*, a gray sea salt from France with a coarse texture and a robust flavor from the bits of seaweed that cling to it. It has a more distinct mineral flavor than Maldon and is great for roast meats and poultry.

I use finishing salts to sprinkle over sliced tomatoes, top off a whole roasted fish, or garnish grilled veggies. I also keep a ramekin of finishing salt at the dinner table; compared to a shaker, it just feels better to sprinkle salt with your fingers.

How to Store

Protected from moisture, salt will last indefinitely. Salts that are blended with spices should be used within six months.

How to Use

The kind of salt you use is not nearly as important as how and when you use it. It takes a long time for most chefs to learn to season properly, and most home cooks are timid about this.

HONING YOUR SEASONING INSTINCTS HAS A HUGE PAYOFF. However, it takes lots of time and tasting to really get the hang of it. You'll find that most of the recipes in this book provide specific salt quantities but also include a "season to taste" note near the end. This provides a rough starting point for how much salt a dish will require, but leaves some wiggle room to account for variations in ingredients (like homemade versus store-bought broth) as well as personal taste.

GIVE YOURSELF READY ACCESS. Salt is an indispensible ingredient, and the way you store it should reflect that. Seasoning comes much more naturally when you don't have to wrestle with a big box or a pour spout, so keep a good supply of salt (at least half a cup) in a bowl, crock, or other wide-mouthed open container. And although I give precise measurements

for salt in most recipes, I also value the instinctive, tactile approach of just reaching in, taking a pinch, and sprinkling away.

SALT EARLY AND OFTEN. Salt is most effective when you season from the inside out, by which I mean that you give salt a chance to permeate every ingredient. How? Rather than just adding salt at the very end, it's much better to season at regular intervals throughout the cooking process.

The Beef Stew with Peppers and Ale on page 181 is an example. The recipe instructs you to season at several different stages: before cooking the beef, as you add the onions, and when you add the liquid. Building flavor as it cooks helps produce a dish that is evenly seasoned throughout.

If, instead, you make the entire dish and add salt only at the very end, the salt will dissolve and season the brothy liquid, but it won't have a chance to permeate the solid ingredients. The overall effect: uneven seasoning and a flat taste.

Also, the larger and denser the ingredient, the longer it takes for salt to penetrate fully. That's why many recipes instruct you to season large cuts of meat the day before you plan to cook them. I always salt a chicken the day before I roast it.

BI-RITE'S BASICS:

- Bay leaf
- Cayenne pepper
- Chile flakes
- Ground cinnamon
- Coriander seed
- Cumin seed
- Fennel seed
- Mild curry powder
- Whole nutmeg
- *Pimentón* (see sidebar)
- Saffron

PIMENTÓN

This special variety of paprika is traditional to Spain and integral to its cuisine. True *pimentón* is ground from peppers that are dried over wood fires, which gives the final product a distinctive smoky flavor. It can be mild or spicy and is labeled as such: **dulce** (sweet or mild), **agridulce** (medium), or **picante** (hot). Quite a few American spice brands have started offering their own versions, but for the best quality look for Spanish brands from the La Vera or Murcia regions. Use *pimentón* in rubs, marinades, and soups or sprinkle it on as a garnish.

TASTE AS YOU GO. Taste before and after each addition of salt. Before, because you might find that it's plenty seasoned already; after, to see what difference you've made. This will make accidental oversalting less likely and also helps you understand how just a little extra salt can wake up a dish.

SEASON THOUGHTFULLY. Although it is important to take a preemptive approach to seasoning, it is unarguably easier to add salt than it is to take it away. So food should remain slightly underseasoned throughout cooking; it's better to take this cautious approach and perfect the seasoning at the very end. Also, think about the final product as you season and remember that salt becomes concentrated as a liquid evaporates. That perfectly seasoned broth may become too salty by the time it reduces to the desired sauce consistency.

The other thing to keep in mind is that different temperatures require different degrees of seasoning. Cold food always needs a little more salt than it would if it were hot or at room temperature; if you plan to serve a dish chilled, be sure to taste and correct the seasoning if necessary after it has chilled.

. . . .

Acid can help temper salt, so if you fear you've over-seasoned, a squeeze of lemon juice may help.

. . . .

Pepper

Used in moderation, black pepper can be a magical ingredient; a turn or two of the pepper grinder releases intoxicating floral notes as well as a delicate heat. However, I find that it's used too often and too heavy-handedly. Black pepper is most effective when used as the finishing touch on a dish—just a few grinds right before serving. Use fresh tellicherry peppercorns and always grind them yourself. Pepper mills vary in their quality and efficiency; Peugeot and Unicorn both make excellent versions.

Other Dry Herbs and Spices

Freshness is critical to getting the most out of the spices you use; the essential oils that give spices their flavor start to disappear in as little as six months. But when jarred spices run $4 to $6 a pop, it's hard to convince yourself to replace a spice you already have at home. The solution is simple and can be found at most natural food stores: **BUY YOUR SPICES IN BULK.** The benefits are many:

- **Higher turnover of inventory**—so the spices are fresher to start with
- **Custom quantities**—you can buy as much or as little as you need, thus minimizing leftovers destined to go stale
- **Less expensive**—often significantly lower than jarred spices
- **Less packaging**—so you can reuse whatever jars you have at home
- **More organic options**—better flavor, better for you, better for the environment

In my home kitchen I keep only a small collection of spices on hand, which also helps keep the supply as fresh as possible. The recipes in this book are written in the same spirit and tend to rely on a handful of readily available, versatile spices.

How to Store

Once opened, keep spices in individual, airtight containers and away from light and heat. Use within six months of opening.

How to Use

FOR MAXIMUM FLAVOR, BUY WHOLE SPICES AND GRIND THEM YOURSELF. Once ground, spices start to lose their potency, so it's always preferable to grind them just before using. Spices that come in seed form (like coriander and cumin) lend themselves especially well to this. A mortar and pestle is ideal, as it pulverizes spices and releases the essential oils more thoroughly. However, a coffee grinder works, too—just be sure to wipe it out before and after using it.

Toasting spices in a dry skillet also develops and transforms their flavor. It's easiest to do this when they're still whole, but you can also do it with ground spices as long as you stir constantly and thoroughly. Two minutes over medium heat is usually enough; you'll know they're ready when they darken slightly and become aromatic. Immediately transfer to a plate to prevent burning from the residual heat of the pan.

SUGAR

Like salt, sugar and other sweeteners have become a cheap ingredient that food manufacturers add to processed foods to give them "flavor." Over time we've become not just desensitized to sugar, but also addicted to it. In fact, we consume 50 percent more sugar and sweeteners annually than we did in the 1950s, much of that hidden in processed foods. The best rule of thumb? Avoid those processed foods, and treat sugary foods as an occasional indulgence.

How to Buy

Once upon a time, all granulated sugar was made from sugarcane. Over time, however, the industry also started using the sugar beet (a variety very different from the beets found in the produce section) as a cheaper and easier way to produce sugar. Big deal, you think—sugar is sugar, right?

Actually, it's not so simple. Beet sugar falls short in multiple ways: it does not melt as smoothly or caramelize as readily, and in baked goods it produces inferior texture and flavor. For the best flavor, texture, and overall quality, **BUY SUGAR THAT SPECIFICALLY STATES**

> ### LOOK FOR SUGAR THAT IS:
> - **Made from sugarcane, not sugar beets, to ensure non-GMO**
> - **Organic**

"PURE CANE SUGAR" ON THE PACKAGE. Many sugars do not specify whether they are beet or cane, so take a close look before you make your selection.

BUY ORGANIC SUGAR WHENEVER YOU CAN; sugar beets are almost always genetically modified, and any conventional sugar is typically heavily sprayed with pesticides and other chemicals. (For one possible exception to this recommendation, see "How to Use.")

How to Store

Sugar absorbs moisture and odors, so store it in an airtight container at room temperature. It will keep indefinitely.

How to Use

Sugar is available in various forms, each uniquely suited to a specific range of uses. For best results, stick with whatever form is called for in a recipe; making

OTHER SWEETENERS OF NOTE

Agave nectar has become popular as an alternative to sugar because of its lower glycemic index (GI). Most of it, however, is highly processed; raw agave nectar is the exception and is preferable to the processed kind.

Corn syrup is what gives pecan pie filling that rich, decadent quality. As a corn derivative, most corn syrup is made from GMO corn. There are some organic corn syrups available, which by definition are GMO-free, but they are much runnier than conventional corn syrup and produce a similarly runny final product.

Tapioca syrup is a good, GMO-free substitute for corn syrup.

Maple syrup is made by tapping the sap from maple trees and reducing it . . . and reducing it . . . and reducing it to make a thick syrup (it usually takes forty gallons of sap to produce just one gallon of syrup). Be sure to buy pure maple syrup, not "pancake syrup," which often contains artificial flavors. Grade A light amber maple syrup has a very light, delicate maple flavor. Grade A medium amber syrup, while more flavorful than light amber, still has a mild maple flavor; this is the grade that most people buy. Grade A dark amber has a deeper, more full-bodied maple flavor. Grade B maple syrup

has a deep, robust flavor, even more flavorful than grade A dark amber. Grade A dark amber and grade B are the best choices for cooking.

Molasses is a byproduct of the sugar-making process. Different grades are available; light molasses is the least processed and has a mild flavor, whereas dark molasses has been further reduced and is slightly bitter. Blackstrap molasses is the most highly processed type and has a very robust flavor. Many producers add sulfur dioxide to clarify and preserve molasses; buy unsulfured molasses if it's available.

substitutions can lead to surprising (sometimes undesirable) textures and flavor combinations.

GRANULATED SUGAR is your all-purpose baking and sweetening sugar. It's also the best kind to use for any kind of caramelizing or candy making; organic sugar is slightly more temperamental in this regard, so you may want to stick with conventional granulated sugar for those recipes.

TURBINADO OR "RAW" SUGAR consists of large, pale beige crystals that make an attractive garnish for cookies and pie crusts.

BROWN SUGAR is usually made by incorporating processed sugar with molasses (which is itself a byproduct of the sugar-making process). It adds a deeper flavor to baked goods, and also produces a soft, chewy texture.

DEMERARA OR "NATURAL BROWN" SUGAR is made solely from sugarcane (rather than adding molasses back to sugar). It is light brown in color and is somewhat drier than brown sugar but produces similar results. **MUSCOVADO,** a similar product, is even darker and more robust in flavor.

POWDERED OR CONFECTIONERS' SUGAR has been processed to a fine powder that dissolves quickly and smoothly. (It's also called icing sugar, for good reason.) It usually has some amount of cornstarch added to help keep it dry and clump-free.

VINEGARS

Acids, including vinegars, are a kind of culinary magic wand: they temper salt, add depth, and heighten flavors. They put all the elements in balance. So if you have any desire to improve your cooking, acids are a great place to start, and vinegars are one way to make your food taste brighter.

A Primer on Vinegars

When we talk about vinegars, we're generally speaking of **WINE-BASED VINEGARS** (with the exception of balsamic—more on that shortly).

Most wine vinegars on the market are blended: they're made from a mishmash of wines that represent a variety of grapes, growing locations, and winemakers. These are cheaper because the vinegar producer can use just about any kind of wine available regardless of quality or quantity. Blending helps ensure consistency across batches, but it also means vinegars with less distinctive personalities.

There are red and white wine vinegars, of course, but some wine vinegars are more specific as far as the grapes, region, and/or techniques represented.

- **Single varietal grapes**—Sauvignon Blanc and Zinfandel vinegars may be aged in oak barrels, just like wine, to mellow and further develop flavors. These are fabulous in vinaigrettes or in meat and seafood dishes.
- **Region and technique**—Jerez (sherry) vinegar and Banyuls vinegar are region-specific wines from Spain and Southern France, respectively. Both vinegars are aged in oak barrels, imparting a nutty, vanilla quality. Jerez employs a special blending process that involves careful mixing of previous years' batches into the newest barrels. Banyuls wine ages in the sun, which leads to maderization—a process that lends a cooked, raisiny flavor to the resulting wine. In both varieties, the wines are then made into vinegars, which are intriguingly complex. These vinegars are great for deglazing a sauté of vegetables or pan-fried lamb or chicken.
- **Fruit vinegars** are made from the fermented juice of any fruit. These tend to be light to medium in acidity and have a clean, somewhat neutral flavor that makes them good all-purpose acids. Toss with fresh fruit for fruit salads with zing; mix with sparkling mineral water for a refreshing beverage.

BI-RITE'S BASICS:

- Wine vinegar: one red, one white/champagne, and one sherry or Banyuls
- Fruit vinegar: apple cider, raspberry, plum, or cherry
- Balsamic vinegar
- Unseasoned rice vinegar

KATZ & COMPANY: Albert Katz

Albert Katz's story is not too different from my own; like me, he's a former restaurant chef who decided to start a new venture outside of the kitchen. In Albert's case, he used his understanding of great ingredients as the basis for making small-batch, artisanal vinegars. Albert focuses on producing vinegar that is harmonious with food—not just in vinaigrettes, but also in sauces and desserts. To accomplish this, he grows most of his own grapes, turns it into wine, and then employs the traditional Orleans method of producing vinegar, which takes time and effort but produces a more complex and food-friendly product. He also raises chickens on his property and produces olive oil. It's a symbiotic relationship, as the chickens fertilize the trees and in turn enjoy the shade the trees provide. I have a lot of respect for the way Albert has created a self-sustaining operation.

- **Balsamic vinegar** is sort of an outlier, because it is the product of direct fermentation; that is, the grape must (pressed juice, skins, seeds, and stems) is unfermented when it's added to the mother. True balsamic is called aceto balsamico and comes from one of two designated regions in Italy: Modena and Reggio Emilia. A hundred-year-old aged balsamic will take your palate on a journey to remember. But a $15, eight-year-old bottle of balsamic—domestic or Italian—will also take you far. Whatever balsamic you buy, just make sure it's made without added sweetening or colorants; grape must and wine vinegar are the only ingredients you should see on the label.
- **Rice vinegar** is made from rice wine and is used extensively in Japanese and Chinese cooking. "Seasoned" rice vinegar contains sugar and salt and is typically added to sushi rice; it's a pleasant

sweet-sour addition to vinaigrettes and other items as well. Both seasoned and unseasoned rice vinegars are great with noodle salads, cucumbers, and seaweed. Unseasoned rice vinegar is more versatile and gives you more control over the sugar and salt levels.
- **Flavored vinegars** are made by infusing herbs, fruits, and/or spices into the vinegar, which gives them a little more dimension. Naturally flavored ones are best; some also contain sugar and other ingredients that give them a saucier, more viscous consistency.

How to Buy

You can drop an astonishing amount of cash on premium vinegars—$100 or more for a tiny three-ounce bottle. And you can bet that it's good stuff—but you can also get some really great, high-quality vinegars for just a little bit more than the regular supermarket brands.

AOC/DOC, AND OTHER PROPS

Certain products from the European Union (particularly wines, cheeses, and cured meats) hold "protected origin" status, which guarantees that a product was made in a specific location using prescribed, traditional techniques. Champagne, Prosciutto di Parma, and Manchego cheese are all regulated and certified according to this system. (For instance, in order to be called Champagne, it must not only be made in the Champagne region of France but also contain only certain approved grape varietals and be made using the traditional *méthode champenoise*.) Each certified product has a unique set of requirements, indicated by an AO, DO, AOC, DOC, DOP, PDO, or IGT (depending on the product, the certifying country, and the level of certification) along with some sort of identifying stamp, seal, or insignia. Looking for these "protected origin" products is one way to support global food traditions and ensure that the products you buy are made the old-fashioned way.

- **When shopping for vinegars, generally the smaller the producer, the better**—Focus on brands whose primary focus is vinegar; specificity has a high correlation with expertise.
- **Bonus points for anything that has a DO, DOC, AO, or AOC designation**—This means that the product comes from a specific region (see above) and is made using prescribed, traditional techniques.
- **Look for unfiltered vinegar**—You'll know it by its cloudy appearance, similar to that of apple cider. Unfiltered vinegars are more flavorful and complex than filtered ones.

> **LOOK FOR VINEGARS THAT ARE:**
> - From small producers
> - With a DO, DOC, AO, or AOC designation
> - Unfiltered

How to Store

Vinegars will last nearly indefinitely, although their flavors will evolve over time, especially if your vinegar contains a mother (the wispy or slimy-looking remnants of a naturally fermented vinegar).

How to Use

Use your very best vinegars "raw"—that is, in dressings or drizzled on a finished dish. When cooking with vinegar, add it at the beginning so that it has time to mellow out; if you add it at the end, its flavor will be too dominant. Also, reduce the vinegar in the pan *before* you add any other liquids so you can concentrate its flavor and subdue its harshness.

CUPBOARD ESSENTIALS

Here are a few other basic items that are useful to have around.

Dijon Mustard

A good Dijon can do a lot more than perk up a sandwich. It goes into nearly every vinaigrette I make, for both its emulsification properties and the subtle heat and flavor it adds. True Dijon mustard (that is, the kind made in France) really is the best. Whole grain mustard is great for spreading and serving with meats and salumi, but in vinaigrettes it doesn't emulsify as well as the smooth kind. Look for brands like Edmond Fallot that are still artisanally produced.

Canned Tomatoes

It's always good to keep a couple of cans of whole peeled tomatoes in the cupboard. Whole tomatoes generally are of better quality than the diced or crushed kind, and they give you the flexibility to dice or puree them however you like. San Marzano tomatoes are generally recognized as the best. Read the label carefully, though: San Marzano is not just a variety of tomato, but also a DOP region in Italy with rich volcanic soil for which the variety is named. If you're going to pony up for the San Marzano variety, make sure you're getting the Italian ones with the DOP label.

Fire-roasted tomatoes are another good option, as the charring gives an added dimension of smoky flavor.

Tomato paste is a great way to add depth and a hint of natural sweetness without the overt tomatoeyness of whole tomatoes. I like to add it near the end of the sautéing so that the paste fries a little bit and infuses the oil.

Nuts

I love all nuts, but I have a special place in my heart for a few particular varieties.

Nuts are rich in fats and therefore prone to rancidity, so always smell them before using. For best flavor, buy them raw and toast them as you need them. To prolong shelf life, store nuts in an airtight container in the freezer.

- **Marcona almonds**—This is yet another Spanish product that I can't do without. Marcona almonds have a unique, extra-crunchy texture that is a step above your typical almond. They're usually fried in oil and sprinkled with salt, which makes them perfect for snacking and also makes them incredibly addictive. The mouthfeel, the saltiness, and that little slick of oil make them the quintessential bar food. Marconas are almost always blanched (skinless). Add to salads, drizzle with honey, or use them in desserts and pastries.
- **Hazelnuts**—The best hazelnuts come from Oregon and the Piedmont region of Italy. Both regions produce nuts with a high oil content and deep, intense flavor. Be extra careful when toasting hazelnuts, as the toasting occurs from the inside of the nut out, so it's difficult to monitor the progress. Using pretoasted hazelnuts will save you the possible anguish of overtoasting. I love hazelnuts ground and mixed into pastry crusts, added to ravioli filling, or sprinkled onto butternut squash risotto.
- **Pistachios**—Although I love the warm, round flavor of toasted nuts, I prefer to leave pistachios raw because toasting can mask their delicate flavor. They're beautiful and delicious in cookies and cakes; I also like them as a garnish on roasted brussels sprouts or squash.

Salt-Packed Capers

You may have to go out of your way to find salt-packed capers, but you'll be glad you did. The familiar capers mostly taste like the vinegary brine they're packed in; salt-packed capers preserve the true essence of caper flavor. Soak them in water before using—otherwise they're too salty. Fifteen to twenty minutes, with a few changes of water during that time, is plenty. Coarsely chopped and mixed with mayonnaise, lemon juice, and mustard, they make a fabulous quick sauce for fish or vegetables. They perk up pan sauces, are delicious in potato salads, add zing to vinaigrettes, and are indispensable in an Italian salsa verde.

Vanilla

Whoever decided to equate "vanilla" with "boring" must have been referring to artificial vanilla. Real vanilla contains 250 different flavor components, which is why it's so heady, aromatic, and intoxicating. Artificial vanilla (or "vanilla flavoring") consists of only one of those components and is extracted from wood pulp. It really pays off to buy pure vanilla extract and/or whole beans.

Be sure to read the label of pure vanilla extract; some brands add corn syrup, which you should avoid.

Terroir is just as important to vanilla as it is to wine. Tahiti, Madagascar, Indonesia, and Mexico all produce great vanillas, each with unique flavor characteristics. Look for vanilla that specifies one of these countries of origin. Read the label carefully, as some producers use country names to describe the type of vanilla plant, even though they're grown elsewhere.

Some companies offer organic vanilla, but in most cases they're produced no differently from their nonorganic versions. (The higher price reflects the costs of certification.)

You get a fresher, truer vanilla flavor by using vanilla beans, but they can be more expensive. A few of the baking recipes in this book (especially custardrich ones) call for beans specifically because they showcase vanilla particularly well. However, substitutions are given if you prefer the liquid form.

THE FREEZER CASE

The freezer aisle is not exactly the sexiest section of the grocery store. It's chilly, the lighting is unflattering, and it's full of products designed for solo eating. Supermarkets haven't done much to improve the experience, but perhaps that's because the freezer aisle contributes relatively little to a store's bottom line—usually less than 10 percent of the store's total sales.

As in most grocery stores, the freezer in our Market is pretty small. But our freezer section is unique in that about half of it is filled with things that we make in-house—everything from stocks and duck fat to cookie dough, puff pastry, and ice cream. The reason is simple: homemade is always better, especially when you compare homemade to commercially produced frozen food.

A closer look reveals a number of unsavory things about packaged frozen foods, particularly those of the TV dinner style:

- **Artificial ingredients**—Most frozen meals are loaded with stabilizers, emulsifiers, and other artificial ingredients that help control the consistency and texture of food when it's frozen and then reheated.
- **Wasteful packaging**—More than any other department, the freezer aisle contains products that are wrapped in layers upon layers of packaging—from cellophane-sealed plastic trays to bags inside boxes. Although they're designed to protect the food and make it easy to reheat, they are also resource-intensive.
- **Very little food for the dollar**—Most frozen food is a waste of money. You pay a premium for convenience, partly thanks to all that packaging, but also because of all the resources required to keep the food frozen as it's shipped and sold.
- **Taste that leaves you cold**—I couldn't resist. Seriously, though, frozen foods are often developed by food scientists, whose primary aim is to please a lowest-common-denominator palate. I believe that TV dinners are called that because you need to be distracted to enjoy them! These foods are not just boring, but soulless at their very core.

When you do buy frozen foods, a little scrutiny will take you a long way in terms of quality, value, and sustainability.

- **Look for real ingredients**—The shorter the ingredient list, the better. Avoid preservatives, stabilizers, or emulsifiers, as well as artificial colors and flavors. The ingredient list should look like a recipe you'd make at home.
- **Choose products with minimal packaging**—The humble frozen burrito is actually a good example of minimal packaging; it's just a thin sheath of plastic that takes up minimal space in the landfill. Avoid items that come in layers on layers of packaging, and choose paper over plastic whenever possible.
- **Recycle (or reuse) the packaging when you can**—Take the time to recycle cardboard and plastic to the extent allowed in your area.
- **Treat frozen foods like a splurge**—Don't rely on convenience foods for your everyday, weeknight dinner.

TRY OUR STORE'S APPROACH: FILL THE FREEZER WITH STUFF *YOU* MADE. I'm not saying you should painstakingly assemble your own compartmentalized dinners, make dinner from scratch every single night, or give up convenience foods. I mean you can create those conveniences yourself by **USING THE FREEZER STRATEGICALLY.** It can save you just as much time—and a lot more money.

Here's how to get started:

- **Tuck away leftovers**—This is a great way to prevent the inevitable boredom that ensues when you have lots of leftovers (especially in smaller households). They won't seem so boring a month or two later!

AT THE VERY LEAST, LOOK FOR FROZEN FOOD THAT IS:

- Made of the same ingredients you'd use if you were to make it yourself
- Minimally packaged

AND DON'T FORGET TO:

- Reuse or recycle packaging
- Treat frozen foods as a splurge

- **Make a double batch, stash half**—Doubling a recipe usually requires only marginally more time and effort, yet you get twice as many meals out of it. So bump up the yield and freeze half right away.
- **Freeze key ingredients in user-friendly portions**—Think of all those ingredients where you might only use a little bit at a time—things like bacon, tomato paste, and demiglace. Freezing keeps any remainders from going bad (as they inevitably do in the fridge).

To facilitate their use and speed thawing, portion these ingredients out before freezing: separate the bacon into 3- or 4-strip sections, scoop tablespoonfuls of tomato paste onto a baking sheet, and divide the demiglace into an ice cube tray. Freeze until solid and then consolidate into smaller containers.

To show you what I mean, here's a rundown of what I typically keep in my home freezer:

- **Butter**—Stock up when it's on sale and save! It keeps practically forever this way, and is especially useful for unsalted butter (which is more perishable than salted).
- **Ice cream**—This is one of the few commercially produced frozen items worth buying. Look for short ingredient lists and hormone-free milk—local and organic if possible!
- **Peas**—Compared to some other veggies, peas hold up pretty well to freezing, and commercial ones certainly save you all that shelling time. I puree them into dips like the English Pea and Green Garlic Dip on page 118, or throw them directly into soups and stews for a little extra green.
- **Frozen stock, soup, and sauce**—Things like homemade beef broth, leftover minestrone, and an extra batch of Delfina's Spaghetti sauce (page 61).
- **Nuts**—Freezing keeps the oils in nuts from going rancid. They don't need to be thawed before using (unless you're just snacking on them).
- **Pizza**—I do keep a couple on hand for emergencies. But I make sure they're preservative-free, and ideally organic. I keep my own pizza dough and par-baked crusts in there, too.

- **Pie dough**—Whenever I make pie dough, I make a double batch and freeze half. With an overnight thaw in the fridge, it's as good as freshly made.
- **Pesto cubes**—I throw these into a soup for extra flavor, or toss with hot pasta, or spread on a sandwich.
- **Pancetta cubes**—Cut into 1-inch chunks and thaw as needed.
- **Phyllo**—Phyllo is a great way to transform leftovers into tasty little appetizers or snacks.
- **Breadcrumbs**—I just blitz leftover bread in the food processor and toss into a zip-top freezer bag. They're ready to go whenever I need them, and not a crumb goes to waste. Toasting them just before using helps revive them a bit.

DO'S AND DON'TS OF FREEZING

Liquidy foods such as soups, stews, and sauces are generally well suited to freezing. But resist the urge to freeze cheese or cream-based soups; freezing makes the fats and proteins in unemulsified dairy products separate in an unappealing way. (Butter, being a pure fat, is an exception.)

Hummus

MAKES ABOUT 1½ CUPS

Good hummus is hard to find; I find that most lack the acid needed to balance the nutty richness of tahini and olive oil, making it fall flat on your tongue. A little extra lemon juice completely transforms hummus to something much brighter in flavor. That's why the best hummus is homemade—besides, nothing could be simpler or more satisfying.

I firmly believe that my mother's hummus is the benchmark for all other hummus out there. She personally taught our chef Eddy how to make it, and he in turn has trained all of our crew to make exceptionally delicious hummus.

I keep a blend of ground toasted cumin and coriander in my spice set; it's a great addition to Middle Eastern and Mexican dishes. I usually toast 2 tablespoons each of the whole spices in a sauté pan on low heat until aromatic and lightly toasted, about 2 minutes. Once cooled, I grind in a coffee grinder reserved for spices; a mortar and pestle also works.

- 2 large cloves garlic, smashed
- 1½ cups cooked garbanzo beans (from a 15-ounce can, rinsed and drained)
- 3½ tablespoons freshly squeezed lemon juice, more as needed
- 3 tablespoons warm water, more as needed
- 2 tablespoons extra-virgin olive oil
- 1½ tablespoons tahini
- ¼ teaspoon ground toasted cumin/coriander combo (or ⅛ teaspoon each if not making the blend)
- Pinch of cayenne pepper
- Kosher salt

Put the garlic in the bowl of a food processor and pulse a few times to chop. Add the remaining ingredients, along with ¾ teaspoon salt. Blend until smooth, scraping down the bowl as you go.

Taste and add more lemon juice or salt as needed; to get the right balance of flavors, it should taste bright with lemon juice, rather than heavy with beans and tahini. You can also adjust the consistency with a little more water, if you like (keep in mind that it will stiffen considerably when chilled).

The Bi-Rite Vinaigrette

MAKES 1⅔ CUPS

If you've been looking for an excuse to stop buying bottled salad dressing, this is it. Delicate and well balanced, this dressing complements just about any veggie or grain you choose—in fact, it is the backbone of some of our most popular deli salads. One batch is enough for many salads, so make this, keep it in the fridge, and don't look back.

You can use different vinegars with equally successful results, but you might need to adjust the quantity of vinegar depending on its acidity. Use good-quality extra-virgin olive oil—the flavor will be well worth it on your beautiful greens.

- 1 cup extra-virgin olive oil
- ¼ cup freshly squeezed lemon juice
- ¼ cup champagne vinegar
- 1 small shallot, minced
- 2 teaspoons kosher salt
- 1½ teaspoons Dijon mustard
- 1½ teaspoons honey

Combine all ingredients in a Mason jar, cover tightly, and shake vigorously.

Refrigerated, it keeps for at least 2 weeks. Whisk or shake well before using; as always, be sure to taste the dressed ingredients and adjust the vinegar, lemon juice, or salt before serving.

Tip: You can also add fresh garlic, finely grated lemon or orange zest, or fresh herbs such as chives, thyme, or basil to this vinaigrette. If you do so, add them only to the portion of dressing you're using right away (these fresh ingredients will discolor and change flavor during storage).

Romesco Sauce

MAKES ABOUT 1³/₄ CUPS

This incredible sauce is particularly versatile and serves as the backbone for the Romesco Chicken Salad on page 187. It's important to avoid over-processing the sauce; not only does heat cause the mixture to become gelatinous, but the sauce simply tastes better when left a little chunky.

If you can't find piquillo peppers, roasted red bell peppers would work, too. Roasting and peeling them yourself is the ideal, because it gives you more of that nice smoky flavor.

1 medium Roma tomato
3 tablespoons extra-virgin olive oil, plus more
   for the tomato
¹/₃ cup toasted blanched almonds, preferably
   Marconas
1 (10-ounce) jar roasted piquillo peppers, drained,
   seeds picked out (about 1¹/₄ cups)
1 medium clove garlic, smashed and peeled
1 tablespoon sherry vinegar, more as needed
1 teaspoon smoked Spanish paprika
Kosher salt

Rub the tomato with a few drops of olive oil to very lightly coat. Using tongs, hold the tomato over a gas flame until charred all over (3 to 4 minutes). If you don't have a gas range, you can put the tomato under the broiler, turning it frequently and watching carefully so that it doesn't go up in flames! Let the tomato cool enough to handle, then remove and discard the skin and seeds. Set aside.

Put the almonds in a food processor and pulse until they're just coarsely chopped, about 10 pulses. It's okay if they're uneven; you just want to start the chopping process. Transfer to a bowl and set aside.

Put the tomato, peppers, garlic, vinegar, paprika, and 1 teaspoon salt in the food processor (you don't need to wash it after chopping the almonds). Blend until it forms a coarse paste, 10 to 15 seconds. Add the almonds and olive oil and pulse just until coarsely chopped; it should still have distinct pieces of almonds. Taste and stir in more vinegar or salt as needed.

Bagna Cauda

MAKES ABOUT ¹/₂ CUP

Bagna cauda ("warm bath") is a traditional Tuscan condiment for dressing veggies and greens. It is meant to showcase the two simple ingredients of anchovy and garlic, which are brought together with oil and butter and tempered by lemon juice.

Raw or lightly steamed vegetables are the simplest pairing, but you can also use it to dress fish, especially tuna or swordfish, or dress beans. With a little extra lemon juice, it makes a fantastic salad dressing for sturdy greens.

¹/₂ cup extra-virgin olive oil
3 large anchovy fillets, rinsed, dried, and finely
   chopped
3 large cloves garlic, minced
1 tablespoon unsalted butter
¹/₄ large lemon
Kosher salt, as needed

Combine the oil, anchovy, and garlic in a small saucepan over medium-low heat. Cook gently and slowly, swirling occasionally, until the garlic is very soft and the anchovy has dissolved completely, about 10 minutes. The garlic should remain pale in color; if it threatens to brown at any point, lower the heat. Off the heat, slowly whisk in the butter and add a squeeze of fresh lemon juice. Taste and season with salt as needed. (You may or may not need additional salt, depending on the anchovies you use.)

For best results, keep the bagna cauda warm as you serve it—a butter warmer (a stand that holds a ramekin over a votive candle) works perfectly.

Clockwise, from top left: Romesco Sauce, Bagna Cauda, and English Pea and Green Garlic Dip (page 118)

EAT GOOD FOOD

Red Quinoa and Tofu Salad with Ginger and Pickled Daikon

SERVES 6 TO 8

Even if you think you hate tofu, or if you've never cooked quinoa, do try this salad. Together, the quinoa and tofu offer a variety of chewy textures, which get a refreshing lift of flavor from ginger, rice vinegar, and daikon radish. It's also a favorite among the staff at the Market; the wallop of protein offers steady fuel for working a hectic shift!

$1/2$ cup grated daikon radish (from a 2-inch chunk)
$1/2$ cup rice vinegar, more as needed
Kosher salt
1 cup (6 ounces) uncooked red quinoa (white is fine too, but isn't as pretty)
2 tablespoons soy sauce, more as needed
2 tablespoons finely grated ginger
1 tablespoon grapeseed or other neutral oil
1 tablespoon toasted sesame oil
$1/2$ teaspoon Asian chile-garlic paste or sriracha
16 ounces baked or smoked tofu, diced
1 cup frozen shelled edamame beans, thawed
2 scallions, thinly sliced

In a small bowl, combine the daikon radish with 2 tablespoons of the rice vinegar. Set aside to marinate while you cook the quinoa.

Bring a large pot of well-salted water to a boil over high heat. Add the quinoa, give it a good stir, and cook until the grains are plump and just tender, about 15 minutes. Drain in a fine-holed colander and spread on a large plate or rimmed baking sheet to speed cooling.

In a large bowl, whisk together the remaining 6 tablespoons rice vinegar and the soy sauce, ginger, grapeseed oil, sesame oil, and chile-garlic paste. Add the quinoa, tofu, edamame, and scallions. Drain the pickled daikon, reserving the liquid, and add to the bowl as well. Toss gently to combine. Taste and add more soy sauce or some of the reserved rice vinegar as needed.

Note: You can make this sturdy salad a day ahead of time, but for best results, reserve the scallions and add them closer to serving time (within an hour or two is fine).

Winter Lentil Salad with Roasted Root Veggies

SERVES 6 TO 8

This flexible salad relies on pantry staples and long-lasting veggies, so it's easy to keep the ingredients around for making on the fly. It's also the perfect place to use infused olive oils, especially herby ones like tarragon oil.

Kosher salt
$1^1/_4$ cups dried green or black lentils
2 stalks celery, cut into $1/2$-inch dice (1 cup)
4 cups diced root vegetables (carrots, parsnips, rutabaga, turnips, or a mix)
$1^1/_2$ teaspoons coarsely chopped fresh thyme
3 tablespoons extra-virgin olive oil, more as needed
3 tablespoons finely chopped parsley
$1^1/_2$ tablespoons sherry vinegar, more as needed

Bring a medium pot of well-salted water to a boil and rinse the lentils in two or three changes of water. And the lentils to the pot and cook just until tender, about 25 minutes. Drain well and set aside.

Position a rack in the center of the oven and heat to 400°F.

Pile the celery, root vegetables, and thyme on a large rimmed baking sheet and drizzle with 2 tablespoons of the oil and $1/2$ teaspoon salt. Use your hands to mix and coat the vegetables evenly with the oil, and then redistribute in a single layer. Roast the vegetables, stirring after 10 minutes or so, and continue to cook until tender and golden on the edges, about 15 minutes longer.

Combine the lentils, vegetables, and parsley in a large bowl. Drizzle with the vinegar and another 1 tablespoon oil and toss to combine. Taste and add more vinegar, oil, or salt as desired.

Serve right away or refrigerate for up to 3 days. If making ahead, let it come to room temperature before serving; you may also want to refresh the salad with a little extra olive oil.

Farro Salad with Mushrooms and Butternut Squash

SERVES 8 TO 10

Farro is an ancient grain that, despite its popularity in central Italy, was once impossible to find in the United States. With rising demand for it, more and more domestic growers are starting to cultivate it, including Eatwell Farm in Northern California and Bluebird Grain Farms in Oregon.

This hearty fall salad works well as a vegan entrée or a side dish, or even warmed and served as a Thanksgiving stuffing. I like to add diced or pulled roasted turkey to turn this into an entrée salad. Small cubes of good-quality Pecorino Romano are also a nice addition and give the dish added richness and *umami*.

FARRO
Kosher salt
1 1/2 cups farro, soaked in water for 1 hour and drained (see Note)
1 medium butternut squash, peeled, seeded, and diced (about 5 cups)
4 tablespoons extra-virgin olive oil
Freshly ground black pepper
1 pound cremini mushrooms, quartered (about 4 cups)
4 large sage leaves, chopped (about 1 tablespoon)
1 tablespoon sherry or Banyuls vinegar, more as needed
5 inner ribs of celery, halved lengthwise and sliced 1/4 inch thick (about 1 1/2 cups)
4 scallions, thinly sliced
2 tablespoons chopped parsley

VINAIGRETTE
1/2 cup freshly squeezed lemon juice, more as needed
1/4 cup extra-virgin olive oil
2 tablespoons minced shallots
Kosher salt

To cook the farro and vegetables:

Bring a medium saucepan of well-salted water to a boil over medium-high heat. Add the farro and cook until tender, approximately 20 to 45 minutes (see Note). Drain and spread on a large plate or rimmed baking sheet and let cool to room temperature.

Meanwhile, position racks in the top and bottom thirds of the oven and heat to 400°F.

Mound the butternut squash on a large rimmed baking sheet and drizzle with 2 tablespoons of the olive oil, 1/2 teaspoon salt, and a few grinds of pepper. Use your hands to mix and coat the squash evenly with the oil, and then spread into a single layer. Repeat with the mushrooms on a separate baking sheet, using another 2 tablespoons oil, 1/2 teaspoon salt, the sage, and the sherry vinegar. Roast the vegetables, rotating the sheets after 10 minutes or so, and continue to cook until the squash is just tender and starting to brown and the mushrooms have released their juices, about 20 to 25 minutes total. (Depending on the size and shape of your vegetables, the two may require different cooking times.) Set aside and let cool to room temperature.

To make the vinaigrette and assemble:

In a small bowl, whisk together the lemon juice, olive oil, shallots, and 1/4 teaspoon salt.

Combine the farro, squash, mushrooms and their juices, celery, scallions, and parsley in a large bowl. Mix gently to combine. Add the vinaigrette and toss just until blended. Taste and adjust the seasoning with more salt, vinegar, or lemon juice if necessary.

Let the salad sit for at least 30 minutes before serving to let the flavors blend.

Note: Cooking farro can be confusing, because there are two different grains that are often marketed under the same name. True farro (*Triticum dicoccum*) must be soaked and will remain chewy even after its 45-minute (or longer) cooking time. The other "semi-perlato farro" is actually spelt, which does not require soaking and cooks in about 20 minutes; it becomes mushy if overcooked. Look closely at the package to determine which one you have, and prepare it accordingly.

White Bean Puree with Prosciutto Crespelle

MAKES ABOUT 8 CUPS

This silky, sophisticated soup is proof that beans can be so much more than humble peasant food. Serve it as a warming first course or main dish.

You can use cannellini beans or white navy beans in this soup, but given the choice, I prefer the cannellinis. They're larger and have comparatively less skin, so they produce a creamier soup.

    2 tablespoons extra-virgin olive oil, plus more
        for brushing
    1 medium yellow onion, diced
    2 stalks celery, diced
    1 medium carrot, diced
    4 large sage leaves, chopped
    3 cloves garlic, chopped
    1 bay leaf
    6 cups chicken or vegetable stock (or low-sodium
        broth), more as needed
    3 cups cooked cannellini beans or white navy beans,
        (two 15-ounce cans, drained and rinsed)
    Kosher salt and freshly ground black pepper
    8 thin slices prosciutto
    1¹/₂ teaspoons freshly squeezed lemon juice, more
        as needed

In a large (8 quart) pot, heat the oil over medium-low heat. Add the onion and cook, stirring occasionally, until soft and translucent, about 8 minutes. Add the celery and carrot and continue to cook, stirring occasionally, until they are somewhat soft, about 10 minutes. Add the sage, garlic, and bay leaf and continue to cook for 2 more minutes, or until aromatic.

Add the stock and beans, 2 teaspoons salt, and a few grinds of black pepper. Increase the heat to medium-high and bring just to a boil, then lower the heat to maintain a gentle simmer. Continue to cook, uncovered, until the vegetables are completely soft and have started to break down a bit, 45 minutes to 1 hour.

Meanwhile, position a rack in the center of the oven and heat to 350°F.

Brush both sides of the prosciutto slices lightly with oil and arrange them in a single layer on a parchment-lined baking sheet. Bake just until they are slightly darker and wrinkly, 10 to 15 minutes. Let them cool undisturbed on the baking sheet—they will crisp up as they cool. Break into large shards and set aside. (You can make these up to 6 hours ahead of time.)

To finish the soup, remove and discard the bay leaf and, working in batches, carefully puree the soup in a blender. If you prefer a thinner soup, add up to 2 cups more broth to adjust the thickness.

Stir in the lemon juice and taste. Adjust with more lemon juice, salt, or pepper as needed and reheat as necessary.

Just before serving, divide the soup among bowls and garnish with the prosciutto crespelle.

Tip: For a vegetarian garnish, you can fry whole sage leaves instead of making the crespelle. Just heat a bit of olive oil in a small skillet and add the sage leaves, a few at a time. Fry just until bright green (15 to 30 seconds), and then immediately transfer to a paper towel–lined plate. Make more than you need—they're so delicious you'll find yourself nibbling on them as you go.

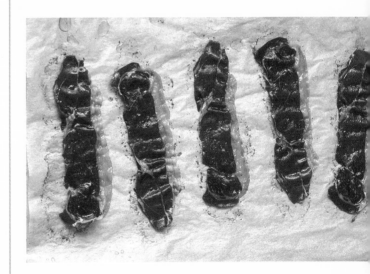

Buttery Black Lentil Dal

MAKES ABOUT 5 CUPS

There are as many varieties of dal (the nourishing lentil soup) as there are towns and villages in India. Our recipe is inspired by the one served at Kasa Indian Eatery, just down the street from the Market. It gets a dose of butter, which makes the soup incredibly rich in flavor, and pureeing half gives it extra creaminess.

This recipe can easily be doubled.

- 1 cup black (beluga) lentils (see Note)
- 1 bay leaf
- 4 tablespoons unsalted butter
- 1¼ teaspoons cumin seeds, lightly crushed or chopped
- 1 small onion, finely diced (about ¾ cup)
- 4 large cloves garlic, chopped
- ½ jalapeño or serrano chile (more to taste), seeded and finely chopped
- Kosher salt
- 1 medium tomato, seeded and chopped (see Note)
- 1 teaspoon freshly squeezed lemon juice, more as needed

Rinse the lentils and pick out any stones or foreign objects. Put in a bowl, add water to cover by 1 inch, and soak overnight, changing the water a couple of times in the process.

Drain the lentils and put in a medium saucepan with the bay leaf and 5 cups water. Bring to a boil over medium-high heat and then lower the heat to a simmer. Cook, skimming the scum periodically, until the lentils are very tender and starting to disintegrate, 30 to 40 minutes. Remove from the heat.

Melt the butter in a medium skillet over medium-high heat. Add the cumin seeds; when fragrant (about 1 minute), add the onion, garlic, chile, and 1 teaspoon salt. Cook, stirring frequently, until the onions are soft and translucent, 3 to 4 minutes. Add the tomato and another 1 teaspoon salt and continue to cook, stirring, for 1 minute longer.

Add the tomato-onion mixture to the lentils and return to a simmer. Cover the pot partially, lower the heat, and simmer gently for 1 hour to blend the flavors. Remove and discard the bay leaf. Carefully puree half of the dal in a blender (working in batches, if necessary) and add it back to the pot.

If the dal is runnier than you like, continue to simmer uncovered until it reaches the desired consistency. Stir in the lemon juice, then taste and season with more lemon juice or salt if necessary.

Note: Indian black lentils are more traditional, but the beluga variety we use are a little easier to find. You can, of course, use Indian black lentils instead, adjusting the cooking times as necessary.

If tomatoes are not in season, you can certainly use canned. For the best flavor, get the whole canned ones, and seed and chop them yourself. You'll need about 1 cup chopped tomatoes.

Mujadara

SERVES 4 TO 6 AS A MAIN COURSE, OR 6 TO 8 AS A SIDE

This dish comes straight from my mom, who made it nearly every Friday during Lent. It's hearty and savory, and the rice and lentils together make it a perfect vegetarian protein. The burnt onion garnish is key; it adds depth and richness to the overall effect. Mom often served this with a rustic tomato, cucumber, and red onion salsa seasoned with lemon and mint, which lend acidity, texture, and fresh flavors to the plate.

1 cup uncooked black or green lentils
1/4 cup extra-virgin olive oil
3 medium or 2 large onions, diced (about 4 1/2 cups)
Salt and freshly ground black pepper
1 cup uncooked long-grain rice, such as jasmine or basmati
2 tablespoons mild curry powder

Rinse the lentils and pick out any stones or foreign objects. Put in a bowl, add water to cover by 1 inch, and soak for at least 2 hours or up to 6 hours. Drain the lentils and set aside.

In a Dutch oven or soup pot, heat 2 tablespoons of the oil over medium heat. Add half the onions and a pinch of salt and cook, stirring occasionally, until the onions are soft and translucent and golden on the edges, about 4 minutes. Add the lentils, rice, curry powder, 1 tablespoon plus 2 teaspoons salt, and 1/4 teaspoon pepper and cook for 1 minute, stirring constantly.

Add 3 cups water, increase the heat to high, and bring the liquid to a boil. Then lower the heat to maintain a gentle simmer and cover the pot. Cook until the rice and lentils are tender, 15 to 20 minutes. At this point, it's okay if there's still a tiny bit of bite to the lentils; they will continue to absorb water. Remove from the heat and let rest with the lid on for 10 to 15 minutes.

While the rice mixture is cooking, caramelize the remaining onions: heat the remaining 2 tablespoons oil in a large skillet over medium-high heat. When hot, add the remaining onions and a pinch of salt. Cook, stirring occasionally at first and more frequently as you go, until the onions are soft and almost at the brink of burning, 9 to 11 minutes (lower the heat if the browning seems to be progressing more rapidly than the softening). Set aside.

To serve, fluff the rice mixture with a fork and transfer to a serving platter.

Top with the caramelized onions.

Serve hot or at room temperature. You can make this up to 2 days ahead. If desired, reheat in a covered, shallow ovenproof dish in a 350°F oven for about 30 minutes.

Orecchiette with White Beans and Chard

SERVES 6 AS A MAIN DISH

This simple, filling one-dish meal is perfect for weeknights. The secret ingredient is the white beans; crushing them slightly helps them break down into a luxurious light sauce for the pasta. If fresh shelling beans happen to be in season, this is a great way to use them (you'll need to cook them separately first). The beans nestle perfectly into the cup shape of the "little ear" pasta, so be sure to use orecchiette for this dish.

Pancetta adds a boost of flavor, but you could also substitute a few tablespoons of olive oil to make this dish vegetarian. And for a spicy kick, you can also add a pinch of chile flakes when you sauté the onions.

I large bunch chard, about 14 ounces (see Note)
Kosher salt
I pound dried orecchiette
$^{1}/_{2}$ cup (about 2 ounces) finely diced pancetta
$^{1}/_{4}$ cup extra-virgin olive oil
I medium yellow onion, finely diced
3 large cloves garlic, chopped
I$^{1}/_{2}$ cups cooked white beans (one 15-ounce can, rinsed and drained)
2 teaspoons chopped thyme or sage, or a combination
I tablespoon freshly squeezed lemon juice, more as needed
$^{1}/_{2}$ cup grated Parmigiano-Reggiano

To prepare the chard, strip the leaves off the stems. Coarsely chop the leaves and dice the stems into $^{1}/_{2}$-inch chunks, keeping them separate.

Bring a large pot of well-salted water to a boil. Add the orecchiette and cook until just barely al dente (2 to 3 minutes less than the package instructs). Scoop out and reserve about 2 cups of the pasta water. Drain the pasta well; do not rinse.

Return the empty pot to the burner on medium-high heat. Once the pot is dry and hot, add the pancetta with 1 tablespoon of the extra-virgin olive oil and cook, stirring frequently, until golden and most of the fat has rendered out, about 2 minutes. Add the onion and $^{1}/_{2}$ teaspoon salt and continue to cook until the onions are softened and translucent, about 4 minutes. Add the chopped chard stems and continue to cook until softened, about 2 minutes. Add the garlic and cook, stirring, for 1 minute longer.

Add the beans and use a potato masher or spoon to gently mash about half of them (to break them down and thicken the sauce). Add the thyme or sage, $^{1}/_{2}$ teaspoon salt, and 1 cup of the pasta water and stir to combine. Cover the pot and cook, stirring occasionally, for 5 minutes to blend the flavors. Stir in the chard leaves, cover, and cook until the chard is tender, 2 to 3 more minutes.

Add the drained pasta to the pot and stir to combine. Cook, stirring constantly, until the pasta is just al dente and the liquid has reduced to a creamy coating of sauce, 1 to 2 minutes longer. (Add a little more pasta water if it seems too dry.)

Remove from the heat and stir in the remaining 3 tablespoons olive oil, the lemon juice, and $^{1}/_{4}$ cup of the Parmigiano. Taste and add more lemon juice or salt as needed. Garnish with the remaining $^{1}/_{4}$ cup Parmigiano.

Note: Just about any type of chard will do, although red chard's pigment will bleed into the dish, and it also has a tendency to become bitter. You can also use kale or spinach instead of chard; kale will take a little longer to cook, spinach a little less.

Delfina's Spaghetti

**SERVES 2 OR 3 AS A MAIN COURSE,
3 OR 4 AS A FIRST COURSE**

———————

Delfina is one of my favorite restaurants in San Francisco, and it happens to be just two doors down from the Market! Although much of their menu changes daily, this spaghetti is always on offer, and I think it's one of the best things they make. It's a great example of how a few high-quality ingredients (most of them pantry items) can come together for a simple but nourishing meal.

Chef-owner Craig Stoll was generous enough to share his recipe. Craig employs the classical Italian technique of par-cooking the pasta and then finishing the cooking with the sauce. This not only thickens the sauce but also lets the sauce cook *into* the pasta. He says, "The result should be juicy and shiny and full of flavor, but with no residual sauce. All of the sauce should be contained within the body of the spaghetti. The last bite of pasta should bring the last bit of sauce with it."

I (28-ounce) can peeled whole plum tomatoes
   (such as Di Napoli)
3 medium cloves garlic
Kosher salt and freshly ground black pepper
$^{1}/_{4}$ cup extra-virgin olive oil
$^{1}/_{8}$ teaspoon chile flakes, more as desired
14 large basil leaves
8 ounces spaghetti
Freshly grated Parmigiano-Reggiano for serving

Working over the opened can of tomatoes, break open each tomato, scrape the seeds back into the can, and put the seeded tomato in a bowl. Squeeze the seeded tomatoes in your hand to break them up slightly, then strain the juice from the can into the bowl with the tomatoes. Discard the seeds.

Chop the garlic coarsely, sprinkle with a pinch of salt, and use the side of a chef's knife to smash and press the garlic into a paste. Put the garlic paste and the olive oil in a medium heavy-bottomed skillet, cover, and put over medium-low heat. Cook the garlic

very slowly until soft and feathery-looking but still creamy in color, 5 to 6 minutes (lower the heat if it starts to brown).

Add the tomatoes and juice, along with the chile flakes, $1^{1}/_{2}$ cups water, $^{1}/_{2}$ teaspoon salt, and a few grinds of pepper. Increase the heat to medium-high and bring just to a boil, skimming off and discarding any foam (be careful not to skim off the oil, though). Lower the heat to a rapid simmer and cook, continuing to skim the foam, until the sauce has reduced to a scant 2 cups, about 45 minutes. (Stir occasionally as the sauce thickens to prevent sticking or burning.)

Remove the sauce from the heat. If you have an immersion blender, pulse the sauce a few times to break up some of the larger chunks. Otherwise, remove one-third of the sauce and puree in a food mill or pulse in a food processor. Return the pureed sauce to the pot and tear the basil leaves into the sauce.

Bring a large pot of lightly salted water to a boil. (Any more than a tablespoon or so of salt will make the final dish too salty.) Add the spaghetti, cook for 6 minutes, and drain, reserving at least 1 cup of the cooking water.

Put the sauce in the same pot you used to cook the pasta, adding another pinch of chile flakes if desired. Add the spaghetti and $^{3}/_{4}$ cup of the cooking water and bring to a rapid simmer. Cook, stirring frequently, until the pasta is cooked to al dente, the liquid is completely absorbed into the pasta, and the sauce is reduced to a very thick purée, 5 to 7 minutes longer. (Add up to $^{1}/_{4}$ cup more of the pasta water if the sauce reduces before the pasta is al dente.)

Taste and season with more salt as needed. Top each serving with Parmigiano and serve right away.

Note: You can make the sauce up to 2 days ahead. Because it also freezes well, consider making a double batch of the sauce and freezing half of it for a rainy day. If making ahead, reserve half the basil leaves and add them when you combine the sauce with the spaghetti.

Spaghetti with Tuna, Capers, and Chile Flakes

SERVES 4

There are so many things I love about this dish, but what I love most is that it's made from basic pantry ingredients, so it can be made on the fly when you really don't want to go shopping for food. It's in the spirit of the classic linguine with clams, but made with canned tuna instead.

Because of the simplicity of this dish, the quality of all the ingredients is critical to the final result. The breadcrumbs are optional but do add great texture.

Kosher salt
1 pound regular or whole wheat spaghetti
1/2 cup extra-virgin olive oil
1 medium onion, finely diced
1 tablespoon chopped garlic
1 teaspoon chopped fresh thyme
1/2 teaspoon chile flakes (or more to taste)
1 (6-ounce) can line-caught albacore tuna, packed in its own juices (do not drain)
2 tablespoons capers, coarsely chopped
3 tablespoons chopped fresh parsley
Finely grated zest and juice of 1/2 lemon
1/2 cup coarse toasted breadcrumbs (see Tip)

Bring a large pot of well-salted water to a boil. Add the spaghetti and cook for 2 minutes less than the package instructs. Reserve about 1 1/2 cups pasta water, then drain the pasta (do not rinse).

Heat 1/4 cup of the olive oil in a large skillet over medium-low heat. Add the onion and a pinch of salt and cook, stirring frequently, until the onions are soft but have not taken on any color, about 8 minutes. Add the garlic, thyme, and chile flakes and sauté until the garlic has softened, about 2 minutes longer.

Add the tuna, juices and all, and the capers. With a wooden spoon, break the tuna up into small pieces as you stir the mixture.

Transfer this mixture to the empty pasta pot (no need to rinse it first) along with the spaghetti and 1 cup of the pasta water. Put the pot over medium heat and continue to cook, stirring constantly, until the pasta absorbs the water and is just al dente, about 1 to 2 minutes longer. Remove from the heat.

Stir in the remaining 1/4 cup olive oil, the parsley, and the lemon zest and juice. Add another 1/4 cup pasta water to moisten; add another tablespoon or so if it still seems too dry.

Sprinkle each portion with breadcrumbs.

Tip: I make the breadcrumbs by slicing day-old, quality bread into 1/4-inch rounds, brushing with extra-virgin olive oil, and baking in a 375°F oven until crisp and lightly colored. Once cool, I crush them with the back of a frying pan until coarse; they should not be uniform in size.

Vinegar Spritzer

SERVES 1

Far too few people are familiar with the vinegar spritzer. It may sound strange to the uninitiated, but it's actually a lovely and highly refreshing drink. It's the perfect thing to wake up your taste buds or cleanse your palate.

1 1/2 cups (one 12-ounce can) seltzer water or sparkling mineral water
1 tablespoon good-quality vinegar (champagne, Banyuls, white balsamic, or fruit vinegars are especially good), more to taste
Honey or simple syrup (optional; see Tip)
Lime, lemon, or orange twist, for garnish

Combine the seltzer and vinegar in a large glass and stir to combine. If you like, add sweetener to taste. Add ice and top with the citrus twist.

Tip: Simple syrup is easy to make and is great to have on hand for sweetening cocktails, iced coffee or tea, or this simple spritzer. Combine equal parts sugar and water in a saucepan (2 cups is a good amount), bring to a boil, and cook until the sugar is completely dissolved. Cool and refrigerate for indefinite shelf life.

Citrus Olive Oil Cake

SERVES 12

Olive oil cakes are a traditional Italian treat; this one is unusual in that it uses whole oranges and lemons, not just their zest. This barely sweet dessert—a sophisticated amalgam of heady olive oil, aromatic fruits, and toasted almonds—will win you friends wherever you serve it.

Be sure to use good-quality olive oil in this recipe. I prefer a Tuscan blend with a bit of peppery bite to give the cake an interesting dimension. I love serving this cake with whipped crème fraîche that has been lightly sweetened.

- 3^1/$_2$ cups sugar, more as needed
- 2 cups water
- 2 medium oranges
- 1 medium lemon
- 1^2/$_3$ cup (6 ounces) sliced almonds, toasted (see Note)
- 1 cup (4^1/$_2$ ounces) all-purpose flour
- 1 tablespoon baking powder
- ^{2}/$_3$ cup extra-virgin olive oil, plus more for the pan
- 4 large eggs
- ^{1}/$_2$ teaspoon table salt

Combine 2 cups of the sugar and the water in a medium saucepan. Bring to a boil over medium-high heat. When the sugar has dissolved, add the oranges and lemon. Make sure there's enough liquid to cover at least two-thirds of the fruit—if needed, add a little more water and an equal amount of sugar directly to the pan (you don't need to dissolve it separately). Cover the pan and lower the heat to maintain a very gentle simmer. Cook, turning the fruit occasionally, until the fruit is very soft and easily pierced with a skewer, about 40 minutes. Carefully transfer the fruit to a plate and let cool enough to handle (save the syrup for another use—see Tip for ideas).

While the fruit is cooking, put the almonds in the bowl of a food processor and pulse until finely ground. Transfer to a large bowl and whisk in the flour and baking powder. Set aside.

Oil a 9-inch springform cake pan (or a regular 9-inch-round by 3-inch-tall cake pan) and line the bottom with parchment. Position a rack in the center of the oven and heat to 350°F.

Cut the fruit into quarters and remove and discard any seeds or large pieces of membrane. Put the fruit in the food processor (you don't need to wash the bowl first). Pulse, scraping down the sides as needed, until the fruit is pureed and fairly smooth—a few small lumps are okay.

Put the eggs and salt in the bowl of a stand mixer fitted with the whisk attachment. Beat on medium-high speed until lightened in color and foamy, about 2 minutes. With the motor running, gradually add the remaining 1^1/$_2$ cups sugar and continue to beat until very thick and creamy white, 3 to 4 minutes longer. Reduce the speed to medium, and with the motor running, drizzle in the olive oil.

Add the pureed fruit and continue to mix until blended, about 30 seconds. Remove the bowl from the stand and gently fold in about a third of the flour mixture. When incorporated, add the rest of the flour mixture and fold until smooth.

Pour into the prepared pan and smooth the top. Bake until the cake is dark golden brown and springs back after a light touch, about 1 hour 10 minutes. (Resist the urge to use a toothpick to determine doneness; it will cause the cake to sink in the center.)

Let cool in the pan for 25 minutes and then run a knife around the perimeter. Turn out onto a rack to cool completely.

This cake is even better the next day, and keeps for up to 5 days at room temperature.

Note: To toast the almonds, spread them on a large rimmed baking sheet and bake in a 350°F oven until light- to medium-golden brown, 10 to 15 minutes. You can also use an equal weight of whole or slivered almonds, but they won't grind to as fine a consistency as the sliced.

Tip: It's a shame to waste the poaching syrup with its lovely flavor of orange and lemon. It will last nearly indefinitely in the refrigerator. Mix a couple of spoonfuls with seltzer water to make an Italian soda, or use in your favorite cocktail recipe (it goes especially well with bourbon and gin).

Chocolate Sour Cream Bundt Cake with Chocolate Glaze

SERVES 10

This rich cake is one of the all-time best sellers from the Creamery. We use this recipe to make cakes of all different shapes and sizes, from cupcakes to tea cakes to ice cream cake bases. The cocoa powder gives the cake a more intense chocolaty flavor. Be sure to use a high-quality cocoa powder; it makes a huge difference in the final product. For the glaze, we prefer to use 60 to 65 percent bittersweet chocolate.

This bullet-proof recipe translates easily to the home kitchen. Unlike many cakes, this one is mixed entirely by hand. No electric mixer needed! And the cake stays moist for days.

CAKE

I cup (8 ounces) unsalted butter
$1/3$ cup (I ounce) cocoa powder
I teaspoon kosher salt
I cup water
2 cups (9 ounces) all-purpose flour
$1^3/_4$ cups sugar
$1^1/_2$ teaspoons baking soda
2 large eggs
$1/_2$ cup sour cream
I teaspoon pure vanilla extract

GLAZE

4 ounces bittersweet chocolate, finely chopped
$1^1/_2$ tablespoons agave nectar or corn syrup
$1/_2$ cup heavy cream
$1^1/_2$ tablespoons sugar

To make the cake:

Position a rack in the center of the oven and heat to 350°F. Butter and flour a 10- or 12-cup Bundt pan and set aside.

In a small saucepan, combine the butter, cocoa powder, salt, and water and put over medium heat. Cook, stirring, just until melted and combined. Remove from the heat and set aside.

Put the flour, sugar, and baking soda in a large bowl and whisk to blend. Add half of the melted butter mixture and whisk until completely blended (it will be very thick). Add the remaining butter mixture and whisk. Add the eggs one at a time, whisking each to blend completely before adding the next. Whisk in the sour cream and vanilla until smooth.

Pour the mixture into the prepared pan and bake until a toothpick inserted into the center of the cake comes out clean, 40 to 45 minutes.

Let the cake cool in the pan for 15 minutes and then invert onto a rack. Let cool completely before making the glaze.

To make the glaze:

Put the chopped chocolate and agave nectar in a medium bowl and set aside.

Combine the heavy cream and sugar in a small saucepan and put over medium heat. Stir constantly until the cream is hot and the sugar is dissolved. Pour the hot cream over the chocolate and whisk until melted and smooth. If it's very runny, let it sit for a minute or so to thicken. Drizzle over the cake.

Chocolate Pots de Crème

MAKES 8

These pots de crème are ridiculously easy and ridiculously good. Don't despair if you don't have eight 4-ounce ramekins; you can use a variety of teacups, prep bowls, or even canning jars of any size.

You can also make these a few days ahead of time if you like. Just be sure to wrap them tightly in plastic and remove any particularly stinky items from the refrigerator (chocolate is prone to absorbing neighboring odors).

6 ounces semisweet or bittersweet chocolate, chopped (see Note)
2 cups heavy cream
³/₄ cup plus 2 tablespoons (7 ounces) half-and-half
¹/₈ teaspoon kosher salt
6 tablespoons sugar
9 large egg yolks
¹/₂ teaspoon pure vanilla extract
Whipped cream and shaved chocolate, for garnish

Put the chocolate in a medium heatproof bowl and set aside.

Combine the cream, half-and-half, salt, and 3 tablespoons of the sugar in a medium saucepan and put over medium-high heat. Cook, stirring occasionally, just until it starts to approach a simmer, about 4 minutes—you'll know it's ready when small bubbles appear around the edge of the pan. Remove from the heat.

Combine the egg yolks and the remaining 3 tablespoons sugar in a medium bowl, and whisk until combined and smooth. Whisking the eggs constantly, slowly pour in about 1 cup of the milk mixture. Then pour the yolk mixture into the pan, whisking constantly until smooth.

Put the pan over medium-high heat and cook, stirring constantly with a heatproof rubber spatula, until the mixture is thick and about the consistency of a pureed soup, 2 to 3 minutes.

Pour the cream mixture over the chopped chocolate and let stand for 3 to 5 minutes. Then slowly and gently stir with a whisk—try not to incorporate any air. When smooth, add the vanilla extract and stir again to blend. Pour the mixture through a fine strainer into a large-lipped measuring cup.

Divide evenly into eight 4-ounce cups or ramekins and refrigerate, uncovered. After 2 hours, cover with plastic wrap and refrigerate for at least 4 hours longer.

To serve, let the ramekins come to room temperature (about 30 minutes) and then top with the whipped cream and shaved chocolate.

Note: The type of chocolate you use has a significant impact on the flavor and texture of this luscious dessert. With bittersweet chocolate (60 to 65 percent cacao), the pots will be intensely chocolaty and almost truffle-like; using semisweet chocolate (around 52 percent cacao) yields a sweeter, mellower, more pudding-like treat.

Sam's Sundae

SERVES I

This unique combination of ice cream, citrus-infused olive oil, and salt is one of the Creamery's best-selling sundaes; it was even featured on the Food Network's show *The Best Thing I Ever Ate*. It may seem strange, but believe me, it's really good. The oil congeals as it cools and creates a luscious mouthfeel, while the salt brightens the flavors and provides an interesting crunchy texture. The whipped cream is optional but really balances out the richness of the sundae.

Our friend Giuseppe Cagnoni, an artisan food producer in Umbria, inspired this dessert when I tasted his Eturia brand oil infused with bergamot (which gives Earl Grey tea its distinctive taste). You can also try other intensely flavored oils, including orange or lemon oil, citrus-infused olive oil, or even toasted sesame oil.

> Chocolate ice cream (preferably a deep, dark variety)
> Bergamot-infused extra-virgin olive oil
> Maldon salt, fleur de sel, kosher salt, or other large, flaky salt
> Freshly whipped cream (optional)

Put a few scoops of ice cream in a bowl, drizzle with about a teaspoon of oil, and sprinkle with a pinch or two of salt. Garnish with a large spoonful of whipped cream.

Tip: Vanilla ice cream with blood orange oil and sea salt is another great combo—it's like a cream pop.

The line at Bi-Rite Creamery often wraps around the block

3

THE DELI

What's most satisfying about my role here is that we start in the morning with cases of produce and meats that came in as raw materials, and by the end of the day people have put it in their mouths and their eyes light up with joy. They trust us to give them something that we'd be happy to have on our own tables.

It's important to maintain the tradition of fresh cooked food—the way your grandma and your parents used to make it. Our guests buy our prepared foods and reheat them for dinner, and it tastes like home. It's more than just a product that you buy; it's what is going to feed your body and your family after a hard day. It's the one moment where you sit down. It's kind of spiritual. I don't think anything could replace sharing a meal with someone.

— Eduardo Martinez, chef

WHEN I AGREED TO TAKE OVER the Market, my one condition was that I could put a full kitchen into the store. More than anything, I didn't want my cooking career to end, and putting a kitchen in the store would allow me to continue on that path while pursuing this new grocery venture.

I knew that I wanted an open kitchen situated in the middle of the store. It would act as a sort of hearth—a central point of focus for the space. I wanted our guests to know, without any doubt, that we were making the food that we were selling every day. The open kitchen, with its sounds and aromas permeating every corner of the Market, would be a constant reminder of that. There was no reason to hide it in the back behind closed doors.

As a restaurateur, I was also attuned to the importance of not wasting food. I viewed the kitchen—and by extension, the deli—as a way to stretch and repurpose the perishable ingredients we carried. If we were going to sell raw meat out of the case, what would happen if it didn't sell after a couple of days? What about the small, oddly shaped ends of fish left over after portioning a fillet? Or a case of peaches with slight blemishes? Without a kitchen, the product would languish and eventually be discarded. But with a kitchen, we could cook that food and sell it as a finished dish, not only salvaging the ingredients themselves but also extending their shelf life *and* giving our guests a convenient dinner option. It was a win-win from a business perspective and from an environmental perspective as well—too many resources are wasted when we throw food away.

Wherever you happen to shop, look for deli cases filled with house-made, seasonally inspired foods. All too often, prepared food counters contain prepackaged, canned, and bagged foods made in a factory and served year-round. Look for salads that look bright and carefully prepared, that represent a variety of cooking styles and preparations (as opposed to endless variations on mayonnaise-based dressings). If you buy

rotisserie chickens, make sure the chicken itself meets the same criteria that I recommend for buying raw chicken. It's okay to buy and eat deli foods, as long as they're homemade using quality, "clean" ingredients. Be sure to ask.

REINVENT, REPURPOSE, AND REVIVE

Learning how to repurpose ingredients that linger in your fridge is a practice that pays off not just in reducing waste but also in making you a more creative cook. This applies to raw ingredients that are about to expire as well as cooked leftovers that are losing their luster. All you have to do is pick up that container of leftover veggies or remnants of last night's roast and ask yourself, "What can I add this to?" Some of the best candidates are pasta sauces, soups and stews, salads, sandwiches, and omelettes and fritattas.

SALADS

Our salads are some of the most exciting and tasty offerings in the deli. We have access to beautiful, farm-direct produce, of course (including vegetables from our own mini-farm in Sonoma), but also a team of chefs who understand what makes a good salad.

SALADS ARE BEST WHEN THEY HAVE FOCUS AND FEATURE JUST A HANDFUL OF INGREDIENTS. Think of it as mixing watercolor paints: blend just a few colors and you'll get something unique and pretty, but blend *all* the colors and you just get muddy brown. So be creative with what you put in your salad, but exercise restraint in the number of items. For a well-balanced salad, start with one or two "base" ingredients for the bulk of the salad, then "accessorize" with smaller amounts of a few other items.

Although there's nothing really wrong with buying and using bottled salad dressing, we're baffled by how much of it we sell. **MAKING YOUR OWN SALAD**

EAT GOOD FOOD

DRESSING IS RIDICULOUSLY EASY AND INFINITELY FLEXIBLE; it can be done in less than a minute and can be as simple or as complicated as your pantry and inclination allow. Make enough for just one salad, or a whole bottle's worth to keep for future salads.

HOW TO MAKE A VINAIGRETTE: You will need good olive oil and an acid (vinegar or lemon juice or a combination), and salt. That's it! A little minced shallot, honey, and Dijon mustard are even better; they add flavor, and the mustard and honey also help keep the oil and vinegar suspended in an emulsion.

Dip a small whisk into the jar of Dijon and use it to pick up about $1/2$ teaspoon of mustard. Splash a little of your acid into a small bowl (a rather deep, narrow bowl works best), drizzle in $1/2$ teaspoon honey, and add a good pinch of salt and a few grinds of pepper. Whisk to blend and dissolve the salt.

Whisking constantly, add the oil in a slow, steady stream—if you pour slowly and whisk thoroughly enough, it will become a smooth, uniform mixture. (If it separates, or "breaks," no worries. Just rewhisk right before you add it to the salad.) I like to alternate whisking in oil and vinegar, because it makes it easier to manage the final yield. Tasting as you go along also helps you get a better handle on how to balance the oil and vinegar. (Most vinaigrettes have 3 to 4 parts oil to 1 part vinegar.) When you reach a flavor you like and quantity you need, taste again and add more salt and pepper as necessary; a properly seasoned dressing will seem slightly too salty on its own. You can also dip a leaf of lettuce into the dressing to taste it "in context."

If you are more recipe-inclined, then the recipe for The Bi-Rite Vinaigrette on page 51 is an excellent place to start.

· ·

Choose the right salad for the occasion. Leafy salads start to wilt the instant you dress them. It's not a problem if you're going to serve right away, but sometimes you need more staying power. For picnics, buffets, and other occasions that require longevity in a salad, choose a grain-, pasta-, or vegetable-based salad rather than one that's mostly leafy greens.

· ·

How to Dress a Salad

How you dress a salad is just as important as what you dress it with. This is how the pros do it, and it can really take your own salads to the next level:

1. **Toss the greens with the dressing.** A salad tastes so much better when dressing is evenly dispersed among every leaf, rather than just drizzled on top. If it's a composed salad, you can toss ingredients separately and then arrange them on your serving platter.

2. **Don't add all the dressing at once.** You can always add more dressing if you need it, but you can't take away if you add too much.

3. **Use a big bowl for tossing.** This gives lettuce and veggies plenty of room to move around. Pour the dressing on the sides of the bowl as opposed to on top of the greens. This will make it easier to evenly dress the salad.

4. **The best tools are your hands.** They're gentle and precise, and have lots of surface area for spreading dressing.

5. **Taste the salad after tossing.** Sometimes you have enough dressing, but still need a little extra acid or salt. Tasting is the only way to know that!

SANDWICHES

Lots of foods are eaten out of hand, but a sandwich is comfort food that begs to be held—hugged, practically—with both hands. Whether exotic or familiar, ornate or simple, a solidly executed sandwich is greater than the sum of its parts. It's food that makes you feel good.

IT STARTS WITH GOOD BREAD. You can't make a sandwich without bread. It's what makes a sandwich a sandwich. But a *great* sandwich must have a good foundation.

The sandwich exemplifies some of the most important principles of cooking. If you can master these in a sandwich, you can do anything! A great sandwich will have these key qualities:

- **Texture**—A little textural contrast makes a sandwich infinitely more satisfying to eat. *Examples: crusty bread, cole slaw, onions, chunky peanut butter, even potato chips.*

- **Acid**—Every sandwich needs a little acid; why else do you think mustard is so popular? It adds brightness and cuts through the richness. *Examples: mustard, balsamic vinegar, pickles, chile sauce, vinagrette.*

- **Fat**—Fatty spreads not only serve as a lubricant, but also help the flavors of other ingredients linger in your mouth. *Examples: mayonnaise, olive oil, butter.*

- **Balance**—Neither the condiments nor the fillings should dominate; rather, they should complement one another. So ease up on that spicy mustard, lest it obliterate the ham and cheese.

- **Seasonality**—If it's the dead of winter and the tomatoes are all pink and crunchy, perhaps it's not the best time to make that caprese sandwich you've been craving. Save it for the summer—or revamp the sandwich with some roasted winter veggies or sun-dried tomatoes instead of fresh tomatoes.

- **Seasoning**—We finish nearly every deli sandwich with a sprinkle of salt and pepper to pull the flavors together.

MAYONNAISE

Mayonnaise is not just for sandwiches. It can take center stage in creamy salad dressings or dips, or can go undercover as a binder or subtle flavor enhancer. You can certainly make your own mayo if you are so inclined, but for convenience and shelf life, I often use store-bought. Here are just a few ideas for how to use it:

- **Instant aioli**—Aioli is basically gussied-up mayonnaise. Mash fresh garlic and salt into a paste, mix into mayo, and thin with a bit of lemon juice. Presto! Perfect as a dip for raw veggies or a spread for a sandwich.
- **Herb dip or salad dressing**—Combine mayonnaise, plain yogurt or sour cream, garlic and/or scallions, and herbs like parsley, chives, and thyme in a blender. Puree until smooth. Add a splash of vinegar or lemon juice to adjust the acid and/or consistency.
- **Binder**—Mayonnaise is great when you need a little glue to hold things together. I use it for breadcrumb stuffings and in crab and salmon cakes.

SOUPS

We offer two hot soups at the deli every day, one of which is always vegetarian. Sometimes, especially on San Francisco's infamously cool and damp days, we can hardly make the soup fast enough to meet the demand. Its popularity is understandable; soup is both food and beverage, and thus an all-in-one source of nourishment. It does not like to be eaten on the go; its high temperature forces you to slow down and sip one spoonful at a time.

I have a dichotomous view of soups: on one hand, they're the ultimate recycler, taking on whatever scraps and tidbits you happen to have. On the other hand, soups are also the perfect place to exercise restraint by showcasing just one or two seasonal ingredients: think of asparagus, so tender they're barely blanched before being pureed into a silken expression of pure spring.

A good vegetable soup doesn't require much in the way of prep or cooking time. If you have very fresh, tender vegetables, focus on cooking them just until they are done to help retain their texture and bright flavor.

CHARCUTERIE

"Charcuterie" is a fancy-sounding word used to refer to the category of nibbles that includes pâté, salami, prosciutto, and pancetta. Although they take many different shapes and forms, there's a common thread: you start with raw meat and, through the use of salt, bacteria, time, or heat, or a combination of these, turn a perishable raw product into one that not only has a longer shelf life but is also uniquely delicious. It's sort of the meat equivalent of cheesemaking, when you think about it—and both are the ultimate in "slow food."

Curing meat in this way is a centuries-old tradition, born of a need to preserve as well as use every last bit of meat on an animal. Whereas prosciutto and country hams use a single muscle, salami and pâté and all those "chopped" versions are the perfect destiny for little scraps of meat left clinging to bones. Although today we tend to think of them as luxury items, charcuterie was actually born out of thrift and necessity in a time when refrigerators and freezers didn't exist.

Thanks to pork's resurgence in popularity and the rekindled interest in nose-to-tail cooking, charcuterie

has experienced a notable renaissance in recent years, particularly among American chefs and ambitious foodies. They're not only learning the complicated art of balancing salt, sugar, air, and temperature, but also giving charcuterie the time and care it requires. As an example, producer Cristiano Creminelli of Utah-based Creminelli Fine Meats literally sleeps with his salumi in the days after they're put up to hang, waking himself every few hours to check on his product. He does this not just to monitor the temperature and humidity of the curing room, but also to manually rotate and turn the salumi logs so that they dry evenly and develop the proper coat of surface mold. That kind of expertise and human oversight is a big part of what makes their salumi so delicious and special.

Although you can make charcuterie out of beef, duck, or even chicken, the vast majority of charcuterie is pork-based. And because of the many problems surrounding the pork industry (see The Butcher Counter chapter for details), it's particularly important to **MAKE SURE THAT WHATEVER CHARCUTERIE YOU BUY IS MADE WITH GOOD-QUALITY, "CLEAN" MEAT.** The good news is that this "new guard" of artisan charcuterie producers has similar leanings; many are sourcing organic and/or heritage pork as their primary ingredient.

There are endless varieties of charcuterie—some are centuries old, and new ones are invented all the time—but you really only need to know about the basic categories and variations within each.

• •

Very high-quality, artisanally made charcuterie takes not just skill and good raw ingredients, but also time and care. As a result, a handmade salami can cost twice as much as a mass-produced version made with cheap ingredients. Keep in mind that high-quality cured meats beg to be savored and enjoyed in moderation. If you have a really beautiful salami, 2 ounces is more than enough to put on a sandwich, and 1 ounce is enough for an appetizer platter.

• •

The other key to success is in how you buy charcuterie. For dry-cured items like salami and prosciutto, **GET THEM SLICED TO ORDER** rather than presliced in

THE WORLD OF CHARCUTERIE

CATEGORY	WHAT IT IS	EXAMPLES
Fermented	This is perhaps the most familiar category, since good ol' salami is an example of fermented charcuterie. The meat (usually pork) and fat are ground together, mixed with bacteria starter culture and nitrites, stuffed into casings, and hung to cure. During the aging process, a white mold grows on the outside of the casings; it aids in preservation of the meat and also contributes to its overall flavor.	Salami (fine grind, mild seasoning) Soppressata (coarse grind, flavorings vary) Toscano (medium grind, robust garlic seasoning)
Whole muscle, cured for eating as is	Muscles are cured whole, often with various spices as part of the mix. Although the muscles are kept intact, they are often pressed or shaped by casing as they cure. These are typically served "raw" in thin slices.	Prosciutto, Jamón serrano, Jamón iberico, and speck (cured pork leg) Coppa (cured pork shoulder) Bresaola (cured beef) Bundnerfleisch (cured beef)
Whole muscle, cured for cooking	Muscles or slabs of fat are cured whole, often with various spices as part of the mix. The process both preserves the meat and fat and transforms its flavor and texture. These are primarily used for cooking, such as the base for sautéing aromatic vegetables.	Pancetta (cured and rolled pork belly) Bacon (cured and smoked pork belly)* Guanciale (cured pork jowls) Lardo and salt pork (cured pork back fat)
Cooked	Meat is either left whole or ground with fat and either stuffed into casings or packed in a vessel. Instead of hanging to cure, these items are gently baked or simmered until cooked through.	Mortadella Pâtés and mousses Prosciutto cotto Salame cotto Smoked and boiled hams

*For more information on bacon, see page 195 in The Butcher Counter chapter.

TOP ROW: Jamón serrano   SECOND ROW: Prosciutto di Parma
THIRD ROW: Salami Toscano, salami picante, and Genoa salami   BOTTOM ROW: Salameti secchi,
salami nostrano, wild boar salami, salami barolo, and rosette de Lyon

a package. The flavors of the charcuterie start to evolve and diminish with exposure to air, so the longer the item stays whole, the better. It also allows you to get it sliced to the exact thickness of your liking. The other benefit to sliced-to-order meats is that you can—and should—**ASK FOR A TASTE**. It lets you make sure the quality is up to snuff, and a freshly sliced sample is the best indicator of what it *should* taste like. It also lets you compare and contrast similar products: say, a classic prosciutto di Parma against a Spanish version and a domestic artisan version.

AT THE VERY LEAST, LOOK FOR CHARCUTERIE THAT IS:

- Ask for a taste before you buy

- Get your charcuterie sliced to order

IDEALLY, LOOK FOR:

- Charcuterie made with "clean" meat using artisanal techniques

---

THE MEANING BEHIND THE MEAT

Salumi and charcuterie represent a wide variety of grinds, sizes, and flavors (see opposite), each one with its own wonderful unique attributes. Each variety gives you an expression of a particular culture, tradition, and history. For instance, Genoa salami, with its signature fine grind texture, has been made that way in its namesake town for centuries. The Toscano salami is coarser, using the red wine indigenous to the area, which helps with preservation and flavoring.

OLIVES

I'm always baffled when I hear someone say, "I don't like olives." But I grew up with olives on the table at every meal—natural, fresh, delicious olives—and I realize that most Americans know olives only from the commercially canned and jarred varieties. At the store, I love seeing people get their first tastes of just how wonderful olives can be.

AT THE VERY LEAST, LOOK FOR OLIVES THAT ARE:

- Taste olives before you buy

- Avoid canned pitted olives

- Buy pit-in olives

- Marinate your own olives

IDEALLY, LOOK FOR:

- Unpasteurized olives

BUY UNPASTEURIZED OLIVES IF YOU CAN. The vast majority of olives are pasteurized, which makes it possible to keep them out in nonrefrigerated or semi-refrigerated displays. Although it doesn't completely destroy the olives' flavor and texture, it does alter them significantly. Unpasteurized olives have a much fresher flavor and firmer texture that more clearly speaks of the olive fruit itself.

"NO GRAZING" IS NOT THE SAME AS "NO TASTING." Olives are so different from one variety to the next, and it's important to taste before you buy. Even if signs tell me otherwise, I always ask if I can taste before I fill up my container. Look for olives that are firm and plump, have good texture, and most of all, taste good to you.

AVOID PITTED OLIVES. When olives are pitted, the fruit starts to break down and soften faster than they would if the pit were left in. Stick with the unpitted kind and pit them yourself. It takes just a few extra seconds, and the flavor is superior.

TRY MARINATING YOUR OWN OLIVES. You'll get brighter flavors and more flexibility in terms of what spices and herbs you use. To marinate olives, rinse the olives with warm water and drain well (I do this whether marinating or not, just to get some of the extra salt off). In a small sauté pan, combine some extra-virgin olive oil, a bay leaf, some fresh rosemary and thyme, a few smashed cloves of garlic, and maybe a little lemon or orange rind . . . a dried chile or two if you like. Warm it over low heat just until aromatic, remove from the heat, and then stir in the olives. Let the flavors mingle for at least 20 minutes. Serve at room temperature, or as I prefer, ever so slightly warm.

BLT&E with Harissa Mayo

SERVES 2

This gussied-up version of a BLT boasts a poached egg whose runny yolk acts as a lusty sauce for the sandwich. Lightly dressed bitter greens stand in for the traditional lettuce; their bite provides a nice counterpoint to the richness of the egg. They're dressed just as you would a salad, so if you have extra, just serve them on the side.

- 2 tablespoons mayonnaise
- 1 teaspoon harissa (see Note)
- 4 slices bacon
- 1 tablespoon plus 1 teaspoon cider vinegar
- 2 eggs
- 2/3 cup lightly packed frisee or shredded radicchio, or a mixture
- 1 teaspoon minced shallot
- 1/2 teaspoon extra-virgin olive oil
- Kosher salt and freshly ground black pepper
- Four 1/2-inch slices good-quality sandwich bread, such as pain de mie
- 1 small ripe tomato, thinly sliced

Combine the mayonnaise and harissa in a small bowl and stir until blended. Set aside.

Cut the bacon in half crosswise, arrange in a medium skillet, and put the skillet over medium heat. Cook, turning the bacon frequently, until cooked through and crispy but still a little chewy, about 8 minutes. Transfer to a paper towel–lined plate and set aside.

Bring about 4 cups of water to a boil in a small saucepan. Lower the heat to a bare simmer and add 1 tablespoon of the vinegar. Crack an egg into a small cup or ramekin and, holding the cup just above the surface of the water, carefully pour the egg into the water. Repeat with the second egg. Cook the eggs until the whites have cooked through but the yolk is still runny, 2 to 3 minutes. (To check, carefully lift an egg out of the water with a slotted spoon. Prod the white—it should feel firm and bouncy all the way through.) With a slotted spoon, transfer the eggs to another paper towel–lined plate.

In a small bowl, combine the frisee or radicchio, the remaining 1 teaspoon vinegar, the shallot, and the olive oil. Sprinkle with a pinch of salt and pepper and toss to blend.

Toast or grill the bread to your liking, then spread the mayo evenly over two pieces. Top with the bacon, tomato, frisee, and egg. Sprinkle the egg with a little salt and pepper, then top with the other two pieces of bread.

Serve right away (with plenty of napkins).

Note: Harissa is a chile-and-spice paste that hails from North Africa. For a slightly different effect, you could substitute a mild Thai curry paste or other Asian chile sauce.

Grilled Manchego and Serrano Ham Sandwich with Membrillo
MAKES 2

This is a simple sandwich, but the combination of classic Spanish ingredients is nothing short of stellar. Try serving with cornichons, pickled carrots, or a brightly dressed green salad to counterbalance the sandwich's richness. To make it vegetarian, just omit the serrano ham—it will still be delicious.

2/3 cup (about 2 ounces) grated Manchego or other semifirm Spanish sheep's milk cheese

Four 1/2-inch slices from a rustic artisan loaf of bread

4 very thin slices serrano ham or prosciutto (about 1 1/2 ounces)

2 ounces membrillo, thinly sliced (see Note)

1 1/2 tablespoons unsalted butter

Spread half of the cheese evenly over two slices of the bread. Top with the serrano, the membrillo, and the remaining cheese. Top with the other two bread slices.

Heat 1 tablespoon of the butter in a medium skillet over medium-low heat. When hot, add the sandwiches and cook slowly until deep golden on one side, 4 to 5 minutes. Then add the remaining 1/2 tablespoon butter, flip the sandwiches over, and scoot them around the pan to pick up more of the butter. Continue to cook until the other side is also golden and the cheese is melted, 2 to 3 minutes longer.

Let the sandwiches rest for about 30 seconds before slicing (it gives the sandwich a chance to firm up so it doesn't slide apart when you cut it). Then serve right away.

Note: Membrillo is a jamlike paste made from quince fruit, traditionally served alongside Manchego cheese. As such, it's often found in the cheese section of grocery stores. If you can't find membrillo, use a very thin layer of fig or apricot jam.

Summer Corn and Tomato Salad
SERVES 6 TO 8

This colorful and refreshing salad is one of the most eagerly anticipated items in our deli case. We don't start making it until the tomatoes are really ripe and the corn is sweet and abundant.

Because the ingredients are fairly sturdy, this salad holds up for quite a while after you make it. It's a great candidate for bringing to a picnic or barbecue, and it's the perfect side for a burger! It's also nice as a salsa or spooned onto a grilled fish fillet.

Kosher salt

3 large ears corn

3 tablespoons extra-virgin olive oil

2 tablespoons red wine vinegar, more as needed

1 large shallot, minced

1 teaspoon honey

1 teaspoon Dijon mustard

Freshly ground black pepper

2 medium tomatoes, cored and cut into 1-inch chunks

1 medium bell pepper, finely diced

1/2 small red onion, finely diced

1/2 medium cucumber, peeled, seeded, and cut into 1/2-inch chunks

1/4 cup coarsely chopped cilantro

Bring a medium pot of well-salted water to a boil. Cut the kernels from the corn, add the kernels to the pot, and cook for 1 1/2 minutes (they should still be a little crunchy). Pour into a colander and run cool water over the corn to stop the cooking. Set aside.

In a small bowl, combine the olive oil, vinegar, shallot, honey, mustard, 1 teaspoon salt, and a few grinds of black pepper and whisk to combine. Combine the corn, tomatoes, pepper, onion, cucumber, and cilantro in a medium bowl, drizzle with about half of the dressing, and toss gently with your hands. Add more dressing as needed to coat the vegetables lightly and toss again.

Taste and add more salt or vinegar as needed.

Butternut Squash Latkes

MAKES 18

Our customers are an incredibly diverse group of people, but there's one thing that unites them: their love for our latkes. We used to make them only for Jewish holidays, but now they're a staple in our deli for Jews and non-Jews alike. Our version includes butternut squash and fresh herbs, which give the latkes a freshness that most other kinds lack.

This recipe employs a trick that we use extensively in our commercial kitchen: we brown the latkes on the stove top and finish the cooking in the oven. It not only minimizes the time you spend standing over a hot pan but also reduces the amount of oil needed and frees up the stove top for whatever else you might want to make.

I love these as a first course or a light supper, especially when paired with smoked salmon or trout. Applesauce and sour cream are great, too.

> 1½ cups grapeseed or other neutral oil, more as needed
>
> 1 large yellow onion, halved, peeled, and thinly sliced lengthwise
>
> Kosher salt and freshly ground black pepper
>
> 1½ pounds russet potatoes (about 2 large)
>
> 1½ pounds butternut squash (about ½ medium)
>
> 4 large eggs
>
> 1 cup matzo meal
>
> ⅓ cup finely chopped fresh parsley
>
> ¼ cup finely chopped fresh sage
>
> 1 tablespoon chopped fresh marjoram

Position racks in the top and bottom thirds of the oven and heat to 350°F.

Heat 2 tablespoons of the oil in a medium skillet over medium-high heat. When hot, add the onion and sprinkle with ½ teaspoon salt and a few grinds of black pepper. Cook, stirring frequently, until the onions are golden all over and very soft, about 10 minutes. Remove from the heat and set aside to cool.

Peel and grate the potatoes and butternut squash. Put in a large bowl, along with the onions, eggs, matzo meal, parsley, sage, marjoram, 1 tablespoon salt, and 1 teaspoon pepper. Toss gently to combine thoroughly.

Heat 3 tablespoons of the oil in a large skillet over medium-high heat. When the pan is hot, use a ⅓-cup dry measure to scoop a mound of the mixture into the pan. With a fork, spread and flatten the mixture to a 4-inch disk. Repeat 3 more times. When the first side is golden brown (about 2 minutes), carefully flip the latkes over and brown the other sides, about 2 minutes more. Transfer the latkes to a rimmed baking sheet and continue to scoop and brown the remaining latke mixture in batches, adding another few tablespoons of oil before each new batch. Arrange the latkes in a single layer on the baking sheet; you'll probably need at least 2 sheets to accomplish this.

When all the latkes have been shaped and browned, transfer the baking sheets to the oven and bake until the latkes are cooked through, about 15 minutes. Serve hot.

4

THE PRODUCE DEPARTMENT

When we started out, we got our produce from one local grower, and now we work with over thirty. Here at the store, we talk a lot about creating community, and some people might think we're just referring to the neighborhood. But to me it's way bigger—it's in Placerville, it's in Salinas. We commit to having a relationship with local growers. We're going the extra step to, perhaps, make the difference in helping a farm stay in business.

We are very aware of the trials and tribulations that farmers go through, but until you experience it yourself, you get only a limited view of what it takes to grow food. That's why we're growing some of our own produce for the store. But even for the products we don't grow, we stand behind them as if we grew them ourselves. We go big in ordering items we're excited about, we'll talk about them with our guests, and we'll even bring the grower in to talk with people. We're really proud of them and the work they do. It's all about celebrating great food and community.

— Simon Richard,
produce buyer

T HE PRODUCE SECTION is one of my favorite parts of the Market—not just because it is so bright and bountiful and full of delicious samples, but also because it is ever-changing and evolving. It is, more than any other department, a true

and direct reflection of the farmland surrounding us, the season we're in, even recent weather patterns. Fresh produce is alive, and it should look and feel that way.

Unfortunately, today's consumer has gotten accustomed to the uniform, waxy, highly polished look and feel of what is available in the supermarket. The same product can be found in nearly every supermarket across the country. Most of the industrially grown produce is controlled by a few behemoth growers and packers, who have narrowed their offerings down to a few varieties in each category—those that grow fast, large, and uniform in size. Varieties that have a long shelf life and withstand long transport are also prized. As a consequence, the vast array of heirloom and other unique varieties has pretty much disappeared from the retail landscape. Fortunately, with the rise and increasing success of farmers' markets, there is still hope and opportunity for tasting "uncommon" fruits and veggies. Ask your retailer to go to the farmers' market and meet some of the growers and to taste the difference. Farm-direct relationships start one at a time.

USE YOUR SENSES as you shop for produce. Smell, taste, and feel as you check for ripeness and quality. Keep in mind that looks can be deceiving; ugly fruits and vegetables sometimes taste better than ones that look "perfect." Of course, avoid items that are wrinkled, discolored, or otherwise beyond edibility.

LET THE SEASONS INSPIRE AND GUIDE YOU. Buying fruits and vegetables that are abundant and in season usually means riper and more flavorful products, lower prices, and (often) fewer "food miles" due to shipping.

ORGANIC PRODUCE IS GENERALLY PREFERABLE OVER CONVENTIONAL (NONORGANIC). It's better for the environment, the people who grow and harvest it, and our own health, and it's also the best and easiest way to avoid GMOs. (By definition, organic food is GMO-free.) However, if you do buy conventional produce, know that some crops are more commonly or heavily sprayed than others. I've made note of these "worst offenders" in the appropriate sections of this chapter. (See the Dirty Dozen information, page 284.) Buying organic versions of these particular items will give you the biggest bang for the buck to minimize your exposure to chemical fertilizers and pesticides and also maintain the health of our waterways and fish supplies.

· ·

Integrated Pest Management (IPM) is another farming approach that, while not organic, ensures limited and judicious use of pesticides.

· ·

BUY LOCAL PRODUCE WHENEVER IT MAKES SENSE FOR YOU. For instance, depending on where you happen to live, your local options may be extremely limited during the winter. In those cases, buy local when you can, but also expand your focus to how the product was grown: organic or unsprayed produce from farms that exercise good stewardship of the land.

READ SIGNS. The country of origin is required on all signage (you'll generally find it on the stickers on supermarket fruits), but also look for more specific information. The name of a particular farm is ideal; seeing this information displayed is a good sign that you're buying from a conscientious retailer.

WHENEVER YOU CAN, TRY HEIRLOOM (NON-HYBRIDIZED) VARIETIES of your favorite produce items—you'll be helping to preserve varieties that would otherwise go extinct.

ASK LOTS OF QUESTIONS, INCLUDING, "MAY I TASTE THAT?" This not only gets you closer to understanding more about how and where produce is grown, but it makes you a better cook as well. Some questions you might ask include:

- "I see that these carrots are from a local farm. Do you know which one? Are they organic, and if not, what sort of practices do they employ?"
- "I am planning on making a pie today. Which fruits are in season right now? Which varieties would be best for a pie?"
- "I hate when peas are starchy . . . may I taste one to make sure they are sweet and tender?" Or . . . "I've never seen a tomato that looks like that. May I taste it to make sure I like it before buying it?" (Note that the latter example requires the clerk to cut a sample for you—something they should be happy to do.)
- "My recipe calls for eggplant, but I see they're not in season right now. What could I use as a substitute that will still work in this recipe?"

WINTER

People who know me expect that summer would be my favorite time of year for produce. As much as I love the bounty of berries and stone fruits, I yearn for winter's citrus, greens, and avocados. The three together make incredible salads that I just can't get enough of. So don't despair when winter hits; that's when some of the most exciting produce is in stores.

AVOCADOS

Someone once told me that a lot of Hollywood executives invest in avocado orchards. It's true that there's a lot of money to be made in avocados, largely thanks to a strongly united front of growers who name their own price. That price influences what wholesalers, distributors, and retailers pay, and everyone feels it when prices swing upward. (Because avocados fetch a fairly high price to start with, most grocers choose to take a lower margin when the cost really skyrockets.) Whatever the price, it's amusing to think that a single Hollywood bank account might be fed by avocados as well as by the box office.

How to Buy

Most people think of avocados as a summer crop, perhaps because they can only be grown in warmish climates. But if you taste avocados throughout the year, you'll find them to be richer and creamier in the wintertime, when they're most abundant in the northern hemisphere.

FROM THE OUTSIDE, IT'S HARD TO TELL THE DIFFERENCE BETWEEN A PERFECTLY RIPE ONE AND AN OVER-THE-HILL ONE, which makes choosing them a challenge. No matter how perfectly ripe an avocado feels on the outside, there's always the possibility of finding streaky blackened flesh on the inside. It's particularly important to buy from someone who cares about the quality of their produce and will happily exchange a bad one. After all, for such a pricey fruit, you shouldn't have to risk losing your money on a dud.

But there are some tricks. Some people use the "nubbin test" to determine ripeness: if you push on that bit of stem and it goes into the fruit, it means that it's ripe . . . or it could mean that it's too ripe. Avocados ripen only after they're picked, so **I FIND IT'S JUST AS EASY TO BUY A SLIGHTLY UNDERRIPE AVOCADO AND MONITOR THE RIPENING** process myself. I buy avocados that *don't* pass the nubbin test at the store, and at home I do the test every day. As soon as that nubbin pops in, I know it's time to eat it.

Even if you want to buy a ready-to-eat avocado, avoid ones that feel spongy or have loose-feeling skins; they're already too far gone. Some varieties, like Haas and Fuerte, start out with green skin and turn black as they ripen. But they're not all like this; Reed and Bacon varieties are green even when ripe.

. . . .

Larger avocados have a higher fruit-to-pit ratio, so you'll get more for your money by picking out a big one!

. . . .

Haas and Reed avocados are some of the most commonly available varieties of avocados. Even though they are slightly more expensive, California-grown Haas are superior to South American–grown Haas; the domestic ones are richer and creamier and consistently delicious. However, there are many other types out there, each with its own unique variations in fat content, pit size, and flavor notes. If you see unusual varieties like the Bacon or Pinkerton, give them a try.

. . . .

> **LOOK FOR AVOCADOS THAT ARE:**
> - **A little underripe**
> - **Somewhat firm (not squishy or spongy) with taut skins**

How to Store

Avocados are at their best when they're kept in cool but not cold temperatures. Let them ripen at a cool room temperature (say, with your potatoes and onions); once they're ripe, you can stabilize them for a few days in the refrigerator.

If you use only half the fruit, wrap the remaining half (pit still in, ideally) in plastic wrap and refrigerate it for a day or so. Or if they're really ripe, just scoop out the flesh, mash it up with lemon or lime juice, and make a quick guacamole instead; the lemon will slow the browning process.

How to Use

I love the creamy taste of pure avocado, whether eaten with a spoon right out of the skin or spread on toast and sprinkled with good salt. (Avocados are a great, healthier alternative to butter on toast.)

Avocados also add a wonderful flavor and texture to salad dressings (Green Goddess is a classic), chilled soups (such as the Garden of Eden Soup on page 235), salsas, and seafood dishes like ceviche. Avocados pair well with other fruits, especially tropical ones like mango, papaya, and pineapple. But I think there's no better match than avocado with citrus, like the Fennel, Blood Orange, and Avocado Salad on page 98.

BRASSICAS: BROCCOLI, CAULIFLOWER, AND THEIR KIN

You don't need genetic engineering or clever hybridization to come up with exciting new vegetables. Sometimes you just have to look at an existing vegetable in a new way. That's exactly what Andy Griffin of Mariquita Farms did when he started clipping the delicate sprouts and blossoms of an heirloom broccoli varietal, thus "developing" broccoli di cicco. At the time, nobody in the States had seen this kind of broccoli before, so Andy taught his customers how to prepare it. The sprouts, which are a little like a leafy broccolini, are so flavorful that they quickly became a local favorite; at the Market, we sell it raw in the produce department and sautéed with garlic and chiles in the deli.

How to Buy

When they're harvested at their peak, brassicas—broccoli, cauliflower, broccoflower, spiky romanesco, and their relatives—are sweet and tender; overly mature ones will be woody and fibrous, no matter how much you cook them. Look for tight, firm heads with consistent, even color and perky leaves. Avoid ones with cracks or splitting in the cut end of the stem or brown or black burns on the edge of leaves—all signs of a too-late harvest and overmaturing. For broccoli, wide-open or yellowed florets are also bad signs. Steer clear of any with black spots, a sign of mold developing.

Poor storage, including rough handling or prolonged exposure to water, can cause even young, tender brassicas to become limp, blackened, and slimy—give these a pass.

Cellophane, often used to protect cauliflower heads over long periods of transit, also encourages the condensation that leads to breakdown; try to buy unwrapped heads instead and put them in a loose plastic bag when you get home.

Cauliflower comes in many colors now—orange, purple, and green, in addition to the classic white—so have fun with them. And if you see purple sprouting broccoli, don't pass it up; it is sweet, tender, and one of my all-time favorite veggies.

How to Store

Keep brassicas in a perforated plastic bag (just poke a few holes in it) and put it in the coldest part of the refrigerator. The natural sugars begin to convert to starch once harvested, so the sooner you use them, the sweeter and more tender they will be. Use within a few days to ensure peak condition.

How to Use

These veggies feature lots of little crevices where dirt and bugs can hide, so be sure to give them a good

> **LOOK FOR BRASSICAS THAT ARE:**
> - Bright in color
> - Firm, with uncracked stems and perky leaves
> - Free of black or slimy spots
> - Unwrapped

cleaning. Immerse them in a bowl of warm water and scrub the sturdier ones with a brush.

In my opinion, brassicas are all much nicer when they're cooked enough—and by that I mean the crunch is gone and your teeth don't have to fight their way through them. You can accomplish this in several ways:

- **Dry heat** (roasting or grilling) drives off much of the moisture and intensifies the flavors of the vegetable. Grilled blanched broccoli is one of my favorite dishes in the world—the slight charring really complements the inherent flavor of the vegetable.

- **Frying** makes everything better, but fried cauliflower is truly something special. With or without batter, the high heat of frying transforms the texture of any brassica. My favorite version is fried (without batter) until golden and soft, and seasoned with capers, garlic, and anchovy with a squirt of lemon. Heaven!

- **Moist cooking** does a lot to tenderize brassicas. It can be difficult to cook brassicas completely just by sautéing them, so it helps to first briefly blanch them in salted water. Or braise them by starting the sauté, adding some liquid, and covering the pan. With this technique, I like to cook the brassicas until they're quite soft and just starting to fall apart; at this point, they become almost creamy and seem to melt on your tongue. Cooked this way, they're great for pasta sauce.

Brassicas, regardless of the variety, do well when paired with pungent, salty flavors. You don't need much more than extra-virgin olive oil, garlic, and chile flakes or capers to create a flavorful side dish. The Roasted Cauliflower and Brussels Sprouts with Caper Lemon Butter on page 99 is a great place to start.

EAT GOOD FOOD

CHICORIES: BITTER LEAFY VEGETABLES

For the first few years we were open, chicories—the category of bitter greens that includes frisee, endive, and escarole—were a tough sell. Over the years, though, chicories started showing up on restaurant menus, and our guests became increasingly interested in cooking with them at home. Now our guests anticipate the arrival of the chicory season and eagerly seek out new varieties. The demand is so great that there are more farmers growing chicories—it went from one or two when we first started to at least a dozen now. Chicories are some of my favorite vegetables, and it makes me happy to see other people catch on, too.

How to Buy

I encourage you to become familiar with a few of the many varieties of chicories that exist, starting with the photo on page 88. If you haven't cooked with or eaten many chicories, you may first be won over by their ruffly elegant curls, their speckled and solid shading, and their general loveliness.

A LIGHTER COLOR USUALLY CORRESPONDS TO LESS BITTERNESS, a sweeter flavor, and a tender texture. If you're not yet on the bitter bandwagon, choose ones with the palest leaves you can find.

When shopping for chicories, **LOOK FOR LEAVES THAT ARE ALERT AND PERKY**, and avoid ones that are weathered or limp. The heads should feel firm and somewhat heavy—a sign that they'll have some texture to them when you eat them.

A RUSTY DISCOLORATION ON THE CUT END IS INEVITABLE and not necessarily a bad sign. Avoid any that seem heavily "rusted" (that is, harvested long ago) or otherwise worse for the wear. Steer clear of heads

---

LOOK FOR CHICORIES THAT ARE:
- Perky and alert
- Firm and heavy
- Light in color (if less bitterness is what you want)

---

whose leaves have started to blacken on the edges—a sign of old age or poor storage.

How to Store

Storing chicories is easy: put them in a plastic bag and keep them in the refrigerator. Depending on when they were harvested, you may have up to a week before they start to lose their verve.

How to Use

Most chicories are just as enjoyable raw as they are cooked, whether grilled, drizzled with a hot dressing, or braised. Chicories are at their best when in the company of acids, fats, and pungent ingredients like anchovies, garlic, and hard grating cheese, which together help temper the bitterness and round out the flavors. A generous dusting of freshly grated Parmigiano-Reggiano will balance and deepen the flavor of the final dish.

Because of the wide variety of shapes, sizes, and flavors of chicories, it's worth talking about a few of them individually:

- **Radicchio, Treviso, and Castelfranco**—I like to quarter or halve the heads through the core so that the wedges stay intact, drizzle with balsamic vinegar, and then grill or sauté them. The high heat caramelizes the sugars in the balsamic and tempers the bitterness.

- **Frisee**—My favorite salad of all time, salade Lyonnaise, stars this frilly chicory. With crispy bits of bacon, a poached egg, garlicky croutons, and a Dijon vinaigrette, it has everything you need to stand up to the gently assertive frisee.

....

If you're looking for a buffet-worthy salad, consider one that's heavy on the frisee. Whereas tender lettuces quickly wilt under the weight and acid of salad dressing, frisee not only holds up but also seems to benefit from a little advance "marination."

....

- **Escarole**—I use escarole two ways. The tougher, darker outer leaves are best when cooked in liquid, because it breaks down into a nice silky-yet-robust texture that I find appealing. You can do this with a

little liquid—by sautéing the greens, adding ¹/₂ cup water or broth, and covering the pan—or by adding them to chicken soup near the end of cooking. I like using the tender, pale yellow inner leaves in salads—they are great in place of romaine lettuce in a Caesar salad.

- **Belgian endive**—Citrus, crab, and avocado seem designed to go with Belgian endive; not only are

they in season at the same time, but the flavors and textures marry perfectly. To use in a salad, julienne the heads or cut crosswise into thin half-moons. I also like to separate the leaves and use the little cups as a base for an hors d'oeuvre: a crumble of blue cheese, a sprinkle of nuts, and a drizzle of honey is a simple but winning combo. Or for a side dish, you can braise or grill whole or lengthwise-cut half heads.

EAT GOOD FOOD

CITRUS

Washington, D.C., is a pretty happening food town. Aside from the White House vegetable garden, there's an exciting restaurant scene and farmers' markets filled with high-quality, locally grown produce. Which is why I was so surprised when, at a grocery conference there, a salad on the lunch buffet featured canned mandarin oranges. The concept was good and the chef had clearly put some effort into picking the beautiful frisee and toasting the almonds perfectly. But it was all ruined by the mushy texture and tinny taste of the canned mandarins. It was winter—the height of citrus season—so there was no reason to use canned. When it comes to citrus, canned just doesn't cut it; it should be fresh or none at all!

How to Buy

In San Francisco, we are lucky to be half a day's drive away from quite a few citrus growers, who provide the store with a mind-boggling array of citrus varieties. And when this fruit is in season, there's no question about it: our displays become a sea of orange and yellow orbs of many shapes, sizes, and flavors. We've had as many as thirty varieties at one time! (Simon, our produce buyer, affectionately calls it The Citrus Bomb.)

But for the vast majority of people in the United States, locally grown citrus simply doesn't exist. So how is it that oranges, lemons, and limes are available year-round? Distributors source from many different regions (and countries) to ensure a constant supply. **BUT BECAUSE CITRUS IS ALWAYS AVAILABLE, IT'S EASY TO FORGET THAT IT GOES IN AND OUT OF SEASON** just like everything else.

I'm all for eating locally produced food, but I won't ask you to pass on lemons if you live in a place where they're not grown. I propose that you **BUY DOMESTIC**

> **LOOK FOR CITRUS THAT IS:**
> - Domestic and in season
> - Firm, with taut skin and no soft spots

CITRUS WHEN YOU CAN, AND CELEBRATE IT WHEN IT'S IN SEASON AND AT ITS PEAK.

And while you're at it, **TRY A VARIETY YOU HAVEN'T HAD BEFORE.** Across varieties of citrus, you'll find a huge spectrum in color, sweetness, acidity, seediness, and fruit-to-pith ratio. (See the photo on page 91 for examples of the physical variations, as well as tasting notes and ideas on what to do with them.)

TASTE, AND PAY PARTICULAR ATTENTION TO THE SUGAR/ACIDITY BALANCE, because that affects how it can be used. For instance, you might not want that super-sour grapefruit if you hope to eat it unadorned, but it might be perfect for topping a custardy tart. Keep in mind that citrus gets sweeter the longer it hangs on the tree, so early season fruits are more likely to be on the tart side and will get sweeter as the season progresses.

FIRM, HEAVY FRUITS ARE BETTER; taut skin and fruit that is heavy for its size suggest a high level of juice inside. (There are a few exceptions, like Satsuma mandarins, which naturally have a loose-feeling skin.) Regardless of the variety, avoid any with soft spots, which indicate damage due to rain or rough handling.

• •

There's one notable exception to citrus being a wintertime fruit: Valencia oranges, used for juice, actually peak in the summertime.

• •

Lemons with thin, taut-looking skin are juicier than the ones with thick, pocked skin. That means more juice for your buck!

• •

How to Store

Citrus skins are highly permeable, so they're prone to drying out if left on the counter. Even though the interior might still be juicy, a lemon whose skin is dried out and hardened is difficult to love (not to mention slice). So for longer storage, put citrus fruits in a plastic bag and refrigerate. Wash them only when you're ready to use them, because the excess moisture in storage will cause the peels to decay and break down.

How to Use

Considering my griping about canned mandarin oranges, I feel obligated to mention **CITRUS'S STRENGTH AS A SALAD COMPONENT**—when fresh, that is! Small, easy-to-peel varieties like tangerines can simply be peeled and separated into sections before adding. For larger varieties, like oranges, grapefruits, or tangerines, the classical technique is to segment each section out and away from the white pith with a paring knife. With smaller and less pithy fruit, I prefer to peel the fruit and slice it crosswise; it's not only speedier but also gives you a much higher yield of usable fruit.

ONE OF MY FAVORITE CITRUS SALADS DOESN'T EVEN NEED GREENS: just arrange slices of citrus (I like to use a variety) along with feta, oil-cured black olives, and very thinly sliced red onion on a large platter. A drizzle of fruity olive oil is all you need to dress it.

Citrus juices—both sweet and sour varieties—are wonderful in dressings and vinaigrettes. If you're using a sweet citrus, try simmering the juice until reduced by half before adding it in; the syrupy juice is more concentrated and helps emulsify the dressing.

I TRY TO USE THE ZEST WHENEVER POSSIBLE— not only does it contain floral aromatic oils, but I also love to get that little extra bit of mileage from the fruit. It's like free flavor! Peel it into strips with a vegetable peeler and throw it into braises or brines, or grate it finely with a microplane to add to baked goods, spice rubs, or plain ol' sugar for a gussied-up sweetener. Meyer lemon zest is my favorite.

Because the zest is the outermost part of the fruit, it comes in direct contact with any pesticide or herbicide sprays that are applied. So if you're going to use the zest, it's particularly important to buy organic.

Citrus juice and zest are integral to so many desserts; the acidity complements sweetness and adds nuance to other fruit flavors. It shouldn't always play a supporting role, though; try the Citrus Olive Oil Cake on page 63 (which uses the entire fruit) or the Blood Orange Granita on page 104.

Even if a recipe calls for only a teaspoon of lemon juice, go ahead and juice the whole thing and refrigerate any leftovers. You're much more likely to use the juice if it's already squeezed, and it saves you from washing the juicer next time around. I prefer to use a bar-style juicer (the kind that squeezes and presses the fruit inside out). It's fast and easy to clean, and it strains the juice as you go.

Always use fresh-squeezed lemon and lime juice in your cooking; the juice from those little lemon-shaped bottles has been pasteurized and just doesn't have the same flavor. And when you think about it, the time you save is really quite trivial. Go for the real thing!

THE IMPORTANCE OF ACID

In the Market (and in the food industry in general), we talk a lot about balance of flavors. When we taste the soup each morning, or sample a test run of a new deli salad, we don't just decide whether it tastes good: we're looking for harmony in flavor, texture, color, and acidity.

That last one, acidity, is incredibly important, and is also a bit of a sleeper element—because if there isn't enough acid, the uninitiated palate doesn't necessarily miss it. Whatever it is, an underacidified dish probably tastes okay, but it doesn't grab you. The potato-leek soup tastes like . . . well, potatoes and leeks and celery and onion and whatever else you put in it. But when you add a squirt of lemon juice, suddenly the flavors pop. It

tastes fresher. Your taste buds start to dance, and your salivary glands start to kick in. You want more!

Acids are a kind of culinary magic wand: they temper salt, add depth, and heighten flavors. They brighten the flavor of sweet, earthy vegetables and diffuse the richness of sauces and braises. They make just about everything better. So if you want to take your cooking to the next level, all you have to do is reach for a lemon.

A CROSS-SECTION OF CITRUS

1 **Lemon**—Where it all begins. Always good to have a couple on hand. Lisbon and Eureka varieties are the most common and are interchangeable.

2 **Persian lime**—Can be used in place of lemon juice. Avoid using the zest—it can be unpleasantly bitter.

3 **Meyer lemon**—A cross between a lemon and a sweet orange, this fruit is aromatic and ever so slightly sweet. Can be used in place of regular lemon juice, but you may want to boost the acidity with a splash of vinegar. Great for lemon curd. Always use the zest, even if just to flavor some sugar for future use.

4 **Seville orange**—This bitter orange is the classic for making marmalade; its bitterness provides the perfect balance for the added sugar.

5 **Sweet lime**—Still quite acidic, despite its name. Also makes a fantastic marmalade or syrup.

6 **Navel orange**—A great eating orange. Relatively low in acid. Because they're seedless, navels are great for eating out of hand and in salads.

7 **Valencia orange**—The juicing orange of choice; its high acidity not only gives a balanced flavor but also acts as a natural preservative.

8 **Moro blood orange**—Not just gorgeous, but offers unique flavor as well.

9 **Minneola tangelo**—A variety of tangelo, which means it's a cross between a tangerine and a grapefruit or pomelo. Easy peeling and just a few seeds make it great for eating out of hand.

10 **Satsuma mandarin**—A seedless tangerine variety that's especially easy to peel.

11 **Clementine tangerine**—Another thin-skinned, easy-to-peel variety whose mild acidity is tempered by a nice sweetness.

12 **Page mandarin**—A little brighter acidity compared to the Clementine. I always think of Page mandarins as having the same flavor as a Tangerine Life Saver.

13 **Calamondin**—Similar to a kumquat, the pulp is sour but the skin is sweet. Eat them whole (really!); also wonderful sliced and tossed into fizzy water.

14 **Cara cara orange**—Cross between a grapefruit and a navel orange. Beautiful color and great for slicing.

15 **Ruby grapefruit**—Sweeter and less acidic than white grapefruits. Avoid pith and membranes.

16 **Oro Blanco grapefruit**—A juicy, intense, fragrant gold grapefruit.

17 **Star Ruby grapefruit**—The best ruby grapefruit there is! From Texas, which has a thriving grapefruit industry.

18 **Pomelo grapefruit**—This giant, fluffy-peeled fruit is sort of like a very mellow grapefruit. Typically eaten by pulling apart sections and peeling off the thick membranes.

DARK LEAFY GREENS

I learned to cook chard at my first restaurant job, where Jimmy taught me to carefully wash the giant leaves before stripping off and discarding the stem. We'd chop the leaves or blanch them, or whatever we were going to do with them, and go on our merry way. So once I got to Switzerland I did the same thing, only to be reprimanded by the chef. "We don't eat the leaves," he scolded, "those are pig's food!" Turns out that in Europe, white chard stems are highly prized for rich, gratin-like dishes, and the nutrient-dense leaves are tossed aside to our four-legged friends. Now, years later, I cook and enjoy both parts of the leafy green, and not a bit of it goes to waste.

How to Buy

If you've ever received a CSA or farm-share box, you're probably well acquainted with leafy greens like chard, kale, mustard, and collards. Why? Because CSA boxes are *full* of them in the winter months! These sturdy greens are prolific and hardy, much more so than any other cool-season crop, it's no wonder we see so much of them. Winter is also when kale and chard are at their sweetest.

Once harvested, greens start to lose their perky texture and are susceptible to becoming slimy. If you are getting your greens from a CSA box, they're likely to be very freshly cut. If you're shopping at the market, though, you'll have to be a little more vigilant. Look for these elements:

- **A local grower.** This minimizes the time from harvest to you, which means more tender and flavorful leaves, and even a shorter cooking time.

GREENS FOR BREAKFAST?

Nothing beats greens first thing in the morning. I take a little cooked chard (leftover or otherwise), top it with a poached or fried egg, and accompany it with a hunk of crusty toast. A sprinkle of salt and a drizzle of olive oil . . . there's no better way to start your day!

- **Leaves with near-reflective sheen**—You see this fleeting quality only when the leaves are just harvested. Over the next two or three days, the sheen fades and the leaves start to dull. If you can't find greens with this elusive sheen, don't despair. But definitely buy any that do have it!
- **A few little holes from bug bites**—This tells you that the greens are grown in a pesticide-free environment. A few holes are harmless (but if the leaves are lacy with holes, they're not worth your money).
- **Full saturated color**—If you see yellowing, it means a too-late harvest or extended storage.
- **Moist stem ends** with no discoloration. Look for ones that are relatively slender and not too "stalky" looking. (After harvesting, the cut stem ends will gradually become dry, brown, and split.)

Some growers have started to package mixes of baby chards or braising greens for sale alongside prewashed spinach and arugula. Requiring only a quick sauté or a drizzle of warm vinaigrette, these mixes are a great option for last-minute dinner shopping.

How to Store

Try to use leafy greens as soon as you can after buying them; having said that, keeping them in a plastic bag in the refrigerator will buy you up to five days' storage. (Without the bag, they will wilt and degrade faster.)

How to Use

You most often see recipes for cooked leafy greens, but don't think that's the only option you have. Chards and kales, especially young tender ones, can be eaten raw in salads, like the Lemony Kale Caesar Salad on page 97. The wonderful concentrated flavor of the kale marries perfectly with the robust Caesar dressing—after trying it this way, plain ol' romaine may not seem adequate anymore!

IF USING YOUNG, TENDER LEAVES, just wash them well and snap off the stem end. (The rib in the center of the leaf is tender enough to cook along with the leaf.) For larger, more mature leaves, hold the stem in one hand and "zip" your other hand along it, pulling off the leaf as you go.

YOU CAN EAT THE STEMS OF WHITE AND GREEN CHARD. Just separate them from the leaves and cook them first, until almost tender. Then add the leaves. (If you add them at the same time, the leaves will over-cook before the stems have a chance to tenderize.) The stems of red and gold chard can sometimes be bitter, but they are still edible.

LEAFY GREENS CONTAIN A SURPRISING AMOUNT OF WATER—something to consider as you plan your cooking strategy. If you're sautéing greens, the water they release can dilute the flavor of whatever aromatics you're using. I prefer to blanch the leaves in boiling salted water very briefly (about 30 seconds), which softens them enough to let me squeeze out excess water before adding them to the other ingredients. (If you're doing anything other than sautéing, you can skip the blanching and just throw them right in.)

My favorite thing about leafy greens is that they retain a beautiful texture even when fully cooked. Whereas spinach can become slimy and almost disappear into a soup, kale and chard tenderize enough to meld with other ingredients while still remaining distinct.

HARD SQUASH

In my mind, hard squash is one of the most underutilized vegetables out there. They're easy to keep on hand, packed with vitamins, and most important, they're delicious. Not only that, but they're inexpensive, and you can make one squash stretch over several meals. There's so much to like about squash, yet many people find them intimidating. Whatever the reason, it's worth giving them another shot and incorporating them into your routine.

How to Buy

The great thing about shopping for hard squashes is that it's pretty hard to go wrong, as long as you buy them fresh and in season. They are also sturdy enough to survive travel and fairly long periods of storage, so even if you can't find local squashes, you can still find good-quality ones from elsewhere. All that means that regardless of where you live, you're pretty much set up for success in the squash shopping department.

As squashes ripen on the vine, their colors become more and more saturated, which also corresponds to a sweeter flesh. So choose the most deeply colored squashes for the best possible flavor; if they have started to lose their pigment and turn yellow, it's a sign that they're well past their prime. Look for ones that are firm and have unwrinkled flesh. They should also be heavy for their size (they dry out and get lighter—and less flavorful—as they age).

In supermarkets, the hard squash selection is generally limited to a few basic varieties that are grown for their familiarity among consumers and for their productivity. Farmers' markets and stores with direct relationships with growers are great options for finding unusual heirloom varieties. Two of my favorites are rugosa (a rich butternut variety originally from Italy) and Long Island Cheese, named because of its resemblance to a wheel of cheese, which was the pumpkin of choice for pie in the Northeast until the 1960s.

How to Store

As long as they're kept at cool room temperature, hard squashes will keep for at least a month. (The shelf life varies according to how long they've already been in storage when you buy them.) Once they're cut open, wrap any leftovers in plastic and refrigerate.

LOOK FOR HARD SQUASHES THAT ARE:

- **Deeply colored**
- **Firm, with unwrinkled flesh**
- **Heavy for their size**
- **Heirloom or unusual varieties**

How to Use

HARD SQUASHES ARE MORE OR LESS INTERCHANGE-ABLE. If your recipe calls for butternut squash, you should be able to swap in acorn, kabocha, hubbard, or just about any other variety with little difficulty. This makes it easy to experiment and try new varieties when you see them.

THE EXCEPTIONS: AVOID MAKING SUBSTITUTIONS FOR SPAGHETTI OR DELICATA SQUASHES. When cooked, the flesh of spaghetti squash becomes stringy like spaghetti and just isn't interchangeable with other squashes. And because delicata squashes have that delicate, edible skin it's best to leave it on rather than attempting to peel it; even scooping out the cooked squash (for mashing) can be a troublesome affair. Why fight it? I leave the skin on, remove the seeds, and slice the squash into pretty half-moons before roasting (as in the Delicata Squash Salad with Fingerling Potatoes and Pomegranate Seeds on page 103).

IF YOU'RE NEW TO WINTER SQUASHES, START WITH BUTTERNUT OR DELICATA. Butternuts have a high flesh-to-skin ratio, which means you get a lot of

CATALÁN FARM: Juan Catalán

It all started in 1994 when mother Maria Catalán, an immigrant from the state of Guerrero in Mexico, began farming at what is now the Agriculture and Land-Based Training Association (ALBA) in Salinas, California (see page 141). In fact, Maria was one of the first Latina organic farmers in the state. Maria eventually struck out on her own and now runs her own organic farm in Hollister, California, with the help of her daughter and three sons (including Juan, pictured here). The family grows a huge variety of vegetables, many of which are expressions of the family's heritage, including corn, cabbage, squash, tomatillos, and pipicha (a lemony herb). Maria's trailblazing farm and her family are a great example of the American Dream realized—and a true inspiration to us.

squash for minimal peeling, and the smooth, elongated shape makes the process easier, too. Delicata squash don't need to be peeled at all! They have thin, edible flesh that's covered with beautiful orange and green striations.

Store winter squash in a cool, dark place in your kitchen; they will last for a couple of months that way.

BE SURE TO WASH ALL SQUASHES THOROUGHLY in hot water before prepping them. After all, even the organic ones grow directly on the ground. (And even if you remove the skin, your knife will transfer contaminants from the surface as you slice.)

It can be challenging and dangerous to cut into bigger squashes, especially ones with thick skins. You can make it a little easier on yourself by flashing the whole squash in a hot oven for 10 to 15 minutes, which softens the skin a bit, and also by putting a kitchen towel on top of your cutting board—it creates a grippier surface and helps prevent the squash from slipping out from under your knife.

SQUASHES ARE COMPATIBLE WITH JUST ABOUT ANY FLAVORS OR SPICES you want to combine them with. Unlike milder vegetables, you can add lots of assertive flavors without masking the flavor of the squash itself. Try any of the following:

- Butter
- Chile
- Lime
- Ginger
- Sage, thyme, or savory
- Curries
- Sweet spices like cinnamon and nutmeg
- Soy sauce
- Coconut milk

MUSHROOMS

The first time I visited Seattle's Pike Place Market, I was overwhelmed by the number of stalls that were literally overflowing with wild-foraged mushrooms: chanterelles, trumpets, goldfoots, bluefoots, and many more varieties. They were abundant, inexpensive, and wonderful. I'm not sure why we don't have the same mania for mushrooms here in the Bay Area (it could be a supply problem due to our highly seasonal rain), but I would be overjoyed if we saw the same abundance a little closer to home.

How to Buy

Most mushrooms you find in the supermarket are **CULTIVATED** indoors in a sterile growing medium. You're probably familiar with many of these varieties: white button, brown button (cremini), portobello (actually mature creminis), shiitake, oyster, and enoki. These are the most common ones because they're easy to cultivate; others are less so and must be **WILD-HARVESTED**. To me there's nothing more exciting than a bag of these beauties: think porcinis, morels, and chanterelles. Aside from their incredible flavors and

> ### FORAGING
>
> Foraging for wild mushrooms is an important culinary tradition that harkens back to our hunter-gatherer roots. Sadly, though, this knowledge seems to have been lost in the United States, so **wild mushroom foraging is best left to the experts.** (If you're interested in gaining that knowledge, look for expert-led workshops and field trips.) I'm saying this not to scare you off, but rather to encourage you to buy from reliable sources. Unfortunately, there's no certification program for mushroom foragers—it's all about expertise and experience. But you can be fairly certain that wild mushrooms sold in a store are coming from a reputable, safe source. *The Wild Table* by Connie Green and Sarah Scott is a great resource.

textures, their elusive nature and their refusal to be tamed make them all the more appealing.

AVOID MUSHROOMS IN SHRINK-WRAPPED CONTAINERS: they trap moisture and encourage condensation, which shortens the mushrooms' shelf life significantly. I always prefer to buy mushrooms from open bins, which give them the air circulation they need. If you have no other choice but to buy packaged mushrooms, get the whole ones and slice them yourself: the extra surface area on presliced mushrooms can absorb other flavors and aromas.

WHATEVER THE VARIETY, MUSHROOMS SHOULD BE FIRM AND DRY when you buy them. A slimy surface or funky smell indicates poor storage or old age, and cooking won't cure this.

BIGGER MUSHROOMS ARE NOT NECESSARILY BETTER. I prefer smaller mushrooms; they're denser and have less moisture than the larger ones. There are

> ### LOOK FOR MUSHROOMS THAT ARE:
> • Displayed in loose bins (not packaged)
> • Whole, not sliced
> • Firm and dry

some exceptions, of course: it's hard to resist the rich, meaty flavor of a portobello.

How to Store

Paper bags are the ideal storage container for mushrooms: they're permeable enough to let just the right amount of moisture in and out of the bag as they sit in the refrigerator.

How to Use

BECAUSE OF THEIR SENSITIVITY TO MOISTURE, DON'T WASH MUSHROOMS UNLESS IT'S REALLY NECESSARY, and definitely wait until you are ready to use them. If there's just a little dirt on the mushrooms, wipe with a paper towel or rinse quickly under water. If particularly dirty, immerse in a bowl of water and swirl gently. Leave for a few minutes to let the dirt settle, then lift the mushrooms out and spread them

between two layers of towels to dry. If you're sautéing them, be sure to dry them really well, or they won't brown. Note: Morels tend to trap dirt on the inside and must always be soaked. Split them lengthwise first to expose the inner grit.

SOME VARIETIES NEED MORE TRIMMING THAN OTHERS. Shiitakes and portobellos have unpleasantly tough stems that should be removed and discarded, because they are not too edible. Others can be trimmed to your liking; save any trimmings and stems and throw into your next batch of veggie broth.

Mushrooms have long served vegetarians as a meat alternative (especially the ubiquitous portobello burger), but they are also complementary to meat, fish, and poultry. Sautéing mushrooms really highlights their special flavor and texture. Stir the mushrooms in a hot pan with butter until the liquid is released and evaporated. Add garlic, shallots, and a little more butter. When everything is tender, add a dash of sherry vinegar (or wine), cook until reduced, and finish with a sprinkling of chopped fresh herbs. You can do this with any mushroom, from the humblest of button mushrooms to sophisticated chanterelles.

Oyster mushrooms, a widely cultivated variety, are one of the best mushroom values out there. They're inexpensive, you use the whole thing, and their flavor is superb.

DRIED MUSHROOMS

Many varieties of mushrooms can be dried to extend their shelf life: shiitakes, porcinis, morels, and black trumpet mushrooms are great examples. The texture is not exactly the same as what you'd get with the fresh version, but in most cases it's close enough. After just a 20-minute soak in hot water, dried mushrooms are ready to throw into pastas, sauces, risottos, and more. Hold on to the soaking water and use it, too; it's packed with flavor. Just avoid the sandy grit that sinks to the bottom.

Lemony Kale Caesar Salad

SERVES 4 TO 6

This salad is inspired by the incredible version I had at New York City's Il Buco restaurant. One bite will convince you that compared to romaine, kale is a better match for assertive Caesar dressing. You can omit the egg yolk if you want to play it safe, but don't try this without anchovy; it makes the dish. This version is crouton-less; if you add them, make a bit more dressing.

> 1 medium bunch dino or lacinato kale
>   (about 10 ounces) (see Note)
> 2 medium cloves garlic
> Kosher salt
> 2 anchovy fillets, minced (about 1 teaspoon)
> 1 large egg yolk
> 2 tablespoons freshly squeezed lemon juice,
>   more to taste
> 1/2 teaspoon Dijon mustard
> 1/4 cup extra-virgin olive oil
> 1/3 cup grated Parmigiano-Reggiano cheese,
>   more for garnish
> Freshly ground black pepper

Strip off and discard any thick stalks from the kale. If the leaves are very tender, you can tear them into bite-size pieces. Otherwise, cut them by stacking 6 or 8 of the leaves, rolling into a tight cigar, and slicing crosswise into 1/4-inch strips. Repeat with the remaining kale; pile any particularly wide strips on the cutting board and cut across the pile once or twice. Put in a large bowl and set aside.

Coarsely chop the garlic and sprinkle with a generous pinch of salt. Use the flat side of a chef's knife to smash and press the garlic into a paste (you should have about 3/4 teaspoon). Transfer to a small bowl and add the anchovy, egg yolk, lemon juice, and Dijon. Whisking constantly, slowly drizzle in the oil until completely incorporated. Dip a leaf of kale into the dressing and taste. Add more lemon juice or salt as needed.

Put the kale into a large bowl and drizzle about 1 1/2 tablespoons of the dressing over the kale. With your hands, gently toss until the leaves are evenly coated, adding just enough dressing to coat the leaves lightly. Sprinkle the cheese over and toss again to blend. Taste and add more dressing or salt as needed.

Garnish with an extra sprinkling of cheese and a grind or two of pepper. You can serve the salad right away, but you can also let it sit for a few minutes before serving (in this time, the acid in the dressing will tenderize the leaves a bit).

Note: We've used regular kale, red leaf kale, and others to make this salad, and they're all delicious. Whatever the variety, the younger and smaller the leaves, the more tender they are and the better for eating raw. You can also use tender inner young escarole leaves, radicchio, or a mix of chicories.

Clockwise, from top left: Lemony Kale Caesar Salad, Cocoa-Cumin Beef Roast (page 180), Butternut Squash and Potato Gratin with Fresh Sage (page 104).

Fennel, Blood Orange, and Avocado Salad

SERVES 4

This salad demonstrates how fresh winter can taste. The raw fennel is clean, aromatic, and crisp, the citrus sweet and a touch bitter, and the avocado rich and smooth.

You can substitute other citrus with similar success or even use several types. To really take this salad over the top, I love to top it with fresh plucked Dungeness crab meat (another winter wonder); about 8 ounces is perfect for four servings.

> 4 medium blood oranges
> 1 large or 2 small heads fennel, with fronds
> 1 small shallot, minced
> Juice from $1/2$ medium lemon (preferably Meyer lemon)
> $1^1/_2$ tablespoons champagne vinegar
> $1/4$ teaspoon honey
> Kosher salt and freshly ground black pepper
> 3 tablespoons extra-virgin olive oil
> 2 medium avocados

Slice the tops and bottoms off the oranges to expose the flesh. Using a paring knife, cut off the remaining peel and pith. Slice the oranges crosswise into $1/4$-inch slices and arrange on 4 salad plates, leaving room in the center of each for the fennel salad. Set aside.

Trim off all but about $1/2$ inch of the fennel stalks, reserving the bulb and fronds. Remove the first outer layer of fennel and discard or save for vegetable stock. Rinse the remaining bulb and set aside.

Chop 1 tablespoon fennel fronds and put them in a small bowl along with the shallot, lemon juice, vinegar, honey, a pinch of salt, and a few grinds of pepper. Whisk to blend, then drizzle in the olive oil as you continue to whisk. Taste for salt.

Halve the fennel bulb, cutting lengthwise through the narrow side of the bulb (this will make it easier to shave thinly). Using a sharp knife (or a mandoline or food processor), slice the fennel crosswise as thinly as you can—about $1/16$ inch is ideal. (Too thick and it will dominate the salad; too thin and it wilt and lose its texture.) Transfer to a bowl and drizzle with half the dressing. Toss, taste, and add salt and pepper as needed. Divide the fennel among the 4 plates, mounding in the center of the orange slices.

Halve the avocado lengthwise, remove the pit, and cut $1/4$-inch slices into the flesh. Using a large spoon, scoop the slices out and nestle them on and around the mounds of fennel. Sprinkle a little salt over the avocado and then drizzle the remaining vinaigrette all over the salad. Finish with a bit of pepper.

Roasted Cauliflower and Brussels Sprouts with Caper Lemon Butter

SERVES 6 TO 8

Plain roasted veggies are fantastic as is, but tossing them with butter, capers, and lemon really takes them over the top.

> 1 medium head cauliflower (1³/₄ pounds), separated into 1-inch florets
>
> 2 tablespoons extra-virgin olive oil
>
> Kosher salt
>
> 1 pound brussels sprouts, halved or quartered into ³/₄-inch pieces
>
> 4 tablespoons unsalted butter
>
> ¹/₄ cup minced shallot
>
> 3 tablespoons capers, rinsed and chopped
>
> 1 tablespoon fresh thyme leaves, chopped
>
> ¹/₂ teaspoon honey
>
> Juice and finely grated zest from 1 large lemon

Position racks in the top and bottom thirds of the oven and heat to 400°F.

Mound the cauliflower on a large rimmed baking sheet. Drizzle with 1 tablespoon of the oil and ¹/₂ teaspoon of salt. Use your hands to mix and coat the vegetables evenly with the oil, and then redistribute in a single layer. Repeat with the brussels sprouts on a separate baking sheet, using the remaining 1 tablespoon oil and another ¹/₂ teaspoon of salt.

Place the pans in the oven and roast the vegetables, stirring and rotating the pans after 10 minutes or so, and continue to cook until tender and golden on the edges, 10 to 15 minutes longer. (Depending on the size and shape of your vegetables, the two may require different cooking times.) Transfer the roasted vegetables to a large bowl.

Put the butter in a small saucepan over medium heat. When the butter is melted, add the shallot and ¹/₂ teaspoon salt. Cook, stirring occasionally, until the shallots are translucent and aromatic, about 2 minutes. Add the capers and thyme and cook for 1 minute longer. Remove from the heat and stir in the honey, lemon zest, and 1 tablespoon of the lemon juice. Drizzle over the vegetables and toss to combine. Taste and season with more salt or lemon juice as needed.

Serve right away or keep at room temperature for up to 1 hour.

MARIQUITA FARMS: Andy Griffin

It's no stretch to say that Andy Griffin is a rebel farmer. Early in his career, he worked for a large organic farm, where he saw the beginnings of the industry's shift toward ever bigger and more corporate practices. So he broke away to do his own thing, choosing to farm "beyond organic"—using organic philosophies, but outside of the structure of organic certification. (To him, the standards aren't stringent enough and weaken the integrity of the product itself.) Andy is also a champion of unique and heirloom varietals, for which he creates awareness and demand; the broccoli di cicco I mentioned earlier, as well as padrón peppers, are just two items that he's responsible for popularizing. Andy is a great writer and storyteller, and his newsletter and blog are constant sources of inspiration for our staff. Read more about Andy by subscribing to his newsletter at ladybugletter.com.

Chicken Soup with Fennel, Chickpeas, and Chard

MAKES 12 CUPS

This simple but luscious soup has all the basic elements of minestrone: broth, beans, and veggies. If you can find it, erbette chard is my favorite variety to use. It's sweet and nutty, with an incredible silky texture when cooked. Serve with grilled or toasted crusty bread, rubbed with the cut side of a halved garlic clove, and drizzle with olive oil.

- 1 large bunch green chard (about 13 ounces)
- 2 tablespoons unsalted butter
- 1 small yellow onion, diced
- Kosher salt and freshly ground black pepper
- 1 medium head fennel, diced
- 4 large cloves garlic, minced
- 1 bay leaf
- 8 cups chicken stock (or low-sodium broth)
- 1¹/₂ cups diced cooked chicken (preferably thighs)
- 1¹/₂ cups cooked chickpeas (one 15-ounce can, rinsed and drained)
- 1 tablespoon freshly squeezed lemon juice, more as needed
- 2 teaspoons chopped fresh marjoram

Strip the stems from the chard and chop the leaves coarsely. Chop the stems and set aside separately from the leaves.

Heat the butter in a Dutch oven or soup pot over medium heat. When hot, add the onion, a pinch of salt, and a few grinds of pepper. Cook, stirring, until the onions start to brown, about 4 minutes. Add the chard stems (if using), fennel, garlic, and bay leaf and continue to sauté until the fennel starts to soften, about 5 minutes longer.

Stir in the reserved chard leaves and the stock, chicken, chickpeas, and 1 teaspoon salt and increase the heat to medium-high. Bring just to a boil, then cover the pot partially and reduce to a simmer. Cook gently for 30 minutes.

Remove the pot from the heat and stir in the lemon juice and marjoram. Taste the soup and add more salt, pepper, or lemon juice as desired.

Pan-Seared Broccolini

SERVES 4

Letting the broccolini brown slightly in the pan gives it a boost of flavor. To accomplish this, the broccolini must be absolutely dry when it goes into the pan; otherwise, it'll steam and won't take on any color. A large cast-iron skillet is the ideal cooking vessel for this dish.

- Kosher salt
- 2 bunches broccolini or broccoli di cicco or broccoli spears (about 1 pound)
- 2 tablespoons extra-virgin olive oil
- 4 medium cloves garlic, minced
- 1 teaspoon chile flakes

Bring a large pot of well-salted water to a boil. Add the broccolini and cook until the florets are tender and the stalks start to soften a bit, 2 minutes or so. Drain in a colander and run cool water over them to stop the cooking. Drain, pat very dry with towels, and set aside.

Heat the oil in a large skillet over medium-high heat. When hot, add half the broccolini and arrange it in a single layer. Let the broccolini cook undisturbed until it starts to brown on the bottom, 2 to 3 minutes.

Transfer the broccolini to a plate, add the remaining broccolini to the pan, and sear in the same way. When the second batch is seared, combine all the broccolini in the pan along with the garlic, chile flakes, and a couple pinches of salt. Continue to cook, tossing constantly, until the garlic is aromatic, about 1 minute longer.

Season to taste with more salt and serve warm or at room temperature.

MARTIN'S FARM:
Martin Bournhonesque

At the potato planting party I describe on page 113, it was no coincidence that all of Martin's volunteers were chefs. After all, he was working at San Francisco's Hayes Street Grill when, in the late 1980s, he began farming as a hobby. He eventually quit his kitchen job in order to devote his full attention to what he describes as a "gigantic kitchen garden"—basically, a place where he customizes crops for the specific (and evolving) needs of restaurant chefs. Now operating on nine acres in Salinas, California, Martin and his small team produce a huge variety of salad and cooking greens, beans, beets, and, of course, potatoes for our Market as well as some of San Francisco's best restaurants. Martin travels extensively, always looking for inspiration and new things to grow. In doing so, he finds crops that he's excited about, which helps generate excitement among his customers.

Delicata Squash Salad with Fingerling Potatoes and Pomegranate Seeds

**SERVES 6 TO 8 AS A SIDE DISH,
OR 4 TO 6 AS AN ENTRÉE SALAD**

This autumnal salad is a kaleidoscope of shapes and colors, thanks to the scalloped half-moons of squash, wispy leaves of baby arugula, and shiny red jewels of pomegranate seeds. It's as visually pleasing as it is delicious.

Boasting both tender greens and roasted potatoes, this dish is sort of a half salad, half starchy side dish. As such, you can serve it alone as an entrée or in smaller portions as an accompaniment. You can roast the potatoes and squash and make the dressing well ahead of time, then assemble at the last minute.

1¹/₂ pounds fingerling potatoes (about 16 medium)

¹/₂ cup plus 3 tablespoons extra-virgin olive oil

Kosher salt and freshly ground black pepper

2 medium delicata squash (about 2¹/₂ pounds)

2 tablespoons minced shallot

2 tablespoons freshly squeezed lemon juice, more as needed

2 tablespoons champagne vinegar, more as needed

1 teaspoon Dijon mustard

1 teaspoon honey

10 cups packed baby arugula (about 8 ounces)

Seeds from 1 medium pomegranate (about 1 cup)

1 cup shaved or grated Parmigiano-Reggiano cheese

Position a rack in the center of the oven and heat to 425°F.

Cut the potatoes lengthwise into ¹/₄-inch-thick slabs. Mound on a large rimmed baking sheet, drizzle with 1 tablespoon of the oil and ¹/₄ teaspoon salt, and toss to coat the potatoes evenly. Arrange in a snug single layer and roast until just tender and starting to brown, 20 to 25 minutes.

While the potatoes are roasting, prepare the squash. Trim the squash, halve them lengthwise, and scoop out and discard the seeds and strings. Slice into thin half-moons, about ¹/₈ inch thick. Transfer to a large bowl, drizzle with 2 tablespoons of the olive oil, and sprinkle on ¹/₄ teaspoon salt. With your hands, gently toss to coat evenly.

When the potatoes are out of the oven, line 2 large rimmed baking sheets with parchment or a nonstick liner and arrange the squash slices across them. Roast, rotating the pans after 10 minutes, until the slices are just tender and starting to brown, 20 to 25 minutes. Be sure not to overcook, or the squash will dry out. Note: Some slices will be darker than others even when cooked perfectly; this provides textural interest and depth of flavor. When done, set aside and let cool to room temperature.

In a small bowl, combine the shallot, lemon juice, vinegar, mustard, honey, and ¹/₈ teaspoon salt. Whisk to blend, and slowly drizzle in the remaining ¹/₂ cup olive oil, continuing to whisk vigorously.

Just before serving, put the potatoes and squash in a large bowl and drizzle with the vinaigrette. Toss well with your hands, taste, and adjust with more vinegar, lemon juice, or salt as needed.

Add the arugula, half the pomegranate seeds, and half of the Parmigiano and gently mix in with your hands. To serve, sprinkle the salad with the remaining cheese and pomegranate seeds and top with a few grinds of black pepper.

Butternut Squash and Potato Gratin with Fresh Sage

SERVES 4 TO 6

Every time I make this gratin I get the same response: "This is *so* good!" Honestly, though, when you combine potatoes and squash with cream, sage, and cheese, how could it *not* be amazing? This gratin is especially well suited for dinner parties or any other time you need a hearty, make-ahead side dish. It scales up easily (just increase the ingredients and baking dishes accordingly), and it reheats wonderfully.

- 2 tablespoons unsalted butter, plus more for the pan
- 1 large shallot, minced
- 1¼ cups heavy cream
- 5 large sprigs fresh thyme, leaves chopped
- 12 large sage leaves
- Kosher salt and freshly ground black pepper
- 3 medium russet or Yukon gold potatoes (about 1½ pounds), peeled and sliced into ⅛-inch thick rounds
- ¼ small butternut squash (preferably from the stem end), peeled and sliced ⅛ inch thick
- 1 cup grated Parmigiano-Reggiano cheese

Position a rack in the center of the oven and heat to 350°F.

Melt the butter in a small saucepan over medium heat. Add the shallot and cook, stirring, until it softens and becomes translucent, about 30 seconds. Add the cream, thyme, 5 of the sage leaves, 2 teaspoons salt, and a few grinds of pepper and bring to a boil. Remove from the heat and let the sage infuse in the cream for 10 minutes. Then remove and discard the sage leaves.

Generously butter an 8 by 8-inch baking dish and arrange one-third of the potatoes and one-third of the squash across the bottom, overlapping them slightly to make a relatively even layer. Pour one-third of the cream mixture over the potatoes and sprinkle with one-third of the cheese. Build 2 more layers in the same way; on the last layer, add the remaining potatoes and cream, then arrange the remaining 7 sage leaves decoratively over the top. Finally, sprinkle on the remaining cheese.

Cover the dish with foil and bake for 30 minutes. Then remove the foil and continue baking until the top is golden and a skewer goes into the potatoes with no resistance, about 30 minutes longer.

Let rest for about 10 minutes before serving.

Blood Orange Granita

MAKES 1 QUART

Because of its seductive red color, this granita is the sexiest slushy on earth. It's incredibly easy to make and requires the simplest of equipment. To take it over the top, serve with whipped cream or, for that Creamsicle effect, with a scoop of vanilla ice cream.

If blood oranges are not available, you can also use ruby grapefruit, Valencia oranges, pomelos, or Meyer lemons. Tarter citruses will require additional sugar, so taste a bit of the mixture before you freeze it.

- 6 tablespoons sugar
- ½ cup plus 2 tablespoons water
- 2¼ cups freshly squeezed blood orange juice
- 2 tablespoons freshly squeezed lemon juice
- ⅛ teaspoon kosher salt

In a small saucepan, combine the sugar and water and whisk to blend. Cook over medium-high heat just until the sugar dissolves. Let cool slightly, then combine with the orange juice, lemon juice, and salt in a medium bowl. Whisk all the ingredients together and pour into an 8- or 9-inch baking dish (or similar vessel).

Freeze uncovered until ice crystals start to form, about 1 hour. Stir the mixture with a fork to break up the crystals. Return the dish to the freezer and stir every 30 minutes until the mixture is icy throughout, 2½ to 3 hours total.

At this point, you can transfer the granita to a resealable container and store in the freezer for up to 2 weeks. Break up the mixture with a fork just before serving.

Lemon Curd Tart

SERVES 8

Before we were married, my wife, Anne, used to court me with this tart. She was a pastry chef at San Francisco's now-razed 42 Degrees restaurant, and they sourced cheese from the same distributor as we did at the Market. Whenever the restaurant got their cheese shipment, Anne would give the delivery guy this tart, and he in turn would deliver it to me on his next stop. I guess the way to *my* heart truly is through my stomach!

Whether you're being wooed or not, this is a fabulous, timeless tart featuring an easy-to-mix shortbread crust and a tart, rich filling. Top it with whatever fruit is pretty and in season. If you are lucky enough to have access to Meyer lemons, you can replace up to two-thirds of the regular lemon juice with Meyer lemon juice.

SHORTBREAD CRUST
2 cups (9 ounces) all-purpose flour, more for rolling
1 cup (2 sticks) unsalted butter, cubed, left out to soften but not yet room temperature
1/2 cup confectioners' sugar, sifted
1/2 teaspoon kosher salt

LEMON CURD
3/4 cup sugar
7 large egg yolks
1/2 cup freshly squeezed lemon juice (from about 2 lemons)
6 tablespoons (3 ounces) unsalted butter, cut into 1/2-inch cubes

GARNISH
Fresh fruit of your choice: berries, or sliced peaches or nectarines

To make the crust:

Combine the flour, butter, sugar, and salt in the bowl of a stand mixer fitted with the paddle attachment. Mix on low speed, gradually increasing to medium speed, until the dough is a uniform consistency and comes together in a ball, about 1 1/2 minutes.

Transfer to a large sheet of plastic wrap, form into a 7-inch disk, and wrap in the plastic. If using the dough the same day, leave at room temperature. Otherwise, refrigerate for up to a week; allow it to come to room temperature before proceeding.

To make the lemon curd:

Put an inch or two of water in the bottom of a double boiler or medium saucepan and bring to a simmer over medium-high heat. In the top of the double boiler or a stainless steel bowl, whisk together the sugar and yolks, then whisk in the lemon juice. Put the pan or bowl of eggs over, but not touching, the simmering water. (If you're not using a double boiler, you can first carefully invert a small heatproof bowl on the bottom of the pan—this will help support the upper bowl holding the egg mixture.) Cook, whisking frequently, until the mixture is thick and nearly pudding-like, about 10 minutes.

Meanwhile, position a rack in the center of the oven and heat to 350°F.

When the curd has thickened, remove from the heat and whisk in the butter, a few pieces at a time, until completely blended. Pour through a fine-mesh strainer into a bowl. (You can make the curd ahead of time; lay plastic wrap directly on the surface of the curd and refrigerate for up to 1 week.)

To assemble and bake:

On a lightly floured surface, roll the dough to a scant 1/4-inch thickness. Transfer to a 9 1/2-inch tart pan, gently pressing the dough into the corners. Remove excess dough from the edges.

Bake until the crust is set and light golden brown, 15 to 20 minutes. Remove from the oven and let cool on a rack for 10 minutes, leaving the oven on. Pour the curd into the tart shell; it should come just to the top of the crust. Return the tart to the oven and bake for 10 minutes longer.

Let cool completely on a rack, then arrange the berries or other fruit on top of the curd.

SPRING

Spring—who doesn't love this time of year? The days are getting longer, temperatures rise, and the earth rewards us with fresh veggies we have been dreaming of all winter long. At the Market, farmers we have not heard from in a few months start sending us their availability lists, and the goods start rolling in: crisp young radishes, sweet English peas, tender greens. And then there's artichokes. Ah, artichokes!

ARTICHOKES

Farmers in Italy have the right idea when it comes to artichokes. At the farmers' market there, I was fascinated to see them pare and prep the artichokes for you. At each table stood a little old lady, expertly trimming and peeling the heads, producing beautiful little ready-to-cook artichoke hearts. As each choke was finished, she would toss it into a bucket of acidulated water to await purchase. I've never seen this nice service offered Stateside. It's a market just waiting to be tapped!

How to Buy

Consumers have been led to believe that bigger is better when it comes to artichokes. And there's nothing wrong with that; those giant heads give you a big, meaty heart and plenty of succulent leaves to nibble on. But I personally prefer baby artichokes, which are smaller and haven't yet developed that super-hairy choke. I find that you can cook them in more interesting ways (more on that in a bit), and they're cheaper to boot.

LET HEFT AND FIRMNESS BE YOUR GUIDE. Look for heads whose leaves are tightly packed, rather than fanned out away from the head. Also, squeeze the head at its widest point, right around where the heart is inside; choose ones that feel nice and firm. Ones that have a lot of "give" to them are older and won't taste as good.

ARTICHOKES HAVE TWO HARVEST SEASONS. The first runs from March to May, the second September to November. **THE FALL ONES ARE BETTER,** as they

---

> **LOOK FOR ARTICHOKES THAT:**
> - **Have tightly packed leaves**
> - **Feel firm around the base**
>
> **IDEALLY, LOOK FOR:**
> - **Baby or "frost-kissed" artichokes**

---

have benefited from summer heat prior to the icy blast. **KEEP AN EYE OUT FOR "FROST-KISSED" ARTICHOKES,** so named when the plants are exposed to cold temperatures. The result is a brown and downright ugly exterior, but the interior is richly flavored and incredibly delicious.

How to Store

Despite their robust, tough-looking form, artichokes are actually fairly delicate and prone to wilting. They need to stay moist and cold in order to keep their firm shape, which is why some grocers keep their artichokes nestled in a bed of ice. At home, keep them in a perforated plastic bag (just poke a few holes in it) in the coldest part of the refrigerator.

How to Use

Most people don't know that, thinly sliced on a mandoline, **BABY ARTICHOKE HEARTS ARE DELICIOUS RAW,** and they have a gorgeous shape to boot. Just peel the tough outer layers and then toss them with extra-virgin olive oil, lemon juice, and salt. They're wonderful just like that, but a grinding of black pepper and a grating of Parmigiano really takes it over the top. I think it's one of the best ways to enjoy a baby artichoke.

POACHING IS A USEFUL TECHNIQUE, although I prefer it as a precursor to other cooking methods (ideas follow). Whether you're doing the classic poached artichoke with drawn butter or getting ready for the grill, **MAKE SURE YOUR COOKING LIQUID IS FLAVORFUL AND ACIDIC.** It not only prevents them from browning but also infuses the spongelike artichokes with lots of flavor. So spike your poaching water with lemon juice, maybe some white wine, a bay leaf, a few garlic cloves, some salt, and a few sprigs of thyme. Cook

Unless you're serving artichokes with the leaves on (either halved or whole), you'll need to trim the heads down to the hearts before you cook them. You can leave the stem on baby artichokes, but otherwise snap it off. Then cut the top inch or two off of the head to make it easier to handle. Starting at the base and working all the way around, trim the leaves and tough flesh off until you're left with just the heart and tender inner leaves. Halve this lengthwise and use a spoon to scoop out the hairy choke. Immediately transfer to a bowl of lemon juice–spiked water to prevent discoloration.

them just until a small knife pierces the heart with a little resistance; any further and they become mushy and fall apart.

As with other vegetables, **ROASTING CONCENTRATES THE FLAVOR OF ARTICHOKES,** and the caramelization is a particularly nice overlay to the inherent grassy notes. You can roast whole or trimmed artichokes.

- **Whole:** Blanch the heads in flavorful, acidic water until just tender, halve lengthwise, and scoop out the hairy choke. Then stuff with any kind of sautéed veggie mixture—I like ones that feature chopped eggplant or mushrooms—and roast in a 400°F oven until golden. Prepared this way, they're pretty, self-contained servings that make an elegant vegetarian entrée.
- **Trimmed:** Quarter or halve your trimmed artichokes, toss with olive oil, chopped garlic, and herbs— maybe even some fingerling or new potatoes—and roast in a 400°F oven until tender and golden. These wonderfully textured, nutty little flavor bombs are great additions to pastas and risottos, as a topping for polenta, or as a base for grilled fish or meat.

GRILLING IS ANOTHER NICE APPROACH. It's best to blanch large artichokes first, as cooking them on the grill alone makes them tough. Blanch first, then grill just until they develop good color.

ARTICHOKE HEARTS ARE WONDERFUL ADDED TO BRAISES AND ROASTS. I especially love to throw them in with roasted chicken legs: they suck up all that beautiful chicken fat flavor as they cook.

ASPARAGUS

When my brother Sal was about nineteen, he visited a friend who lived near Hanover, Germany. His arrival coincided with the beginning of the asparagus season, and both were considered special occasions. At dinner that first night, the mother proudly announced, "Today we have . . . asparagus!" She brought out boiled fat white asparagus, melted butter, and fresh black bread. That was the whole dinner! And there was Sal, this big muscular growing boy struggling to fill his hungry stomach. But for that family, such a simple dinner was significant and potent: it meant the end of winter, the rebirth of the fields, and the resurgence of fresh green vegetables. The arrival of asparagus was cause for celebration.

How to Buy

White asparagus are just one of several varieties of this vegetable, all of which are part of the lily family:

WHITE ASPARAGUS are not a specific variety, but rather have been shielded from sunlight to prevent chlorophyll from developing. The result is a sweet, almost nutty vegetable, entirely devoid of the grassiness that chlorophyll usually contributes. The white asparagus cultivated in Europe are supple and tender, but I'm usually disappointed by the ones available here in the States. Most are imported from South America,

---

LOOK FOR ASPARAGUS WITH:

- Firm, tight tips
- Fresh-cut ends
- No "off" odor

where they're grown with volume and efficiency in mind rather than flavor. Even in Europe, much of the white asparagus available is now being imported, and the celebration for this once local crop is waning.

PENCIL ASPARAGUS, named for their slender diameter, are delicate and don't require much cooking. They're so sweet and tender, you can even eat them raw!

LARGE AND JUMBO ASPARAGUS are a little meatier and can handle more extended cooking times. I prefer these to pencil asparagus, because I think the skin-to-interior ratio is better. "Asparagus tips" are also in this category—they're asparagus that have been trimmed to a uniform length of 5 inches or so.

FRESHNESS IS KEY FOR ASPARAGUS, as they become limp and slimy with time. Look for three telltale signs of fresh asparagus:

- **Firm, tight tips, with no signs of sliminess.** Run your finger against the grain of the "petals"—avoid ones that feather out easily.
- **Moist, freshly cut ends.** Even if the asparagus are stored in a moist environment, the flesh will gradually start to recede, making the lengthwise-running fibers stick out a bit. Choose those with a clean, straight cut.
- **A fresh, grassy smell.** If you get a whiff of mildewy odors, it's over the hill.

How to Store

Asparagus will keep for a week if you store them correctly. Wrap the bottom of the bundle in a damp paper towel (secure with a rubber band), leaving the tips exposed. Put the bundle, towel end in first, into a plastic bag and refrigerate.

How to Use

When I worked in Switzerland, I spent an entire month doing nothing but meticulously peeling asparagus, so you'd think I'd have had my fill of that somewhat tedious technique. However, **PEELING IS STILL MY PREFERRED METHOD OF PREPPING ASPARAGUS**; you get a much better yield this way, compared to simply snapping off the ends. You only need to peel the bottom half; the skin of the top half is tender enough to enjoy.

Asparagus are wonderful in pureed soups or shaved, raw, into salads. Otherwise, **HIGH-HEAT COOKING METHODS ARE BEST,** whether it's grilling, frying, or roasting. It minimizes the cooking time and preserves that fresh "green" flavor that's lost in extended cooking.

ASPARAGUS NEED ACID TO BRIGHTEN THEIR FLAVOR, BUT WAIT UNTIL THE LAST MINUTE; acids quickly turn the bright green stalks a sad, drab color. A squeeze of lemon is all you need; add it as a final tableside flourish before serving. Pickling asparagus is a fun, simple, and delicious way of preserving a taste of spring for later in the year.

For ideas on what to pair with asparagus, look no further than the rest of spring's bounty. Eggs, tarragon, and spring onions are the perfect combination and make a wonderful omelet—add a little Gruyère or fresh goat cheese if you like. And it doesn't get any better than the classic spring combo of morels, peas, and asparagus; it's equally good as a risotto or pasta dish.

CARROTS

In cooking school they taught us the classical preparation for carrots Vichy, named after the town in France that's blessed with not just incredibly sweet carrots but also naturally effervescent pure mineral water. Traditionally, you'd take your sweet Vichy carrots and braise them in the mineral water with some butter. But we in San Francisco didn't have Vichy water, and our commercial carrots weren't nearly as sweet as the famed French ones. So our instructors taught us to make do by braising our domestic carrots in 7-Up, which—in theory at least—contributed both the needed sweetness and the fizz. This was a clumsy

---

LOOK FOR CARROTS THAT:

- Have bright, stiff greens (if attached)
- Are firm and show no splitting
- Have a diameter somewhere between a dime and a quarter.

IDEALLY, LOOK FOR:

- Unique varieties in interesting shapes and colors

compensation for subpar ingredients; I'd much rather just seek out sweet carrots and use pure water!

How to Buy

There's a lot more to carrots than your standard orange type; a huge variety of colors and shapes await your exploration—white, red, and purple carrots, long and thin or round and radishlike. You'll be surprised how much more flavor and sweetness they have compared to regular carrots. Rainbow carrots add color and texture, but orange carrots (such as the fat, cylindrical Nantes variety) tend to be sweeter.

The green tops of carrots are the first part to wilt and decay, so some producers leave the tops on as proof of their freshness. If you buy top-on carrots, make sure they're bright green and stiff, rather than wilted or blackened.

Make sure the carrots themselves are firm and not wilty. Avoid those that are split, a sign they have seen too much water. Very large carrots can be woody; go for ones with a diameter somewhere between that of a dime and a quarter.

How to Store

Kept cool and moist, carrots hold up fairly well (otherwise they dry out and become limp). Store in a plastic bag in the refrigerator.

How to Use

AS LONG AS THEY'RE ORGANIC, I GENERALLY DON'T PEEL CARROTS, especially if they're on the smaller side. Just give them a good scrub to remove any dirt. It's less wasteful and you hold on to more of the vitamins.

ROASTING IS MY FAVORITE WAY TO COOK CARROTS. I toss them with melted butter and a bit of balsamic vinegar, season with salt and fresh pepper, and roast until the carrots are tender and caramelized. The rich, concentrated flavor pairs beautifully with grilled meats or roast chicken. Steaming is also nice, as long as you don't overcook them; you want to keep them from falling apart and maintain a little of their texture. I love to treat them as my grandmother did, steaming, then tossing with a dressing of tahini, lemon juice, garlic, and olive oil; the nutty earthiness of the tahini really complements the sweet carrots.

PEELED "BABY" CARROTS

These are not made from baby carrots at all, but rather larger ones that are ground down to those little rounded nubbins. It is a convenient, nutritious snack, but it's a fairly processed food that doesn't represent how sweet and deep a carrot's flavors can be. I prefer to start with whole carrots and cut them into sticks myself—it's so worth the time and will save you money.

You can of course grate carrots for a salad or pickle them. I also love to shave them with a vegetable peeler into thin, elegant ribbons. These need little more than a squeeze of lemon juice and a drizzle of olive oil (try the carrot salad on page 117 as an example).

FENNEL

Some people are turned off by the anisey flavor of fennel. I'm completely enamored with fennel; to me, it's just as addictive as it is versatile.

How to Buy

Look for pale white or light green fennel bulbs that show no bruising. The fronds are usable as well, so seek out heads with at least some of the fronds still attached.

How to Store

When you get them home, wrap fennel in a moist paper towel, put in a plastic bag, and refrigerate. They'll keep for up to a couple of weeks this way.

How to Use

Dirt tends to collect between the layers of the bulb, so they'll need a good washing when you're ready to use them: halve the bulb lengthwise and peel off and discard the outer layer. Then rinse the remaining inner bulb under water, gently separating the layers as much as you can.

Fennel's possibilities are nearly infinite. Raw, you can shave it thinly or leave it chunky and coarse. You can sauté it, roast it, grill it, or poach it, and serve it warm or at room temperature. If the feathery fronds are attached, chop them and use just as you would dill. And although the stalks are too fibrous to eat on their own, they're a wonderful addition to broths.

The easiest way to use fennel is as an aromatic ingredient. You can add it any time a recipe calls for carrots, celery, or onions. Or pair it with citrus and avocado (such as the Fennel, Blood Orange, and Avocado Salad on page 98), fish and seafood, tomatoes, or potatoes. They work particularly well in gratins, chowders, and other creamy dishes, where the fennel infuses its flavor beautifully into the liquid. And as a sturdy yet light vegetable, fennel is a nice complement to starchy, earthy vegetables such as parsnips, carrots, and rutabaga. It's also fabulous on a crudité platter with your favorite dip.

. . . .

Because it's less susceptible to frost, fennel is a crop that bridges winter into spring.

GREEN GARLIC

Regular bulb garlic is a pretty addictive ingredient, but I find green garlic to be even more so. Green garlic comes from the same plant as the regular bulb garlic you buy, but it's harvested young, when the bulb hasn't yet developed and the aboveground shoots are still tender and green. The garlic is planted closely together so the space for the bulb to grow is limited, enabling the shoots to stay slender and tender.

How to Buy

Look for green garlic with bright, firm green leaves. Avoid those that are yellowing or slimy; they're too old. For the mildest flavor, avoid any whose root end has started to take on a bulbous shape. (The round ones are usable, but the flavor is more pungent.)

How to Store

Store in a plastic bag in the refrigerator. When ready to use, halve lengthwise and wash thoroughly between the layers, just as you would a leek.

How to Use

Think of green garlic as a robust scallion or very mild garlic that's taken on a different shape. That's all you need to know in terms of how to use them. Use the entire stalk, from the white root end to the green tips.

Try throwing whole stalks onto the grill and serving alongside grilled meats. Or slice and tuck under the skin of a chicken before you roast it. Use it in pestos and risottos or as a ravioli filling.

To use as part of a dressing for new potatoes, whisk together sliced green garlic, olive oil, and some vinegar, then toss it with the just-drained boiled potatoes. The heat of the potatoes softens the pungency of the green garlic a bit and makes it more aromatic.

LETTUCES

If there's one glaring irony in the produce aisle, it's the unwavering, year-round presence of "spring mix" lettuces. It's a fairly recent development; when I first started working in restaurants, we had to trim, wash, dry, and mix all our lettuces by hand. It was expensive not just because of the lettuces themselves, but also because of the labor we put into them.

How to Buy

Increased demand has made premixed, prewashed lettuces available and affordable for restaurants and consumers alike, although the quality has suffered for the most part. Most commercial producers go heavy on "filler" greens like radicchio and frisee that add bulk and have a longer shelf life, but at the expense of overall quality. Instead of choosing individual greens to achieve a balance of flavors and textures, it's more like a bunch of stuff that's just thrown together.

FOR THE BEST FLAVOR AND VALUE, MAKE YOUR OWN MIX. It's been years since I've bought spring mix, and flavor is just one reason for that. Cost is another—pound for pound, you'll always pay less and get more by buying lettuces individually. But more than anything, I like being able to mix lettuces according to my own taste: sometimes I want to go heavy on the sweet nutty leaves or perhaps emphasize peppery lettuces.

I can customize the flavors and textures in ways that commercial mixes don't.

IF YOU WANT TO BUY PREMIXED LETTUCES, THE FARMERS' MARKET IS YOUR BEST BET. There you can find some wonderful baby lettuce assortments that are blended with flavor in mind above all else. Additionally, the product is usually harvested just a day or two before it's sold, which means amazing, fresh-picked flavor and texture.

AT THE GROCERY STORE, ALWAYS BUY LETTUCE FROM OPEN BINS OR AS BUNDLED HEADS, rather than sealed bags. Sealed lettuces are prone to contamination; a recent study found alarmingly high frequency of fecal contamination in these products. To combat this, these prewashed lettuces are bathed in a chlorine solution to help kill any lingering bacteria. I don't know about you, but I'd rather wash the lettuce myself and leave the chemicals out.

When buying whole-head lettuces, check the base. Look for a freshly trimmed end with no rusty discoloration. (A conscientious retailer will trim the ends periodically to keep any rusting from spreading.) Look for vibrant, perky leaves. If they're limp, wilted, or blackening, it's a sign the lettuces are old and haven't been stored properly.

FEEL FOR HEFT. Whole heads are usually sold on a per-unit price rather than by weight, so pick out the heaviest heads you can find. A heavy head with tightly packed leaves means a lot of salad for your buck.

TASTE LETTUCE BEFORE YOU BUY. It should be flavorful and taste like more than just water and chlorophyll.

ALWAYS BUY ORGANIC LETTUCE. ALWAYS. Lettuce is one of the most pesticide-intensive crops out there. Aside from heavy application of pesticides, the high surface area of lettuce means we end up ingesting more of those pesticides (versus vegetables that have less surface area or can be peeled). I recently visited one of our organic growers in the Salinas Valley, where 80 percent of the country's lettuce is grown, and

---

LOOK FOR LETTUCES THAT ARE:

- Organically grown, ideally from a local grower or farmers' market
- From open bins or bundled heads— no sealed bags
- Pert and lively
- Heavy heads with fresh-cut ends

watched in amazement and disgust as planes drenched the other nearby fields with chemicals. Not only was I concerned for the folks that would eventually eat the crops, but I could not stop thinking about the migrant workers that spent all day in contact with the pesticide-laden land. Fortunately, there was enough of a buffer zone between the conventional and organic fields that there wasn't any cross-contamination. Even still, I could not help but think about what would happen on a windy day.

Lettuces exhibit so many distinct varieties, shapes, and flavors beyond the familiar red leaf and romaine. Some of my favorites include:

- **Red Oak Leaf**—slightly nutty in flavor
- **Lollo Rosso**—with beautiful red ruffles, it tastes almost citrusy
- **Little Gem**—the small, compact heads are perfect single-serving sizes
- **Butter**—its perfectly velvety texture lives up to the name

How to Store

Lettuces need to be kept cold and moist; otherwise, they become limp and start to rot. Grocers regularly mist their lettuces to compensate for moisture lost in the open display cases. However, this is often too much moisture for home storage and can accelerate the path to sliminess. So if the heads feel heavy with water, give them a good shake, wrap in a dry paper towel, and put into a plastic bag. This will minimize the amount of water in direct contact with the leaves.

How to Use

CAREFUL, THOUGHTFUL DRESSING OF GREENS CAN REALLY ELEVATE A SALAD TO THE NEXT LEVEL. I am constantly inspired by Judy Rogers's description of her Caesar salad in her *Zuni Café Cookbook*. Although she goes by a written-out recipe, she also recognizes that each component of the salad—including the lettuce— varies from day to day and season to season. To adjust for these variations, she adjusts and tweaks the recipe each time she makes it. I encourage you to take a similar approach when you dress greens.

TASTE THE LETTUCES ALONE and consider their texture, flavor, and robustness when you build your vinaigrette. **AVOID OVERDRESSING DELICATE LETTUCES**— often a lightly whisked (but not emulsified) oil and lemon vinaigrette is plenty and will keep the greens from wilting prematurely. And with all but the most robust lettuces, **SERVE THE SALAD IMMEDIATELY AFTER YOU'VE TOSSED IT** with the dressing. You'll get the very best flavor and texture by doing so.

More information on making and using salad dressings is on page 71.

PEAS AND FAVA BEANS

Fresh peas in the pod were the ultimate car snack whenever my family went on summer vacation. Like strawberries, for every handful of pea pods you'll find just one or two that are really outstanding.

How to Buy

Whether you're buying English peas, snap peas, or fava beans, get the freshest ones you can find. As soon as the pods are picked, the sugars start to convert into starch, thus changing the character of the flavor and texture. Ideally, you'd buy and use beans within three to four days of their being picked. But they can last up to two weeks and still hold up pretty well; it's just that the flavor and tenderness diminish somewhat over time.

LOOK FOR BRIGHTLY COLORED PODS WITH NO DRY SCARRING ON THEM; avoid pods that are shriveled or have dry-looking ends—telltale signs of age.

WHENEVER YOU BUY PEAS, POP ONE OPEN AND GIVE IT A TASTE. More than anything, look for a sweet flavor and a creamy, delicate texture; it's a good sign if the pea gives a little squirt when you bite into it. Pass on any that taste chalky or pasty.

LOOK FOR PEAS AND FAVA BEANS THAT ARE:

- **As fresh as possible**
- **Bright with no scarring**
- **Sweet and almost juicy when you taste one raw**

How to Store

Keep peas and beans in a plastic bag in the refrigerator. If they were at room temperature when you bought them (for instance, from a farmers' market), give them plenty of circulation at first to prevent undesirable condensation from forming. To do that, make sure the bag is wide open for the first few hours of refrigeration. Then twist it closed.

How to Use

What you do next depends on your specific variety:

ENGLISH PEAS need to be shelled (their pods are too fibrous to eat) and cooked only briefly. Blanch them for a minute or two in well-salted water, or toss them directly into soups or risottos.

Farro and other hearty grains are a beautiful match with peas; the grains' nutty chew counters the bright freshness of the peas.

Peas and morels with some cream and butter make a simple but unforgettable treatment for pasta.

FAVA BEANS change dramatically as they mature. If they're very young, small, and tender, you can eat them pod and all. First remove the strings by snapping off and pulling the stem end. Then sauté, roast, or even fry them tempura-style.

As favas mature, the pod toughens and the membrane surrounding the bean itself thickens and becomes unpleasantly chewy. These must be shelled and blanched for a minute or so, which makes it possible to peel the membrane off. It's somewhat time-consuming, but with their fleeting season it's a once-a-year labor of love that pays off in deliciousness.

Fava beans, mint, and pecorino make a classic combination for pastas and salads, but you could just as easily use any fresh pea.

- -

You can shell peas and beans up to a day or so before you cook them.

- -

SUGAR SNAP AND SNOW PEAS offer the ultimate in terms of ready-to-eat-ness and minimal waste. Just break off the stem (and string, if present) before using. Although you can eat snap and snow peas raw,

DRIED FAVAS

When very mature, fava beans become starchy and beanlike. This is the type favored in many Mediterranean and Middle Eastern cuisines, where they're dried and treated more as a traditional legume. It produces a completely different product—one that, although delicious and nutty, is less exciting to me than the fresh sweetness of the younger version.

blanching them for a minute (or less) will brighten the flavor and get rid of any chalky residue on the surface. In particular, be careful not to overcook snow peas, which take on an unpleasant, dirty-dishwater taste when cooked beyond barely tender.

Chopped, both of these varieties are a reasonable substitute for English peas in recipes where the peas are left whole (it doesn't work well for purees).

- -

To prevent overcooking, transfer peas and beans to a bowl of ice water immediately after blanching. This halts the cooking process and keeps the colors bright.

- -

If you ever see pea shoots on offer, grab them! These lovely, elegant tendrils have all the fresh flavor of green peas but in a different, tangly form. They're great in salads, for sautéing, or adding to pastas or risottos.

POTATOES

My first adult experience growing food was around 1999, when my friend Martin Bournhonesque rallied a crew of restaurant folks for a potato planting party at his farm in San Gregorio, California. Row by row, we dropped the sprouty, smelly, somewhat funky pieces of sprouted potatoes into the freshly tilled ground, covered them with soil, and ended the day with a family-style dinner. When we gathered again six months later for harvesting, I was amazed at the field's transformation—from a barren, desolate landscape to one covered in green leafy vines. Getting my hands in the dirt, digging up those potatoes, and then putting them up for sale in my store was a powerful experience for me. I was so proud of it that I made a little sign for the store's display that proclaimed: *"I helped plant and harvest these potatoes!"* From then on I knew I wanted to get more involved in the soil.

I realize now that Marty was creating community through food. Some of the chefs I met then are still friends today. I now use the same tactic with our own farm, enlisting help from our store's employees and friends. It works beautifully; we get lots done and have a ball while we're at it, and everyone gets a chance to learn firsthand where their food comes from.

How to Buy

Although my first potato growing experience was pretty straightforward, I've since learned that **POTATOES ARE ACTUALLY A CHALLENGING CROP TO PRODUCE.** The vines need plenty of space in which to stretch out and ramble, so it's an acreage hog as far as land goes. And because the tubers grow underground, they're susceptible to mold as well as gophers and other subterranean plights. To combat this, most commercial potatoes are subjected to heavy sprays of pesticides and fungicides.

Organic growers simply resign themselves to losing a certain percentage of their crops, so they end up growing significantly more potatoes than they actually end up being able to sell. On top of all that, consumers have come to take potatoes for granted; they expect a rock-bottom price for this staple food. But given how many chemicals are applied to the conventional version, **ORGANIC POTATOES ARE THE WAY TO GO.**

When you're shopping for potatoes, **LOOK FOR VARIETIES THAT GO BEYOND YOUR STANDARD RED-SKINNED AND RUSSETS.** There are so many unique and interesting varieties out there, and they're slowly but surely starting to show up in the markets. Fingerlings, a favorite of mine, come in gorgeous hues from rose-tinged to deep amethyst. But that's just a start: there are literally thousands of varieties of potatoes in the world, each with their own personality and characteristics, and the only way to ensure continued cultivation of these unique varietals is to buy them.

Seek out **dry-farmed potatoes**, especially at farmers' markets. These potatoes are from fields that have not been irrigated; the longer growing time necessary for nonirrigated crops produces densely flavored, concentrated flesh that's truly incomparable.

NEW POTATOES ARE SPECIAL AND WONDERFUL, but most "new potatoes" at the grocery store are not truly new—they're just small. Actual new potatoes come from the very first potato harvest in late spring or early summer. They're so young and delicate that their skins practically flake off if you handle them too much. These new potatoes are also more tender and less starchy than their mature brethren. They barely need to be cooked, and they offer a once-a-year reason to celebrate an otherwise everpresent vegetable.

A slightly shiny skin—almost glowing—is the telltale sign of a freshly dug potato.

If not harvested as new potatoes, the tubers are left in the ground not only to grow, but also to allow the skins to cure and harden, which makes them better suited for long-term storage. Their flesh also becomes somewhat starchier in this process.

LOOK FOR POTATOES THAT ARE FIRM AND UNIFORM IN COLOR. Avoid those that are shriveled or have started to turn green, which indicates that they've been exposed to light. And although sprouting is a sign of extended storage, it's not so much a concern as long as the rest of the potato looks good. Just be sure to remove the sprouts and eyes before cooking.

LOOK FOR POTATOES THAT ARE:
- Organic
- Firm, with no green areas

IDEALLY, LOOK FOR:
- Unique varieties of potatoes
- "Dry farmed" potatoes

How to Store

Store potatoes in a cool (50° to 60°F), well-ventilated place. Don't refrigerate potatoes, which alters the starches and prevents them from becoming tender when you cook them. And try to keep them away from light, as overexposure causes them to turn green.

How to Use

Because potatoes represent a spectrum of textures, flavors, and shapes, how you cook them largely depends on what kind you have:

- **New potatoes** are the perfect roasting potato. Just toss them with olive oil and salt and roast in a tightly covered pan (it helps the potatoes steam as they roast). Or poach them lightly in a flavorful broth, as you would poach fish or other vegetables.
- **Russets** have a fluffy, starchy interior that makes them best suited for mashed potatoes, french fries, and good ol' baked potatoes. Cut into wedges and tossed with olive oil, they also make perfectly crispy oven fries.
- **Fingerlings** are densely flavored and somewhat waxy in consistency, which means they hold up nicely in salads or folded into other dishes. They're best roasted, whether whole, halved, or sliced. Although they brown nicely, they don't crisp up in the way that other varieties do.
- **Yukon golds** are my favorite mashing potato. Rich and buttery, they require a minimum of butter and cream to make that perfect comfort food.

But don't let these guidelines limit you! Seek out and try new varieties, even ones you've never heard of. If you're not sure how to cook them, just ask; **A GOOD RETAILER OR FARMER WILL KNOW THE BEST COOKING METHOD FOR EACH VARIETY HE OR SHE SELLS.**

RHUBARB

Rhubarb is a funny vegetable; with its bracing, sugar-friendly acidity, it's more like a fruit. In fact, it's quite versatile, and one that can be used in sweet or savory recipes.

How to Buy

Because its leaves are poisonous, rhubarb is always sold sans foliage. Look for stalks that are firm and brightly hued, whatever the color (some stalks are all red, others nearly completely green).

How to Store

Wrap stalks in plastic and refrigerate for up to a week. For longer storage, you can also chop the stalks and freeze them in an airtight container.

How to Use

When ready to use, trim and slice or chop the stalk as you would celery.

If you've never had rhubarb, think of it as the flavor of cranberries in the shape of celery. When cooked, it disintegrates into a loose jammy consistency, which makes it a good addition to compote, chutney, or jam recipes. Or you can cook it down with nothing more than sugar and lemon zest; the sweet-tart puree pairs nicely with ice cream or with cake and whipped cream to make a trifle. Frozen, the puree makes a delicious and palate-cleansing sorbet.

Rhubarb goes well with everything from strawberries and apples to ginger and black pepper.

From left to right: green garlic, baby leeks, red torpedo onions, white spring onions, cippolini onions, scallions, ramps

SPRING ONIONS

Contrary to popular belief, spring onions are not the same as scallions. Despite their visual similarity, scallions are a species unto themselves, whereas spring onions are simply young specimens of "regular" onion varieties. Just like green garlic, spring onions are harvested before the bulb has a chance to fully develop and form the paper skin of a cured onion. The flavor is similar to but milder than the fully mature onion.

How to Buy

Like fully cured onions, spring onions come in different colors, sizes, and shapes, depending on the variety and when they're harvested; my favorites, 1 or $1^1/_2$ inches in diameter, are sweet and more tender. Because they lack the papery outer layer of cured onions, look for ones that are bright in color and firm.

How to Store

Store them in a plastic bag in the refrigerator.

How to Use

Spring onions work amazingly well as a tempura-fried snack. Use your favorite beer batter recipe, or simply toss with a little flour, salt, and pepper.

They also work wonderfully well in pastas. I like to sauté a little bacon or pancetta, add chopped spring onions, and then add some fresh sage and chicken stock. When the pasta is just shy of al dente, I add it to the onion mixture and do the last minute or two of cooking there.

Spring onions are great as a pickle—just cover with vinegar and refrigerate for a few days—or braised in a little chicken stock. However you treat them, pair them with other mild ingredients so you don't overpower the delicate flavor of the onions.

Heirloom Carrot Ribbons with Pine Nuts and Golden Raisins

SERVES 6 TO 8

Heirloom carrots, with their deep varied hues of orange, yellow, and purple, are ideal for this salad, but you can use regular carrots and it will be just as delicious. Just make sure they're organic and smaller in size to ensure the same tender, sweet results.

You can use a vegetable peeler or a mandoline to make the ribbons. The vegetable peeler takes a little longer, but produces beautifully thin, delicate strips. A mandoline, on the other hand, is faster but makes thicker ribbons if you are not careful. If you go this route, let the ribbons sit for a few minutes after tossing with the dressing so they soften somewhat.

- $1/3$ cup golden raisins
- $1^1/2$ tablespoons extra-virgin olive oil
- $1^1/2$ tablespoons Banyuls or sherry vinegar, more as needed
- $1/2$ teaspoon Dijon mustard
- $1/2$ teaspoon honey
- Salt and freshly ground black pepper
- 15 small heirloom carrots (about $1^1/4$ pounds)
- $1/3$ cup toasted pine nuts (see Tip)
- 3 tablespoons chopped parsley

Put the raisins in a small bowl and add about $1/2$ cup very hot or boiling water. Set aside to soften for about 10 minutes.

In a small bowl, whisk together the oil, vinegar, mustard, honey, $1/2$ teaspoon salt, and a few grinds of pepper. Set aside.

With a vegetable peeler or mandoline, peel the carrots into thin ribbons and put in a large bowl along with the pine nuts and parsley. Drain the raisins, pat dry, and add them to the bowl as well.

Drizzle the dressing over the carrots and mix well with your hands. Taste and season with more salt or vinegar as needed. Serve right away.

Tip: To toast pine nuts, heat a small skillet over medium heat. Add the pine nuts and stir frequently until golden and toasted, 3 to 4 minutes. (Be careful—they go from golden to burned in an instant!) Transfer to a plate and let cool before using.

Any-Green Pesto

MAKES ABOUT I CUP

Don't limit yourself to basil in pesto. You can use just about any tender green herb—even baby arugula or spinach, or a combination of herbs. It's a great way to use up whatever lingers in the bottom of your fridge.

This flavorful sauce is perfect for a simple pasta dish. The nuts are optional, but they add a nice viscosity and flavor. Without them, you get a cleaner flavor and more of the true essence of the herbs. On the other hand, a nut-free version is looser and the oils don't incorporate quite as well.

Pesto definitely tastes best as soon as it's made, but it also freezes incredibly well. Freeze in an ice cube tray and then transfer to a zip-top bag. The cubes are the perfect size for a single portion of pasta, veggies, or a sandwich.

2 large cloves garlic, smashed
2 cups packed fresh leafy herbs: basil, cilantro, parsley, arugula, or a mixture
$1/2$ cup extra-virgin olive oil, more as needed
$1/4$ cup nuts: pine nuts, walnuts, almonds, or pistachios, toasted if you like (optional)
I tablespoon freshly squeezed lemon juice, more as needed
Kosher salt and freshly ground black pepper
$1/2$ cup grated Parmigiano-Reggiano cheese (or other salty grating cheese)

Put the garlic in the bowl of a blender or food processor and pulse a few times to chop. Add the herbs, olive oil, nuts, lemon juice, $3/4$ teaspoon salt, and a few grinds of pepper. Pulse and blend until smooth. Add the cheese and blend just until incorporated. Taste and add more lemon juice or salt as needed; you can also thin the pesto by adding more olive oil.

Tip: Keep the pulses on the food processor to a minimum; overprocessing the pesto will heat up the mixture, leading to discoloration and muted flavors. For a true taste of the Old World, try making the pesto by hand in a mortar and pestle, mashing and mixing everything until smooth.

English Pea and Green Garlic Dip

MAKES ABOUT I²/₃ CUPS

This is one of my favorite ways to showcase the fresh and delicate flavors of spring: sweet peas, tender green garlic, and mint. Serve with crostini or fresh spring veggies as a dip (pictured on page 53), or spread it on sandwiches. You can also use fava beans in place of the peas, or use a combination. Truffle pecorino would also work well in this recipe.

$1/3$ cup plus I tablespoon extra-virgin olive oil (see Tip)
I small yellow onion, finely diced
Kosher salt and freshly ground black pepper
I cup chopped green garlic (from 2 stalks)
$3/4$ teaspoon chopped fresh thyme
$11/2$ cups English peas (or frozen peas, thawed—if so, skip the blanching step)
$1/3$ cup grated Pecorino Romano (or other salty, gratable sheep's milk cheese)
2 tablespoons freshly squeezed lemon juice, more as needed
6 large mint leaves, coarsely chopped

Heat 1 tablespoon of the oil in a medium skillet over medium heat. Add the onion, a pinch of salt, and a grind or two of black pepper. Cook, stirring frequently, until the onions are soft but not browned, 3 to 4 minutes. Add the green garlic and thyme and cook until the garlic is wilted and fragrant, another 2 to 3 minutes. Remove from the heat and let cool.

Bring a small pan of well-salted water to a boil. Add the peas and cook until just tender, 2 to 3 minutes. Drain, rinse with cold water, and drain again.

Put the peas in the bowl of a food processor along with the onion mixture, pecorino, lemon juice, mint, and $1/4$ teaspoon salt. Pulse a few times to blend, and with the motor running, pour in the remaining $1/3$ cup oil, blending just until combined. Taste and add more salt or lemon juice as needed.

Tip: Don't compromise on the olive oil; its quality can make or break this recipe, so use the best oil you've got. A peppery Tuscan oil would be my first choice; its "back of the throat" heat is perfectly balanced by the sweetness of the peas.

EAT GOOD FOOD

Seared Wild Salmon with Late Spring Succotash

SERVES 4

This dish is one of the first things I make once the Pacific salmon season has opened. It is the first sign that summer is near. Later in the summer, I make a similar dish with corn, zucchini, and tomatoes with fresh basil. Any combo of fresh, perfectly sweet, just-picked veggies will be a great complement to the fish.

It's especially important to buy wild salmon—even self-proclaimed "sustainable" salmon farms are dangerous because of the parasitic lice that thrive on farmed salmon; when the infested fish escape (a frequent occurrence), the lice threaten the wild salmon population. If wild salmon isn't in season, use any sustainable fillet or steak that is of similar thickness.

If available, use 1/4 cup chopped green garlic instead of the garlic cloves. And if you can find them, rainbow carrots are beautiful here.

3 tablespoons unsalted butter
1 large spring onion, chopped (about 1 cup)
Kosher salt and freshly ground black pepper
2 large cloves garlic, minced
9 medium stalks asparagus, sliced on the diagonal into 3/4-inch pieces (about 1 1/2 cups)
3 small carrots, cut into 1/4-inch-thick half-moons (about 3/4 cup)
1 cup shelled English peas (if using frozen, no need to thaw first)
1/2 cup vegetable broth (homemade or low-sodium store-bought)
1 tablespoon extra-virgin olive oil
4 (6-ounce) scaled skin-on salmon fillets, about 1 to 1 1/2 inch thick (see Note)
1 tablespoon chopped tarragon
1 teaspoon freshly squeezed lemon juice
Lemon wedges, for serving

In a medium saucepan, melt 1 tablespoon of the butter over medium heat. Add the spring onion and a pinch of salt and cook until softened, about 2 minutes. Add the garlic and cook until fragrant but not browned, about 1 minute. Add the asparagus, carrots, peas, broth, 3/4 teaspoon salt, and a few grinds of pepper. Bring to a gentle simmer, cover the pan partially, and cook until the vegetables are just tender, about 5 minutes. Remove from the heat.

Meanwhile, heat the olive oil and 1 tablespoon of the butter in a large nonstick or cast-iron skillet over medium-high heat. Season the salmon all over with 1 teaspoon salt and add the salmon, skin side down, to the pan. Let cook undisturbed for at least 2 minutes, then carefully peek at the underside to check the browning. When the skin is crispy and golden brown, flip the fillets over and lower the heat to medium. Cook until the salmon is just barely firm to the touch, 2 to 4 minutes longer.

Rewarm the succotash, if necessary, and stir in the tarragon, lemon juice, and remaining 1 tablespoon butter. Taste and season with additional salt if necessary.

Spoon succotash onto each of 4 individual plates, reserving some of the liquid in the pan. Place a salmon fillet, skin side up so it stays crisp, on top of the veggies and drizzle with a little of the reserved liquid. Serve with a lemon wedge on the side.

Note: The crispy fried salmon skin is one of the best parts of this dish. It's full of omega-3 fatty acids, helps keep the fillet moist, and provides textural contrast. The dish will work with skinless fillets, but it won't be quite as good.

Strawberry Rhubarb Pie with Ginger Crumb Topping

MAKES ONE 9-INCH PIE

The combination of strawberry and rhubarb is a classic for good reason: the juicy-sweet strawberries are perfectly balanced by the tart rhubarb. Our version features a crumb crust on top, which works well with a very juicy fruit filling such as this one; a traditional pie crust topping would get soggy. The crumb also provides crunchy textural contrast to the soft fruit inside.

CRUST

1 cup (4 1/2 ounces) all-purpose flour, more for rolling

7 tablespoons (3 1/2 ounces) cold unsalted butter, cut into 1/2-inch cubes

1/2 teaspoon sugar

1/4 teaspoon kosher salt

2 tablespoons ice-cold water, more as needed

1 1/2 teaspoons apple cider vinegar

FILLING

2 1/2 cups (about 3 large stalks) rhubarb, sliced 1/4 inch thick on the diagonal

2 1/2 cups hulled and halved strawberries (quarter any very large ones)

2/3 cup packed light or dark brown sugar

1/3 cup all-purpose flour

1 teaspoon cinnamon

CRUMB TOPPING

2/3 cup (3 ounces) all-purpose flour

5 tablespoons (2 1/2 ounces) cold unsalted butter, cut into 1/2-inch pieces

1/2 cup granulated sugar

3 tablespoons packed dark or light brown sugar

3/4 teaspoon ground ginger

1/8 teaspoon kosher salt

To make the crust:

Put the flour, butter, sugar, and salt in the bowl of a stand mixer and put in the freezer for 20 minutes.

Remove the bowl from the freezer and put it on the mixer fitted with the paddle attachment. Mix on low speed until the mixture resembles a coarse meal, about 2 minutes. Combine the ice water and vinegar in a small measuring cup. With the mixer running, slowly add it to the flour mixture. Add just enough for the mixture to come together into shaggy clumps; if you use all the liquid and it is still not holding together, add cold water 1 teaspoon at a time until it does. Be careful not to overmix the dough, or it will become tough.

Turn the dough out onto a large piece of plastic wrap, shape into a 5-inch disk, and wrap in the plastic. Chill for at least 30 minutes or up to a few days.

On a lightly floured surface, roll the dough into a 12 1/2-inch circle about 1/8 inch thick.

Transfer to a 9-inch pie dish by either folding the dough into quarters and unfolding it in the dish or rolling the dough around a rolling pin and unrolling it into the dish. Tuck the excess dough under the edges to create a double thickness and a smooth edge. Then pinch the dough every 2 inches to form a decorative border. Refrigerate while you prepare the filling and crumb topping (at least 20 minutes).

To make the filling:

Position a rack in the center of the oven and heat to 350°F.

In a medium bowl, combine the filling ingredients and toss gently to combine.

To make the crumb topping:

In another medium bowl, combine the crumb topping ingredients. Using a pastry blender or two table knives, cut the mixture until the biggest pieces of butter are about the size of small peas. The mixture will still be very dry and floury looking.

To assemble and bake:

Spoon the rhubarb mixture into the pie crust, then top with the crumb mixture. Place the pie on a large rimmed baking sheet and bake until the crust is dark golden brown, the filling is bubbling, and some juices are spilling over the edge, about 1 hour 15 minutes.

Let cool completely on a rack.

Tip: If the dough has been in the fridge overnight or longer, let it come to room temperature for 30 minutes prior to rolling. (It needs to have a bit of give.) If it has been refrigerated for only a couple of hours, you can roll it out immediately.

If you choose to buy baked goods instead of making your own, be sure the ingredients list is short and free of preservatives and artificial flavors or colors

Strawberry Rhubarb Pie w/Crumb Topping

INGREDIENTS:STRAWBERRIES*,RHUBARB*,FLOUR*,BUTTER,BROWN SUGAR,CINNAMON*,GINGER*,SUGAR*,WATER,CIDER VINEGAR*,SALT(*ORGANIC)

$16.99

BIRITECREAMERY.COM

Potato, Parsnip, and Celery Root Soup

MAKES ABOUT 8 CUPS

This is a great basic recipe that allows for interchangeable veggies. You can use any combination of root veggies, including rutabagas, turnips, or different potatoes. The cream adds a nice richness and velvety texture, but you can get a similar effect without the cream if you use a rich, creamy potato like a yellow finn or German butterball. And when it's available, spring green garlic is a great substitute for the regular garlic for an added burst of flavor.

1 tablespoon unsalted butter

1 tablespoon extra-virgin olive oil

2 large leeks, white and light green parts only, sliced

Kosher salt

2 large Yukon gold or other waxy potatoes (about 1 pound), peeled and diced

2 medium parsnips (about 8 ounces), peeled and diced

1 medium celery root (about 10 ounces), peeled and diced

2 large cloves garlic, chopped

1 teaspoon ground mustard

4 large sprigs thyme

1 bay leaf

$1/4$ cup dry white wine or dry vermouth

4 cups homemade vegetable broth (or low-sodium store-bought broth)

1 cup water

$1/4$ cup heavy cream (optional)

1 tablespoon freshly squeezed lemon juice, more as needed

In a soup pot or large Dutch oven, heat the butter and oil over medium-low heat. Add the leeks and $1/2$ teaspoon salt and cook, stirring occasionally, until soft and translucent, 6 to 8 minutes. Add the potatoes, parsnips, celery root, and garlic, cover the pot, and stir occasionally until the veggies are heated through and softening a bit on the edges, about 10 minutes. Add the mustard, thyme, and bay leaf and continue to cook for 2 more minutes, or until aromatic. Add the wine and cook until the liquid has completely evaporated, about 1 minute.

Add the broth and water, cover the pot partially, and increase the heat to medium-high. Bring just to a boil, then lower the heat to maintain a gentle simmer. Continue to cook, partially covered, until the vegetables are completely soft and have started to break down a bit, 45 minutes to 1 hour.

To finish the soup, remove and discard the thyme stems and bay leaf and, working in batches, carefully puree the soup in a blender (or use an immersion blender). If you prefer a thinner soup, add a little more water to adjust the thickness.

Stir in the cream and the lemon juice and taste. Adjust with more lemon juice or salt as needed and reheat as necessary.

Tip: This soup is wonderful garnished with fresh croutons sautéed in butter and some chopped chives.

SUMMER

Nothing gets our guests more fired up than when cherry season starts. It's the first sign that summer's bounty is near and the plethora of sweet stone fruits is about to hit. It also means that tomatoes, eggplants, squash, and tender beans soon will overflow our shelves.

ARUGULA

Everybody who has ever worked on the bottom rung of a restaurant kitchen has a tale of drudgery, whether it's peeling potatoes or scaling fish. The most memorable for me was at Kimball's in San Francisco in 1987, where I was tasked with washing arugula (which we called "rocket") for the arugula salad we served nightly at dinner. The arugula that we got at the restaurant was a far cry from the triple-washed and bagged baby arugula that we now are accustomed to; it was mature bunch arugula and full of sand and silt, which made prepping it a laborious process. I didn't mind it that much, but it was definitely slow work; now I love washing greens, and I find it almost meditative.

How to Buy

Regardless of how you intend to prepare or cook arugula, I think that smaller, younger leaves are always better than more mature ones. Baby leaves have a better balance of sweet and spicy bite; as they mature, that bite becomes too strong and can overpower many dishes. **BABY ARUGULA IS SIMPLY MORE PALATABLE AND MORE VERSATILE THAN MATURE ARUGULA.**

YOUR NOSE KNOWS. Whenever we receive a delivery of arugula at the Market, we open a case, "fluff" the contents a bit, and take a big whiff. If it smells mildewy, musty, or anything other than fresh and grassy, we send it right back to the grower. That funky smell means the arugula has been sitting around for too long and has begun to break down. The odor becomes apparent before any visible changes take place, so if in doubt, rely on your nose rather than your eyes. For this reason, **OPEN CONTAINERS (LIKE BASKETS OR BINS) AND RESEALABLE CONTAINERS (LIKE ZIP-TOP BAGS) ARE PREFERABLE FOR ARUGULA,** because they allow you to get up close and personal with the leaves before you buy.

IF THE ARUGULA SMELLS GOOD, TASTE A LEAF OR TWO. It should be tender and moist, with both heat and sweetness. If it tastes overpoweringly bitter, pass it up (but if you have no other choice, consider substituting in some baby spinach to mellow out the overall effect).

Let's say, though, that sealed plastic bags of arugula are all that's available to you. **THE LEAVES SHOULD BE GREEN—NO YELLOW ONES—AND SHOULD LOOK PERT AND BOUNCY.** Watch out for evidence of moisture inside the bag; it might just be condensation from temperature fluctuation, but it might also be "slime" from decaying leaves. Pass on any bags that look suspect.

AT THE VERY LEAST, LOOK FOR ARUGULA THAT IS:

- **Young (or "baby"), rather than mature (2 to 4-inch leaves are ideal)**
- **Fresh smelling, rather than funky or musty**
- **Bright green and lively looking**

IDEALLY, LOOK FOR:

- **Open bins or resealable containers**

How to Store

Store arugula in a closed (sealed or tied) plastic bag in the refrigerator. Keep an eye on it, and use it before it starts to wilt or become slimy.

How to Use

You don't need me to tell you that arugula is great for salads. What you might not know, though, are a few tricks I learned from some of my grower friends. For one thing, arugula is already very flavorful, so it only needs to be dressed lightly. Also, the tiniest, most delicate arugula leaves are easily overwhelmed with dressing; a teaspoon too much and they all but collapse under the extra weight. **SO ADD THE DRESSING CAUTIOUSLY AND SLOWLY, AND HANDLE THE LEAVES AS GENTLY AS POSSIBLE.**

More mature arugula is more robust, not just in structure but also in flavor. That means it can handle a little more dressing, but may also demand a different kind: **LEAVES WITH A STRONG PEPPERY BITE ARE BALANCED AND TEMPERED WITH ACID**, so go a little heavier on the vinegar when you make your dressing. Slight sweetness, whether it's in tomatoes or figs or pears, is also a nice counterpoint to assertive arugula. Good Parmigiano also mellows the bitterness.

In hot dishes, arugula is easy to work with. I think arugula loses something when it's cooked to obliteration, so I just **THROW IT IN AT THE VERY END OF COOKING** risotto or pasta dishes or soups; it softens in a matter of seconds and still keeps its fresh flavor that way.

Leftover arugula can easily be made into a simple pestolike sauce. Puree fresh arugula with garlic, lemon juice, olive oil, and a little salt in the blender. (Try it in the Any-Green Pesto on page 118.) It's a perfect verdant drizzle over soup and grilled fish or chicken. The sauce freezes beautifully, either in a single container or portioned into ice cubes.

(STRING) BEANS

Our first Thanksgiving at the Market was a learning experience, to say the least. We had been open for only five months, so we had no idea how many turkeys we would sell or which ingredients people would want us to have on hand. We did a pretty good job anticipating those needs, with one glaring exception. As a seasonally driven market, we didn't have fresh green beans in November; after all, their season had been over for more than a month. Well, our customers were used to having green beans at Thanksgiving, and they really freaked out when they found out that we didn't have any! At that moment I realized that for some guests, tradition trumps seasonality. (And yes, we have had green beans every Thanksgiving since!)

Before we get too far into beans, let's talk about bean categories. There are **STRING BEANS**, which we cook and eat whole; these are the focus of this section. The group includes varieties such as green beans, haricots verts (the delicate French ones), wax beans, and Romano beans. Then there are **SHELLING BEANS**, whose beans we cook and eat outside of the pod. That includes cranberry beans, garbanzos, cannellini beans, and my personal favorite, the large creamy butter beans. (For information on shelling beans, see the sidebar at right.)

How to Buy

String beans should be firm and plump but not bulging with the beans themselves (that's a sign the beans are overdeveloped). The beans should also be rich in color and have no spots of discoloration or "rust." **THE STEMS AND TAILS SHOULD BE STIFF AND BRIGHT**; steer clear of beans whose tails are wilted or starting to break down or have turned black.

THE POD SHOULD BREAK IN HALF READILY AND FAIRLY CLEANLY; if it bends or buckles back on itself, either it is so mature that it has developed air pockets, or it has been in storage for too long and has begun to dry out. The snapped-off end should be wet and glistening.

TASTE A STRING BEAN; IT SHOULD BE SWEET AND TENDER AND ALMOST MELT IN YOUR MOUTH A BIT. Pass on any that are chewy, fibrous, or woody; no amount of cooking will completely save them. Be especially careful to taste yellow wax beans, which are particularly prone to being woody; they're also more expensive than green beans, so it's worth the money to check.

STRING BEANS ARE ANOTHER CROP THAT IS OFTEN HEAVILY SPRAYED WITH PESTICIDES AND HERBICIDES (I always get a headache after eating a conventionally grown green bean). Buy organic ones whenever possible.

LOOK FOR STRING BEANS THAT ARE:

- Firm, unblemished, and plump (but not bulging)
- "Snappy"—that is, they break in half cleanly and look moist
- Sweet and tender when sampled raw
- Organic

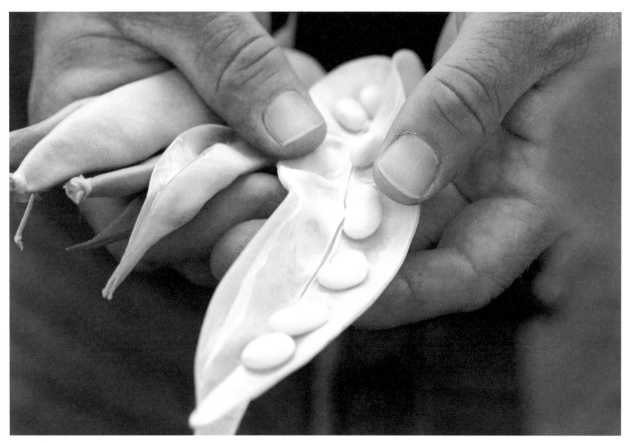

Fresh canellini beans from Martin's Farm

SHELLING BEANS

Shelling beans are admittedly hard to find. They have a very short season in the late summer and early fall, so if you find them at all, it'll only be for eight to ten weeks or so. But they have an incomparable creaminess that I find irresistible.

If you get your hands on fresh shelling beans, cook them just as you would dried beans, but skip the soaking step. They'll cook more quickly than their dried counterparts—usually from half an hour to an hour.

At this point, you can toss beans with pasta, cooked greens, or even green beans (they make wonderful partners). If using with pasta, reserve a little of the bean cooking liquid and reduce it with a little olive oil and some sage leaves; it'll yield a lovely silky sauce that you can toss with the warm pasta.

How to Store

Keep string beans in a plastic bag in the refrigerator. They'll stay good for about a week.

How to Use

ALL STRING BEANS SHOULD BE BLANCHED IN WELL-SALTED WATER before you do anything else to them. For years I cooked them just until al dente, and no longer, but after experimenting with longer cooking times, I realized that I preferred them cooked to full tenderness. So now when I blanch string beans, I cook them thoroughly—still being careful not to overcook. I suggest you do your own experiments and discover your own preference.

You can then take the beans in many different directions. Use them as is, tossing while still warm with vinaigrette and split cherry tomatoes for a lovely salad. (The vinaigrette will adhere better if you dry the beans thoroughly before tossing them.) You can also grill broader varieties like Romanos, which gives them a lovely smoky flavor. Sauté them with garlic and shallots, or mix them with pasta, pesto, and boiled potatoes for a classic Ligurian dish.

String beans also pair wonderfully with pork fat (especially bacon fat), as well as herbs like sage, thyme, and tarragon. Or all of the above!

BERRIES

I think everyone should go berry picking at least once. It's a delicious and rewarding endeavor, and it also gives you an appreciation for how challenging berry farming must be. First, the often-thorny bushes create a prickly obstacle course for your hands and arms as you reach toward that perfect berry. It's laborious, too; an hour's work may yield only three or four pounds of berries. Because of this, I never hesitate to pay whatever price a berry farmer wants to charge. I know that whoever did the picking really earned that money, so to me it's worth it as long as the berries taste good.

How to Buy

As with most foods, the best way to judge a good berry is to **TASTE A FEW**. They should be sweet and flavorful and heavy with juice.

Why taste a few, and not just one? Well, berries on a single bush or plant don't all ripen at the same time. So even at the height of the season, a single bush or plant is likely to contain berries at different stages of ripeness. A good, conscientious farmer will harvest the same bush multiple times throughout the season, each time picking only the berries that are truly ripe; a careless farmer will harvest less often, picking unripe as well as ripe ones. So as you shop, **LOOK FOR BERRIES THAT ARE RELATIVELY CONSISTENT IN COLOR AND TEXTURE**; it's a good indicator that they were grown and harvested with care.

THE CONTAINER IS CRITICAL TO BERRIES' SHELF LIFE. Berries are particularly sensitive to moisture, and too much of it will cause the fruit to break down quickly. It's unfortunate that plastic "clamshell"

containers are so common, because they trap heat and moisture, creating exactly the wrong environment. (Commercial growers and packers like these containers because they provide more protection for fruit traveling long distances.)

Stashed at the bottom of these plastic containers, you'll often find a little paper pad, which acts as a cushion and a juice picker-upper. **TAKE A PEEK AT THAT PAD BEFORE YOU DECIDE TO BUY**; if it's stained, it means the fruit has already started to break down, and mold is just around the corner. Avoid those.

PREFERABLE TO CLAMSHELL CONTAINERS ARE OLD-FASHIONED WOOD OR PULP PAPER CONTAINERS, OR PLASTIC BASKETS; their open-top design allows air to circulate freely and keeps moisture from collecting around the berries. Because open-top containers are more difficult to transport, they're a clue that the berries haven't traveled very far to get to you.

Aside from that, what you should look for depends on the type of berry.

BLACKBERRIES are really delicate when they're at their peak; really ripe ones will almost stain your fingers when you pick them up. Blackberries with green tinging will be sour, so look for darker berries. Bigger blackberries are not necessarily better (it could simply mean they're bloated from overwatering).

BLUEBERRIES should all be wrinkle-free; even if just a few are wrinkled, it still means the basketful is fairly old. Steer clear if the berries still have stems attached; it's a sign they were harvested mechanically or with a comb-type tool, which picks the berries regardless of their ripeness. Unlike other types of berries, smell won't help you much in determining blueberries' ripeness; they don't smell like much even when they're ripe! Look for berries that are rich in color, avoiding unripe green or lavender berries. Size is not an indicator of quality; both large bluets and smaller wild blueberries can taste fabulous when harvested at the right time.

RASPBERRIES are hollow inside, which means they are less structurally sound than other kinds of berries. When they're ripe, they'll become even more fragile and will collapse under too much weight; this is why raspberries are usually packaged in shallow half-pint containers rather than deeper pints. Aside from the usual red variety, gold raspberries are increasingly available but have a very short shelf life. Still rarer are black raspberries, which are a bit sturdier than gold raspberries and have an incredible flavor reminiscent of violets. Look for deeply colored berries with just enough give to indicate ripeness.

- -

QUICK STRAWBERRY JAM

Most people don't realize that you can make jam without going through the canning process. Combine a pint of berries (hulled and halved), a cup of sugar, and the zest and juice of half a lemon in a saucepan. Cook just until it boils and the sugar has dissolved. Remove from the heat, mash it up a bit, put it in a jar, and refrigerate. Done! It'll keep for a few weeks, if you don't devour it sooner.

- -

> **LOOK FOR BERRIES THAT ARE:**
> - Flavorful and juicy
> - In open containers rather than plastic clamshells, with no evidence of breaking down
> - Unsprayed or organic (especially for strawberries)

STRAWBERRIES are finicky little things. They must be picked by hand, one by one. If they're picked by grasping the fruit, they'll eventually turn brown wherever they were touched. To avoid this, strawberries must be picked by grasping the stem, not the fruit itself. So unlike blueberries, a little stem on a strawberry can be a sign of careful picking; look for pert green stems and leaves, which indicate a freshly picked berry.

The large, hulking strawberries you see at most supermarkets are generally grown for their looks and their ability to withstand travel—not for flavor. Whenever possible, look for a varietal designation, like Chandler or Seascape. This specificity often means you'll get a more flavorful strawberry. Whatever the variety, truly flavorful berries will smell irresistible, and they'll be red all over, even on the "shoulders" near the stem.

Strawberries are one of the most highly sprayed crops, and with new pesticides like methyl iodide (a known carcinogen) garnering FDA approval every year, it keeps getting worse. So it's particularly important to seek out organic strawberries.

· ·

Strawberry picking is backbreaking work and dangerous, as workers can be exposed to cancer-causing chemicals. It's an industry that relies on migrant workers, many of whom earn only a few dollars a day for their efforts.

· ·

How to Store

You'll get maximum longevity from berries if you **REFRIGERATE THEM AS SOON AS YOU GET HOME.** If your berries did come in a plastic clamshell container, pop the lid open before putting them in the fridge; this will keep condensation from collecting inside. And you can double berries' shelf life by storing them between layers of paper towels inside a resealable container.

How to Use

Because of their sensitivity to moisture, **DON'T WASH BERRIES UNTIL JUST BEFORE YOU ARE READY TO USE THEM.** Submerge them in a bowl of cold water, shake them around a bit, and lift them out of the water. Repeat in a fresh bowl of water if necessary, and dry gently on a layer of paper towels.

ASIDE FROM EATING OUT OF HAND, MACERATION IS ONE OF THE EASIEST WAYS TO ENJOY BERRIES. Maceration essentially means to marinate fruit in sugar, which causes the fruit to break down and become somewhat saucy. It's ridiculously easy, requires no measuring, and is ready in minutes. Just put berries (whole, sliced, or slightly crushed) in a bowl, toss with a little granulated sugar, and stir occasionally. After 15 minutes, the berries will have released some liquid; the longer they sit, the more juicy the mixture will get.

You can also add in one or more of these enhancements:

- Brandy, cognac, or tequila
- Aged balsamic vinegar or saba
- Maple syrup
- Lemon, lime, or orange zest or juice
- Vanilla bean mixed with sugar, or vanilla extract
- Fresh mint or basil (but serve right away, because the herbs blacken quickly)

Macerated berries are incredibly versatile. Try them with:

- Pound cake, cheesecake, or panna cotta
- Waffles or pancakes
- Yogurt, granola, or oatmeal
- Rice pudding
- Sweetened whipped cream
- Sorbet or ice cream

When berries are in season and cheap, buy lots and freeze them. You can later fold them into muffins, cakes, or pancakes, or make a sauce out of them.

CORN

Super-sweet varieties of corn dominate the marketplace—partly because of our culture's obsession with sugar—but heirloom varieties are worth trying if you can find them. I recently served two different varieties (a sweet and an heirloom) mixed together in a sauté, and the contrast was remarkable. The sweet corn was familiar and delicate, with its tiny, tender kernels that pop when you bite into them. The heirloom corn, on the other hand, was starchier and more robust in flavor, and downright chewy in texture. Some folks liked the sweet corn better; others preferred the fuller-flavored heirloom corn.

How to Buy

These days it's hard to think about corn without immediately thinking about Big Agriculture and genetic modification. But the fact that most U.S. corn is nonorganic and genetically modified doesn't mean we should avoid corn altogether. And because conventionally grown corn is one of the most heavily sprayed crops, it's particularly important to **BUY ORGANIC CORN, WHICH BY DEFINITION IS UNSPRAYED AND GMO-FREE.**

FOR THE FRESHEST FLAVOR, AND TO GET THE MOST CLUES ABOUT FRESHNESS AND QUALITY, BUY CORN WITH THE HUSK AND TASSELS STILL ON. The silk, or tassels, are the first part of the ear to show signs of age, as it will eventually turn slimy and mildewy; many grocers simply remove the silk to keep the ears presentable-looking longer. But if the grocer has left the tassels on the ear and they still look fairly

---

AT THE VERY LEAST, LOOK FOR CORN THAT IS:
- Organic
- Husk on, with tassels
- Full of plump, juicy kernels

IDEALLY, LOOK FOR:
- A unique or heirloom varietal; Silver Queen is a tender, sweet, white varietal

---

kernel (the fresher the corn, the more easily it will pop off) and taste it for sweetness and texture.

How to Store

For the best flavor, eat corn the same day you buy it, because the sugars in corn begin converting into starch as soon as the ears are picked. However, if you need to store it for longer than that, keep it in a plastic bag in the refrigerator for up to five days.

How to Use

However you choose to prepare your corn, **DON'T SHUCK THE EARS UNTIL YOU ARE READY TO COOK.** Once those husks come off, the flavor starts to go downhill, so resist that big garbage bin at the grocery store and save the shucking for later. And by all means, avoid those three-packs of shucked, plastic-wrapped ears if you can. They will not be sweet and tender.

When super fresh, corn can even be eaten raw. As long as the sugars have not yet begun converting into starch, the kernels are tender, super sweet, and incredibly juicy.

• •

If you happen to live near the coast, use a technique I learned on the East Coast: soak the ears (husk on) in a bucket of seawater for a few hours. Then throw them straight onto the grill and cook, turning every few minutes, until the outer layer is charred. You'll get perfectly seasoned, plump kernels of corn on the cob with a hint of smoky flavor. (If you don't live near the ocean, you can replicate the effect with a bucket of heavily salted water.)

• •

For an assertive roasty-toasty flavor, you can grill whole shucked cobs—brined or not—until the kernels are charred in spots. Corn cooked this way is perfect for salsa, especially if you grill a couple of hot peppers at the same time. Grilled corn on the cob is wonderful drizzled with mayonnaise or aioli, squirted with a wedge of lime, and sprinkled with chili powder.

Indoor cooking can be equally easy. You can always boil corn (either as whole shucked ears or cut kernels) in well-salted water; a few minutes is all it takes to tenderize the kernels of a really fresh ear.

dry, it's a good sign; not only is the grocer's turnover high enough that they don't have to worry about tassel decay, but also **A DRY TASSEL INDICATES A RECENTLY PICKED EAR.**

The husk forms a protective barrier that keeps the corn fresh and sweet, so be sure to **LOOK FOR HUSKS THAT ARE BRIGHT GREEN AND ALIVE LOOKING,** not dry or brown. Also take a look at the stem end, where the ear once attached to the stalk. If it looks wet and moist, the ear was recently harvested; as it sits around, it starts to dry out and the cut surface starts to recede a bit (similar to the way asparagus ends dry out).

Next, peek at the kernels themselves. Pull down a bit of the husk enough to expose a couple inches' worth of the ear. You may see evidence of a worm or two, which is fine as long as it's just at the very end of the ear (you can just lop it off before cooking). **THE KERNELS SHOULD BE PLUMP AND SWOLLEN; PASS ON ANY THAT LOOK SHRIVELED OR TIRED.** Pop off a

Cut kernels can be added to stews, braises, pastas, and salads. Sautéing is an easy, fast way to cook corn, especially if you're going to combine it with other sautéed ingredients anyway. You'll be most successful if you use a super-hot pan, and plenty of fat.

Corn plays well with flavors such as tomatoes, cucumbers, peppers, okra, sweet onions, chorizo, and chanterelle mushrooms, and adds a little burst of freshness to risotto and pizza.

CUCUMBERS

Cucumbers get a bad rap from some, which is too bad. But if you've only ever had standard, wax-coated cucumbers, it's no wonder—to me, those just taste like water suspended in a thick, bitter skin.

How to Buy

English cucumbers (the long, skinny ones that are often shrink-wrapped in plastic) are a step up from the fat, waxy kind, as their thinner skins and delicate seeds make the whole package more palatable.

THE WRAPPING ON ENGLISH CUCUMBERS GIVES THEM A MUCH LONGER SHELF LIFE, but even they have their limits. When buying them, give the ends a little squeeze. If they have any give at all, they're getting up there in age. (Same thing goes if the plastic wrapping is loose on the ends—a sign of moisture loss in the cucumber itself.)

ANYTIME YOU SEE A WEIRD, UNUSUAL CUCUM-BER AT THE GROCERY STORE OR FARMERS' MARKET, BUY, BUY, BUY! Then it's easy to discover how wonderful cucumbers can be. Some varieties, especially Persian cucumbers, are increasingly available in supermarkets and are often available at ethnic markets as well.

In general, the smaller the diameter of the cucumber, the sweeter, more tender, and perishable it will be.

LOOK FOR CUCUMBERS THAT ARE:

- Taut, not soft or wrinkly
- Unusual varieties
- Relatively small in size

How to Store

Cucumbers get slimy if they're too wet, and they wilt if they're too dry, too warm, or overexposed to the airflow of a refrigerator. This is why most supermarket cucumbers are usually either waxed or wrapped in plastic. But for uncoated or unwrapped cucumbers, **YOU CAN STRIKE THE PERFECT BALANCE BY DRYING THEM WITH A TOWEL, TOSSING THEM IN A PLASTIC BAG, AND STORING THEM IN THE REFRIGERATOR.**

How to Use

WHEN YOU GET YOUR HANDS ON OFF-THE-BEATEN-PATH VARIETALS, RESIST THE URGE TO PEEL THEM AUTOMATICALLY. Many of them have delicate, flavorful skins that are a shame to waste, plus there's a lot of nutrition in the skin. Besides, a little bitterness adds balance and depth to any dish. As with everything, taste as you go. I've found one cucumber's skin sweet and delicate, another's too bitter to tolerate.

CUCUMBERS HAVE A TENDENCY TO RELEASE WATER WHEN THEY'RE IN CONTACT WITH SALT; over time, this can dilute salads and make them runny. You can counteract this by pre-salting the cukes and letting them hang out in a colander for 15 to 20 minutes. Squeeze well or pat dry before using, and use a light hand in salting after that.

PICKLES ARE AN OBVIOUS USE FOR CUCUMBERS, AND ANY KIND OF CUCUMBER WILL WORK. For quick pickles, slice the cukes thinly, toss with a little vinegar and salt, and set them aside for 15 minutes or more. Then serve them on a burger or eat them all by themselves. If you use rice vinegar and add a little sesame oil, it's a wonderful topping for grilled or poached fish.

. . . .

The best cukes for pickling are small (about 1½ inches in diameter) and have no yellowing on the skin.

. . . .

CUCUMBERS GET ALONG PARTICULARLY WELL WITH GREEN HERBS AND YOGURT; dice or slice them thinly and toss with yogurt, garlic, and mint or basil. It's great as a dip or garnish for grilled meats. (And goat or sheep's milk yogurt, if you can find it, is especially good this way.)

TRY CUCUMBER SLICES AS AN ALTERNATIVE TO CRACKERS when serving hummus or a yogurt-spiked ranch dip.

EGGPLANT

Eggplant can be so wrong, but it can also be so right. I used to hate it—I thought it was either too slimy and slippery or spongy and squeaky—but that all changed with my first restaurant job at Kimball's, where eggplant was a mainstay on the menu. We halved or sliced the heads, tossed them with extra-virgin olive oil and balsamic vinegar, and grilled them until charred on the outside but still soft inside. The eggplant stayed moist and took on a sexy, smoky quality. It's still my favorite way to cook and eat them!

How to Buy

Purple globe eggplants are still the most common at the grocery store, but you're also likely to find white varieties (sporting clever names like Ghostbuster and Cloud Nine) as well dappled lavender Rosa Biancas. Some are rounded and bulbous, others long and slender.

EGGPLANTS HAVE VERY DELICATE SKINS AND BRUISE EASILY, ESPECIALLY WHEN THEY COME IN CONTACT WITH WATER, which is why some high-end packers wrap the eggplants in tissue paper and line them up carefully in shallow crates. As eggplants ripen on the vine, they go from a dull matte finish to a shiny bright one; after they peak, they lose their gloss. So look for the shiny ones; if they're dull, it means they're either immature or over the hill.

AT THE VERY LEAST, LOOK FOR EGGPLANTS THAT ARE:

• Shiny, unbruised, and firm

IDEALLY, LOOK FOR:

• Unusual varietals

GIVE THEM A GENTLE SQUEEZE: perfectly ripe eggplant should be firm, with hardly any "give." If they feel spongy, it means three things: the flesh has become sinewy, the seeds have gotten fat and bitter, and it'll take longer to cook.

How to Store

Store eggplants wrapped in a paper towel in a plastic bag in the refrigerator for up to five days or so.

How to Use

You only need a couple of tricks to make eggplant delectable. **YOU CAN PEEL IT IF YOU LIKE, BUT I LIKE THE SLIGHT BITTERNESS THAT THE SKINS CONTRIBUTE.** If you leave the skin on, just make sure you coat it with a little oil—otherwise, the skin will get tough as it cooks. Some recipes instruct you to pre-salt eggplant to leach out the bitter liquid, but as long as you have youngish, vibrant eggplant, I think this step is unnecessary.

GRILLING EGGPLANT is the best way to introduce it to newbies, or to convert those who think they hate it. Slice into $1/2$-inch-thick rounds, toss with olive oil, balsamic vinegar, and salt, and grill until slightly charred and tender to the touch. That's all you really need for a perfect side dish, but you can make it even better by topping the warm eggplant with a simple salsa of tomato, garlic, olive oil, and balsamic vinegar. It's so good, I've seen people who claimed to hate eggplant fight for the last piece!

Slender eggplant—the Chinese and Japanese varieties—are also great grilled in the same manner, and they're divine for roasting or quick sautés as well. Roasting is ideal if you have an especially large batch of eggplant (more than would fit in one or two sauté pans); just toss with lots of olive oil and roast in a 400°F oven until soft and tender. If you're sautéing, be sure to cut the eggplant into relatively thin slices (about $1/4$ inch thick) or smallish dice ($1/2$-inch cubes). This helps ensure that the eggplant cooks through without overbrowning the outside.

Basil

To store: Put the stems in a glass of water, cover loosely with a plastic bag, and refrigerate. (The bag and refrigeration are critical to keeping the leaves from wilting.)

Friendly flavors: Tomatoes, white beans, Parmigiano, mozzarella, eggplant, peppers.

When to add to a dish: Near the end of cooking.

Tip: The more you chop basil, the faster it will turn black. Unless you need very finely chopped basil, try tearing it into bite-size pieces with your hands. This will minimize oxidization and will also keep bitterness at bay.

Bay leaf

To store: Stash fresh bay leaves in a plastic bag and keep in the refrigerator.

Friendly flavors: Stews, beans, pickles, braises, stocks, game, poultry.

When to add to a dish: At the beginning of cooking.

Tip: The bay leaves you can buy at the store are of the Mediterranean variety. You can substitute the California bay leaf, but they're about twice as potent.

Cilantro

To store: Wrap loosely in a paper towel, put in a plastic bag, and keep in the refrigerator.

Friendly flavors: Vegetables, ginger, hot chiles, soy sauce, garlic, chicken, tomatoes, salsas.

When to add to a dish: At the end of cooking or just before serving.

Tip: You'll get maximum life if you untie the bunch to give the sprigs a little breathing room before putting them in the paper towel.

Fennel fronds

To store: Wrap loosely in a paper towel, put in a plastic bag, and keep in the refrigerator.

Friendly flavors: Fish and seafood, lemon, fresh salsas, soups, paellas, pastas.

When to add to a dish: In the middle or near the end of cooking.

Tip: Bronze fennel is my favorite variety; it has a gorgeous hue and incredible flavor to boot.

Marjoram

To store: Wrap loosely in a paper towel, put in a plastic bag, and keep in the refrigerator.

Friendly flavors: Cauliflower, tomatoes, onions, garlic, chicken, pork.

When to add to a dish: Near the end of cooking.

Tip: Fresh marjoram is worth exploring; it's a little like oregano, but more fragrant and not as earthy.

Mint

To store: Wrap loosely in a paper towel, put in a plastic bag, and keep in the refrigerator.

Friendly flavors: Fruit, especially berries, citrus, and melon, chocolate, cucumbers, yogurt.

When to add to a dish: At the very end, or use uncooked.

Tip: Fresh mint is easy to grow, but be sure to plant it in a pot, as it will take over your garden.

HERB IT UP!

HERBS

I don't think I'm alone in saying that I didn't grow up with fresh herbs. My mom, like so many others, relied on dried herbs in little metal tins and glass jars for all her cooking. That all changed in the early 1980s with the arrival of French nouvelle cuisine, which brought lighter, brighter flavors and fresher, less adulterated ingredients. With it came a new interest in fresh herbs, which inspired the development of California cuisine and eventually took hold across the country.

How to Buy

There are a few quality indicators that hold true, regardless of the variety of herb. **LOOK FOR VIBRANT, GREEN HERBS WITH LIVELY LOOKING STEMS.** Avoid any that have yellowing or blackened leaves. Avoid herbs that have been sitting under the mister, if possible; although herbs like cilantro and parsley require moisture to stay lively, that moisture quickly leads to decay once you put them in a plastic bag.

How to Store

Once you get home, various herbs require different means of storage; see the details above.

How to Use

Fresh herbs are delicate, and they can become bitter if mishandled. You can minimize this by chopping them with a very sharp knife; a dull one will crush and bruise the herbs, which affects the flavor. Similarly, try to use as few knife strokes as possible, and err toward a coarser chop if you have to.

Oregano

To store: Wrap loosely in a paper towel, put in a plastic bag, and keep in the refrigerator.

Friendly flavors: Tomatoes, lemon, fish, olives, onions, chicken, pizza.

When to add to a dish: Near the end of cooking.

Tip: Fresh oregano can be overpowering, so add a little at a time if you're not sure how much to use. Easy to dry if you have extra.

Parsley

To store: Wrap loosely in a paper towel, put in a plastic bag, and keep in the refrigerator.

Friendly flavors: Everything! Parsley's pure "green" flavor brightens and livens just about any dish. It should also be used as an ingredient, not just a garnish.

When to add to a dish: Just before serving.

Tip: I personally prefer Italian (flat-leaf) parsley; if you use curly parsley, be sure to chop it fairly finely, otherwise, it can have a scratchy, fibrous mouthfeel.

Rosemary

To store: Stash in a plastic bag and keep in the refrigerator.

Friendly flavors: Lamb, chicken, goat, eggplant, potatoes, garlic, lemon.

When to add to a dish: At the beginning or middle of cooking.

Tip: Use sparingly (too much tastes resiny). Easy to grow and then dry.

Sage

To store: Wrap loosely in a paper towel, put in a plastic bag, and keep in the refrigerator.

Friendly flavors: Root vegetables, autumn squash, chicken, turkey, white beans, pork, potatoes.

When to add to a dish: At the middle or end of cooking.

Tip: Fried sage leaves make a beautiful and delicious garnish. Fry them in a little olive oil until crisp (less than a minute), drain on a paper towel, and sprinkle with salt.

Tarragon

To store: Wrap loosely in a paper towel, put in a plastic bag, and keep in the refrigerator.

Friendly flavors: Fat, fat, fat! Infuses wonderfully into mayonnaise, butter, or cream (béarnaise sauce is a classic example). Also seafood, chicken, pot pies.

When to add to a dish: Near the end of cooking. Tender leaves can be left whole and tossed into salads like the Fennel, Blood Orange, and Avocado Salad (page 98) for additional flavor.

Tip: Use fresh tarragon unless you have no other choice. (Dried tarragon has only a fraction of the flavor of fresh.)

Thyme

To store: Stash in a plastic bag and keep in the refrigerator.

Friendly flavors: Seafood, chicken, potatoes, lemon, soups, stews, braises.

When to add to a dish: At the beginning or middle of cooking.

Tip: I use thyme more than any other herb. For brothy dishes, you can add whole sprigs of thyme and simply fish out the stems at the end of cooking.

- -

You'll chop more efficiently if you roll or fold the herbs up tightly before slicing through them. Make a series of close-laid slices across the bundle, and then make just a few more cuts in the opposite direction. These ten or twelve strokes are usually enough to achieve a fairly fine consistency, whereas chopping willy-nilly might require twice as many strokes for the same effect.

- -

I generally think that fresh herbs are preferable to dried ones; not only do herbs' flavors change and diminish when dried, but also most commercial dried herbs are of poor quality to start with. Plus, dried herbs have a limited shelf life, and it's difficult to know exactly how old they are.

Fresh herbs are perfect for omelets, soups, roasted chicken or potatoes, and tuna or egg salads. They're a wonderful addition to green salads, as well; keep in mind that the smaller, tender leaves are milder in flavor and better suited for this use. Leafy green herbs like basil, cilantro, and parsley are also prime candidates for the Any-Green Pesto on page 118.

- -

It's helpful to gauge the intensity of herbs before you add them to a dish. To do this, rub a few leaves between your fingers and take a sniff to learn how robust that particular herb is. It's also a good idea to do a taste test once you've chopped the herbs, as they sometimes become more bitter and assertive once the knife hits them. Remember that it's easy to add more, but impossible to take it out once stirred into a dish.

- -

MELONS

Unique melon varietals have exploded of late, and it seems like every year brings at least five new kinds to try. Be sure to explore the myriad flavors and textures on offer.

How to Buy

When shopping for melons, many use the "thump test" to determine whether the melon is ripe or mealy. An *unripe* melon sounds like rapping your forehead; a *ripe* one sounds like thumping your chest; and an *overripe* melon sounds like thumping your abdomen. Try these on your body and get to know the different sounds, then compare on melons.

IF YOU CAN, LOOK AT THE CROSS-SECTION OF A CUT WATERMELON, which will tell you about the melon's texture. It should feel firm rather than spongy; avoid any that have air pockets around the seeds, because they tend to be mealy. And contrary to popular belief, deeply colored flesh does not necessarily correlate to sweetness. (Prayer is your best bet for that.)

FOR OTHER TYPES OF MELONS, LIKE CANTALOUPE OR HONEYDEW, A HEADY, TROPICAL FRAGRANCE IS A GOOD INDICATOR of a melon's ripeness. Melons are prone to molding, which is preceded by a musty smell; avoid any that seem headed in that direction.

MELONS DO NOT GET SWEETER AFTER THEY'RE PICKED. An underripe melon will get slightly more aromatic as it sits on the counter, but nothing compares to a melon that's picked at its height of ripeness. Look for ones that have a little give in the indentation where the stem was. Size doesn't matter much as far as flavor goes, so just try to find a ripe one in whatever size you need.

LOOK FOR WATERMELONS THAT ARE:
- Dense at the center (if it's already cut)

LOOK FOR OTHER MELONS THAT ARE:
- Heady and fragrant
- Ever so slightly soft at the stem end

How to Store

A good melon is so fragrant that its scent fills the entire house, and a successful melon hunt pays off before you even eat it. **LEAVE IT ON THE COUNTER AND ENJOY THE SMELL IF YOU'RE GOING TO EAT IT WITHIN A DAY OR SO**; otherwise, store it in the refrigerator to help prevent breakdown.

How to Use

Melons require high-nutrient soil, and in this effort many growers use manure as fertilizer. So **IT'S PARTICULARLY IMPORTANT TO THOROUGHLY WASH (EVEN SCRUB) MELONS** before you cut into them to prevent foodborne illness. To be extra safe, wash your knife and cutting board after you've removed the skin and before you cut any deeper into it. This not only reduces the likelihood of contamination but also keeps the skin's unpleasant earthy flavor from contaminating the rest of the flesh.

If you're going to use only half a melon, don't peel or seed the other half. Just wrap it in plastic and refrigerate for maximum shelf life.

A cold slice of melon can be so refreshing, it hardly needs anything else. I do sometimes like to emulate my Mexican friends and sprinkle the fruit with a little salt and lime juice, and sometimes even a tiny pinch of chili powder.

Melons are also wonderful pureed into chilled soups and smoothies or diced into a salsa. Topping cubes with yogurt and honey is also a great simple dessert.

Melons are just starting to get recognition as a worthwhile ingredient in savory dishes. Of course, there's the classic Italian technique of wrapping melon slices with prosciutto or other cured ham, but there have been many innovations as well. One of my recent revelations was at a restaurant in New York City called Fatty Crab. There, watermelon is paired with pork belly that has been braised and then fried crispy and dressed with a tangy dressing; the watermelon contributes a unique sweetness, texture, and cooling effect that is a perfect counterpoint to the rich pork, hot out of the fryer.

PEPPERS

In my mind, fancy restaurant food of the late '80s and early '90s was defined by two things: squiggles of sauces from squeeze bottles, and bell peppers. Not just any bell peppers, though: multicolored ones, cut into perfect tiny "confetti" and thrown onto a plate as a final garnish. It was so precious and fussy and it didn't add much flavor to the dish. But because of that little omnipresent flair in restaurants, grocery stores began to branch out beyond green bell peppers and started carrying yellow, orange, and red varieties.

How to Buy

Unfortunately, the peppers you see in the supermarket were grown for color and uniformity, rather than flavor. If you were to close your eyes, you probably wouldn't be able to taste the difference between a red and a yellow pepper or a yellow and an orange pepper. These sweet peppers, mostly hothouse-grown in Mexico, Holland, and Israel, are beautiful and perfectly shaped, but also fairly flavorless.

Peppers (sweet and hot alike) are a late summer/early autumn crop, but their constant availability in the supermarket has made it easy to forget that. Once you taste true in-season peppers, you'll find they have a deeper, richer flavor compared to one-note hothouse peppers. **SO TRY THINKING OF THEM AS A SUMMER CROP: GET THEM WHEN THEY'RE GOOD, AND LEAN ON OTHER PRODUCE WHEN THEY'RE NOT.** Unfortunately, most supermarkets carry only hothouse peppers

Harvesting peppers on our Sonoma Farm

AT THE VERY LEAST, LOOK FOR PEPPERS THAT ARE:

- In season
- Unwrinkled, with stiff green stems

IDEALLY, LOOK FOR:

- Unique varietals

---

even at the peak of the season, so seek out field-grown, true summer peppers. They are worth it.

LOOK FOR PEPPERS THAT ARE SHINY AND FIRM, WITH STEMS THAT ARE STIFF AND GREEN rather than black and dry. Avoid any that have black spots on the skin; they're about to break down and mold. And a wrinkled pepper is an old one.

DON'T BE AFRAID OF STRANGELY SHAPED, TWISTY BELL PEPPERS; at the very least, it's a clue that they weren't grown solely for uniformity and may be more flavorful than cookie-cutter peppers. (Though if you plan to roast the peppers, relatively straight-sided ones will be easier to deal with.)

HOT SAUCE

When hot peppers are in season, making hot sauce is an easy way to use a lot of them at once. Just sauté stemmed, seeded peppers in a little olive oil for a few minutes, then add a little distilled white vinegar, salt, and sugar, plus enough water to come about halfway up the peppers. Simmer until the peppers are tender, then puree in the blender. Strain and adjust with more water or vinegar as needed. Refrigerated, it will keep for several months.

Any time you encounter an interesting variety of pepper, pick up a few for experimentation. Small frying peppers like Spanish padróns, Japanese shishitos, and Italian friarielli are particularly worth exploring. They're intensely flavorful—proof that there's much more to peppers than the standard bell.

How to Store

Peppers need to breathe, so try to buy them loose and keep them that way in a paper bag. If you do buy them in the shrink-wrapped trays, remove the plastic as soon as you get home, put them in a bag, and refrigerate.

How to Use

I think peppers are vastly improved by roasting, which concentrates the flavors and sweetens the flesh. It also improves the texture, going from a watery, applelike crunchiness to a creamy, silky consistency.

You can roast peppers in any kind of direct, high-heat source, whether it's a gas stove top, a broiler, or on the grill. Rub the peppers with a little oil first, then put them on (or under) the flame until the skins are charred and blistered all over. Then put them in a bowl, cover with plastic wrap, and let them steam for a few minutes to further loosen the skins.

Once you've skinned and seeded the peppers, you add them to soups and salsas, of course, but my favorite thing to do is to turn them into a salad that I used to serve at my restaurant. Slice peeled, roasted sweet peppers into $1/2$-inch ribbons and toss them with capers, minced shallots, sherry vinegar, and olive oil. (If good Valencia oranges are available, peeled slices with seeds removed are a nice addition, too.) The result is vibrant and succulent, midway between a condiment and a side dish; it's an amazing accompaniment to grilled beef or fish.

So many cultures around the world have a tradition of stuffed peppers, either hot or mild, and there are hundreds of different fillings you can use. My favorite is to roast piquillo peppers (a small, sweet variety from Spain), stuff them with fresh goat cheese, and drizzle with good olive oil. Three ingredients, and you're done! It's the perfect little pre-dinner nibble.

Piquillo peppers are hard to find fresh in the United States; mine were grown from seeds smuggled back from Spain in a suitcase! You can, however, find roasted, jarred, ready-to-use piquillos in many specialty stores. Their small size and thin skins make them ideal for stuffing.

ANY TIME YOU'RE WORKING WITH HOT PEPPERS, PROCEED WITH CAUTION. Minimize the spread of their hot oils by handling the cut hot peppers as little as possible. And once you've finished chopping, wash your hands, your knife, and your cutting board before moving on to anything else! Most of the heat is held in the white ribs of the pepper, so trim those off if you want to tone it down a bit. And carefully taste a bit of any pepper before adding it to your dish; even within a single variety (like jalapeños), individual peppers have very different levels of heat; knowing if a particular pepper is very hot or very mild makes it easy to adjust the recipe to your taste.

STONE FRUITS

If you've never heard them called this, stone fruits are the category of tree fruit that have a hard, stonelike pit in the center. Cherries, apricots, peaches, plums, and nectarines are a few examples.

I can't eat apricots without thinking of my mother. Mom loves apricots. She would stone the fruit, saving the pits, and then make the most wonderful jam or fruit leather. Then she would crack open the pits to reveal the kernel inside and we'd eat them like nuts. Their gelatinous texture and the bitter almond flavor (called *noyeau* in French) is a delicacy that really stays with you. You also can steep the kernels into a crème anglaise and then make ice cream or a sauce. You can serve either with apricot galette—a beautiful way to make use of the whole fruit.

How to Buy

Among all fruits and vegetables, stone fruits are the most frequently and most heavily pesticide-sprayed crops around (a study by the Environmental Working Group showed that 97 percent of conventionally grown peaches and nectarines are pesticide-ridden). **SO IF NOTHING ELSE, BUY ORGANIC APRICOTS, PEACHES, NECTARINES, PLUMS, AND CHERRIES.**

THE BEST WAY TO SHOP FOR ANY STONE FRUIT IS TO PICK ONE UP. If it feels noticeably heavy for its size, it's fully ripe, dense with juice, and recently harvested. Smell it: does the aroma make you want to take a bite, or is it as anonymous as the cardboard box it arrived in? Picking stone fruit is one task where you want to use all your senses. The fruit needs to look good (not necessarily perfect), smell good, and feel good. Most important, they should taste good, so be sure to ask for a sample.

FIRMNESS IS ANOTHER GOOD INDICATOR, BUT TO DIFFERENT DEGREES ACROSS VARIETIES. With a really ripe peach or nectarine, you'll sense a delicateness to the skin and the flesh just under it; at its peak you might even be afraid to handle it too much. On the other hand, apricots, plums, and cherries are fairly firm even when ripe—but they should still have a little give.

For cherries, look for shiny ones with bright green stems. Dark stems are a sign of age, and although it's not necessarily a bad sign, it is an indicator that the cherries spent time in a storage facility and did not come straight from the tree.

As some stone fruit continues to ripen, you'll see a couple of things happening. You'll see small, slightly dark patches appear on the fruit's skin; these "sugar spots" may resemble bruises, but are actually areas of super-concentrated sweetness. And eventually some of the moisture will evaporate through the skin, leaving a slightly wrinkly appearance. But this process actually results in more concentrated sweetness and flavor (the same principle is what makes late-harvest wines so special).

How to Store

THE BEST WAY TO STORE STONE FRUITS IS AT ROOM TEMPERATURE. Stashing them in the fridge will buy you a little time and discourage mold, but you'll lose some of the more delicate flavors. Buy just what you will eat within a few days so you can savor them at their peak.

> ### AT THE VERY LEAST, LOOK FOR STONE FRUITS THAT ARE:
>
> - **Organic (or not sprayed)**
> - **Heavy for their size**
> - **Firm with a bit of give (not spongy)**
> - **Fragrant**
>
> ### IDEALLY, LOOK FOR:
>
> - **Sugar spots**

How to Use

Great stone fruit is glorious as it is. Our neighbor Pizzeria Delfina offers a lovely dessert consisting of plain Bing cherries accompanied by a bowl of mascarpone cheese. Like everything Delfina does, it is understated and perfect. Still, that's not to say that stone fruits don't play well with others—not only in desserts like cobblers and pies, but also in savory contexts.

One special—and incredibly simple—way to treat peaches is to halve them and grill them (cut side down) just until they get grill marks and are heated through. I like to pair them with blue cheese, aged vinegar, and nuts; see the recipe on page 249 for my favorite version.

That slightly darker spot isn't a bruise—it's an area of concentrated sugar, and something to look for if you want sweet fruit!

And even if you don't consider yourself a canning type of person, you can easily "put up" any stone fruit in brandy. Just pit and slice the fruit of your choice (cherries may be left whole), pack in a clean jar, and pour in equal parts brandy and simple syrup to cover. After a week or so, the fruit will have taken on the brandy flavor and vice versa. Brandied cherries make a knockout cocktail garnish; nectarines are a divinely boozy accompaniment to vanilla ice cream. The brandy itself is ideal for late-afternoon sipping, either solo or mixed with soda water.

Peach and nectarine varieties can be classified as either freestone or clingstone. Freestone means that the pit pulls cleanly away from the fruit, and clingstone means that the pit doesn't separate easily. Freestones are the easiest to work with when slicing, but if you need to slice clingstone fruit, try cutting wedges directly from the fruit. Start by making two long cuts that meet in a V near the pit. Remove the first wedge, and then make another lengthwise cut at the desired interval, keeping the knife in place. Use your thumb to brace the section against the knife and pull the wedge to free the section from the pit. Continue all the way around.

SUMMER SQUASH

My all-time favorite squash dish is, unfortunately, not an everyday kind of recipe. It's called *mahshi*, which means "stuffed" in Arabic, and my mom is the master of it. To make it, she first cores out little squashes and stuffs them with a mixture of parcooked rice, ground lamb, onions, and garlic. Then she arranges them in tight concentric circles over a bed of lamb ribs, tomatoes, and onions, and tops it all with a layer of grape leaves. She then steams it until everything is tender, about four hours. It takes about half a day to make from start to finish. She puts so much love and effort into that dish, and it makes every bite that much more delicious.

How to Buy

As summer squash grows, the flesh gets less dense and the flavor becomes less concentrated. If allowed to grow too big, the seeds become large and holes will develop alongside them. (They're still fine to eat, but

they are less flavorful and not ideal for eating raw.) **SO GO FOR THE SMALLEST, CUTEST SQUASHES** you can find! Most commercial growers grade their squashes by size, which means that your supermarket is probably going to carry only one of those size grades. If all you can find are big hulking zucchinis or yellow squash, don't be afraid to ask your grocer to carry the smaller grades instead.

Regardless of their size, take a good look at squash before you buy them. **PASS ON ANY THAT ARE DISCOLORED ON THE STEM END**; a rusty brown color indicates that they're too old. The optimal squash will have unblemished, bright skin and a firm, unyielding feel.

Squash that still have the blossoms attached are extremely fresh. Buy them any time you see them.

COMPARED TO THE GREEN VERSIONS, YELLOW SUMMER SQUASH ARE MORE FRAGILE AND PRONE TO BECOMING SLIMY. So if you aren't going to cook it right away, you're better off with green summer squash.

Also, some summer squash is genetically modified, so buying organic is the safest bet.

How to Store

Those spray misters in the supermarket produce aisle make the veggies look nice, but they're terrible for summer squash because the moisture makes them break down faster. So if your squash is still moist, **DRY THEM OFF AS SOON AS YOU GET HOME**. Store them in a plastic bag in the refrigerator.

How to Use

Summer squash bakes beautifully. I like to layer slices of zucchini along with tomato in a casserole, drizzle it with extra-virgin olive oil, herbs, and cheese, and bake until tender. Diced, roasted squash is a great

> **AT THE VERY LEAST, LOOK FOR LOOK FOR SUMMER SQUASH THAT ARE:**
> - Smallish, with a firm feel and unblemished skin
> - Organic, to avoid possible GMOs

addition to pasta or risotto, too. And let us not forget frying—not just the squash itself, but also their gorgeous blossoms. Try my favorite batter recipe below—it's incredibly simple and fries up light and crispy.

· ·

EASY TEMPURA BATTER: Mix equal parts rice flour and all-purpose flour (or cornstarch) in a bowl, along with a little salt and pepper. Slowly and gradually whisk in enough ice-cold water to get a thin batter—it should be slightly thicker than heavy cream. Dip slices or spears of squash, or blossoms, into the batter and immediately transfer to hot frying oil.

· ·

Summer squash brings a nice fresh-tasting element to an omelet. Grate the squash, sauté in a little olive oil, then stir right into the omelet as it cooks, along with some Gruyère cheese.

TOMATOES

With the recent resurgence of farmers' markets and renewed interest in seasonal eating, it's easy to take good tomatoes for granted. But a recent experience made me really appreciate good tomatoes. I ordered a BLT at a restaurant, and for some reason the chef made it with raw green tomatoes. It was awful! If the chef had only fried or grilled the green tomatoes, the sandwich would have been awesome.

How to Buy

As beautiful as tomatoes can be, the true test is in tasting them. That's easy enough to do at the farmers' market, but you have to be a little proactive in the supermarket. Don't hesitate to ask a staffer to sample a tomato or two.

But you can—to a degree—judge a tomato by its cover. Tomatoes with full, saturated color all over are ideal. However, many commercial tomatoes are mechanically harvested while still green (when they are sturdier and better able to withstand travel) and later artificially ripened with ethylene gas. This treatment makes the tomato look red on the outside, but the core will still be pink; for this reason it's useful to check out the cross-section of a cut tomato if you can.

AT THE VERY LEAST, LOOK FOR TOMATOES THAT ARE:
• **In season and flavorful (ask for a taste)**
• **Have some green stem attached**
• **Show no splitting in the skin**

IDEALLY, LOOK FOR:
• **Organic or unsprayed**
• **Naturally ripened (not gassed)**
• **Unique and heirloom varietals**
• **Dry-farmed (see the profile on page 140)**

Ideally, the color will be consistent from the skin to the very center.

BUY ORGANIC TOMATOES WHENEVER POSSIBLE. Most commercial tomatoes are heavily sprayed with pesticides and then treated with fungicides after harvest to prolong shelf life. Organic and unsprayed tomatoes are becoming more readily available, especially at farmers' markets, so look for and purchase those if you can.

TWO DOG FARM:
Mark and Nibby Bartle

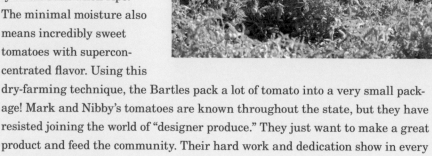

There are a lot of good tomatoes out there, but Mark and Nibby Bartle's tomatoes are life-changing. At Two Dog Farm, their property near Santa Cruz, California, they practice dry-farming techniques on the Early Girl tomatoes they grow. Dry-farming is just as it sounds; it means no irrigation, and the plants depend on the cool, moist coastal air for their water. Because the plants get only enough water to survive, and no more, the tomatoes grow slowly and remain fairly small even when ripe.

The minimal moisture also means incredibly sweet tomatoes with superconcentrated flavor. Using this dry-farming technique, the Bartles pack a lot of tomato into a very small package! Mark and Nibby's tomatoes are known throughout the state, but they have resisted joining the world of "designer produce." They just want to make a great product and feed the community. Their hard work and dedication show in every tomato they sell.

TOMATOES THAT STILL HAVE A BIT OF GREEN STEM ATTACHED ARE OPTIMAL. The stems themselves have a short shelf life, as they dry and brown fairly quickly. Not only are stem-on tomatoes more work as far as picking goes, but also a bright green stem is a good sign that the tomato was recently picked.

AVOID TOMATOES WITH SPLIT SKINS; it indicates a late rain or general overwatering, and that exposed flesh is vulnerable to mold.

IT SEEMS OBVIOUS TO RECOMMEND BUYING TOMATOES IN SEASON, BUT ITS IMPORTANCE CANNOT BE OVERSTATED. Many folks associate tomatoes with summer, so guests start asking for them as soon as the weather warms up. However, because tomatoes are a late-planted crop (they can't go into the ground until after the final frost), and they require an extended period of heat and sun to reach maturity, tomatoes aren't ready for harvest until mid-July or later, depending on the weather and where you are.

Farmers' markets are almost always the best places to find good tomatoes—but you can often find pretty good tomatoes at the supermarket if you know what to look for:

CHERRY AND GRAPE tomatoes tend to be a little more flavorful than other varieties of supermarket tomatoes. Their small size makes it easy to sneak a little taste and evaluate the goods. Sungolds and Sweet 100s are a couple of varieties that tend to have good flavor.

HEIRLOOM tomatoes are mind-boggling in their variety and proliferation. Some are utterly incredible; others are just so-so. When you're shopping, it's important to realize that "heirloom" refers only to the varietal category and doesn't have anything to do with the way the tomato is grown. Some commercial growers have hopped onto the heirloom bandwagon and grow heirlooms just as they grow their other tomatoes: for size and appearance, not for flavor. So you might buy a huge, gorgeous heirloom, only to find that it's bloated and flavorless from overwatering. They can be pricey, too—all the more reason to ask for a taste!

ROMA AND OTHER "PASTE" tomatoes are the ideal choice for cooking if you have to buy fresh tomatoes out of season. San Marzano is my favorite variety in this category; they're perfect for canning.

SLICER tomatoes, like Beefsteak, New Jersey, and Early Girl, are so named because of their hefty size and round shape. "Vine ripe" tomatoes also fall into this category; they are generally hothouse-grown in Holland. Their flavor is decent, but not great.

DON'T FORGET CANNED TOMATOES as a reasonable alternative to fresh tomatoes in the off-season. In the dead of winter, tomatoes from a can will have worlds more flavor than crunchy, underripe ones. They work perfectly if you're going to cook the tomatoes anyway and even make great salsas.

How to Store

Do not refrigerate tomatoes (and don't buy refrigerated ones, either); the chill adversely affects the texture and diminishes the flavor. If you buy slightly underripe tomatoes, put them in a paper bag and let them sit on the counter for a few days; they will soften and become a bit sweeter.

How to Use

When you have really excellent tomatoes, especially organic heirlooms, all you need is a sprinkle of salt and a drizzle of high-quality extra-virgin olive oil.

Basil is a natural accompaniment to tomatoes; tarragon, thyme, oregano, and cilantro are good partners.

CHERRY tomatoes are excellent in salsas, tossed with tender green beans, or briefly sautéed and mixed with pasta. (For a quick meal, toss good spaghetti or linguine with sautéed tomatoes and garlic, basil, extra-virgin olive oil, and salt and pepper. Five minutes is all it takes to make the sauce, start to finish.)

ROMA tomatoes are well-suited to making tomato paste and sauce.

HEIRLOOMS are at their best when you leave them raw; their subtleties and distinct personalities diminish when cooked. If you can get your hands on a few different heirloom varieties, try conducting a side-by-side tasting of your own. Pay attention to what's happening in your mouth. You'll find a surprising spectrum of textures, flavors, and seed structures. Some will seem incredibly sweet, and others will be almost salty.

If you find yourself with a surplus of tomatoes of any type, the gazpacho recipe on page 144 is a terrific way to use them up.

Strawberry farmer Domitila Gayton

ALBA and Their Farmers

Farmers grow food, but how are farmers "grown"? With the help of the Agriculture and Land-Based Training Association (ALBA). This Monterey County, California, nonprofit (situated in an area that grows 80 percent of the country's lettuce supply) provides education and training to small-scale minority farmers. ALBA's programs include workshops, field days, and leadership development. They also lease farmland, at below-market rates, to farmers who are just starting to strike out on their own. ALBA does an incredible job in helping make the food system more just and sustainable, starting with the people who produce our food. We need an ALBA in every state!

Fire-Roasted Tomato Salsa

MAKES ABOUT 2¹/₂ CUPS

Our chef Eddy developed this recipe based on the salsa he grew up with in Mexico City. It's a favorite among our customers, especially at the height of summer when the tomatoes and peppers come from our own mini-farm. I love to spoon it over fried eggs after a late night of drinking, but it's also perfect for picnicking or just snacking. For a milder salsa, remove the seeds from the jalapeño before roasting it.

4 medium tomatoes, halved and cored
(about 1¹/₂ pounds)
1 medium yellow onion, peeled and cut into 8 wedges
1 medium red bell pepper, quartered and seeded
1 or 2 medium jalapeño or serrano peppers, halved
6 cloves garlic, peeled
1 tablespoon grapeseed or other neutral oil
Kosher salt
¹/₂ teaspoon chile flakes
¹/₂ teaspoon ground cumin
2 tablespoons lightly packed cilantro leaves
¹/₄ cup freshly squeezed lime juice, more as needed

Position a rack in the center of the oven and heat to 400°F.

Pile the tomatoes, onion, bell peppers, jalapeño, and garlic on a large rimmed baking sheet and drizzle with the olive oil and ¹/₂ teaspoon salt. Stir the vegetables around to evenly coat with the oil, then spread them in a single layer. Roast until softened and browned in spots, about 40 minutes. (Check the vegetables periodically, removing any that seem to be getting too brown.) Let cool completely on the pan.

Meanwhile, put the chile flakes and cumin in a small skillet. Cook over medium-high heat, stirring frequently, until the spices are fragrant and slightly darker, about 2 minutes. Remove from the heat.

Put the cooled vegetables, cilantro, and spice mixture in a food processor and pulse just until everything is coarsely chopped. Transfer to a medium bowl, add

the lime juice, and stir to combine. Taste and add more lime juice or salt as needed; the effect should be a little tangy but not particularly salty.

Use right away, or refrigerate for up to 5 days.

Padrón Pepper Poppers

SERVES 4 TO 6

Pimientos de Padrón are little peppers that hail from Spain, where they're simply prepared and served as a tapa or snack. You can eat these tender peppers whole, and they go perfectly with a glass of crisp dry sherry. This preparation hardly requires a recipe, but it's so good that it deserves the formal attention of one.

If you can't find Pimientos de Padrón, look for Italian friarielli or Japanese shishitsu peppers (often stocked at Japanese grocers). In their absence, fresh okra spears make an excellent substitute—they just take a little longer to cook. You may also want to add a sprinkle of chile flakes to replicate the occasional heat of the Padróns.

1¹/₂ tablespoons extra-virgin olive oil, more as needed
¹/₂ pound Pimientos de Padrón
Kosher salt

Put the oil in a large skillet (cast iron is best) and put the skillet over medium-high heat. When the oil is shimmering hot, add half of the peppers (see Tip) and cook, carefully stirring them occasionally, until they are blistered and have started to brown in spots, 2 to 3 minutes.

Using tongs or a heatproof slotted spoon, transfer the peppers to a paper towel–lined plate and sprinkle generously with salt. Fry the other peppers in the same way, adding a little more oil if the pan seems too dry.

Serve warm or at room temperature.

Tip: Make sure the peppers are completely dry before you add them to the skillet, as even a drop of water will cause the oil to spatter vigorously.

Tomato, Cucumber, and Chickpea Salad

SERVES 6 TO 8

When tomatoes are abundant and cucumbers fat and crisp, this salad begs to be made. It's based on a salad my mother makes, and I consider it a summer classic. This recipe is a template for multiple variations: use white beans instead of the chickpeas, cilantro instead of the basil, or whatever strikes your fancy.

> 1 large English cucumber
> 3 medium tomatoes
> 1/4 medium red onion, thinly sliced
> 1 1/2 cups cooked chickpeas (one 15-ounce can, drained and rinsed)
> 2 tablespoons chopped fresh dill
> 2 tablespoons chopped fresh basil
> 2 tablespoons chopped fresh chives
> 2 tablespoons apple cider or sherry vinegar, more as needed
> 1 tablespoon extra-virgin olive oil
> Kosher salt and freshly ground black pepper

Halve the cucumber lengthwise and scoop out and discard the seeds. If the cucumber is very fat, cut it in half lengthwise again. Cut the cucumber crosswise into 1/2-inch-wide half-moons and put in a large bowl.

Core the tomatoes, cut into 1/2-inch wedges, and add to the bowl along with the onion, chickpeas, herbs, vinegar, and olive oil, 3/4 teaspoon salt, and a few grinds of pepper. Toss to combine thoroughly.

Taste and add more salt or vinegar as needed.

Spicy String Beans with Black Sesame Seeds

SERVES 3 TO 4

We have an ongoing war among some of our staff members, and it centers around green beans. Our chef, Eddy, insists on cooking them just until al dente, whereas I cannot abide a crunchy green bean. It's entirely up to you, of course; the timing I give here is for making them the way *I* like them: fully cooked!

> Kosher salt
> 3/4 pound yellow or green string beans, trimmed
> 2 teaspoons rice vinegar
> 1/4 teaspoon sugar
> 1 teaspoon olive oil
> 1 teaspoon fish sauce
> 1/4 teaspoon sesame oil
> 1 small Thai bird chile, minced
> 1 1/2 teaspoons black or white sesame seeds (or a mixture)

Bring a large saucepan of well-salted water to a boil. Add the beans and cook until tender (or to your liking), 3 to 4 minutes. Strain the beans into a colander (do not rinse), then spread them on a towel-lined baking sheet. Let cool.

In a small bowl, combine the vinegar, sugar, and a big pinch of salt and whisk to dissolve. Add the olive oil, fish sauce, sesame oil, and chile and whisk again.

Put the beans in a large bowl and drizzle the dressing over. Sprinkle with the sesame seeds and toss well to combine.

Taste and season with more salt if desired.

Watermelon Agua Fresca with Mint

MAKES ABOUT 6 CUPS

When summer is in full swing and melons are fat and juicy, treat yourself to this delightful, kid-friendly beverage. You can use cantaloupe, honeydew, or a mixture of different melons. Watermelon works best on its own, though—its consistency doesn't jive with other kinds of melons.

For a more adult beverage, try spiking this with tequila or vodka!

- $1/2$ small watermelon (about 3 pounds)
- $1/4$ cup sugar, more as needed
- $1/4$ cup freshly squeezed lime or lemon juice, more as needed
- 16 large mint leaves (optional)
- 2 cups water

Cut off and discard the watermelon rind. Cut the fruit into 2-inch cubes, removing any seeds you encounter along the way.

Put half of the watermelon in a blender, along with half the sugar, half the lime juice, half the mint leaves (if using), and 1 cup of the water. Pulse and blend until you have a smooth mixture. Transfer the puree to another container and repeat with the remaining watermelon, sugar, lime juice, mint, and water.

Strain the puree, if desired. Taste the mixture and add more water, sugar, and/or lime juice as desired. Melons vary significantly in texture, sweetness, and acidity, so it's important to take the time to taste and tweak. (Don't worry if the sugar is still a little gritty; it'll dissolve completely as it chills.)

Refrigerate for at least 2 hours before serving.

Sergio's Gazpacho

MAKES ABOUT 7 CUPS

This is one of our deli's best-selling items in the summer. Two cups may seem like a lot of oil, but the soup really doesn't have the same rich flavor with any less (we've tried). You can, of course, reduce the amount if you like. You can also use any combination of Roma and heirloom tomatoes.

- 2 cups extra-virgin olive oil, more for drizzling (see Note)
- $1/4$ cup sherry vinegar, more as needed
- 1 teaspoon Tabasco or other hot pepper sauce
- $1/2$ medium red onion, peeled and cut into large chunks
- $1/2$ medium cucumber, trimmed and cut into large chunks
- Leaves from 6 large sprigs flat-leaf parsley
- 10 to 12 large fresh basil leaves
- 1 large clove garlic
- Kosher salt
- 4 medium Roma tomatoes, cored and cut into large chunks
- 3 medium heirloom tomatoes, cored and cut into large chunks

Put the oil, vinegar, and Tabasco in the bowl of a blender and blend briefly. Add the onion, cucumber, parsley, basil, garlic, and 1 tablespoon salt and blend until smooth. Add the tomatoes a few at a time, blending as you go. When the blender is about three-fourths full, pour out half of the liquid into a medium bowl. Continue to puree and add the tomatoes a few at a time until all the tomatoes are incorporated and the mixture is smooth. Pour the blender contents into the bowl and stir to blend.

If you want a super-smooth texture, pass the soup through a fine-mesh strainer.

Chill for at least 2 hours before serving. Whisk to blend, then taste and add more salt or vinegar as needed. Garnish each serving with a drizzle of extra-virgin olive oil.

Note: You can also substitute up to half of the extra-virgin olive oil with a mild or neutral oil, if you like.

Plum-Almond Cake

SERVES 10 TO 12

This is a wonderful, simple cake that stays very moist thanks to the almond paste. Although this version calls for plums, you can adapt it for every season by substituting blueberries, cooked apple chunks, ripe fuyu persimmons, or other types of stone fruit.

- 5 tablespoons (2$^1/_2$ ounces) unsalted butter, at room temperature, more for the pan
- 1 vanilla bean
- 4$^1/_4$ ounces (about 1 cup) cake flour
- 1 teaspoon baking powder
- $^1/_2$ teaspoon kosher salt
- 7 ounces ($^3/_4$ cup) almond paste (not marzipan, which is sweeter)
- $^3/_4$ cup sugar
- 5 large eggs
- 1 teaspoon pure vanilla extract
- 2 pounds plums (about 8 medium), cut into $^3/_4$-inch chunks

Position a rack in the center of the oven and heat to 350°F. Butter and flour a round 9-inch-wide by 2$^1/_2$-inch-tall cake pan and line the bottom with parchment.

Split the vanilla bean lengthwise and scrape the seeds from the pod. Transfer the seeds to a medium bowl and add the flour, baking powder, and salt. (To use the pod, place it in a jar and cover with sugar. After infusing for a month, the sugar will take on the vanilla flavor.) Whisk to blend (use your fingers to blend in the vanilla seeds) and set aside.

Combine the almond paste and sugar in the bowl of a stand mixer fitted with the paddle attachment. Beat on low speed until the almond paste breaks apart and starts to resemble fresh breadcrumbs, 1 to 2 minutes. Add the butter, increase the mixer speed to medium, and continue to mix until the crumbs start to aggregate into larger clumps, 2 minutes longer. Increase the speed to medium-high and with the motor running, add the eggs, one at a time, beating well after each addition and scraping the bowl as necessary. Add the vanilla extract and mix briefly to blend.

Add the flour mixture and mix on low speed until the batter just comes together, about 15 seconds. Remove the bowl from the mixer and gently fold in the plums.

Pour the batter into the pan and smooth the top. Bake until the top is dark golden brown and a skewer inserted into the center comes out clean, 65 to 70 minutes.

Let cool in the pan for 15 minutes, and then turn out onto a cooling rack. Let cool completely before serving.

Nectarine Buttermilk Upside-Down Cake

SERVES 10 TO 12

This is my favorite cake of all time. The buttermilk adds a nice acidity and helps create a moist, light crumb that is a perfect complement to the fruit.

This works just as well with pears, apples, and stone fruits; for best results, use fruit that is ripe but not too soft.

- ³/₄ cup (6 ounces) unsalted butter, at room temperature
- ³/₄ cup packed light brown sugar
- 4 medium (about 1¹/₄ pounds) nectarines, cut into ¹/₂-inch slices
- 1¹/₂ cups (6³/₄ ounces) all-purpose flour
- 2 teaspoons baking powder
- ¹/₂ teaspoon kosher salt
- ³/₄ cup granulated sugar
- 3 large eggs
- ¹/₂ cup buttermilk
- 2 teaspoons pure vanilla extract

Position a rack in the center of the oven and heat to 350°F.

In a small saucepan, melt 6 tablespoons of the butter over medium-low heat. Stir in the brown sugar and cook, stirring, until the sugar has melted and the mixture is smooth, about 4 minutes. Transfer to a round 9-inch-wide by 3-inch-tall cake pan, spreading the mixture evenly across the bottom. Arrange the nectarine slices on top of the butter mixture in an overlapping spiral pattern. When you've covered the bottom, build another layer of fruit on top, filling in any blank spaces left by the first layer. Set aside.

In a medium bowl, whisk together the flour, baking powder, and salt and set aside.

In a stand mixer fitted with the paddle attachment, combine the remaining 6 tablespoons butter with the granulated sugar. Beat on medium-high speed until light and fluffy, about 2 minutes. With the motor running, add the eggs, one at a time, beating well after each addition and scraping the bowl as needed.

Add the flour mixture and mix on low speed just until the batter comes together, about 15 seconds. Add the buttermilk and vanilla and mix again just until blended, about 10 seconds longer.

Spoon the batter over the fruit and gently smooth the top, being careful not to dislodge the fruit.

Bake until a wooden skewer inserted into the cake comes out clean, about 1 hour.

Let cool on a rack for 30 minutes. Then run a small knife around the edge of the pan and turn out onto a large plate or cake stand. The cake may resist releasing from the pan—if so, give the inverted pan a gentle up-and-down shake to help the cake slide out.

Let cool completely before serving.

The Portland Cooler

SERVES 1

Portland, Oregon, is one of my favorite places to visit—mainly to visit our dearest friends, but also for the fantastic foods and possibly the best farmers' market in the country. This drink was inspired by a magical afternoon there, spent distillery hopping on a bicycle. The bell pepper is a surprising ingredient; it adds a slight sweetness to this unique, very quaffable beverage.

> 1 strip red bell pepper (about $1/2$ inch wide by 3 to 4 inches long)
> 2 large mint leaves
> 2 ounces ($1/4$ cup) gin
> 2 ounces ($1/4$ cup) lime juice
> 1 ounce (2 tablespoons) strong simple syrup (see Tip)

Fill a cocktail shaker halfway with ice and add the pepper and mint. Use a muddler to crush and bruise the fresh ingredients thoroughly; the goal is to break some of the pepper into a coarse paste and release the aromatics from the mint. Add the gin, lime juice, and simple syrup, cover the shaker, and shake vigorously for 30 seconds.

Strain into a chilled martini glass and enjoy right away. I guarantee you won't stop at just one!

Tip: To make strong simple syrup, bring 1 cup water to a boil in a small saucepan. Add $1^{1}/_{2}$ cups sugar and stir until dissolved. Let cool, then store in the refrigerator.

Berry Simple Syrup

MAKES ABOUT 2 CUPS

This gorgeous syrup is a super easy way to preserve otherwise-fragile berries. Drizzle it over ice cream, mix it with seltzer for an Italian soda, or pair it with bourbon or gin in a cocktail.

> 1 pint (about 12 ounces) berries, any kind
> Juice and finely grated zest of 1 lemon
> $1^{1}/_{2}$ cups sugar
> $3/_{4}$ cup water

Gently rinse the berries, pat them dry, and put them in a medium heatproof bowl. Using a fork or potato masher, crush the berries into a relatively even consistency. Add the lemon juice and zest.

Combine the sugar and water in a small saucepan and put it over medium-high heat. Cook, stirring frequently, until all the sugar has dissolved. Pour the syrup over the berries and stir to combine.

Set aside and let cool to room temperature, then cover and refrigerate overnight. The next day, strain the mixture into a jar or bottle. (Enjoy the leftover fruit with ice cream or plain yogurt; otherwise, just discard it.)

Refrigerated, the syrup will keep for at least a month.

FALL

If I could choose one season to eat from all year long it would be fall. You still get a taste of summer produce—in my opinion, at its best due to extended time on trees or in the ground. Fruit tastes sweeter, tomatoes are more intense, and to top it off, you get to rejoice in all the new fall crops just starting to come to fruition: apples, pears, hard squash, and nuts. It's no wonder it's the time that everyone celebrates the harvest and gives thanks for what the earth has given us.

APPLES

Whenever I travel, I always try to hit the farmers' markets; I'm endlessly fascinated by the way that seasonality and culinary preferences vary from one place to the next. The last time I visited London, in November 2009, I was struck by all the apple varietals, many of which I had never encountered before. And the farmers I talked to were sheer experts, intimately in tune with each varietal's characteristics and unique pace of ripening. We Americans think of apples as "our" fruit, but that visit proved to me that the Brits could teach us a thing or two about them.

How to Buy

APPLES ARE VERY DIFFICULT TO GROW ORGANICALLY, mainly because of the pervasive and invasive codling moth. The moth enters during the tree's blooming phase and the moth's larvae chew their way through the fruit and leave unappetizing (albeit harmless) tunnels in their wake. For this reason, most commercial apple growers spray their trees with pesticides—often several types on a single tree. Many farmers spray only during the budding and flowering stage, which does limit the residue on the fruit itself.

ORGANIC APPLES ARE GREAT, BUT ARE NOT THE ONLY ANSWER. Buying organic apples is a sure-fire way to avoid the plague of pesticides. But don't pass up nonorganic apples without scrutiny; because the codling moth is so aggressive and so difficult to combat, many organically inclined apple farmers choose not to be certified, leaving the option to use pesticides if their crops do come under attack. In doing so, they farm with organic methods as much as possible and still minimize the risk of losing an entire orchard's worth of income. If you find a local source for apples that isn't organic, take the time to ask about their farming methods. You may find that the apples are "practically organic," just without the official certification.

TRY HEIRLOOM APPLES. Heirloom apples have always been around, but until recently they were mostly sold to juice and sauce processors. Now heirloom apple growers have finally found a market for their unique fruit. It's incredible how different one varietal can be from the next: not just in size and color, but also in density, acidity, sweetness, and aroma. They can be tart or sweet, crisp or buttery, honey-flavored or bracing, and everything in between.

Unlike the most commonly available apple varieties, many heirloom apples are not suited for long-term storage—part of the reason for their limited window of availability. Buying and eating heirloom fruits is the best way to ensure their future availability.

BEAUTIFUL APPLES ARE NOT ALWAYS MORE TASTY. Many producers coat their apples with a thin layer of wax to give them a sexy sheen—a practice that makes me cringe. Fruit should not be made up with cosmetics! Don't worry if apples have scarlike blemishes, either. They're sometimes caused by tree-wide disease, in which case the apples are unlikely to make it to market, but more commonly they appear from a

---

AT THE VERY LEAST, LOOK FOR APPLES THAT ARE:

- Organic, or organically grown
- Tasty, even if they look ugly
- Unwaxed

IDEALLY, LOOK FOR:

- Heirloom varieties
- In season, domesitically grown

hail strike or growing in contact with another apple. These blemishes have no effect on the apple's flavor.

You may see quality grades on the side of an apple crate; it simply refers to the size of the apples. If you see a lot of variation in a stack of apples, it probably means that the apples are being sorted manually and may also be from a smaller producer. That's a good thing to support, plus it's nice to choose exactly the size apple you want.

THE OUTSIDE OF AN APPLE WON'T TELL YOU MUCH ABOUT WHAT IT TASTES LIKE. The only way to know an apple's flavor or texture is to ask for a taste. Apples cease to ripen once they're picked, and an underripe-tasting apple isn't going to get any better. Choose apples that taste good now.

How to Store

Apples always taste best when they're freshly picked, but they store exceptionally well under the right conditions. Commercial producers keep their supply in ozone-controlled cold storage rooms, which stabilizes the fruit and keeps it from rotting. At home, keeping the apples as cold as possible is the key to their longevity. Put the apples in a paper bag and tuck it into the coldest part of the refrigerator (usually the back of the bottom drawer).

How to Use

If you plan to cook or bake with apples, be aware that some varieties lend themselves better to such pursuits than others. Generally, the ideal cooking apple has dense flesh that will stay intact when cooked and

PINK LADY

WINTER BANANA

JAZZ

TSUGARU

HAWAII

HONEYCRISP

GALA

JONATHAN

RED GRAVENSTEIN

SUMMERFIELD

MUTSU

GRAVENSTEIN

PINK PEARL

SANSA

JONAGOLD

ELSTAR

PIPPIN

enough acidity (tartness) to stand up to other flavors. Granny Smiths and Pippins are classics, but there are many others that work equally well. The best way to find a good cooking apple is to ask your grocer for advice and a sample.

For desserts, you don't need me to tell you to make an apple pie (but perhaps I can interest you in the Apple Cranberry Turnovers on page 164 instead). And although baked apples are fun, I prefer the sophistication of poached whole apples. To make them, just simmer peeled, cored apples in sweet dessert wine or flavored syrup until barely tender. Then halve them and serve with whipped cream, mascarpone, or a farmers' cheese, and finish with a drizzle of honey.

Apples are wonderful in salads and pair particularly well with fennel, lemon, goat cheese, and nuts. Try raw apples with steamed or roasted beets. Crisp apples are best; my favorites are Fuji, Gala, Mutsu, or the Pink Pearl, with its dramatic rose-colored flesh.

Apples are my secret ingredient for pureed soups; they add a nice sweet-acid kick to soups featuring earthy root vegetables or sweet squashes. I usually dice the apples and sauté them along with the onions and other aromatics before adding the simmering liquid. This addition works in just about any pureed vegetable soup recipe. Pippins, Granny Smith, Graventsteins, and Arkansas Blacks work really well.

If you're planning on cooking apples, you don't have to worry about the discoloration that happens as the cut flesh is exposed to oxygen (cooking darkens the fruit anyway, and the oxidation doesn't affect the taste). However, if you want to use apples raw—especially if you want to prepare them ahead of time—you can stall the oxidation with the addition of acid. Peel and/or slice the apples as desired, then put them in a bowl with a tablespoon or two of lemon juice and toss to coat evenly.

APPLE HILL RANCH:
Ned and Mariette Mogannam

It was the upsell of the century when my parents stopped by Apple Hill Ranch in 2001. They were passing through Placerville, California, an area dotted with apple orchards, roadside stands, and U-Pick operations, on their way back to San Francisco from Lake Tahoe. On a whim, they pulled over for a bushel of apples, but they ended up buying the entire ranch! (They mentioned how beautiful it was, the owner responded with "You think so? It's for sale!" and the rest was history.) My parents now spend about half their time up there. Dad tends to the orchard, which includes apple, kiwi, fig, and Asian pear trees, as well as blueberry and blackberry bushes, tomato plants, and many other fruits and vegetables. Mom "puts up" the fruits as jams, jellies, and preserves, all of which are sold at the Market, along with fresh produce harvested from their ranch.

BRUSSELS SPROUTS

It took us a long time to get our guests to warm up to brussels sprouts. Most people have tasted only sprouts that have been boiled to oblivion, so they're associated with mushy texture, sulfurous odor, and—let's face it—a gassy aftermath. At the Market, we roast our brussels sprouts until golden and tender—a much more appetizing preparation—and we actively give out samples of them to our guests. Now brussels sprouts are one of the most popular veggies in the deli case.

How to Buy

Unless you've seen them at the farmers' market, you may be surprised to learn that brussels sprouts grow on a stalk. They look like a prehistoric weapon of sorts—a clublike stem studded on one end with the little heads. Brussels sprouts are best early in their season (October and November); in the later months they get tougher and a bit more bitter.

THE SMALLER THE SPROUT, THE SWEETER AND MORE TENDER IT WILL BE. But even large brussels sprouts will still be tasty. It helps to pick sprouts that are all about the same size, as they'll cook more evenly if you choose to leave them whole. Choose brussels sprouts whose leaves are bright green and feel compactly formed; expect a few loose leaves on the outside, but pass on any where the head "gives" when you squeeze it.

How to Store

Store brussels sprouts in a plastic bag in the refrigerator for up to a week. When you're ready to cook, remove loose or darker outer leaves, trim any discolored areas off of the stem end, and give them a good soak in a bowl of warm water if they're particularly sandy.

How to Use

If you've only ever had boiled brussels sprouts—and especially if you hate brussels sprouts—do me a favor and try roasting them. **ROASTING DOES ITS MOST IMPRESSIVE WORK ON BRUSSELS SPROUTS.** The high heat not only drives off some of the moisture and concentrates the flavors as it tenderizes the leaves, but it

> **AT THE VERY LEAST, LOOK FOR BRUSSELS SPROUTS THAT ARE**
> - On the small side
> - Bright green, with no yellowing or black spotting
> - Compact and firm

also results in wonderful caramelization. Start with the Roasted Cauliflower and Brussels Sprouts with Caper Lemon Butter on page 99. Or try your own roasting recipe—just make sure the sprouts are all about the same size (halve or quarter them if necessary) to ensure even cooking.

SAUTÉING HAS SIMILAR POSITIVE EFFECTS on brussels sprouts, although you won't get quite the same caramelization as with roasting. One of my favorite stove top preparations is to separate the heads into individual leaves and sauté them in a hot skillet. It's a fairly labor-intensive process to pick off all those leaves; you can achieve a similar effect by cutting the heads into very thin slices, either by hand or in a food processor with the slicer blade.

YOU CAN ALSO EAT THINLY SLICED BRUSSELS SPROUTS RAW. Toss them with a little vinaigrette or a gussied-up mayo to make a delicate coleslaw-type dish, or top them with a warm dressing to gently "melt" the leaves, as in the Brussels Sprout Salad with Pistachios and Warm Bacon Vinaigrette on page 162.

Brussels sprouts like fat and acid, which help smooth over their inherent earthy pungency. Think bacon fat, brown butter, and lemon zest or juice. They also love nuts, especially pistachios, hazelnuts, and almonds.

FIGS

Sometimes the best produce comes from the most unexpected places. Several years ago, a couple of hippies pulled up in front of our store—they had driven down from Humboldt County (about six hours north of San Francisco). They opened up the back of their beat-up sedan to reveal flats of the most beautiful Adriatic figs: their deep green exteriors were elegantly streaked with cracks and seams, and a bite revealed the dark ruby flesh inside. We bought everything they had, but still they were so good that we sold out in a single day. The guys didn't have a phone number, so we had no way to order more from them. We just had to hope they'd come back—which they do, now and again, each time with something different to sell. Whatever it is, it's always incredible.

How to Buy

It's a shame so many people hate figs. I suppose that culturally we tend to be biased against slimy foods, or foods with lots of seeds, but more often, I think premature picking is to blame. When underripe, figs are slightly astringent and have a firm, almost fibrous interior. Figs are often picked prematurely because ripe ones are so fragile and can't withstand traveling long distances. Once picked, underripe figs can soften a bit, but the sugars and flavors will not continue to develop much. But when they're allowed to ripen on the tree, they have a creamy, nectary center that's bursting with luscious sugar. Put simply, a fig's perfection lies in its excess.

FIG LEAVES

Fig leaves are incredible to cook with—they're very common in Provençal cooking, but hard to find here. The leaves are not edible but they perfume other foods with an incredible coconuty aroma. Perfectly sized to wrap around individual fish fillets, they can then be grilled or oven-roasted; when served, peeling away the leaves unleashes a steamy puff of transcendent perfume.

LOOK FOR FIGS THAT HAVE:

- **A soft, delicate feel**
- **Cracked skin**
- **Deep, intense color**
- **Somewhat shriveled stems**

Ripe figs don't have a telltale scent, so most of the sure-fire signs of ripeness are tactile and visual:

- **Soft to the touch**, which indicates fully ripe, mature fruit.
- **Cracked skin**, a sign that the fruit is literally bursting at the seams with sugar and juice.
- **Saturated color**—for black figs, that means a deep purple-blue hue almost like the ink of a ballpoint pen (they start out charcoalish and take on a dark blue hue as they ripen). Green figs become a yellow chartreuse color as they approach peak ripeness, and brown figs become a deep purple.
- **Slightly shriveled stems**, rather than stiff, rounded ones. As figs ripen on the tree, the stem dries out and shrinks, which is what makes the fruit fall from the tree. Full round stems sometimes mean that the fruit was picked before its time.

How to Store

Because of their fragility, you should eat figs within a few days of buying them. Any longer than that and you risk their molding—especially if they're very ripe. If you plan to eat them with in a day or two, keep them at room temperature—otherwise, refrigerate them; to extend their shelf life, spread them in a single layer on a plate to maximize air circulation and forestall mold.

How to Use

Versatile figs can be used in both sweet and savory dishes. Figs pair particularly well with other strongly flavored ingredients.

- **Sweet and/or acidic liquids** like honey, balsamic vinegar, or aged sherry vinegar. Drizzle on directly.
- **Salty, aged, or tangy cheeses** like Parmigiano, creamy Gorgonzola, or fresh goat cheese. Halved lengthwise, the cut surface makes the perfect little platform for any of these cheeses.
- **Peppery and bitter greens** like arugula and radicchio that are tempered by figs' sweetness.
- **Aromatics** like thyme, mint, and citrus zest. Sprinkle them on or mix with whatever cheese or drizzling liquid you're using.
- **Salty or smoked meats** like bacon, pancetta, or prosciutto.

  WHOLE OR HALVED, I ALSO LOVE TO ROAST, GRILL, AND BROIL FIGS. I'm not talking about cooking the figs fully, but rather a quick and strategic blast of heat—just enough for the natural sugars to caramelize. This is the perfect way to try figs if you haven't liked them in the past; I've converted many a fig-hater with a platter of figs that have been wrapped in prosciutto, grilled, and drizzled with a splash of sherry vinegar (as in the recipe on page 160).

· ·

If you happen to buy less-than-fully-ripe figs, cooking them is a great way to go.

· ·

Given their luscious natural sugar and viscosity, figs make the most amazing jam—just dice them and cook with a little sugar and lemon juice until they begin to break down. Refrigerated, this quick jam will keep for two to three weeks.

GRAPES

Before the store got big enough to hire a produce buyer, it was my job (among others) to go to the wholesale produce market every week and place our orders. I would walk the aisles, tasting along the way, and by the end of the excursion I often found myself with a roaring headache. Finally I realized that the headaches came on within minutes of eating conventionally grown grapes; I did some research and found that grapes are one of the most heavily sprayed crops, and I realized that the pesticides and fungicides were affecting me in a big way. Since making that connection, I've tasted (and bought) only organic grapes, and now those headaches are a thing of the past.

How to Buy

Most of the grapes sold in this country are heavily sprayed with pesticides. During the off season, grapes are predominantly sourced from Chile, where pesticides and fungicides are used in even greater quantities. Wherever they're from, make sure the grapes you buy are organic or unsprayed.

Interesting varietals of grapes are increasingly available, from the pink-blushed Bronx (a cross between Concord and Thompson) to the delicate champagne variety (which is not used for winemaking but named after the tiny fruit's resemblance to fizzy bubbles) that dries into currants.

Just-picked grapes will have robust, green stems; however, grapes store exceptionally well, and in that process the stems will start to brown and dry out.

> ### AT THE VERY LEAST, LOOK FOR GRAPES THAT ARE:
> - Organic or unsprayed
> - Taut enough to "pop" when you bite into one
>
> ### IDEALLY, LOOK FOR:
> - Unusual varieties such as Crimson, Concord, Bronx seedless, and Scarlet Royal

TOP ROW: Crimson, Thompson, Concord, Bronx   **MIDDLE:** Pristine, Fantasy, Scarlet Royal, Muscat, Peony
BOTTOM: Kyoto, Champagne, Princess, Black, Chardonnay

The most important quality to look for is in the fruit itself, so go ahead and taste one. **THE SKIN SHOULD BE TAUT AROUND THE FRUIT AND GIVE A GOOD POP WHEN YOU BITE INTO IT.**

If the grapes are already in a bag, avoid any that have moisture collecting at the bottom. It's a sign that the fruit has started to break down.

How to Store

Store grapes in a paper or perforated plastic bag in the refrigerator for up to a week.

How to Use

You rarely see cooked grapes, but I find that it concentrates the fruit's flavors and makes them much more interesting. One easy way to do this is to roast them: just spray a whole cluster of grapes with olive oil and balsamic vinegar and bake in a hot oven until the fruit pops open. These make a fantastic garnish for cheese or crostini, nestled alongside a serving of chicken or pork, or even as a topping for pizza or focaccia.

PEARS

One of my favorite simple pleasures is opening a crate of pears when they come into the store. The fruits ripen a great deal as they're shipped, and in that process the fruit gets incredibly fragrant. The fragrance stays contained within the case until opening, which releases a huge waft of floral and honey aromas. When that happens, I just want to stand there and drink in that perfume of pears!

How to Buy

Pears are one of the few fruits for which full ripening on the tree results in inferior fruit—instead of reaching juicy lusciousness, tree-ripened pears become mealy and unpleasant. So most farmers pick pears when they're still underripe and let them ripen off the tree. In a sense, this makes pears an easy fruit to shop for because **YOU CAN BUY UNDERRIPE ONES KNOWING THAT THEY WILL EVENTUALLY RIPEN AT HOME.** The only real challenge comes in timing (and, perhaps, patience).

> **FOR EATING RIGHT AWAY, LOOK FOR PEARS THAT ARE:**
> - Aromatic
> - A little soft, even with a little bruising or soft spots
> - Slightly wrinkled near the stem
>
> **FOR EATING LATER, LOOK FOR PEARS THAT ARE:**
> - Firm, with securely attached stems
> - Not fully saturated in color

If you see pears with French names, buy them. Comice and Concorde are two of my favorites for their silky texture, perfumey aroma, and delicate sweetness. Bartletts and Warrens are two others worth seeking out. They're firmer, but still delicious. The best cooking pear is the Bosc, which maintains its shape and texture when poached or roasted.

Asian pears are an altogether different breed. More like apples, they should be eaten when firm. They should have a floral aroma and saturated color. These are amazing eaten out of hand or sliced into salad.

FOR EATING RIGHT AWAY, LOOK FOR PEARS THAT ARE AROMATIC, WITH A SLIGHT SOFTNESS and maybe even a few little dings or bruises (a sign that the sugars have developed). Steer clear of pears with excessive surface damage.

CHECK THE STEMS; when ripe, they will have a bit of give, and the skin around them will wrinkle slightly.

IF YOU WANT TO BUY A LITTLE TIME, LOOK FOR PEARS THAT ARE FIRM AND HAVEN'T YET DEVELOPED THEIR FULL SATURATED COLOR. A securely attached (not loose feeling) stem is another sign that you have a few days before the pear reaches its peak.

How to Store

Store pears at room temperature; to speed ripening, put them in a paper bag.

How to Use

You can use pears as a substitute for apples in just about any recipe, whether it's raw in salads or with cheeses, cooked into chutneys or jams, or pureed into soups. I even add them to my Thanksgiving stuffing, along with a chopped apple or two.

RIPE PEARS BREAK DOWN INTO MUSH WHEN THEY COOK, so unless you want to make pear puree, cook with ones that are a day or two away from full ripeness.

Pears don't have much acid of their own, and they really come to life with the addition of lemon juice or other tart ingredients.

Underripe pears have an astringent quality that can be unpleasant. If you have to use pears that are underripe, you can reduce the astringency by peeling them.

PERSIMMONS

The Japanese have a wonderful method of drying persimmons, called *hoshigaki*. Hachiya persimmons are peeled and suspended from threads, and every few days the fruit is massaged to soften the dried surface and break up the pulp inside. After several weeks, the persimmons are firm and dry, with a natural crystalline exterior from the fruit's sugars. This labor-intensive (and increasingly scarce) technique is a prime example of how devoted attention alone can completely transform an ingredient.

How to Buy

The most important thing to know about persimmons is that there are two distinct varieties: the squat and rounded fuyu and the acorn-shaped hachiya. Although their flavors are similar, they have very different textures when ripe, and thus are not interchangeable.

FUYU persimmons are firm and a little crunchy, even when they're fully ripe. Look for deep, saturated orange color (paler ones are likely to be somewhat astringent). A tiny bit of wrinkling around the leaves means they're mature and the flavors are concentrated. If you see black spots, don't worry; they don't affect the flavor.

HACHIYA persimmons ripen in a dramatic way. They start out hard and so tannic as to be inedible. During the ripening process the tannins are replaced by sweetness as the flesh breaks down into a soft, intensely flavored pulp. Once they reach that point, they are highly perishable, so it's pretty rare to find fully ripe hachiya persimmons for sale. However, time is all you'll need to ripen them yourself. As with fuyus, black spots are nothing to worry about (in fact, they're all but inevitable).

How to Store

BOTH TYPES OF PERSIMMONS WILL CONTINUE TO RIPEN AFTER PICKING. If you want to slow down the ripening process, keep them in the refrigerator; to let them ripen at their normal pace, leave them out on your kitchen counter. Hachiyas should be completely soft to the touch and look almost overripe before eating.

How to Use

You can eat fuyus like an apple or sautéed or grilled—they pair especially well with pork or aged cheeses such as Manchego or pecorino. They shine in salads, particularly with peppery greens (try them instead of apricots in the Apricot and Arugula Salad with Fresh Ricotta on page 250).

When fully ripe, hachiyas are soft enough to spoon right out of the skin and eat as is. Their intense flavor also complements desserts that are rich with eggs or cream. Made into a pudding, they are the essence of fall wrapped up in warm spices—and they are also great in ice cream.

POMEGRANATES

Even though I grew up in the Market, my mom would still do some of her shopping at neighborhood produce stands. One day when I was about seven, she sent me out to buy a few pomegranates. Always a savvy shopper, she gave me very specific instructions for the vendor: "Tell him that if they're not good, I'm going to go wring his neck!" I dutifully relayed the message, at which he laughed and laughed! But sure enough, it worked; he went into the back and picked out two enormous pomegranates, telling me, "If you drop them, I'm going to blame you!" I carefully carried them home, and they were some of the best pomegranates I've ever eaten.

How to Buy

A couple of years ago just before Thanksgiving, I came across a couple of my produce staff who were culling out and discarding cracked pomegranates. I rushed over with a "Nooooo!" We opened a few together, and those guys immediately understood that split skin on a pomegranate is actually a good sign.

THE VERY BEST POMEGRANATES ARE HEAVY AND EVEN HAVE CRACKED SKIN—both are signs that the fruit inside is juicy, abundant, and bursting with flavor. Pomegranates are fairly fragile and need to be handled carefully. If they're bumped or beaten around, the fruit inside ruptures and breaks down quickly.

THE SKIN OF A POMEGRANATE BEGINS TO DRY OUT AFTER IT'S PICKED. It's okay if it is a little leathery, but if it looks tight and hard like a dried-out lemon, you know the fruit is past its prime.

How to Store

Store pomegranates in a paper bag in the refrigerator.

How to Use

Pomegranates are a true test of patience. You can't just pick one up and start eating it as you continue on your way, as you can a banana or an apple. Instead, you have to plant yourself down and commit to plucking each little jewel out of its casing. It's so worth it, though!

WITH POMEGRANATES, THE GOAL IS TO BREAK OPEN THE FRUIT WITHOUT RUPTURING THE SEEDS. In some cultures, folks cut the pomegranate in half and beat the seeds out, but that seems so bizarre and counterproductive. I prefer a method that keeps the fruit intact and doesn't result in loss of juice: score the skin all the way around into quarters, and stick a knife into the stem end. Use the leverage of the knife to pry the sections apart, and then use your thumb to pry the seeds from the skin. Once all the seeds are loose, scoop your hands through them, letting the seeds fall through your fingers; the membranes will stick to your hands and can be discarded.

POMEGRANATE SEEDS ADD INTEREST TO SALADS, COUSCOUS, LAMB, OR ANY KIND OF SWEET RISOTTO-TYPE DISH. My mom makes a sort of rice pudding using wheatberries cooked with water, sugar, and cinnamon, which she finishes with butter and pomegranate seeds. The warm, comforting wheatberries are a perfect contrast to the cool freshness of the pomegranate seeds. Plus, it's very healthy, as desserts go.

POMEGRANATE SEEDS ALSO MAKE A STUNNING GARNISH for just about any dessert. Sprinkle them over cupcakes, panna cotta, custard, or pudding for instant glam.

Garlic Confit

YIELDS AS MUCH AS YOU CHOOSE TO MAKE!

In the Market's kitchen, we make this in mass quantities and use it for all kinds of things. The gentle cooking method produces garlic cloves that are meltingly soft and delicate in flavor, making them easy to blend into mashed potatoes, mayonnaise, salad dressings, or even spread onto sandwiches. The poaching oil becomes infused with garlic flavor; use it in place of olive oil in any savory recipe. (Brushed onto baguette slices, it makes incredible crostini, too.)

2 to 3 heads garlic, cloves trimmed and peeled
Kosher salt
Extra-virgin olive oil, as needed

Position a rack in the center of the oven and heat to 325°F.

Put the garlic in a small baking dish (see Note) along with a pinch or two of salt and just enough oil to cover (the exact amount will depend on the size and shape of your vessel). Cover tightly with aluminum foil.

Bake until the garlic is completely soft and just barely starting to turn color, about 40 minutes. (Check the progress periodically and be careful not to let the garlic brown, as this makes the garlic bitter and tough.) Remove from the oven and let cool to room temperature.

At this point, you can leave the mixture as is, or puree all or part of it in a blender or food processor (this makes it easier to add to soups, dressings, and marinades). Transfer to a storage container. Refrigerated, it will keep for several weeks.

Note: You can use just about any oven-safe vessel for this, including a sauté pan or saucepan, as long as you cover it tightly. Deep vessels with a small diameter will require less oil than broad shallow ones.

Sautéed Figs with Prosciutto and Parmigiano

MAKES 16 WRAPPED FIGS; SERVES 4 TO 6

Like the grilled peaches on page 249, these figs can be served as an hors d'oeuvre, as the anchor for a green salad, or as a garnish for roast pork.

Because you're wrapping the prosciutto around the figs, it's best to use slices from the widest part of the ham. If the prosciutto is smaller, buy two slices per fig and use toothpicks to secure the prosciutto around the figs.

1 small chunk Parmigiano-Reggiano cheese
8 large fresh figs
8 thin slices prosciutto
Extra-virgin olive oil for brushing
1¹/₂ tablespoons aged sherry or balsamic vinegar

Use a vegetable peeler to shave the Parmigiano into shards. Set aside.

Cut the figs in half lengthwise, and cut the prosciutto slices in half lengthwise as well. Wrap a piece of prosciutto around each fig, then brush lightly with the olive oil.

Heat a large skillet (ideally cast iron) or a grill pan over medium-high heat. When hot, arrange half the figs in a roomy single layer, cut side down, in the pan. Cook until the prosciutto is browned and crispy, 1¹/₂ to 2 minutes. Then flip the figs and repeat on the other side. Transfer to a serving platter and cook the remaining figs in the same way.

Drizzle the vinegar over the figs and top with Parmigiano shavings. Serve warm or at room temperature.

Savory Pear Chutney with Dried Cherries and Ginger

MAKES ABOUT 3 CUPS

Although it might sound exotic, savory chutney has a time-honored place on nearly every American's Thanksgiving table in the form of cranberry sauce. Chutneys are flexible, versatile condiments that add a nice sweet-sour note to roasted meats, sandwiches, and cheese platters.

Although sour cherries add a lovely tangy punch to this chutney, you could also use golden raisins, dried cranberries, diced dried apricots, or nearly any other dried fruit. Instead of the pears, you can use apples—as long as it's a variety that will hold its shape after cooking.

This is best made a day or two in advance so all the flavors have a chance to come together.

1/2 cup halved dried cherries, preferably a sour variety such as Morello
1 cup boiling water
2 tablespoons extra-virgin olive oil
1 small yellow onion, finely diced
Kosher salt
2 tablespoons minced fresh ginger
1 tablespoon yellow mustard seeds
Pinch of ground cardamom
3 tablespoons champagne or sherry vinegar
2 tablespoons brandy
Scant 4 cups peeled, diced Bosc pears (about 3)
2 teaspoons sugar
Kosher salt

In a small bowl, combine the cherries and boiling water and set aside for at least 10 minutes. Strain, reserving the liquid.

Heat the oil in a medium saucepan over medium-high heat. Add the onion and a pinch of salt and cook, stirring, until soft and golden on the edges, 3 to 4 minutes. Add the ginger, mustard seeds, and cardamom and stir constantly until fragrant, about 1 minute longer.

Add the vinegar and brandy and stir constantly to loosen the browned bits from the bottom of the pan. Cook until the liquid has reduced by half, about 1 minute. Add the pears, sugar, drained cherries, 1/4 teaspoon salt, and 1/2 cup of the reserved soaking liquid.

Bring the liquid to a boil, partially cover the pan, and lower the heat to maintain a gentle simmer. Cook, stirring occasionally, until the pears are just tender and the flavors have melded, about 15 minutes. (It will still be fairly liquidy, but it will thicken as it cools.)

Serve warm or at room temperature. Refrigerated, this keeps for up to 7 days. You can also process it in Mason jars and keep it for up to a year.

GABRIEL FARM: Torrey Olson

Torrey Olson just couldn't leave well enough alone. His fourteen-acre organic orchard in Sebastopol, California, was already known for producing some of the most succulent, perfumey Asian pears, apples, and persimmons around. But Torrey decided to up his own ante and started using his fruit as the base for other products: everything from conserves to Asian pear juice. They're all delicious, but my favorite by far is his Asian Pear Eau-de-Vie. Made in the tradition of France's Poire William, Torrey's pear brandy sports a small Asian pear right in the bottle. It's a subtle but potent reminder that the best spirits start with real produce that's grown with care.

Brussels Sprouts Salad with Pistachios and Warm Bacon Vinaigrette

SERVES 4 TO 6

Brussels sprouts are rarely eaten raw, but they are amazing served this way. This salad is great served solo or as an accompaniment for pork chops, roast chicken, or even game meat. The fresh horseradish garnish is optional, but it lends a wonderful kick!

- 1¼ pounds brussels sprouts
- 6 thick slices bacon, cooked crisp and crumbled, fat drained and reserved
- Extra-virgin olive oil, as needed
- Freshly squeezed juice of 1 lemon
- 1½ tablespoons sherry vinegar
- 1 small shallot, minced (about 1 tablespoon)
- 1½ teaspoons minced garlic
- ¼ teaspoon honey
- Kosher salt
- ¼ cup lightly chopped toasted pistachios
- 1-inch knob fresh horseradish, peeled (optional)

Peel off and discard the darker outer leaves of the sprouts and trim any discolored areas from the stem ends. Cut the sprouts in half lengthwise, then slice them crosswise very thinly—about ¹⁄₁₆ inch. (Alternatively, you can use a food processor fitted with the slicer attachment, but the cuts will not be as clean.) Transfer to a large heatproof bowl, add the bacon, and set aside.

Measure ¼ cup of the reserved bacon fat into a small pan and warm over low heat until liquified (if you don't have enough bacon fat, make up the difference with olive oil). Remove from the heat and whisk in the lemon juice, vinegar, shallot, garlic, honey, and ¼ teaspoon salt. Drizzle the dressing over the brussels sprouts and toss well. Taste and season with more salt as necessary.

If you have time, let the salad sit out for 30 minutes or so before proceeding—in this time, the dressing helps the sprouts soften a bit.

Just before serving, top with the toasted pistachios; if using the horseradish, use a microplane grater to shave a little over the top as well.

Apple, Pear, and Spinach Salad with Walnuts and Blue Cheese

SERVES 4 TO 6

This is one of our all-time classic salads. It's easy to see why it's so popular: it has the perfect combination of sweet fruit, crunchy nuts, tangy cheese, and tender spinach, bound together by a delicate vinaigrette. It's substantial yet not too heavy, perfectly suited as an accompaniment to other dishes.

- 1 tablespoon minced shallot
- 1½ teaspoons champagne vinegar, more as needed
- ½ teaspoon Dijon mustard
- ½ teaspoon minced fresh thyme
- ½ teaspoon honey
- Kosher salt and freshly ground black pepper
- 1 tablespoon extra-virgin olive oil
- 1 medium pear, cored and thinly sliced
- 1 small apple, cored and thinly sliced
- 2 teaspoons freshly squeezed lemon juice
- 3 cups lightly packed baby spinach (about 3¾ ounces)
- ⅓ cup coarsely chopped toasted walnuts or pecans
- ⅓ cup crumbled blue cheese

In a small bowl, whisk together the shallot, vinegar, mustard, thyme, honey, ½ teaspoon salt, and a grind or two of pepper. Continue to whisk as you drizzle in the olive oil. Dip a spinach leaf into the dressing and taste. Add more vinegar or salt as needed. Set aside.

Put the pear and apple in a large bowl, drizzle the lemon juice over them, and toss gently until the slices are evenly coated. Add the spinach and all but a tablespoon each of the walnuts and cheese, and drizzle with 1 tablespoon of the dressing. Toss and taste the salad. Add more dressing or vinegar, salt, and pepper as needed. Sprinkle the remaining walnuts and cheese over the salad.

Curried Coconut
Sweet Potato Mash

MAKES 4 CUPS; SERVES 6 TO 8

So many sweet potato recipes call for lots of additional sugar, which can produce cloyingly sweet results. Wow your guests with this version, which uses mild curry powder, a tiny bit of cayenne, and coconut milk to complement the natural sweetness of the potatoes.

2¹/₂ pounds sweet potatoes (3 or 4 large), scrubbed and cut into 1¹/₂-inch chunks

4 tablespoons (¹/₄ cup) unsalted butter

1 tablespoon mild curry powder

¹/₄ teaspoon ground cinnamon

Pinch of cayenne pepper

³/₄ cup coconut milk (see Tip)

Kosher salt

1 teaspoon freshly squeezed lemon juice, more as needed

6 tablespoons toasted coconut flakes, sweetened or unsweetened (see Note)

Fit a steamer basket into a large pot, add water just to the bottom of the basket, and arrange the sweet potatoes in a snug layer in the basket. Bring the water to a boil over medium-high heat, cover the pot, and lower the heat to maintain a vigorous simmer. Cook until the potatoes are completely tender when pierced with a skewer, 15 to 20 minutes. (Keep an eye on the water level during cooking, and add more if it threatens to boil off.) Remove from the heat, carefully remove the potatoes from the basket, and set aside.

Pour the water out of the pot and return to medium heat. Add the butter, curry, cinnamon, and cayenne and cook, stirring constantly, until the butter is melted and the spices are fragrant, about 2 minutes. Add the coconut milk and 1¹/₂ teaspoons salt, bring to a simmer, and cook for an additional minute to thicken slightly. Remove from the heat and stir in the lemon juice.

Carefully peel off and discard the potato skins. Add the potatoes to the pot and mash until smooth and all ingredients are blended. (At this point you can adjust the consistency of the potatoes by adding up to ¹/₂ cup of water.) Taste and add more salt or lemon juice as needed. If necessary, rewarm over low heat, stirring constantly.

To serve, transfer to a serving dish and top with the coconut.

You can make these potatoes up to a day ahead. Reheat in a covered ovenproof dish in a 350°F oven until heated through, about 40 minutes. Garnish just before serving.

Note: To toast coconut, spread it in an even layer on a rimmed baking sheet and bake in a 350°F oven, stirring occasionally, until golden.

Tip: Make sure you use coconut milk (which is unsweetened) and not coconut cream (which has a hefty dose of sugar added). And because the fatty coconut solids rise to the top, it's always a good idea to whisk the entire contents of the can before measuring out the amount you need.

Apple Cranberry Turnovers
MAKES 8 LARGE TURNOVERS

This dough is quite versatile and works for savory empanadas just as well as for sweet tarts and turnovers. It's also incredibly easy to work with; not only does it resist sticking, but it's almost impossible to overwork. (The secret is the cream cheese!) If you can, make a double batch of the dough and freeze for later use.

1¼ cups (2½ sticks) unsalted butter, at room temperature

6 ounces cream cheese, at room temperature

2⅔ cups (12 ounces) all-purpose flour, more for rolling

Kosher salt

¼ cup packed light brown sugar

4 medium apples (about 1½ pounds), peeled, cored, and sliced ¼ inch thick

¾ cup fresh or frozen cranberries

½ teaspoon freshly squeezed lemon juice

1 large egg, lightly beaten

About ¼ cup turbinado sugar (or granulated), for sprinkling

Put 1 cup (2 sticks) of the butter in the bowl of a stand mixer and beat on medium until smooth, about 30 seconds. Scrape down the sides of the bowl, add the cream cheese, and mix on medium to blend, 30 seconds longer.

Scrape the bowl again, add the flour and ½ teaspoon salt, and mix on low speed just until it comes together in a ball. Divide the dough in half and shape each half into a square slab. Wrap with plastic wrap and chill for at least 3 hours, or overnight.

Meanwhile, put the remaining ¼ cup (½ stick) butter, the light brown sugar, and a pinch of salt in a large skillet over medium heat. When the butter is melted, add the apples and cook, stirring frequently, until they start to soften, 8 to 10 minutes. Mix in the cranberries and lemon juice and let cool completely.

When you're ready to roll the dough, position racks in the top and bottom thirds of the oven and heat to 350°F. Line 2 large rimmed baking sheets with parchment or a nonstick liner.

Transfer one half of the dough to a lightly floured work surface and roll it out into a 12-inch square about ⅛ inch thick. You won't have much excess dough, so trim and reposition pieces of the edge to make a straight-sided square, pressing seams firmly to seal. Cut the dough into four 6-inch squares and set aside. Repeat with the other half of the dough.

Divide the apple filling among the dough squares, leaving at least a ½-inch border around the edge. Brush the borders lightly with the beaten egg and fold each square in half to make a triangle. Use a fork to crimp the edges and ensure a good seal.

Transfer to the 2 baking sheets, spacing them evenly apart. Brush the tops of the turnovers with egg and sprinkle generously with the turbinado sugar. Cut 3 small slits into the top of each turnover.

Bake for 15 minutes and then rotate the sheets top to bottom and front to back. Continue to bake until golden brown and you can see the filling bubbling through the slits, about 15 minutes longer.

Let cool slightly on the baking sheets. Serve warm or at room temperature.

Note: These turnovers can easily be assembled and then frozen. Freeze them on the lined baking sheet; when solid, transfer to a zip-top bag and seal. They'll keep for up to 2 months this way. When ready to bake, arrange on a baking sheet and bake as directed—they'll just take an extra 10 minutes or so in the oven.

Mom's Pear Skillet Cake

SERVES 8

The recipe for this homey cake comes from my mom, who made it for us to sell at my restaurant and then in the early days of the Market.

I think that cast-iron skillets are one of the most versatile and indispensible cooking vessels you can have, and this cake is proof of that!

6 medium Bosc pears (about 3^1/$_3$ pounds)

6 tablespoons (3 ounces) unsalted butter

^{3}/$_4$ cup packed light brown sugar

1^1/$_3$ cups (6 ounces) all-purpose flour

^{2}/$_3$ cup granulated sugar

3 tablespoons minced crystallized ginger

1 teaspoon ground cinnamon

1 teaspoon baking soda

^{1}/$_2$ teaspoon ground ginger

^{1}/$_2$ teaspoon table salt

3 large eggs

^{1}/$_2$ cup grapeseed or other neutral oil

1 teaspoon pure vanilla extract

1 teaspoon finely grated orange zest

Position a rack in the center of the oven and heat to 350°F.

Peel, quarter, and core 4 of the pears and set aside. Peel and grate the other 2 and set them aside separately.

In a 10-inch cast-iron skillet, melt the butter over low heat. Remove from the heat and sprinkle the brown sugar over the butter. Arrange the quartered pears on the sugar; if necessary, trim a few pieces to fit and fill the center.

Combine the flour, granulated sugar, crystallized ginger, cinnamon, baking soda, ground ginger, and salt in a medium bowl and whisk to blend. In a separate large bowl, whisk the eggs, oil, vanilla, and orange zest until blended. Stir in the grated pears. Add the flour mixture and stir just until blended.

Pour the batter over the pears and smooth the top. Bake until the cake is deep golden brown and a toothpick inserted into the center comes out clean, about 40 minutes. Cool the cake in the skillet for 20 minutes, then run a knife around the edge of the pan and turn out onto a plate. Serve warm or at room temperature.

5

THE BUTCHER COUNTER

I started out as a restaurant cook, a job that is all about preparing and nurturing proteins to make a finished product. But here at the Market, I get the chance to delve deeper—I get to develop relationships with ranchers and learn how they treat their animals. It gives you greater respect for what it takes to raise an animal and turn it into food, from the field all the way to the point of enjoying it as a meal.

One of the biggest challenges of working with smaller ranchers, rather than buying industrially produced meat, is teaching our guests that some cuts are just not going to be available 100 percent of the time. Each animal only has a certain amount of parts, so there are only so many tenderloins to go around. We work with our guests to help them adjust their cooking based on what is available, similar to how you would cook seasonally. We get them to realize you don't have to follow a recipe exactly. You can take a recipe, adjust it to what is available, and make it your own.

— Chili Montes, butcher

OF ALL THE AISLES in the grocery store, the butcher section is the most complicated, the most confusing, and the most challenging as far as making good choices. Labels are often limited in the information they provide; including the cut, price, and country of origin is about as specific as it gets. And whereas the produce aisle often offers organic as well as conventional versions of a given item, the butcher aisle doesn't always have the same variety.

It's important to know exactly what you're getting when you buy a piece of meat. It's not easy, though, because there are so many factors to weigh and they're not always easy to find. A store-brand package of beef will probably tell you basic nutritional information and what country the beef came from, but the label won't tell you much beyond that. If you ask the person behind the counter where that chicken was raised, or even where it was slaughtered, you might not get a solid answer. When it's this difficult to know who's behind the meat we eat, it's hard to hold anyone accountable when something goes wrong—or when we want better choices.

The name of the game is **TRACEABILITY**. The more you can determine about a producer or a particular piece of meat, the more likely it is to be a sustainable, flavorful choice. Good producers who take pride in the meat they sell will go out of their way to answer your questions. Get in the habit of asking retailers (the people behind the butcher counter) about what the animal fed on, how it was raised, and so forth. If they won't take the time to answer your questions, don't know the answers, or aren't willing to tell you, it's a red flag.

AS A RULE OF THUMB, THE MORE DETAILED INFORMATION YOU CAN GET ABOUT THE MEAT YOU BUY, THE MORE LIKELY IT IS THAT YOU'RE MAKING A GOOD DECISION. The long and complicated supply chain of the meat industry can be a major roadblock in this investigative process. Big corporate conglomerates have production chains that are not only physically spread out, but also likely to be handled by totally different companies at various points, which makes it even harder to connect the dots from ranch to plate. Smaller, local producers are part of shorter supply chains, which makes it easier to get the information you want.

No matter what kind of meat or seafood you buy, there are several key things to consider:

Who and where did this come from?

In an ideal world, we all would have a personal relationship with the person who raised the animals we eat. It's possible to do, especially if you **FREQUENT FARMERS' MARKETS**. There not only do you know the name of the rancher, but you can actually ask him or her whatever questions you have. Many of them will even let you visit their property to see their operation firsthand.

SMALL-SCALE RANCHERS tend to care deeply about the flavor of their product—just one reason they often avoid the unsavory practices that large-scale producers are notorious for. Instead, they embrace a more natural way of raising and processing their animals. It takes longer and requires more attention, but the products are superior.

If you aren't buying directly from the producer at a farmers' market, then the next best thing is to **LOOK FOR RETAILERS WHO BUY DIRECTLY FROM INDIVIDUAL PRODUCERS**.

AT THE VERY LEAST, LOOK FOR MEAT THAT COMES FROM:

- Brands with lookup codes printed on their packaging
- Cooperatives of ranchers who abide by established protocols and standards

IDEALLY, LOOK FOR:

- Small-scale, local producers who can tell you about their practices
- Retailers who source directly from ranchers

Otherwise, **SMALLER COOPERATIVES ARE ANOTHER WORTHWHILE OPTION** (Niman Ranch and Heritage Foods USA are good examples). These cooperatives tend to have established standards and protocols of operation—which are usually posted on their websites—and maintain close oversight of the ranches to ensure they're adhered to.

Another important consideration is where the animal was slaughtered and processed. Often, especially in large "factory farm" operations, animals are raised in one place and shipped to another facility for slaughtering and processing. Sometimes these facilities are thousands of miles apart. The transport alone causes stress in the animal, and the animals are rarely given time to acclimate once they reach their destination. As a result, the animals are slaughtered with their systems full of adrenaline, and it causes the meat's flavor to be subpar. It's just one more reason to look for meat that was raised, slaughtered, and processed within the same region (and ideally, a region that is close to you!).

What did the animal consume?

There are two basic and opposing philosophies in the world of ranching. There's the "nature knows best" approach, which embraces the fact that animals have evolved to thrive on a varied and natural diet. At the other end of the spectrum is the "science = progress" approach, espoused by most commercial producers. It relies on a formula heavy in corn and soy, most of it genetically modified (GMO) and controlled by a single large company.

There are many benefits to the natural approach, and many drawbacks to the science-driven one. Laboratory-made feed, although designed to bring animals to slaughter weight faster than nature ever could, also causes major health problems for the animals. And the chemical fertilizers used to boost the yield of the feed itself are detrimental to the environment and tether farmers to the seed and fertilizer corporations. Unsurprisingly, the genetically modified seed, fertilizers, and medications used to treat sick animals are often made by the same companies.

One of our ranchers delivering a hog to the store

THE VERY BEST-TASTING MEAT, AND THE MOST SUSTAINABLE, COMES FROM ANIMALS FED PRIMARILY ON WHATEVER THEY WOULD EAT IN NATURE. (It's also the best way to keep the animals healthy.) Ideally, this diet comes in its naturally occurring form: growing on a field for cows, a variety of insects for chickens, and so on. Animals that are allowed to live in open spaces and graze on their natural diet are called pasture-raised.

IF THEY'RE NOT RAISED ON PASTURE, LOOK FOR ANIMALS THAT ARE FED ORGANIC (AND THUS GMO-FREE) GRAINS. However, keep in mind that organic certification is not the be-all, end-all; there are many small farms who choose not to become certified organic but still operate as "beyond organic" producers. Certification is expensive and time-consuming, and some farmers would rather just practice sustainable methods (some of which are more stringent than the government dictates) without having to deal with government oversight. A few go so far as to even grow their own grain to feed their animals! If you're not sure whether a noncertified producer is "beyond organic," ask.

Also consider other things that the animals are given, including:

- **Antibiotics**, given as a regular dose whether the animals are sick or not. This practice, extremely common in feedlots, is used to minimize spread of illness in tight quarters. Not only does this "pulse dosing" of antibiotics reduce their effectiveness over time for the animals, but we end up consuming the drugs ourselves, polluting our water sources, and in turn affecting other species.

"No preventative antibiotics" means that the animals were not regularly dosed but may have been treated individually in the case of illness. Be aware that the use of antibiotics is sometimes necessary and the most humane option; if an animal is sick, treatment limits its suffering. In those cases, the most conscientious ranchers will segregate the sick

---

AT THE VERY LEAST, LOOK FOR MEAT:

- Free of preventative hormones or antibiotics
- Given organic or non-GMO feed
- Raised on a vegetarian diet

IDEALLY, LOOK FOR MEAT:

- A "never ever" program
- Certified organic, or using "beyond organic" practices
- Pasture-raised
- Certified by a reputable, third-party program for humane and/or sustainable practices

---

WHY YOUR MEAT CHOICES MATTER

Meat has come under a lot of fire in recent years, and for good reason. The commercial meat industry is responsible for practices that are inhumane toward both animals and workers. It operates in a way that is destructive to the environment, and the products are unhealthy (or even dangerous) to consume. Here's a breakdown of some of the key issues surrounding meat:

- **Meat production is land- and resource-intensive**, especially compared to plant-based food production. Animal feed alone requires a significant amount of fuel and water to grow, harvest, and ship. The bigger the animal, the more feed and water it requires over the course of its life; it actually requires ten pounds of grain and about two thousand gallons of water to produce one pound of beef. This *conversion rate* is the driving factor for profitability in industrial meat production (it's why growth hormones are so prevalently used). Even more energy and fuel are needed to transport to slaughter and then to subsequent processing, packing, and distribution centers, and retail outlets. And assembly-line meat factories consume enormous amounts of energy, pollute water supplies, and generate significant greenhouse gases.

- **Animals are often treated poorly.** Most large-scale meat producers look nothing like the pastoral scenes pictured on their logos and packages. In actuality, the animals live in confined animal feeding operations (CAFOs)—cramped, poorly ventilated enclosures. The animals are fed grains (primarily genetically modified corn and soy), which their bodies are not suited to digest, so they are prone to illness, aggression, and discomfort throughout their lives.

- **Meat contains a lot of hidden ingredients** in the form of hormones, antibiotics, steroids, and supplements all meant to counteract the health problems caused by an unnatural grain-based diet, as well as prevent the spread of disease in the cramped conditions. These hidden ingredients are never disclosed on labels, and many people, myself included, question whether they're truly safe for human consumption.

- **Workers are often treated poorly.** Jobs in slaughterhouses and meat processing plants are some of the most dangerous in the country. The industry relies on undocumented workers who are subjected to extremely long hours, sub-minimum-wage pay, and constant danger of injury or death.

- **Commercial meat doesn't taste like much.** Factory-farmed meat is produced with efficiency in mind, not taste. Because large producers favor extra-lean breeds, feed the animals a monotonous grain diet, and don't give the animals an opportunity to move around, the resulting meat is bland and uninteresting.

animal and allow it to heal, thus protecting the rest of the herd or flock. After treatment ends, many undergo a waiting period before the animal can be slaughtered so that the antibiotics can be flushed from the animal's system.
- **Steroids and growth hormones**, administered to encourage rapid growth, bring the animals to slaughter weight faster and with less of an investment in feed. These too enter our waterways and adversely affect other species of wildlife.
- **Animal byproducts**, including bodies of sick or "downer" animals—feeding these to cattle led to the mad cow outbreaks of the last few decades.

Meat that is labeled **"NEVER EVER"** means that the animals are never given hormones or antibiotics. If an animal is sick and requires treatment, it is culled from the rest of the herd and, once healthy, sold off to a commodity rancher.

What kind of life did the animal live?

Animal welfare is an important moral issue for many meat eaters, but husbandry also has a direct impact on what the meat tastes like. Raising animals in crowded, confined indoor spaces means their muscles get only a fraction of the exercise they'd get in an open, outdoor space. The result is an unhealthy animal and potentially less flavorful meat.

Even more dramatic is the impact that stress has on the flavor of meat. When animals are treated roughly prior to slaughter, it triggers the "fight or flight" reflex, producing adrenaline, which makes the meat taste decidedly unpleasant. That's just one of many reasons to support producers who are kind to the animals they raise and conscious of the slaughter process.

There are quite a few **CERTIFICATION PROGRAMS** designed to provide the consumer with assurances about how the animals were treated. Some of these programs come out of industry lobbying boards, which are not as strict in their guidelines and enforcement. Third-party programs such as **CERTIFIED HUMANE** and **FOOD ALLIANCE** offer more comprehensive and reliably enforced guidelines.

Being a conscious eater of meat isn't just about the meat itself. Consider this:

QUESTION CHEAP MEAT. Because of the time, effort, and materials needed to raise animals in a sustainable and humane manner, good meat is (and should be) more expensive than commodity meat. Cheap meat is available to us because of government subsidies on the grain, and because producers have put efficiency and profits above quality and conscientious practices. It's easy to balk at expensive meat, but in fact it's the cheap meat that deserves scrutiny.

CHOOSE QUALITY OVER QUANTITY (FREQUENCY AND SIZE). Cheap commodity meat is so widely available that we've seen a cultural shift to eating ever-larger portions of meat with increasing frequency. Not only does this have a negative effect on our health, but also the constantly growing demand for meat seems to demand large-scale meat production. **CONSIDER MEAT A TREAT; EAT IT LESS OFTEN AND IN SMALLER PORTIONS WHEN YOU DO.**

LEARN TO LOVE THE UNLOVED PARTS. To compound the challenge of the enormous public demand for animal protein, over the years we've narrowed our view of what's worth eating. When our ancestors raised and slaughtered their own pigs, they made use of every last bit of the animal—"everything but the squeal," as they say. It may require a mental shift, but other parts can be inexpensive and delicious. It's worth giving these unloved bits a chance.

Given all of these factors and things to consider, your head may be spinning. I understand. This isn't an easy subject. **THE MOST IMPORTANT THING IS TO START ASKING QUESTIONS.** That way, you'll make more informed choices, whatever you end up buying.

Still, when you're standing in the butcher aisle, the best choice is not always obvious, and that can be frustrating. The following strategies will help:

TRY BOTH SHORT-TERM AND LONG-TERM SOLUTIONS. It may take time (and multiple requests) for pasture-raised chickens to show up at your local market. In the meantime, you may choose to keep buying "regular" chicken, or you might steer clear. Keep asking for what you want, and keep looking for other outlets.

BE FLEXIBLE. If a recipe calls for one type of meat—pork chops, say—and you can't find a sustainable option at the grocery store, see what else they have. You may find another kind of meat—organic boneless chicken thighs, for example—that you can substitute fairly easily.

SHOP AROUND. Good meat is really worth going out of your way for—more so than any other ingredient. So suss out the farmers' markets. Ask your local Slow Food chapter for a list of local ranchers and retailers of sustainable meat. Read up on foodie discussion boards. Find out where to go, and then make the time to visit. You can also order online from our friends at Heritage Foods USA.

BUY A SHARE. Find a few friends who will go in on a purchase of a half hog or a quarter steer that you purchase from a local ranch. It's often more economical than buying individual cuts, and a great way to get sustainable meat.

· ·

Although they're hard to find, any butcher who starts with whole (or half) animals and breaks them down in-house is worth your business. You'll support a dying art among retailers and ensure that you're buying from people who know their stuff and want to serve the highest-quality meats to their guests.

· ·

TIPS FOR COOKING MEAT:

- Let all cuts come to room temperature before cooking.

- For best browning, pat meat dry just prior to cooking, and avoid overcrowding the pan.

- Season meat well with salt and pepper just prior to cooking.

- Lubricate your cooking surface. Use a neutral oil like grapeseed oil, or a more flavorful fat like butter, lard, or duck fat.

- An instant-read thermometer is your best friend when it comes to cooking meat. Insert it into the thickest part of the meat for the most accurate reading.

ON COOKING MEAT

When cooking any kind of meat, it's hard to predict when it will be done. It depends on a lot of factors: how thoroughly you like your meat cooked, the size and shape of the meat, the cooking method, how hot your flame is, and whether your oven holds a steady temperature. **PRACTICE IS THE BEST TEACHER. TOUCHING, OBSERVING, AND MONITORING AT EACH STAGE FROM PURCHASING TO EATING HELPS YOU BECOME MORE IN TUNE WITH YOUR INGREDIENTS AND THE COOKING PROCESS.**

Let cooked meat rest, loosely tented in foil, before serving (10 to 15 minutes for roasts and 5 to 10 minutes for steaks, chops, breasts, and other smaller cuts). This helps the meat stay juicy. Slice across the grain if possible.

· ·

It's easier to see the grain's striations when the meat is still raw—so take a close look before you start cooking.

BEEF

A recent conversation at Costco gave me new hope about the future of grocery shopping. I asked a salesperson if they carried any organic beef besides the ground chuck I saw. His response actually made my heart swell! He said, "We used to have organic steaks. People have been asking for them, though, so we might bring them back in." That response is proof that we *all* have the power to change the food system, even at the biggest chains. We just have to make our voices heard.

How to Buy

The beef aisle is particularly overrun with lingo and marketing terms. Some are useful and have very specific definitions established by the USDA. However, producers also muddy the waters with their own similar-sounding—but meaningless—labels, which makes it difficult to get to the meat of the matter.

Let's start with **QUALITY GRADES**, such as Prime, Choice, and Select. These grades are assigned by the

USDA and indicate the meat's overall tenderness and juiciness, based on an animal's physiological maturity and intramuscular fat (marbling). Of the grades given, Prime has the most marbling and is the most costly. Choice is the next highest, followed by Select.

Commercial producers use a plethora of other labels to make it sound like their beef is of special pedigree; they include words like "premium," "reserve," or "master" and are generally meaningless. Ignore them.

The most important factor that determines beef's quality, flavor, and sustainability has to do with what the animal fed on and when.

- **Grain-fed**—The industry standard feed for beef cattle is a mixture of corn, soy, and other grains, most of which is genetically modified. The bovine digestive tract is designed for grass, not grains, and a grain-based diet creates a host of health problems for cattle. (This is one reason for the preventive dosing of cattle.) If the label says nothing about grass or pasture, you can be pretty sure it was grain-fed.
- **Organic**—This label is not only meaningful but also relatively easy to find; organic ground beef is widely available in supermarkets, even when no other type of organic beef is. Under that label, you can be sure that the beef you're eating is free of hormones or antibiotics and is GMO-free.
- **Grass-fed or pasture-raised**—When cattle eat the grass that their bodies are designed to thrive on, you end up with a much different piece of steak. Grass-fed beef has higher levels of omega-3 fatty acids (the ones you want more of) and lower levels of omega-6 fatty acids (the ones you want less of). It also boasts a more robust, true-beef flavor that just doesn't exist in grain-fed beef. Because grass-fed beef tends to be leaner, many producers choose not to have it graded on the USDA scale (which is based on intramuscular fat content). Keep in mind, though, that "pasture-raised" has no legal definition. The best way to find out what a producer means by this term is to ask: What are the conditions? How much time do the animals spend outdoors? What percentage of what they eat is foraged, versus feed?

    You can grow and harvest grass, transport it to a feed lot, and still end up with grass-fed beef.

"**Pasture-raised**" means that the cattle actually grew up on a field, eating the grass growing on it. This requires a higher degree of skill on the part of the rancher, who must be competent as a steward of his or her land (and everything that grows on it) as well as a keeper of cattle. In fact, many great cattle ranchers consider themselves grass farmers. Because grass growth ebbs and flows along with the seasons, pasture-raised beef is a seasonal product.

- **Grass-fed, grain-finished**—Some producers take the middle road by raising the cattle on pasture and feeding them grain for the final weeks before slaughter. This "grain finishing" helps the cattle gain a little extra intramuscular fat and also results in a milder flavor that many consumers are accustomed to.

For flavor reasons, as well as for the well-being of the cattle themselves, **GRASS-FED BEEF IS TRULY PREFERABLE—EVEN IF IT'S GRAIN-FINISHED.**

. . . .

Of all the items in the butcher aisle, **ground beef** is one of the most risky as far as foodborne illness goes. A single package of ground beef might represent hundreds, even thousands of animals from multiple countries, which is part of why *E. coli* outbreaks are so difficult to trace. *E. coli* is most likely present in any preground beef you buy, and will multiply fast, so be sure to use it soon after purchase and cook it through. Some grocery stores grind their own beef daily, though, which reduces the risk significantly. Even if they don't regularly grind beef, the butcher may be willing to grind a package of chuck if you ask nicely.

. . . .

STEP RIGHT UP AND TAKE A NUMBER. There are a few advantages to buying your beef from the service case rather than the self-service displays. For one thing, the service case is better for the beef itself, as it's best when stored with a bit of ventilation; otherwise, it will eventually develop an "off" smell and taste. It also means your beef is wrapped to order in breathable butcher paper. And just as important, it gives you a chance to talk to the butcher, ask questions about the product, and make requests for the types of beef you'd like to see available.

Contrary to popular belief, beef doesn't have to be rosy red in order to be good. Over time, meat that's been exposed to oxygen will turn slightly darker. This is purely a visual change and has no affect on flavor. Leaner cuts tend to oxidize faster than fattier ones.

How to Store

You can generally store beef in whatever packaging it came in. However, if the beef is sitting in a pool of its own blood or juices, you'll extend the shelf life if you repackage it as soon as you get home: unwrap the beef, pat dry with a paper towel, wrap in parchment or waxed paper, and set it on a plate to catch any juices. Use within three days (one day for ground beef); if it starts to smell funky or look slimy, throw it out.

How to Use

Just because a beef recipe calls for a specific cut of meat doesn't mean you have to use it. Many cuts are interchangeable with one another, as long as they fall into the same general category (steaks, roasts, or stewing/braising cuts).

- **Steaks**—"Steak" can mean one of two things: a large piece of meat cut into individual portions prior to cooking, or a smaller muscle that is usually cooked whole and sliced for serving. In both instances, steaks are quick-cooking and perfect for weeknight meals. They are well suited for pan-searing, broiling, or grilling.

  CUTS: *Flank, Bavette, Skirt, Hanger, Flatiron, Top Sirloin, Tri-tip, Ribeye, T-bone, Porterhouse, New York, Tenderloin (filet mignon)*

- **Roasts**—Roasts are medium to large-size pieces of meat and thus take a little more time to cook. But the cooking also tends to be pretty hands-off, and they're a great way to feed a lot of mouths at once. You can cook roasts in the oven or over indirect heat on a grill (in either case, the lower the temperature, the more evenly cooked and succulent the meat will be).

  CUTS: *Prime Rib, Tenderloin, Chuck Roast, Top Sirloin Roast, Tri-tip, London Broil*

- **Stews and Braises**—Stewing and braising are really magical techniques—they turn tough and less expensive cuts of meat into tender, succulent ones. The secret is a low cooking temperature plus a flavorful braising liquid. Stewing and braising are essentially the same technique; stewing uses more liquid. Once you get the hang of braising—our beef cheeks recipe on page 179 is a great start—you can improvise using the same technique.

  CUTS: *Stew Meat, Short Ribs, Brisket, Shanks, Cheeks*

BEEF COOKING TEMPERATURES

120°–125°F: medium-rare
125°–130°F: medium
130°–135°F: medium-well
135°–140°F: well

**TIMING GUIDELINES FOR LARGER
ROASTS (2 POUNDS OR MORE)**

Rare = 9–10 minutes/pound
Medium = 12–15 minutes/pound
Well-done = 18–20 minutes /pound (not recommended, especially for leaner grass-fed beef)

Sicilian Meatballs with Fresh Basil Marinara

MAKES 6 LARGE MEATBALLS

These baseball-size meatballs are a mainstay of the market's deli case. They're flavorful and tender and stay good for several days after they're made. If you have leftovers, they make an incredible meatball sandwich; just slice them up, reheat in the sauce, and put them in the middle of a good crusty roll. Then top with mozzarella or provolone if you have it.

- 1/2 cup fresh breadcrumbs
- 1/4 cup whole milk
- 1 large egg
- 3/4 cup grated Parmigiano-Reggiano, more for sprinkling
- 1/4 cup ketchup
- 2 tablespoons chopped parsley
- 1 teaspoon finely chopped fresh oregano
- 1 teaspoon finely chopped fresh thyme
- 1 small onion, finely chopped
- 4 large cloves garlic, minced
- Kosher salt and freshly ground black pepper
- 1 1/2 pounds ground beef
- 3 tablespoons extra-virgin olive oil
- 1 (28-ounce) can crushed tomatoes
- Sugar, as needed
- 2 tablespoons chopped fresh basil

Put a rack in the center of the oven and heat to 375°F. Line a large rimmed baking pan with parchment or a nonstick liner and set aside.

Put the breadcrumbs and milk in a large mixing bowl, stir to blend, and set aside for 5 minutes. With your hands, squeeze and mash the breadcrumbs so that they make a smooth paste. Add the egg and whisk, then add the Parmigiano, ketchup, parsley, oregano, thyme, half the onion, half the garlic, 2 teaspoons salt, and 1/2 teaspoon pepper. Stir to blend.

With your hands, break the beef into small chunks and add to the bowl. Mix gently but thoroughly; overmixing will make the meatballs tough and dry. When all the ingredients are evenly combined, shape the mixture into 6 balls and arrange on the baking sheet.

Bake until an instant-read thermometer reads 165°F at the center of a meatball, 40 to 45 minutes.

While the meatballs are baking, make the sauce. Heat the olive oil in a medium saucepan over medium heat. Add the remaining half onion and 1 teaspoon salt and increase the heat to medium-high. Cook, stirring frequently, until translucent, about 3 minutes. Add the remaining half garlic and cook until aromatic, about 1 minute. Add the tomatoes, bring to a boil, and lower the heat to maintain a vigorous simmer. Cook, stirring occasionally, until reduced to a thick sauce, 10 to 15 minutes. Taste the sauce and add a pinch or two of sugar if it seems too tangy, and season with more salt if necessary. Stir in the basil and keep warm until the meatballs come out of the oven.

Spoon the sauce generously over the meatballs and bake for another 5 to 10 minutes to blend the flavors. Garnish with a sprinkling of Parmigiano.

Tip: This marinara sauce is as versatile as it is simple. Add some capers, anchovies, and olives for a puttanesca sauce or a pinch of chile flakes for arrabiata.

Pan-Fried Bavette Steak with Red Onions and Chimichurri Sauce

SERVES 4

Chimichurri sauce hails from Argentina and is sort of like a vinegary pesto. The sauce's bright herby notes bring an unexpected freshness to the plate and balance out the rich beefy steak.

Bavette is an underappreciated and fairly inexpensive cut that's common in French bistros, and very similar to (and from the same muscle group as) flank steak. It's flavorful but also tender, especially if you don't cook it beyond medium-rare. If you can't find bavette, flank or skirt steak would be the closest substitute, but any steak cut would work just as well.

If you have leftovers, pile the beef on a baguette or crusty roll, top with onions, and slather on the sauce for a fantastic sandwich.

Kosher salt and freshly ground black pepper

1 1/2 pounds bavette steak

2 large cloves garlic, peeled and smashed

1/2 large bunch parsley, thick stems removed (about 1 1/2 ounces)

1/2 large bunch cilantro, thick stems removed (about 1 1/2 ounces)

1/4 cup plus 3 tablespoons extra-virgin olive oil

1/4 cup red wine vinegar, more as needed

1 large red onion, cut into 1/4-inch rings

Sprinkle 1 1/2 teaspoons salt and a few grinds of pepper over the steaks and set aside to come to room temperature.

Meanwhile, put the garlic in a blender or food processor and pulse just to chop coarsely. Tear the parsley and cilantro into 2- to 3-inch lengths and add to the blender (tender stems and all), along with 1/4 cup of the olive oil, 2 tablespoons of the vinegar, and 1 teaspoon salt. Puree until smooth. Taste and add more salt or vinegar as needed.

Heat 2 tablespoons of the remaining oil in a large skillet over medium-high heat. When the pan is smoking hot, add the steaks and cook undisturbed for at least 2 minutes. Check the browning and lower the heat if they seem to be browning too quickly. Cook, flipping occasionally, until the steaks reach the desired doneness, 4 to 5 minutes per side. (For medium-rare, an instant-read thermometer will read 125°F at the thickest part of the steak.) Remove the steaks from the skillet, place on a cutting board, and cover loosely with foil. Let rest while you cook the onions.

Add the remaining 1 tablespoon oil to the pan, along with the onion and a generous pinch of salt. Cook, stirring occasionally, until the onions have softened somewhat and are golden brown on the edges, 3 minutes. Add the remaining 2 tablespoons vinegar and cook, stirring, until the vinegar has evaporated and the onions are soft, 1 minute longer. Remove from the heat.

Slice the steaks across the grain into 1/2-inch-thick strips, top with the sautéed onions, and serve the sauce alongside.

Braised Beef Cheeks with Lobster Mushrooms

SERVES 4 TO 6

With this dish you can turn an inexpensive, under-utilized cut of beef into a succulent, tender, soul-satisfying stew; once it's in the oven, you need do nothing but enjoy the amazing aromas that fill your house. (Do plan your time accordingly, though, as it spends at least five hours in the oven.)

This dish, like any stew, is best made a day ahead but is fine served the same day. It's great served atop soft polenta or horseradish-spiked mashed potatoes. Leftovers make a wonderful rustic pasta sauce, as well.

A large Dutch oven is best for making this, but a wide-bottomed stock pot with a tight-fitting lid works, too. Just make sure it fits in your oven!

BEEF CHEEKS

4 cups beef stock (or low-sodium broth)

3¹/₂ to 4 pounds beef cheeks, trimmed of glands and silver skin and cut into 3-inch chunks (see Note)

Kosher salt and freshly ground black pepper

3 tablespoons all-purpose flour

¹/₄ cup extra-virgin olive oil, more as needed

2 medium onions, coarsely diced

5 medium carrots, peeled and cut into 1-inch chunks

2 small or 1 large celery root, peeled and cut into 1-inch chunks

8 bushy sprigs fresh thyme

2 bay leaves

16 small cloves garlic, peeled (or 8 large—cut them in half or thirds lengthwise and remove any green germ)

1 (750 ml) bottle dry red wine (one that is hearty but not too tannic, such as Côtes du Rhône)

MUSHROOMS

¹/₂ to ³/₄ pound lobster mushrooms (or any other variety)

2 tablespoons unsalted butter

1 tablespoon chopped shallot

¹/₄ teaspoon chopped garlic

1 tablespoon sherry vinegar

1 tablespoon chopped fresh parsley

Kosher salt and freshly ground pepper

To cook the cheeks:

Position a rack in the lower third of the oven and heat to 250°F.

Heat the beef stock in a medium pan over low heat and keep warm.

Season the beef cheeks with 1 tablespoon salt and 2 teaspoons pepper, and sprinkle the flour evenly all over.

Put a large Dutch oven or wide-bottomed stock pot over medium-high heat. When hot, add 2 table-spoons of the oil and enough of the beef chunks to make a roomy single layer in the pan. Cook, turning the beef as needed, until browned all over, about 6 to 7 minutes. Transfer to a large plate and repeat with the remaining beef, working in batches as necessary and adding another tablespoon or so of oil if the pot seems too dry.

Add 2 tablespoons more olive oil to the pan, then add the onions. Cook, stirring frequently and scraping the browned bits off the bottom of the pan, until they start to soften and are barely brown on the edges, 3 to 5 minutes. Add the carrots, celery root, thyme, bay leaves, garlic, 1 teaspoon salt, and a few grinds of pepper. Cook, stirring frequently, until the celery root starts to soften, about 6 minutes.

Return the beef and any accumulated juices back to the pot. Stir well for another minute or so to combine.

Add the wine and bring just to a boil over medium-high heat. Lower the heat to maintain a simmer and continue to simmer for 5 minutes. Add the warm stock; once the liquid has returned to a simmer, cover the pot and transfer to the oven.

Bake for 4 hours, checking every hour to make sure the liquid is at a bare simmer. (The key to tenderness is to cook at the lowest temperature possible. If the broth is simmering rapidly, reduce the oven temperature.)

After 4 hours, remove the lid and stir. The stew should be very wet; if not, add a cup or so of water to reliquify. Return the uncovered pot to the oven. Continue to bake until the beef is completely tender and offers no resistance when you pull it apart with two forks, 1 to 2 more hours. If the beef is tender but the

continued on page 180

Braised Beef Cheeks with Lobster Mushrooms,
continued

liquid has not reduced much, continue to bake until the liquid is 3/4 to 1 inch lower than the original level. Taste the liquid and season with more salt as needed.

When the beef is done, set aside while you cook the mushrooms.

(If you make this a day ahead, let cool to room temperature before you cover and refrigerate the cheeks. When ready to serve, reheat gently over low heat, stirring frequently until heated through, 30 to 45 minutes.)

To cook the mushrooms:

Using a small knife, scrape any dirt off of the mushrooms. If they are particularly large, cut them into 3/4- to 1-inch pieces.

Put 1 tablespoon of the butter in a large skillet (it should be large enough to hold the mushrooms in a single layer) and put the pan over medium-high heat. When the butter is melted and bubbling, add the mushrooms and cook, stirring frequently, until the mushrooms' juices have released and evaporated. Add the remaining 1 tablespoon butter and the shallot and cook for 1 minute, stirring frequently. Add the garlic and continue sautéing for an additional minute. Add the vinegar and stir until the liquid evaporates. Add the parsley and season with salt and pepper to taste.

To serve:

Arrange the beef in shallow bowls and ladle some of the braising liquid over it. Top with the sautéed mushrooms.

Note: You may need to special order beef cheeks (a specialty butcher is your best bet), but you can substitute with brisket if you can't find cheeks. The glands are marble-size organs that are attached to the cheeks (they may already have been removed from the ones you have).

Cocoa-Cumin Beef Roast
SERVES 4 TO 6

Tri-tip goes by several other names, including corner cut and bottom sirloin, but curiously it's generally only found on the West Coast. It's flavorful and toothsome and worth seeking out, but you can also use an equal weight of flank, bavette, or top round. (Recipe pictured on page 97.)

I teaspoon ground cumin
3/4 teaspoon unsweetened cocoa powder
1/4 teaspoon ground allspice
Kosher salt and freshly ground black pepper
I whole tri-tip, excess fat and silver skin trimmed
(about 2 pounds)
2 tablespoons extra-virgin olive oil

Combine the cumin, cocoa, allspice, 2 teaspoons salt, and 1 teaspoon black pepper in a small bowl, mix well, and rub all over the beef. If the roast has a long, thin end, tuck it under to prevent overcooking. Use butcher twine to tie the roast at 2-inch intervals; tie it a little tighter at the wide end, which will create a more even thickness. Refrigerate uncovered overnight, if time permits, or for a minimum of 2 hours if cooking the same day. Let the beef sit out at room temperature for at least 30 minutes before cooking.

When you're ready to cook, position a rack in the center of the oven and heat to 350°F.

Heat the oil in a large ovenproof skillet (cast iron is best) over medium-high heat. When hot, add the beef and cook undisturbed for at least 2 minutes. Check the underside for browning; if necessary, cook until the bottom is a deep golden brown, up to 2 minutes longer. Flip the roast and transfer the skillet to the oven.

Roast until the beef reaches the desired doneness; it'll take about 25 minutes to reach medium-rare (120°F at the center). (Keep in mind, though, that cooking time will vary depending on the size and shape of the roast. A meat thermometer is your best aid.)

Remove from the oven and let rest for 10 to 20 minutes. Then remove the butcher twine and cut across the grain into 1/3-inch-thick slices.

Beef Stew with Peppers and Ale

SERVES 6 TO 8

This is sort of a cross between chili and beef stew, with delicious wintry results. It has all the flavors of chili—cumin, dried chiles, tomatoes, and beans—but features stew meat instead of ground beef for a more interesting texture. Be sure to give the stew the full two hours of simmering; it's essential to making the beef super tender.

You can make this up to two days ahead and reheat gently on the stove top. It also freezes well; consider stashing leftovers in the freezer for a last-minute dinner or a snowy weekend.

I dried ancho chile (or other sweet dried chile)
2 dried arbol chiles (or other small hot dried chile)
³/₄ cup boiling water
¹/₄ cup all-purpose flour
Kosher salt and freshly ground black pepper
2 pounds beef stew meat, cut into ³/₄-inch cubes
¹/₂ cup diced pancetta or bacon
I tablespoon extra-virgin olive oil (or bacon fat), more as needed
I medium onion, finely diced
2 medium red bell peppers, cored, seeded, and diced
I tablespoon molasses
I teaspoon ground cumin
I teaspoon ground coriander
I teaspoon Dijon mustard
I (20-ounce) bottle amber ale or stout (or two 12-ounce bottles)
I cup beef or chicken stock (or low-sodium broth)
I¹/₂ cups cooked kidney beans (or other sturdy bean)
I cup peeled, seeded, diced tomatoes (from whole canned tomatoes if not in season)
4 sprigs thyme
I large sprig parsley
I bay leaf

In a small bowl, cover the dried chiles with the boiling water and let soak for 20 minutes. Drain the chiles, reserving the water, and remove and discard the seeds. Puree the chiles with the soaking water in a blender and set aside.

In a large bowl, toss together the flour with 2 teaspoons salt and ¹/₂ teaspoon black pepper. Add the beef, mix until completely coated in flour, and set aside.

Put the pancetta in a large Dutch oven or soup pot over medium-high heat. Cook, stirring frequently, until the pancetta is browned and has released most of its fat, about 4 minutes. Remove from the pot and set aside, leaving the rendered fat in the pan. Increase the heat slightly.

Add about one-third of the beef to make a roomy single layer. Cook, turning every couple of minutes, until browned all over, about 5 minutes. Transfer to a plate and repeat with the remaining beef. The meat will not caramelize and brown well if there is not enough fat in the pot, so add more oil 1 tablespoon at a time as necessary.

Add 1 tablespoon olive oil to the pot and add the onion and a pinch of salt. Cook, stirring frequently and scraping any very dark bits from the bottom of the pan, until the onions are translucent, about 4 minutes. Add the bell peppers and continue to cook until softened slightly, 2 minutes longer. Stir in the molasses, cumin, coriander, and mustard and cook, stirring, for 1 minute, or until fragrant.

Add the beer and stir to release the browned bits from the bottom of the pan. Add the reserved beef, pancetta, and chile puree, as well as the stock, beans, tomatoes, thyme, parsley, bay leaf, and 1 teaspoon more salt. Bring just to a boil, partially cover the pot, and then lower the heat to maintain a bare simmer.

Cook, stirring occasionally, until the beef is tender and the flavors have melded into a rich broth, about 2 hours. (At this point you can uncover and increase the heat to a rapid simmer to reduce and thicken the broth if you like.) Remove the thyme and parsley sprigs. Taste and season with more salt as needed.

CHICKEN

Because I have a personal relationship with the ranchers we source our meat from, I've made many farm pilgrimages to see how pigs, cows, goats, and chickens are raised. I've yet to experience slaughtering a chicken for my own dinner, but as a conscious eater, I think it's important to see a chicken from the pasture to the plate at least once.

How to Buy

Any creature allowed to live as nature intended is going to be healthier and taste better. It's no surprise, then, that THE BEST-TASTING CHICKENS ARE PASTURE-RAISED; they get lots of exercise and sunlight, and in addition to their feed they have access to an omnivorous diet of bugs, worms, and other naturally occurring tidbits. So their meat is truly meaty and dense with flavor, and the fat is succulent and savory. Keep in mind, though, that "pasture-raised" has no legal definition. The best way to find out what a producer means by this term is to ask: What are the conditions? How much time do the animals spend outdoors? What percentage of what they eat is foraged versus feed?

A true pasture-raised chicken is hard to find. It's much easier to find "FREE RANGE" and "range-fed" chickens, but those terms are less meaningful because the official definitions are very loose to begin with. ("Free range," for instance, only means that the chickens have "been allowed access to the outside," without specifics on how often or for how long, and no guarantee that they ever made it outside.) Often these birds are crammed into houses in a space no bigger than a sheet of printer paper.

Whether a chicken is pasture-raised, free range, or neither, there are some other signs that let you know a chicken is worth eating:

- **Clean feed**—This means a diet free of animal byproducts (that is, "vegetarian feed"), no preventive antibiotics, and non-GMO feed. Feed—whether it's corn, soy, or barley—that is organically grown in the United States is ideal, as it's difficult to get specifics on imported feed (which is what most commercial chickens are raised on).

- **"Air chilled"**—Most commercial chickens, once slaughtered and cleaned, are submerged in a bath of chlorinated water to minimize bacterial growth and chill the flesh to a safe holding temperature. It also causes the chicken to absorb water, thus diluting the flavor. Commercial producers prefer water-chilled birds because the residual water adds weight to the final product—and consumers wasting dollars on "juices" that leak away in cooking. Air-chilling is an alternative method that does not compromise taste or safety. It also produces a drier bird that browns evenly and doesn't release excess moisture when cooking.

- **Shiny skin and bouncy, firm meat**—A good fresh chicken will have moist, almost translucent skin (an air-chilled chicken will look a bit dry, but that's okay). Chicken meat becomes opaque and mushy as it ages; avoid both qualities.

- **Variety in size**—Factory farms have chicken production down to a science; each chicken lives and dies on a strict schedule and is meticulously sorted by size at slaughter. Most commercial chickens mature in six to seven weeks, whereas a pastured or heritage breed chicken takes eight to ten weeks to get to market. True pasture-raised farm chickens are allowed to grow to whatever size they want to be, which means chickens of many different sizes

ABOUT CHICKENS

Unfortunately, the vast majority of chickens we consume never see a pasture—or even daylight. Factory farms in the form of cramped, dark warehouses are designed with efficiency as the priority. The chickens are debeaked (such stressful living situations make them aggressive) and subsist on laboratory-created feed full of growth stimulants and antibiotics. The overuse of antibiotics creates resistant strains of bacteria, which puts the chickens—and all of us—at further risk of disease.

and shapes. This lack of uniformity shows that nature still has some say in what we eat.

- **Heads and feet**—Some people get weirded out by birds that still have their head and feet on, but we treasure the sight. The head and feet are great for making stock.

And there are some labels you should be skeptical of:

- **Hormone-free**—It's illegal to give chickens hormones. So if a producer boasts that their chickens are hormone-free, you can just nod knowingly.
- **Natural**—According to the USDA, these chickens contain no artificial ingredients or added colors and are "minimally processed" (whatever that means). The term is abused and meaningless; it shouldn't be the only thing you go by.
- **Basted, injected, or otherwise "enhanced"**— Some chicken processors inject or brine chickens with various solutions. This is done not only to bump up the chicken's weight (and price), but also to preserve freshness and compensate for the flavor that is so lacking in commercial chickens. Brining can be a useful technique, but I'd rather do it myself, when I want to, and with clean ingredients.

Most chickens you see at the supermarket represent one of a few breeds specifically developed to mature quickly (and therefore more cheaply) and conform to consumers' desire for more white meat. However, as a result, the breasts are so large that the chickens are not

able to support their own weight. Look for heritage breed chickens such as Plymouth Rock, Jersey Giant, and New Hampshire, all of which reflect chickens' natural body proportions, are allowed to grow at their natural rate, and are exceptionally rich in flavor.

How to Store

You can generally store chicken in whatever packaging it came in. However, if the chicken is sitting in a pool of its own juices, you'll extend the shelf life if you repackage it as soon as you get home: unwrap the chicken, pat dry with a paper towel, wrap in parchment or waxed paper, and set it on a plate to catch any juices. Use within two days; if it starts to smell funky or look slimy, throw it out.

How to Use

Whenever possible, buy and use whole, pasture-raised chickens, and savor every part of them. One 4- to 5-pound chicken can be the base for three meals for two adults: you can braise the legs for one meal, pan-fry the breasts for another, and make broth for soup with the wings and carcass.

Getting the most out of a chicken means enjoying the flavorful legs just as much as the tender breasts. It means taking a few extra minutes to pick every little bit of meat off of the back and wings, then collecting the bones and using them for stock—you can even stash the bones in the freezer until you're ready to take on the project. This might seem like extra work at first, but it's also incredibly rewarding, and it lessens the impact of paying more for a better chicken.

Safety and freshness is of primary importance when cooking chicken. Cook it until an instant-read thermometer reads 165°F at the thickest part of the meat (or, for a whole bird, at the deepest part of the thigh). Thoroughly wash hands, knives, and cutting boards—anything that raw chicken touches—with soap and the hottest water you can stand.

White chicken meat—namely, the breast meat—is very lean and can dry out easily if overcooked. The legs and thighs contain significantly more intramuscular fat and so can withstand longer, slower cooking times and methods.

Ginger-Lemongrass Chicken Skewers with Spicy Peanut Dipping Sauce

MAKES ABOUT 30 SMALL SKEWERS

At the Market we sell platters of these as appetizers, but they're also a great way to make a little bit of chicken stretch into a light entrée. They're always a crowd-pleaser, so make more than you think you'll need.

The skewers are wonderful paired with grilled or steamed veggies and a mound of coconut-infused rice. Leftovers are great on a sandwich, too.

For this recipe, you'll need thirty 6-inch or 8-inch wooden skewers (a few extras never hurt) that have been soaked in water for 2 hours.

- 1 stalk fresh lemongrass
- 1^1/$_2$-inch knob fresh ginger, peeled
- 2 large cloves garlic
- 2 scallions, very thinly sliced
- 1 tablespoon grapeseed or other neutral oil
- 1^1/$_2$ tablespoons freshly squeezed lime juice, more as needed
- 4 teaspoons Asian fish sauce, more as needed
- ^{3}/$_4$ teaspoon honey
- 1^1/$_2$ pounds boneless skinless chicken breasts or thighs
- ^{1}/$_2$ cup smooth natural peanut butter
- 1 teaspoon rice vinegar
- ^{1}/$_2$ teaspoon Asian chile garlic sauce

Cut the pale yellow bottom portion off the lemongrass stalk and discard the green top. Trim about ^{3}/$_4$ inch from the root end, then peel off and discard the tough outer layers. You should end up with a stick of only the more tender inner layers, about ^{1}/$_2$ inch thick and 3 inches long. Finely mince the lemongrass, along with the ginger and garlic; the pieces should be no bigger than ^{1}/$_{16}$ inch. (You can do most of this in a food processor and finish with a little hand chopping.) Put the mixture in a medium bowl and stir in the scallions, the oil, 1 tablespoon of the lime juice, 2 teaspoons of the fish sauce, and ^{1}/$_2$ teaspoon of the honey.

Slice the chicken into ^{1}/$_3$-inch-thick strips about 1 inch wide—slice across the grain and at an angle on breasts, and with the grain on thighs. You should have about 30 strips. Add to the bowl with the lemongrass mixture, stir to coat the chicken evenly, and refrigerate for about 30 minutes.

To make the dipping sauce, put the peanut butter in a small bowl. Stir in enough warm water to make a thick sauce (about ^{1}/$_4$ cup, depending on the peanut butter), then add the vinegar, chile garlic sauce, and the remaining 2 teaspoons fish sauce, 1^1/$_2$ teaspoons lime juice, and ^{1}/$_4$ teaspoon honey. Taste and adjust the saltiness, heat, or acidity to your liking; thin with more water if necessary.

Prepare a medium-hot gas or charcoal grill or heat a large grill pan. Meanwhile, thread the chicken onto the skewers. Grill the chicken, flipping once, until just cooked through, 1 to 3 minutes per side. (Alternatively, you can cook the skewers under a broiler—about 8 minutes total—but they won't brown as well.)

Serve with the dipping sauce.

Wine-Braised Chicken Legs with Root Veggies

SERVES 4 TO 6

This take on coq au vin has it all: tender, moist chicken, flavorful root veggies, and an incredibly rich sauce; to top it off, it's a one-pot meal. Serve with a simple garlicky green salad and lots of steamed white rice to soak up all the chicken broth goodness. Duck legs are a great substitute for the chicken legs, too.

You'll get the best results if you salt the legs the day before you cook, but it's not essential. If you are short on time, skip the salting and jump right in—just season the legs well with salt and pepper before you brown them.

6 large whole chicken legs (thighs and drumsticks; about 2¼ pounds)
Kosher salt and freshly ground black pepper
¼ cup extra-virgin olive oil, more as needed
⅓ cup all-purpose flour
3 thick slices bacon or pancetta, cut into ¼-inch-wide strips
1 large onion, peeled and cut into 1½-inch chunks
2 bay leaves
1 (750 ml) bottle dry aromatic white wine (such as a German or Alsatian Riesling)
4 pounds assorted root vegetables, such as fingerling potatoes, peeled carrots, turnips, and rutabagas, cut into 1½-inch chunks
3 large sprigs fresh thyme
4 cups chicken stock (or low-sodium broth)

Place the chicken legs on a large plate or baking sheet and season with 2 teaspoons salt and ½ teaspoon pepper. Refrigerate uncovered overnight.

The next day, position a rack in the center of the oven and heat to 300°F.

Remove the chicken from the refrigerator, rinse well, pat dry, and let come to room temperature while the oven heats.

In a large Dutch oven (or similar ovenproof pot), heat the olive oil over medium heat. Dredge the chicken legs in the flour, shaking off the excess.

Working in batches as necessary, arrange the legs in a roomy single layer in the pot, skin side down. Cook, turning occasionally, until deep golden brown all over, about 15 minutes per batch. Transfer to a plate and repeat with the remaining chicken, adding a tablespoon or more olive oil if the pan seems too dry.

Set aside the chicken legs and remove all but 1 tablespoon of the fat from the pot. Add the bacon and cook, stirring and scraping the pan frequently, until the bacon is browned and crispy, about 5 minutes.

Add the onion, bay leaves, 2 teaspoons salt, and ¼ teaspoon black pepper and cook, stirring, until the onions just start to brown on the edges, about 5 minutes. Add the wine and cook, stirring occasionally, until the wine has reduced by half and has thickened, about 5 minutes. Add the root vegetables and thyme and continue to cook, stirring, until the vegetables barely start to soften, 5 minutes longer.

Add the chicken legs and chicken stock. There should be enough liquid to just barely cover the chicken legs; add a little water if necessary. Increase the heat to medium-high and bring the liquid to a bare simmer. Cover the pot and transfer to the oven.

Bake until the chicken is cooked through and tender (if you pierce the thigh with a paring knife, you should feel no resistance), about 1¼ hours. Taste the sauce and season with more salt as needed.

Let rest for 30 minutes before serving.

Sumac-Roasted Chicken du Monde

SERVES 2 TO 4

My translation of one of Mom's great recipes, this dish quickly became a favorite among the regulars at my restaurant Rendezvous du Monde. Sumac is a spice used in marinades and salads throughout the Middle East. It has a tangy, citrusy flavor and adds a beautiful pinkish hue to the chicken. It's worth seeking out sumac, but if you can't find it, the recipe will still be delicious. Serve with buttered couscous or grilled country bread drizzled with the pan juices.

BRINE

7 cups water

1 cup dry white wine

6 tablespoons kosher salt

3 tablespoons sugar

2 tablespoons yellow curry powder

CHICKEN

3-pound chicken, cut into two halves

2 medium red onions (about 1 pound)

4 sprigs fresh thyme

2 tablespoons balsamic vinegar

1 tablespoon extra-virgin olive oil

2 teaspoons ground sumac

The day before you plan to cook:

Combine all the brine ingredients in a large pot and stir until the salt and sugar have dissolved. Put the chicken in the pot and top with a plate, if necessary, to keep the chicken submerged. Refrigerate for at least 6 hours or overnight.

When you're ready to cook the chicken:

Heat the oven to 450°F and remove the chicken from the refrigerator.

Peel and trim the onions, keeping as much of the root end intact as possible. Cut into 1-inch wedges, cutting through the root end so the layers stay connected. Put the onions and thyme in a large roasting pan, drizzle with the balsamic, and stir to combine.

Remove the chicken from the brine, dry off with paper towels, and rub with the olive oil. Sprinkle the sumac all over the chicken. Put the chicken halves skin side up in the pan, arranging the onions around them.

Roast, stirring the onions occasionally, until the skin is golden and an instant-read thermometer reads 165°F at the deepest part of the chicken's thighs, about 40 minutes. Remove the chicken from the pan and set aside on a cutting board. Stir the onions so that they pick up some of the juices and browned bits on the bottom of the pan. Taste and add a sprinkle of salt if needed.

To serve, spread the onions across the bottom of a serving platter and top with the chicken.

Romesco Chicken Salad

MAKES ABOUT 2¹/₂ CUPS, ENOUGH FOR ABOUT 4 SANDWICHES

This unique chicken salad is bound together with romesco sauce, the Spanish puree of red peppers, almonds, and olive oil. It takes the classic chicken salad sandwich to another level, but piled on crostini, sliced baguette, or even mini tart shells, you can also turn it into a fabulous hors d'oeuvre.

5 tablespoons Romesco Sauce (page 52)

2 tablespoons mayonnaise

2 teaspoons freshly squeezed lemon juice, more as needed

Pinch of cayenne pepper (optional), more as desired

2 cups shredded or diced cooked chicken (about 8 ounces)

¹/₄ cup finely diced small celery

2 tablespoons finely diced red onion

1 tablespoon chopped fresh parsley

Kosher salt

In a medium bowl, combine the romesco, mayonnaise, lemon juice, and cayenne and stir to blend. Add the chicken, celery, red onion, and parsley and stir to combine. Taste and add more salt or lemon juice as needed.

TURKEYS

The kind of turkey you buy has as much impact on flavor (if not more) as the way you cook it.

How to Buy

If you are new to the world of heritage breeds of meat, **HERITAGE TURKEYS** are a great place to start. Heritage breeds are the animal equivalent of heirloom tomatoes—unhybridized varieties that developed through natural selection rather than human intervention. Unlike common commercial turkeys, heritage birds are intensely flavorful on their own—more like a really good chicken or game bird—and require hardly any adulteration or flavorings. There are many breeds of heritage turkeys, but some of the most common are Standard Bronze, Bourbon Red, and Narragansett.

The other key advantage to heritage turkeys is that they usually live a more natural life. Commercial turkeys are bred to have unnaturally large breasts—so large that the birds can't even support their own weight or reproduce on their own. Heritage breeds, on the other hand, exist just as nature intended. This allows them to move about freely and without difficulty. Additionally, unlike most commercially produced turkeys, **HERITAGE TURKEYS ARE NOT ARTIFICIALLY INSEMINATED**, which is better from an animal welfare perspective.

MANY OF THE "GOLD STANDARD" CRITERIA FOR CHICKENS ALSO APPLY TO TURKEYS. Look for turkeys fed a non-GMO, vegetarian diet, raised on pasture, and not given preventive antibiotics or steroids. Air-chilled is preferable, as well.

There's nothing wrong with frozen turkeys, as long as they've been frozen soon after slaughter and kept that way with minimal temperature fluctuations. In fact, I'd choose a frozen heritage turkey over a fresh commodity turkey.

· ·

If you're cooking for just a few people or for a white-meat-only crowd, consider buying a turkey breast instead of a whole bird.

· ·

How to Store

Keep a frozen turkey in the freezer until a few days before you want to use it. Then let it defrost in the refrigerator (never at room temperature); allow at least three days for this. But even turkeys sold as "fresh" are transported and stored at near-freezing temperatures. So once it reaches your refrigerator, allow at least a day for it to thaw completely.

How to Use

Let the turkey come to room temperature before you cook it; depending on the size of the bird, this could take several hours.

Resist the urge to brine; it actually masks the incredible flavor in heritage turkeys. Instead, try a "salt cure": season the bird generously inside and out with kosher salt and refrigerate overnight.

Heritage turkeys tend to be leaner than commercial turkeys and have comparatively less white meat. For best results and to prevent the breasts from drying out, roast the whole bird until the breasts reach 155° to 160°F in the center. Then carefully separate the legs from the rest of the body and finish cooking the legs on their own in the rendered fat and pan juices. Or braise the legs and roast the breast separately.

AT THE VERY LEAST, LOOK FOR TURKEY THAT IS:

• Pasture-raised

• Fed a non-GMO, vegetarian diet, with no preventive antibiotics

IDEALLY, LOOK FOR:

• Heritage breed

• Not artificially inseminated

• Air-chilled and fresh, if available

LAMB

Lamb was the meat we ate most often in my family—and not just muscle, but offal as well. My mom's specialty was lamb brains, which she roasted under a dusting of Shake 'n Bake. She'd ring the buzzer at the butcher counter and ask the guy, "Got any brains?" The poor man would invariably look confused, and only then would she say, "Oh, I'm sorry! I meant lamb brains." It produced a chuckle every time.

How to Buy

One of the unique things about lamb is that much of it is pasture-raised—even the kind you buy at the supermarket. The reason is surprising: sheep are temperamental animals and have a hard time living in confinement. They don't respond well to excessive handling and may simply stop eating if penned in too closely.

LOOK FOR SMALL PRODUCERS THAT RAISE THEIR LAMB ON OPEN FIELDS AND LET THEM GRAZE ON GRASS. The best also rotate the sheep through pasture and practice other sustainable, controlled grazing techniques.

One challenge with lamb is that **IT CAN BE DIFFICULT TO FIND A LOCAL PRODUCER.** Most lamb sold in the United States comes from Australia and New Zealand, and those come from a few massive collectives. Domestic lamb ranches—concentrated in California and Colorado—tend to be smaller operations that sell under individual ranch or producer brands. Imported lamb can be a solid choice, but the shorter supply chain and the shorter food-miles distance make domestic lamb preferable.

AT THE VERY LEAST, LOOK FOR LAMB THAT IS:

- Raised on pasture and grass-fed
- Domestic, if possible
- Small in size
- Hormone- and antibiotic-free

IDEALLY, LOOK FOR:

- Heritage breeds

Some people don't like lamb because they associate the meat with a strong gamey flavor. However, that flavor is characteristic of mature sheep meat (mutton); it's all but absent in young lamb. Another reason to avoid older, larger lamb? They are likely to have come off of feedlots, where the sheep are fed large amounts of grain in their final months so they rapidly add weight. **IDEALLY, LOOK FOR SMALLER MUSCLES: LEGS THAT WEIGH 6 TO 8 POUNDS BONE-IN OR 4 TO 6 POUNDS BONELESS, AND RACKS THAT WEIGH 10 TO 12 OUNCES.**

Another way to avoid that gamey flavor is **TAKE A LOOK AT THE FAT AS YOU SHOP.** Yellow or darkish fat is an indicator of an older, mature animal; light, creamy fat (and even a slightly lighter colored flesh) tells you it's a young, tender animal.

As with all meat, look for lamb raised without hormones or antibiotics. Heritage breeds are increasingly available, as well; Romney, Tunis, and Targhee are just a few.

How to Store

You can generally store lamb in whatever packaging it came in. However, if the lamb is sitting in a pool of its own blood or juices, you'll extend the shelf life if you repackage it as soon as you get home: unwrap the lamb, pat dry with a paper towel, wrap in parchment or waxed paper, and set it on a plate to catch any juices. Use within three days; if it starts to smell funky or look slimy, throw it out.

How to Use

Because lamb meat comes from relatively young animals, their muscles haven't developed the sinews and toughness of older animals. So most cuts of lamb are fairly tender and lend themselves to quick cooking methods like pan-frying or grilling.

But keep in mind that lamb, especially lamb chops, develops that gamey flavor when well-done or overcooked. For milder flavor, **TRY KEEPING IT TO MEDIUM OR, EVEN BETTER, MEDIUM-RARE.**

Lamb racks are delicious, but demand for them also makes them the most expensive cut. I think the leg is a better value and tastes just as good. Most markets that

NAPA VALLEY LAMB: Don Watson

When Don Watson gives you directions to his ranch, the final turn may surprise you. How on earth could "enter the raceway through the front gate" possibly lead you to 1,500 of California's best-tasting lamb? The name of Don's business, Wooly Weeders, gives you a clue: in return for open pasture on which to raise his sheep, Don provides the Infineon Raceway (as well as other clients) a service in the form of lamb-powered "mowing." Watched over by five Peruvian sheep herders and a Border Collie named Bounce, who live on the property (and carry work visas especially for sheep herders), Don's sheep feast on grass, yellow starthistle, clover, and other flora that grow on

the rolling hills overlooking San Pablo Bay in Sonoma, California. Don personally delivers whole lambs to us at the store every week. I love how Don has found new audiences for sustainable ranching through his Wooly Weeders service.

carry lamb offer both the rack and the leg, so ask the butcher if he or she is willing to sell you just a portion of the leg. **TRY THE TOP SIRLOIN**, a single muscle from the top of the leg; it's perfect for two people, and you cook it just as you would a rack.

Shanks and shoulders are two cuts with a fair amount of connective tissue, so they require slow, moist cooking. (The shoulder can also be ground for burgers, sausage, and such.)

LAMB COOKING TEMPERATURES

125°–130°F: medium-rare
130°–135°F: medium
135°–140°F: well

Moroccan Lamb Meatloaf

SERVES 8 TO 10

This is no ordinary meatloaf. A hefty dose of fresh herbs and dried spices means it's packed with flavor; the yogurt, tahini, and rolled oats help keep it moist. We developed this recipe as a deli sandwich special, but it's just as delicious eaten on its own.

For best results, try to get ground lamb with 15 to 20 percent fat content; ground shoulder usually falls in this range. Meat from the leg is too lean and will result in a dry end product.

1 large onion, minced (2 cups)
1 cup rolled oats
1/2 cup coarsely chopped fresh cilantro
1/4 cup chopped fresh mint
3 tablespoons plain yogurt
2 tablespoons tahini
4 large cloves garlic, chopped
2 teaspoons ground allspice
1 1/2 teaspoons ground toasted cumin (see box page 192)
1 1/2 teaspoons paprika
3/4 teaspoon cayenne pepper
Kosher salt and freshly ground black pepper
2 1/2 pounds ground lamb
1 1/2 tablespoons harissa (see Note)
1 1/2 tablespoons tomato paste

Position a rack in the center of the oven and heat to 350°F. Line a large rimmed baking sheet with parchment or a nonstick liner and set aside.

Combine the onion, oats, cilantro, mint, yogurt, tahini, garlic, allspice, cumin, paprika, and cayenne in a large bowl, along with 4 teaspoons salt and 1 1/2 teaspoons pepper. Mix well to blend. With your hands, break the lamb into small chunks and add to the bowl. Mix gently but thoroughly; overmixing will make the meatloaf tough and dry. When all the ingredients are evenly combined, transfer to the baking sheet and shape into a flat loaf about 13 by 6 by 1 1/2 inches.

Bake until an instant-read thermometer registers 150°F at the thickest part of the loaf, 55 to 60 minutes.

Meanwhile, combine the harissa and tomato paste in a small bowl. When the meatloaf is done, brush the mixture over the loaf and bake for 10 to 15 minutes longer, or until the internal temperature reads 165°F.

Let the loaf rest for at least 15 minutes before slicing (longer is better, as the pooled juices will be reabsorbed into the meatloaf).

Note: Harissa is a chile-and-spice paste that hails from North Africa. For a slightly different effect, you could substitute Asian chile-garlic sauce.

GETTING YOUR GOAT

Long exclusive to ethnic meat markets, goat is enjoying a bit of a renaissance in culinary circles. Adventurous eaters are discovering that goat can be just as tender, succulent, and mildly flavored as lamb. (Just like lamb, smaller and younger goats are the most tender and mild of the herd.) Good domestic goat meat is still hard to find, and fairly expensive when you can find it, but this is likely to change as more people seek it out.

Breed is key in differentiating tough, gamey commodity goat meat from high-quality goat meat. Boer and Spanish brush goats are good meat breeds. Dairy goats need to kid (give birth) in order to produce milk, so the male kids are often processed and sold as meat, even though they are not ideal meat breeds.

Grilled Pimentón Leg of Lamb with Cucumber Raita

SERVES 8

This grilled beauty is the perfect entrée for an outdoor gathering. If you prefer to stay inside, a stove top grill pan (the kind that straddles two burners) works just as well as a "real" grill, although you won't get the smokiness that really makes this dish sing. (Pictured opposite with Padrón Pepper Poppers, page 142.)

1/2 teaspoon cumin seeds

1 1/2 cups Greek-style (thick) plain yogurt, preferably sheep's milk

4 teaspoons minced garlic

2 teaspoons hot pimentón (see Note)

1 teaspoon honey

Kosher salt

3- to 4-pound boneless leg of lamb, butterflied to an even 1 1/2- to 2-inch thickness (see Tip)

1 cup thinly sliced cucumber, preferably a thin-skinned variety like Armenian, Persian, or English

Toast and grind the cumin seeds (see box below). In a small bowl, combine the cumin, 1/2 cup of the yogurt, 3 teaspoons of the garlic, 1 teaspoon of the *pimentón*, the honey, and 2 teaspoons salt and stir to combine. Rub the mixture all over the lamb and refrigerate, covered, for at least 4 hours (overnight is even better).

An hour before you want to grill, take the lamb out of the refrigerator and let it come to room temperature.

Prepare a medium charcoal or gas grill fire. When the grill is hot, grill the lamb, uncovered, until it reaches 130°F at the center, 20 to 25 minutes per side. If the lamb starts to darken too quickly, move it to a cooler part of the grill or lower the heat.

Let the lamb rest for 20 to 30 minutes before cutting into 1/4-inch-thick slices. Sprinkle the slices with a little more salt.

While the lamb is resting, make the raita: Combine the cucumber with the remaining 1 cup yogurt, 1 teaspoon garlic, 1 teaspoon *pimentón*, 1 teaspoon salt, and a few grinds of pepper in a small bowl. Mix well and season to taste with more salt and pepper as needed. Serve alongside the lamb.

Note: Hot *pimentón* (spicy Spanish paprika) gives the dish a lovely heat, which is tempered by the cool yogurt. If you're not into spicy food, or if you're serving children, you can of course use sweet (dulce) or medium-hot (agridulce) paprika instead.

Tip: You can ask your butcher to butterfly the lamb, or you can do it yourself. To start, place the boneless leg skin (smooth) side down on a cutting board. With a sharp knife, make a series of long horizontal cuts through the thickest part so that the leg eventually fans out to a more or less even thickness.

TOASTED, GROUND CUMIN SEEDS

To toast cumin seeds, heat them in a small skillet over medium-high heat until aromatic and slightly darker, about 2 minutes. Let cool and grind in a mortar and pestle or coffee grinder or use the bottom of a sauté pan against a cutting board.

PORK

As a young cook, I never consciously thought about where pigs came from—in the States, where I had done all my cooking, pork came pre-cut and packaged in a box. But when I got a kitchen job in Switzerland, I found how different it could be. There, the staff saved all of their peelings and food scraps for the pig farmer. Every week when he dropped off our hog, he took away our scraps to feed to his herd. I was so impressed by this practice of getting more use out of our waste, and I loved how it fed the pigs that we would eventually serve our guests. That was one of my first lessons in sustainability, and it taught me a lot about where food comes from. So when San Francisco started its composting program for food service establishments, we were one of the first businesses to jump on board. Our food waste is composted and then sold as fertilizer to many of the wineries and farms we buy from—it goes full circle.

How to Buy

Here in America, it's pretty rare to find anyone (retailers or restaurants) who buy and butcher whole hogs, although the practice is gaining momentum across the country. The pork industry is highly concentrated among a few behemoth processors, who portion and package pork for retailers; the largest, Smithfield, puts out six billion pounds of packaged pork every year. These large companies have not just been reluctant to offer sustainable versions of their commodity pork; by intentionally violating many federal regulations and guidelines, they have continued to embrace husbandry and slaughter practices that are detrimental to the pigs, the environment, the workers, and even people who live near the producers' facilities. Additionally,

industrial pork production has put many small farmers out of business—between 1975 and 2008 the number of swine farms was reduced by 90 percent—because they can't compete with the artificially cheap price of mass-produced pork.

Most grocery stores carry only commodity pork. The best, most sustainable pork comes from **ALTERNATIVE SOURCES** such as farmers' markets, co-ops, natural food stores, and artisan butcher shops. Pigs are amenable to living in a variety of climates, so finding a local rancher is easier than you might think.

The benefits of buying from these alternative sources are many, but the biggest is that it offers a level of transparency that is hard to get with a chain retailer. It's much easier to find out what kind of conditions the pigs are raised in, what they're fed, and so forth.

As you shop, keep in mind that **ALL PORK SHOULD BE FREE OF ADDED HORMONES**, per USDA regulations. Producers who label their pork as "hormone-free" are simply restating the obvious.

Here are some of the factors that set good pork apart from the rest—look for them when you shop:

- **Organic, or close to it**—For pork that comes from large processors, or even large cooperatives, the certified organic label gives you specific assurances that might otherwise be elusive. It tells you, for instance, that the pigs were given organic, non-GMO feed, were not given antibiotics, and had access to the outdoors.

- **Antibiotic- and steroid-free**—Antibiotic use is rampant in pork production due to the abusively confined conditions the animals are raised in. They are often sick, bruised, and lacerated. Even though hormones are illegal in pork production, steroids are often added to the antibiotic regime to stimulate faster growth. Steroid levels in industrially raised pork are high enough to fail an Olympic athlete's drug test.

- **No injections or brines**—Many commercial processors "enhance" their pork by injecting the meat with a brine solution—often increasing the pork's weight by 10 percent. This makes the pork more tender and slower to spoil, but it also means you're paying for what is essentially salt water. It's easy to identify and avoid enhanced pork, as the law requires disclosure on the label.

- **Heritage breeds**—Many small-scale producers have rediscovered naturally occurring heritage breeds, the animal equivalent of an heirloom vegetable. These heritage pigs are well marbled with fat and incredibly flavorful. Red Wattle, Berkshire, and Duroc are a few varieties. Because heritage pigs developed through natural selection, each breed displays its own unique traits: varied loin size, intramuscular fat, cap fat (surface), and so on. At the Market, we encourage our guests to celebrate the many shapes and qualities that heritage pigs represent!

- **High-quality feed**—As with all meat, the pig's feed has a big impact on both its health and the flavor of the meat. Most pigs are fed grain—either corn or soy—which is all too often GMO. Look for pig ranchers who give their pigs non-GMO feed, acorns, whey, or like our friend Jude Becker in Iowa, organic grain that he grows himself.

As you shop for pork, keep in mind that fat is not only the key to flavor but also what keeps the meat from drying out as it cooks. The "other white meat"

AT THE VERY LEAST, LOOK FOR PORK THAT IS:

- **Organic**
- **Free of antibiotics and steroids**
- **Free of injections or other "enhancements"**

IDEALLY, LOOK FOR:

- **Heritage breeds, such as Red Wattle, Berkshire, or Duroc**
- **Raised on high-quality, non-GMO food**

---

campaign of the pork industry was brilliant in increasing consumption by Americans, but it resulted in flavorless, almost cardboard-like meat produced with no integrity or care for the animal, the environment, or the people eating it. So **LOOK FOR PORK THAT HAS SOME FAT ON IT**, either as a cap (fat that surrounds a muscle) or ideally in marbling (fat distributed within a muscle).

How to Store

You can generally store pork in whatever packaging it came in. However, if the pork is sitting in a pool of its own blood or juices, you'll extend the shelf life

---

BACON—CONSIDER THE CURE

Bacon is unquestionably America's favorite pork product and so important that pork bellies (the cut from which bacon is made) are traded on the Chicago Mercantile Exchange. There are many styles of bacon to choose from: some sweet, some salty, some smoky. Tasting different bacons side by side is really fun and a great way to discover your preferred level of smoke and seasoning.

All bacon is made from pork bellies that have been cured and then smoked. One factor influencing bacon's flavor is the cure recipe itself; different ratios of salt,

sugar, and spices produce different results. Most cured meat producers also use synthetically produced sodium nitrite to help prolong shelf life and preserve the meat's color and flavor. This additive has been linked to increased risk of cancer, so now many producers also offer nitrite-free versions of their products, using the naturally occurring sodium nitrates in celery juice to "cure" their meat. Because these meats don't contain sodium nitrite, the USDA requires that they be labeled "uncured," even though they are effectively cured.

The curing method also influences the end result. **Dry-cured** bacon is made by rubbing fresh pork belly with a dry mixture

of salt, sugar, spices, and either nitrates or nitrites; this not only transforms the meat and fat but also removes much of the liquid from the belly. The result is bacon that's firmer in texture (before cooking) and intensely flavored. **Wet-cured** bacon is made by submerging the pork belly in a nitrate or nitrite brine solution, which may also contain sugar and spices. This, too, transforms the meat and fat, but maintains the moisture content in the bacon, increasing the yield for the manufacturer. The retained moisture evaporates upon cooking, so wet-cured bacon is cheaper and shrinks significantly more than dry-cured bacon when cooked. Try both types to find your favorite!

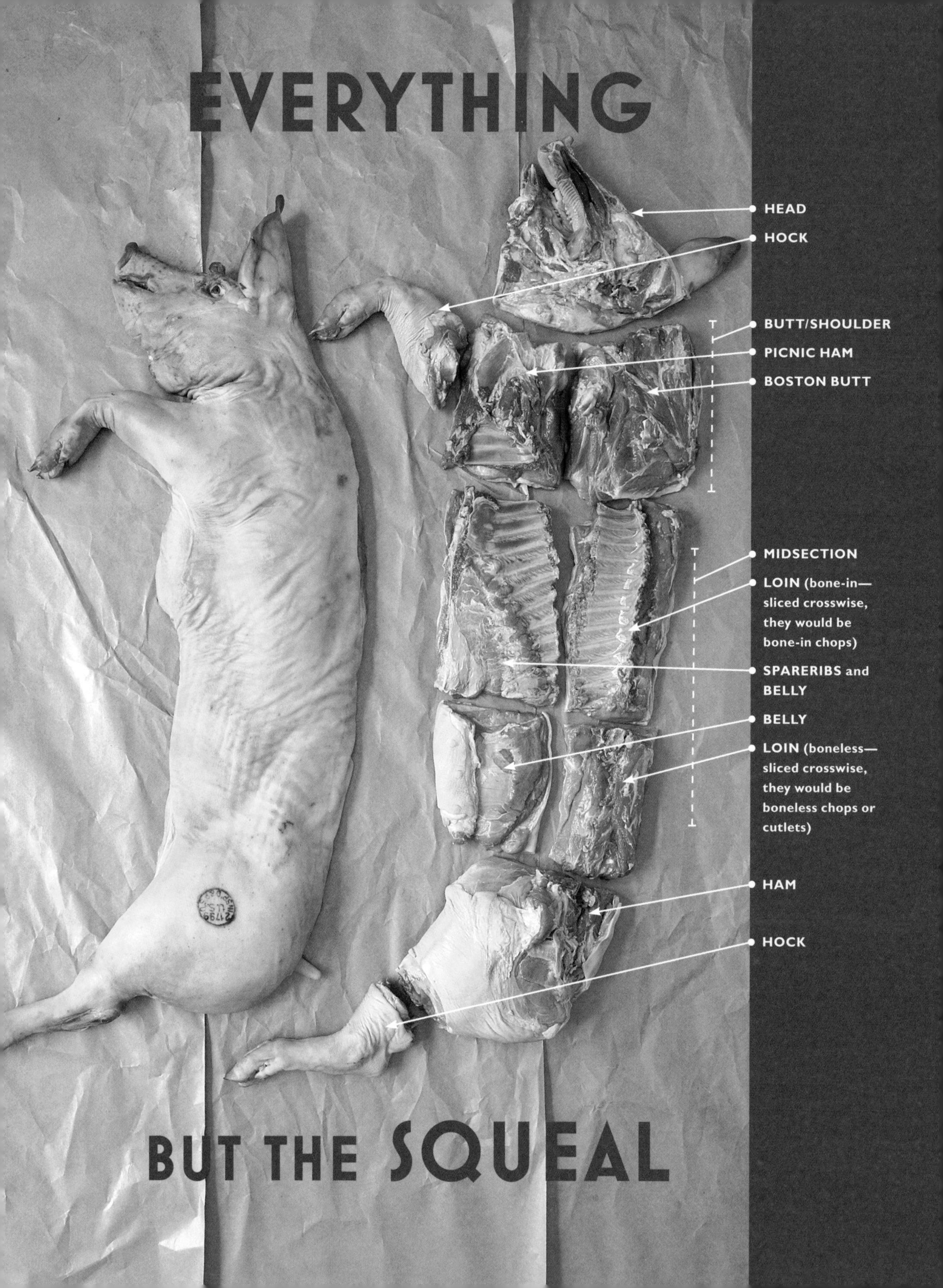

EVERYTHING

- HEAD
- HOCK

- BUTT/SHOULDER
- PICNIC HAM
- BOSTON BUTT

- MIDSECTION
- **LOIN** (bone-in— sliced crosswise, they would be bone-in chops)
- **SPARERIBS** and **BELLY**
- **BELLY**
- **LOIN** (boneless— sliced crosswise, they would be boneless chops or cutlets)

- HAM
- HOCK

BUT THE SQUEAL

if you repackage it as soon as you get home: unwrap the pork, pat dry with a paper towel, wrap in parchment or waxed paper, and set it on a plate to catch any juices. Use within three days; if it starts to smell funky or look slimy, throw it out.

With prolonged exposure to oxygen, the surface of pork will darken somewhat. This is purely a cosmetic change and does not affect the flavor of the meat.

Brining is a great way to add flavor to pork and ensure juiciness. To make a simple brine, combine 8 cups water, 1/2 cup kosher salt, and 1/4 cup sugar and stir until dissolved. Add pork and additional herbs, if desired, and refrigerate for 30 minutes and up to 24 hours (for larger cuts). Drain and pat pork dry before cooking.

DEVIL'S GULCH RANCH:
Mark Pasternak

Pigs are known for their willingness to eat just about anything (they are omnivores), but few ranchers take advantage of that fact quite as much as Mark Pasternak of Devil's Gulch Ranch in Nicasio, California. The area is populated by food producers of all sorts, and the Los Angeles native (who knew from the age of two that he wanted to be a farmer) is more than happy to relieve these companies of their byproducts and stale or unsellable castoffs. Mark believes that animal feed should complement, not compete with, the human food system, and it's a boon for the pigs, too. Their fat bellies betray the whey, soybean pulp, and even tortillas that make up much of their diet, and the meat itself is incredibly flavorful. We sell Mark's heritage breed pigs (which we buy whole and break down ourselves) as well as his rabbits at the Market, and he's developed a cult following among many local chefs.

How to Use

We are all busy people, so it's no surprise that the most popular cuts of pork are those that cook quickly. Peruse the pork section of any supermarket aisle and you'll find that the offerings reflect this: pork loin, tenderloin, chops, and cutlets take up the majority of the shelf space.

Those cuts are fine. But they're not as exciting to me as, say, a pork shoulder. It's relatively inexpensive, has the perfect ratio of meat to fat, and requires very little effort to cook. All it needs is a little salt and plenty of time. This means you must plan accordingly, but you'll be rewarded with silken morsels of succulent, tender pork. There's good reason to venture beyond quick-cooking pork and give some of the other cuts a go.

We used to be warned to cook pork thoroughly to reduce the risk of trichinosis. Unfortunately, if you cook lean pork until all the pink is gone, you're going to end up with one dry, chewy pork chop! Fortunately, the dreaded roundworm is virtually nonexistent in any pork you may buy nowadays. So feel free to keep a little tinge of pink in there; the pork will be more succulent and still (fairly) risk-free. (Still, it's all the more reason to buy good pork.)

> ### PORK COOKING TEMPERATURES FOR CHOPS AND QUICK ROASTS
>
> 130°–140°F: medium (just pink in center)
> 140°–150°F: medium-well
> 150°–155°F: well

> ### TIMING GUIDELINES FOR LARGER ROASTS (2 POUNDS OR MORE)
>
> Medium = 18–20 minutes/pound
> Medium-well = 20–25 minutes/pound
> Well = 25–30 minutes/pound

> ### GLORIOUS DRIPPINGS
>
> When I get a really good piece of pork, I don't want any of it to go to waste. I say this from an economical perspective as well as a philosophical one: good pork can be expensive, but I also appreciate how much time and effort a passionate rancher puts into the product. I collect drippings that come off of pork roasts, chops, and even bacon. Stored in the refrigerator, they keep almost indefinitely and can stand in for oil or butter in just about any savory dish.

- **Chops and Other Quick-Cooking Cuts**—These cuts cook quickly, and because they're so mild, they lend themselves to many different flavors and cuisines. They're well suited to stove top, broiling, or grilling.
  CUTS: *Pork chops, Cutlets (Boneless Chops), and Tenderloins*

- **Quick Roasts**—These cuts are too large to pan-cook and are better suited for the oven or indirect grilling. They're tender enough that they don't require lengthy cooking times.
  CUTS: *Loin Roasts (Boneless or Bone-in), Top Sirloin Roasts, Tenderloins*

- **Slow Roasts and Stewing Cuts**—These cuts are large and have a fair amount of connective tissue, so they require plenty of slow-cooking time to cook through. If you can manage the wait, the payoff is stellar. The cuts are less expensive and the result is tender, moist, and luscious. They're best suited for roasting, indirect grilling, and stewing/braising.
  CUTS: *Shoulders (also known as Picnic Ham and Boston Butt), fresh hams, ribs, belly*

Giant Pork Roast
with Tangy Carolina Slaw

SERVES 8 TO 10

This simple slow roast uses the pork shoulder, one of the least expensive cuts of pork—so go ahead and splurge on heritage breed pork if you can. Regardless of the variety, what makes this roast so good is the dry rub, which gently cures the pork and infuses it with flavor. Two days' marinating time is ideal, but 24 hours is fine, too. Don't do it if you can't wait at least a day, though; the results will not be ideal.

If you're lucky enough to get a roast with the skin on, you'll be rewarded with a bonus: chicharrones! The skin will bubble and puff as the roast cooks; if you want to amplify the crunchiness, after the roast is done, take off the skin and place it on a cooling rack set on the roasting pan. Continue to roast until the fat has rendered off to your liking.

The accompanying slaw is inspired by the kind typically served with Carolina-style barbecue. Its sweet and sour notes complement the rich pork nicely.

ROAST

6 large cloves garlic
Kosher salt and freshly ground black pepper
1 tablespoon chopped fresh thyme
1 teaspoon crushed red chile flakes
3/4 teaspoon fennel seeds, toasted and
    lightly crushed
5- to 6-pound boneless pork shoulder, preferably
    skin-on

SLAW

1 medium head Napa cabbage (about 1 1/4 pounds)
3 medium carrots, peeled and grated
3 tablespoons extra-virgin olive oil
2 tablespoons cider vinegar, more as needed
1 teaspoon Dijon mustard
1/2 teaspoon honey
3/4 teaspoon fennel seeds, toasted lightly and crushed
Kosher salt and freshly ground black pepper

To make the roast:

Coarsely chop the garlic, sprinkle with a pinch of salt, and smash and smear it into a paste with the side of your knife. Transfer to a bowl and add the thyme, chile flakes, fennel seed, 1 1/2 tablespoons salt, and 1 teaspoon pepper. Stir to blend and set aside.

Put the pork skin side up on a cutting board and score the skin (or fat) in a crosshatch pattern of 1-inch squares, being careful not to cut into the meat itself. (If the meat doesn't have a cap of fat on one side, skip this step.) Then turn the pork skin side down and cut the roast in half horizontally so that it opens up like a book, cutting along the natural seams as much as possible. Spread about two-thirds of the spice mixture over the top (cut side) of the pork, then fold it back together in its original shape. Rub the remaining spice mixture on the outside of the roast.

Tie butcher twine around the roast at 2-inch intervals. Put the roast skin side up on a rack set over a roasting pan or large baking sheet and refrigerate uncovered for 24 to 72 hours.

When you are ready to cook the roast, take the pork from the refrigerator and let it come to room temperature (at least 1 hour). Preheat the oven to 425°F.

Remove the rack, put the roast directly on the roasting pan, and roast the pork until its surface starts to turn brown, about 30 minutes. Lower the heat to 300°F and continue to roast for at least 4 hours, basting every 45 minutes or so and spooning off the excess fat as necessary. You'll know it's done when the pork is visibly wobbly (a sign that the connective tissue has broken down) and a fork goes into the meat with little resistance. The roasting time will depend on the size and shape of the roast.

Let the roast rest on a cutting board for at least 15 minutes, then slice into 1/2-inch slabs.

To make the slaw:

Quarter the cabbage lengthwise and then crosswise into thin strips. Place in a large bowl along with the carrots. In a small bowl, whisk together the oil, vinegar, mustard, honey, fennel seed, 1 teaspoon salt, and 1/4 teaspoon pepper. Drizzle over the cabbage and carrots and toss well. Let rest for about 10 minutes, then toss again and taste. If necessary, add more vinegar or salt.

Serve a mound of salt alongside each serving of pork.

Pan-Fried Pork Cutlets
with Bing Cherries

SERVES 2

Cherries are just as delightful in savory contexts as they are in sweet ones; here, they're combined with sage and a little vinegar to complement the mild flavor of pork chops. This is a perfect dish for a romantic dinner for two.

This is a classic example of a simple pan sauce and can be modified for different meats or seasons. Try swapping in different fruits, herbs, or vinegars, depending on your whims and desires. If cherries aren't in season, figs or apricots would be especially good.

3/4 cup Bing cherries (about 18)
6 center-cut, 1/2-inch-thick boneless pork chops
   (aka cutlets; about 14 ounces total)
Kosher salt and freshly ground black pepper
1 tablespoon extra-virgin olive oil
1 large shallot, thinly sliced
1 tablespoon unsalted butter
1 tablespoon cider or red wine vinegar
1/2 teaspoon Dijon mustard
1/4 teaspoon finely chopped fresh sage
1 cup salt-free chicken stock or salt-free broth
   (see Note)

Pit the cherries and cut half of them in half. Set aside.

Season the pork with 3/4 teaspoon salt and a few grinds of black pepper and let come to room temperature.

Heat the olive oil in a large skillet over medium-high heat. When hot, add as many pork chops as will fit in a roomy single layer and let cook undisturbed for 2 minutes. When the first side is golden brown, flip and cook until just firm and cooked through, 2 to 3 minutes longer. Transfer the pork to a plate, cover loosely with foil, and repeat with any remaining chops.

Lower the heat to medium and add the shallot and half the butter. Cook, stirring frequently, until the shallots start to soften, about 1 minute. Add the vinegar, Dijon, sage, and a good pinch of salt and cook, stirring occasionally, until the shallots are soft and the pan is almost dry. Add the stock along with any juices that have accumulated under the cutlets. Increase the heat to high and bring to a boil. Add the cherries and cook, stirring occasionally, until the liquid has reduced to one-fourth of its original volume, 3 to 4 minutes.

Remove from the heat, season with more salt if desired, and swirl in the remaining half of the butter. Pour the sauce over the chops and serve immediately.

Note: Because the liquid gets reduced so dramatically, it's important to use salt-free stock or broth. Otherwise, the sauce can end up too salty.

Pozole

MAKES 16 CUPS

This classic Mexican soup develops its flavors from a series of techniques: braising, roasting, toasting, and frying. The soup itself is fabulous, but this dish is really elevated by the garnishes. Put them out in bowls and let guests help themselves to whatever they want.

The soup is best when made one day in advance to allow the flavors to come together. If you can't wait, be sure to save some for the next day so you can see how much better it gets.

2 fresh pasilla (chilaca) or poblano chiles
3 tablespoons grapeseed or other neutral oil
1 dried ancho chile
1 dried guajillo chile
1 1/2 pounds pork shoulder, trimmed of excess fat and
    cut into 1/2- to 3/4-inch cubes
Kosher salt
1 large white onion, diced
4 large cloves garlic, coarsely chopped
2 teaspoons cumin seeds, toasted lightly and ground
    in a mortar and pestle
1 teaspoon dried Mexican oregano (see Note)
8 cups chicken stock (or low-sodium broth)
2 (29-ounce) cans white hominy, rinsed and drained
2 tablespoons freshly squeezed lime juice
1 cup water
Garnishes of your choice (see list below)

GARNISH OPTIONS

Choose as many of these options as you like; in my opinion, the first four are "must-haves."

  Finely shredded green cabbage
  Fresh limes, cut in half for squeezing
  Crisp fried tortillas (or high-quality store-
      bought tortilla chips)
  Sliced avocado
  Finely diced red onion or scallion
  Thinly sliced radishes
  Sliced fresh jalapeños
  Hot sauce
  Coarsely chopped cilantro leaves

If you have a gas stove top, char the fresh chiles over a medium flame, turning them regularly until black and blistered on all sides, about 8 minutes. Otherwise, char them under the broiler, watching them carefully and turning them until black all over. Let cool enough to handle, then peel, seed, and dice the chiles and set aside.

Heat the oil in a large stockpot over low heat. Add the dried chiles and fry, flipping once, until aromatic and blistered all over, about 1 minute total. (Be careful not to let them burn.) Remove the chiles and set aside.

Increase the heat to medium-high, season the pork with 1/2 teaspoon salt, and add enough of the pork to the pot to make a roomy single layer. Cook, turning occasionally, until browned on all sides, about 8 minutes. Transfer to a plate and repeat with the remaining pork. When all the pork is browned, return it and any accumulated juices to the pot. Add the onion and sauté, stirring frequently, until soft and translucent, about 5 minutes. Add the garlic, cumin, and oregano and cook for 3 minutes more, stirring constantly.

Add the reserved fresh and dried chiles, chicken stock, hominy, and 1 tablespoon salt to the pot and bring just to a boil. Reduce the heat to maintain a bare simmer and cover the pot. Simmer gently for 1 1/2 hours, then remove the dried chiles and set aside.

As the soup continues to simmer, remove and discard the stem and seeds from the dried chiles. Put the chiles in a blender along with the lime juice and water and puree until smooth. Add the puree to the soup and continue to simmer, covered, for an additional 30 minutes to 1 hour, or until the pork is meltingly tender.

Let the soup rest for at least 30 minutes. Then taste and season with more salt as needed before serving.

Note: Mexican oregano is sweeter and more intense than the European oregano you more commonly find at the supermarket; in fact, they're from distinct plant families altogether and are not interchangeable. Mexican oregano is increasingly available at grocery stores and is also found in most Latin markets.

Around-the-World Pork Sausage Patties

MAKES 6 SMALL PATTIES

I'm particularly proud of our house-made sausages, which we have been making and selling at the Market since day one. They're delicious, and they're also free of the fillers, additives, and preservatives common in commercially made sausages.

You don't need a meat grinder or a sausage stuffer to make sausage at home. You can use preground pork shoulder, mix in the spices of your choice, and form them into patties or kebabs. Here I share three of my favorite spice combinations: a classic breakfast sausage, a hot Italian variety, and a sweet Spanish-style chorizo.

If pork is not your thing, ground chicken or turkey that has a 15 to 20 percent fat content will work as well.

1 pound ground pork, plus your choice of one of the following seasoning mixes:

BREAKFAST SAUSAGE
1 tablespoon cold water
1 teaspoon kosher salt
1 teaspoon freshly ground black pepper
1 teaspoon dried sage
3/4 teaspoon dried marjoram
1/2 teaspoon dried savory
1/8 teaspoon dried thyme
1/8 teaspoon ground nutmeg

HOT ITALIAN
2 tablespoons grated onion
1 tablespoon dry red wine
1 tablespoon minced parsley
1 teaspoon kosher salt
3/4 teaspoon paprika
3/4 teaspoon crushed fennel seed
1/2 teaspoon crushed red chile flakes, more to taste
1/4 teaspoon freshly ground black pepper
1 medium clove garlic, minced

SPANISH CHORIZO
1 tablespoon dry white wine
1 teaspoon kosher salt
2 tablespoons sweet smoked paprika (pimentón dulce—or use half sweet and half hot)
1/4 teaspoon freshly ground black pepper
1/4 teaspoon cayenne pepper
1/4 teaspoon crushed fennel seed
1 medium clove garlic, minced

Extra-virgin olive oil, as needed
More kosher salt, as needed

In the bowl of a stand mixer fitted with the paddle attachment, gently break up the pork into chunks. Add the spice ingredients and mix on medium speed, just until blended and the pieces of fat start to look a little "smeared" against the meat (see Tip).

Heat a tablespoon or so of oil in a small skillet over medium-high heat. Form a little of the sausage mixture into a patty and cook, flipping occasionally, until the pork is cooked through. Let cool slightly, then taste for seasoning. Gently mix in more salt as needed and retest if you like.

Shape the remaining sausage into patties or mold around skewers to make kebabs. Cook on the stove top or a grill.

Note: You can make the sausage up to a day ahead of time. Store it covered in the refrigerator, but let it come to room temperature before cooking.

Tip: The key to making good sausage is to beat the mixture just until the fat starts to stretch, but not blend, into the meat; that way, the mixture will hold together and the flavors will be well integrated. It's important to keep all ingredients cool; otherwise, the fat will melt into the meat. The ideal for this is to use a stand mixer with the paddle attachment; rinse the bowl and attachment in icy-cold water to chill them first. But you can also use your hands, as long as you keep them cool (I dip mine in an ice bath).

FISH AND SEAFOOD

We sell a lot of salmon in our Market—more than any other type of fish. Wild salmon is especially popular, as it's a local product with lower risk of chemical contaminants. Pacific wild king salmon isn't always available, though. Governing councils determine the time frame and limits for the fishing season, based on how many fish are out there and when. Some years the Pacific salmon season is called off altogether so that the fish populations can recover from overfishing, human impact on the spawning areas, and other factors. Although our customers are invariably disappointed when local wild salmon isn't available, it's an important reminder that we *should* be dependent on nature's whims, and not the other way around. Fortunately, the Alaska wild salmon fishery is well managed and available every year to supplement any shortfall from the Pacific harvest, though it is often more expensive because of basic supply and demand.

How to Buy

The original source of fish and seafood is often hard to trace. Most fishing (wild fishing, at least) depends on a vast network of small-scale fishermen, who then sell their product to brokers and distributors. Unlike farmers, there's virtually no name recognition with fishermen. It makes sense when you think about it. Whereas farmers actually cultivate and harvest their product, fishermen are not *producing* fish; they're just harvesting it. Also, a fishing expedition may traverse many countries' waters over thousands of miles; on ship, they don't necessarily label exactly where each haul came from. Not much information comes in from the ship, and the retailer is several transactions removed from the people on the boat.

Even for a conscientious, well-meaning retailer such as myself, the waters of information can be quite murky. Things change along the supply chain, and the important facts don't always get passed along. Here's an example:

For some time, we had been buying tilapia from a well-known and very well-respected seafood wholesaler. We chose to get the tilapia from this particular vendor because the fish was responsibly farmed in California. It was a plentiful, sustainable, local product, and our customers loved it. Then we discovered that at some point the tilapia farm had closed. Apparently the wholesaler had switched to Ecuadorian tilapia but neither notified us nor updated their product list. Not only did that company lose some of our trust, but also we were horrified to have unwittingly misinformed our customers about what they were buying.

HERE'S THE RUB: THE WHOLE SEAFOOD SYSTEM HINGES ON TRUST. You have to find a fishmonger who can answer your questions, but more important is that the fishmonger is sourcing from trustworthy wholesalers and fishermen.

But how can you know? You can tell a lot just by talking to the fishmonger. Can they tell you where that fish came from or how it was caught? If they don't know, can they find out from the wholesaler? Do you feel like the fishmonger cares about answering your questions or that you're being brushed off? If the story sounds fishy, it probably is.

SEA CHANGE AT THE FISH COUNTER

Change is under way. At the Market, we recently started working with a new breed of fishmonger: all their fish is 100 percent traceable (down to the name of the boat) and 100 percent sustainable (no bycatch, no negative impact on the environment). It's the project of Kenny Belov of Fish Restaurant in Sausalito, the first West Coast restaurant to be certified by the Monterey Bay Aquarium. He has made a commitment not only to serving only sustainable fish in his restaurant, but also to wholesaling his fish to other restaurants and retailers, because he knows the only way the fishermen he works with will survive and thrive and continue to be motivated to do the right thing is to have a market to sell to. We need to encourage fisherman and the industry to improve their practices and to work with legislators to improve our laws, so that our seafood supply will perpetuate into the future.

To further complicate things, the issues surrounding fish and seafood are entirely different from those surrounding other types of animal protein. Not only are the health concerns different, but also the environmental impact—especially on other species—is much greater.

- **Population management and control**—We Americans eat a lot of fish—more than our oceans and rivers can supply. Although some species (like California salmon) are protected by regulated seasons and catch limits, many more—like swordfish—are not. The very existence of these high-demand species is threatened because of overzealous, unregulated fishing practices and ever-developing fishing technology. Fish have no chance against our fancy sonar, detection devices, and massive nets.

- **Mercury and other contaminants**—Industrialization has done more than pollute our skies. Thanks to runoff from power plants and from dairy and animal factory farms, many larger species such as tuna now contain dangerous levels of mercury, which can cause neurological problems in babies and children. PCBs also accumulate in fish; over time, consumption can lead to serious health problems in babies and adults alike.

- **Impact on other species and on the ecosystem**—Some catch methods, such as trawl nets used to harvest shrimp, also scoop up significant quantities of other species in the process. These "bycatch" critters often die before being thrown back. Other catch methods, and even many fish farms (called "aquaculture") can destroy habitats and leave a wake of pollution.

The concerns are many, and complex, and a little different for each species we consume. Where you live is even a factor. And wild fish and seafood populations are constantly evolving. A fish that's considered sustainable can quickly become less so and then eventually bounce back. Fishing technologies change. Our health priorities shift. It's a lot to keep up with.

THE GOOD NEWS IS THAT THERE IS HELP. The Monterey Bay Aquarium is just one of many organizations offering a plethora of resources to help you make good choices. Their website offers exhaustive information about these issues, as well as species-specific information for just about any kind of seafood you might want to eat. They issue monthly updates on the status of specific fisheries, so check the site often for the most current information. Perhaps best of all are their downloadable pocket guides and mobile phone

FISH FARMING

Because of high demand and widespread overfishing of our wild fish and seafood populations, a sustainable seafood landscape will inevitably include aquaculture (farming) to supplement what our oceans, lakes, and streams provide. Aquaculture is often criticized for its negative environmental impacts and high "feed-to-fillet" ratio (the amount of food required to produce a pound of farmed fish). However, a few producers are finding innovative ways to farm fish sustainably, including land-based tanks (which eliminates the risk of fish escaping and endangering wild populations), filtering and reusing water, and composting the solid waste that's filtered out. Such innovations help make aquaculture a more viable option for supplying the world's future needs.

Unfortunately, as of this writing, there is still no 100 percent sustainable salmon farm operation. A few come close, but due to their large open net pens in the ocean, they cannot guarantee that no fish escape, thus potentially contaminating the wild population. Most salmon farms are major environmental offenders—the ocean's version of a factory farm. The fish feed contains antibiotics (to fight lice infestation and other diseases in the overcrowded pens) and dye to color the fish to look like wild salmon. It also takes three (or more) pounds of food to produce one pound of farmed salmon. If improperly managed, the waste from these factory farms renders the surrounding waters sterile and highly polluted. Entire communities are destroyed and left abandoned once the farming operation, having sucked all the life out of the area, picks up and moves on. **Eating no salmon is better than supporting these operations.**

applications. I have listed contact information for some of these resources on page 285.

Provenance aside, you also want to make sure that whatever fish you buy is high quality, fresh, and delicious. Keep these in mind as you inspect the fish case:

- **Frozen fish is nothing to sniff at.** True, there's nothing quite like a gorgeous, glistening piece of fresh-off-the-boat fish. But that doesn't mean that frozen fish can't be great, too; frozen right on the boat within hours of being caught, it maintains its like-fresh characteristics (like flavor and texture) better than some of its never-frozen counterparts.

- **Fresh fish and seafood should smell bright and briny,** not funky or "fishy." Whole fish should have clear eyes and bright red gills. Bloodlines (the darker streak that runs the length of the fish) should be bright, not gray or drab. Clams, oysters, and mussels should be tightly closed. Feel free to ask your fishmonger to let you smell the fish. He or she should be thrilled to.

- **Be flexible and ask for alternatives.** If you're cooking from a recipe that calls for an unsustainable fish, don't be afraid to substitute for another, more sustainable fish. If you aren't sure which types of fish are interchangeable, ask for help. Good fishmongers are just as well versed in cooking seafood as they are in selling it!

Buying Shrimp (aka Prawns)

If you change only one seafood-buying habit, make it switching to sustainable shrimp. Most shrimp sold in the United States is from Southeast Asia, from either pollution-producing farms or fisheries that employ unsustainable catch methods. Bycatch is the most notable drawback; for every pound of shrimp caught, an average of six pounds (sometimes up to twelve pounds) of additional marine life is caught and left to die. And much of it is harvested using habitat-damaging trawls, which drag along the ocean floor and cause severe damage to ecosystems. Instead, seek out domestic shrimp that is either **SUSTAINABLY FARMED OR WILD-CAUGHT USING TRAPS**. In general, buying American is a better choice, since the U.S. has the strictest standards for managing fisheries.

Shrimp are often labeled with a size descriptor like "jumbo" or "large," but these terms are neither regulated nor consistently applied. Instead, **REFER TO THE MUCH MORE RELIABLE NUMERIC SIZE**—two numbers separated by a slash mark—which refers to the minimum and maximum number of shrimp in one pound of that particular size. So 31/40 means 31 to 40 shrimp per pound. The smaller the numbers, the bigger the shrimp, and vice versa.

UNLESS SPECIFICALLY LABELED OTHERWISE, MOST SHRIMP HAS BEEN PREVIOUSLY FROZEN (retailers often thaw before displaying). Although there's nothing wrong with shrimp that has been frozen and stored with minimal temperature fluctuations, fresh, never-frozen shrimp is a special treat for its superior flavor and unbeatable texture. You can find fresh shrimp from the Gulf area as well as from California's Monterey Bay.

Shrimp is often treated with preservatives such as sodium metabisulfite to prevent the development of

MONTEREY FISH MARKET:
Paul Johnson and Tom Worthington

Since its establishment in 1978, Monterey Fish Market has been revo-
lutionizing the fish industry. At the time of Monterey Fish's founding,
the fish business was insular and unwelcoming to newcomers to the
scene. Instead of forcing his way in with the big players, founder Paul
Johnson, with his partner Tom Worthington (pictured below), focused
on small local fishermen. They were bringing in great product caught
using environmentally friendly catch methods but were unable to
compete with larger fishing operations, and Monterey Fish gave them
a new and viable outlet. The company also began to collaborate with
area chefs not just to understand their needs but also to introduce
and promote species like skate and monkfish, once uncommon on the
West Coast.

The company has grown to a $15 million a year business and is consid-
ered an authority on—and reliable source for—sustainably harvested fish
and seafood. And in 2007, Paul Johnson published the award-winning
*Fish Forever: The Definitive Guide to Understanding, Selecting, and
Preparing Healthy, Delicious, and Environmentally Sustainable Seafood.*
I recommend it to anyone who wants to delve deeper into this realm.

EAT GOOD FOOD

dark spots on the shrimp. Some of these chemicals can be dangerous to workers who handle the shrimp.

The heads of shrimp are especially perishable, which is a major reason that most shrimp in the United States is sold headless. However, **IF YOU SEE HEAD-ON SHRIMP AT THE MARKET, TRY THEM!** The flavor is truly amazing, plus all those leftover heads make for excellent shrimp stock.

Buying Lobsters and Crab

If you live near the coast and have a local source of lobsters and/or crab, you probably already know how lucky you are! Wherever you live, **TRY TO BUY THESE CRITTERS FROM AS NEARBY AS POSSIBLE, AND TAKE ADVANTAGE OF THEM WHEN THEY'RE IN SEASON.**

IDEALLY, BUY LIVE LOBSTERS AND CRAB; THEY SHOULD BE FAIRLY WRIGGLY AND ACTIVE, not sluggish or lethargic. Buy them the same day you want to cook them. However, if you choose to buy them already cooked, make sure they were cooked on site (wherever that might be) in the past 24 hours.

Buying Scallops

Scallops are sometimes treated with a sodium solution, which acts as a preservative and also keeps the scallops white and plump. The preservatives themselves are unappealing, and they also prevent scallops from browning properly. **ALWAYS BUY "DRY" SCALLOPS, WHICH MEANS THEY HAVE NOT BEEN TREATED IN THIS WAY.** They should also be consistent in color and smell briny (not like iodine). The fresher they are, the more translucent and firm they will appear.

THE BEST SCALLOPS ARE CALLED DIVER SCALLOPS. These are collected by hand by divers and thus have minimal negative impact on the sea floor. They are generally the largest in size, with 5 to 20 of these scallops per pound. The next best are **DAY BOAT SCALLOPS,** which refers to boats that fish for scallops just for the day, rather than the traditional practice of being at sea for up to ten days before returning to harbor. Day boat scallops can range in size from 10 to 30 per pound. Look for scallops that are trawl caught as opposed to dredged, as there is less damage to the sea floor.

BAY SCALLOPS are much smaller in size, about 50 to 90 per pound.

Buying Mussels, Clams, and Oysters

AS A GROUP, THESE BIVALVES TEND TO BE PRETTY SUSTAINABLE; they're small, they reproduce fairly quickly, and they serve as natural filters for their ecosystems. Look for mussels, clams, and oysters that are tightly closed (if they're slightly ajar, they should close up when lightly tapped on a counter). **TRY NOT TO BUY ONES THAT ARE PREPACKAGED IN MESH BAGS,** as this makes it difficult to determine whether the shells are closed.

How to Store

Freshness is of paramount importance in cooking seafood. Not only is the flavor at stake, but less-than-fresh seafood can put you out of commission temporarily, as well. For the best quality and freshness, follow these simple guidelines:

- **If you buy it frozen, keep it that way**—Similarly, if you buy previously frozen, thawed fish or seafood, do not refreeze it (it diminishes the flavor and texture).

- **Keep it as cold as possible**—At the store, ask for a bag of ice to help keep it cold on the way home. Then keep it in the coldest part of the refrigerator. You can leave fish in whatever wrapping they came in, but clams, mussels, and oysters should come out of their plastic bag and go into an ice-filled colander set into a larger bowl. (They will suffocate and die if kept in a plastic bag.)

- **Store properly**—Wrap live lobsters and crabs loosely in damp newspaper and set in a roasting pan or similar container.

- **Cook seafood within a day or two of purchasing it**—If you aren't able to cook fish right away, you can buy a little time by dipping it into a saltwater solution before you refrigerate it. This keeps microbial action at bay and keeps the fish fresher longer.

- **If in doubt, throw it out**—It's not worth risking getting sick just to avoid wasting money. If seafood smells strong, funky, ammoniated, or otherwise "off," toss it into the garbage and don't look back.

DRAKES BAY FAMILY FARMS:
The Lunney Family

Nestled into a picturesque bay in the Point Reyes National Seashore, the Drakes Bay oyster farm is a self-sustaining part of its ecosystem in more ways than one. Whereas most oyster farms buy their larvae from farms in the Pacific Northwest, Drakes Bay is the only farm in California to hatch its own larvae. The Lunney family also runs the last surviving

oyster cannery in the state, just a few steps away from the briny estuary where the oysters are grown. The thriving business is an important part of the local economy as well. In a region where men dominate the agriculture-heavy workforce, half of Drakes Bay's thirty-some employees are women. And in an effort to counteract the "seafood trade deficit" of Northern California, the Lunneys limit most of their distribution to local restaurants and markets. Although this limits the number of folks who enjoy their sweet, briny oysters, it helps ensure a more sustainable business—not just in terms of the ecosystem, but for the community and local economy as well.

How to Use

Some people are intimidated by cooking fish, whether it's fretting over cooking times or anxiety over flipping a fillet. It's actually not that hard if you use the right equipment and pay attention to a few key areas:

- **If frozen, thaw fish and seafood before you intend to cook it**—If time permits, the ideal is to thaw it overnight in the refrigerator. Otherwise, to thaw it more quickly, put it in a bowl in the sink and run a steady stream of cool water over it until thawed (timing depends on the size and thickness of the item). This works equally well for fish fillets and shrimp.
- **Use fish-friendly cookware**—I don't use nonstick cookware very much, but it does come in handy

when cooking fish. A well-seasoned cast-iron skillet is another great tool and can work just as well.
- **Use plenty of fat**—A generous amount of butter or oil (enough to coat the entire bottom of the pan) will minimize sticking and also encourage browning.
- **Try a fish spat**—A slotted fish spatula is invaluable in turning and transferring fish. The low-profile metal slides underneath a fillet without damaging the delicate flesh, and the widely spaced tines make it easy to check the progress of browning.
- **Keep your eyes on the sides**—Watch the side of the fish as it cooks; when it looks cooked about halfway up the side, you know it's time to flip it over. (This works well for scallops, too.) Cook for less time on the second side to avoid overcooking.

- **Better to undercook than overcook**—Because seafood is relatively low in fat and also quick-cooking, the window of proper doneness—of that silky, moist texture—is very narrow before it veers into dry, overcooked rubber or paste. An easy way to check doneness is to insert a paring knife into the thickest part of the fish. The flesh will be just barely opaque when done. It will continue to cook once you remove it from the heat, and if you wait until it flakes easily, as some recipes suggest, it'll be overcooked.

Using Shrimp

- **You don't always have to devein shrimp**—Do a visual inspection first and a test devein on a couple of shrimp before making this decision. To do this, make a shallow cut along the back of the shrimp. If you see a dark vein, use your fingers or a tooth-pick to fish it out; this means you probably need to devein all of the shrimp. If there's no vein, or if you have fresh whole (head-on) shrimp, you don't need to devein the batch.
- **For the best flavor, cook shrimp in the shells.**
- **Different sizes of shrimp are more or less inter-changeable;** just adjust your timing accordingly to avoid overcooking.

Using Lobsters and Crab

IF YOU STEAM OR BOIL LOBSTERS OR CRAB, IT ISN'T NECESSARY TO KILL THEM BEFORE THEY GO INTO THE POT. However, some people find it more humane to kill them without heat, and you'll need to do so if you're using any other cooking method (like grilling).

- To dispatch a lobster or crab, first freeze it for 20 minutes; this numbs the animal and also slows it down, making it easier to work with.
- For a lobster, place it belly side up on a cutting board and starting about 2 inches from the head end, make a lengthwise incision through the belly and toward the head.
- For a crab, grab it by the legs and wedge it against a counter edge (or similar surface) to pry the top shell away from the body.

These techniques will kill the animal instantly.

Using Scallops

- **Diver and day boat scallops are large and ideal for searing**—Cook them just until opaque in the center; any longer and they become rubbery.
- **Bay scallops are smaller (about the size of a marble) and better suited for chowders, stews, pastas, and risottos.**
- **If searing scallops, pat them very dry with a paper towel just before cooking;** this helps ensure that they brown rather than simply steam in the pan. Pan-fry them in a cast-iron pan in a mixture of butter and olive oil. To get the best browning without overcooking, cook scallops longer on the initial side and then finish briefly once flipped over, just to cook through.

Using Mussels, Clams, and Oysters

- **Most mussels have already been fairly well cleaned for you;** however, give them a scrub and pull off any fuzzy "beards" if necessary.
- **Mussels and clams are wonderful simply steamed** with shallots and white wine, or with curry paste and coconut milk. Be sure to serve with lots of bread or rice to soak up the extra-tasty liquid they release.
- **You can serve oysters either raw or quickly grilled**—Purists eat them as is, but I sometimes like a squirt of lemon juice or mignonette sauce (champagne vinegar mixed with a little minced shallot and cracked black pepper).

LOOK FOR FISH AND SEAFOOD THAT ARE:

- Sustainably caught or farmed and certified by one or more third-party organizations
- Bright and briny smelling, rather than funky or fishy
- Local when available and in season
- Live or cooked on site, wherever you buy it (for lobster and crabs)
- Not treated with preservatives (for scallops and shrimp)
- Sold loose, rather than prepackaged (for mussels, clams, and oysters)

Grilled Sardines with Charred Lemon and Chile Sauce

SERVES 4 AS A MAIN OR 6 AS A FIRST COURSE

Sardines are small and abundant and have a short life cycle, making them one of the most sustainable fish out there. They're low in mercury and other toxins that build up in larger fish. Plus, the method used to fish them produces very little bycatch and has minimal environmental impact. Best of all, they are quick-cooking, versatile, and tasty! They can hold up to the bold flavors of the accompanying sauce. This is finger food at its best, perfect for outdoor cooking—and eating.

If you have any seasoned fruit wood or grapevines, add to the coals or use to build the fire—the flavor will take you directly to the Mediterranean. If it's not grilling season, you can make this indoors in a well-seasoned cast-iron skillet instead.

1/2 cup extra-virgin olive oil, more as needed
3 medium lemons
3 medium-hot dried chiles, such as arbol, stems removed
2 tablespoons chopped fresh parsley
3 large cloves garlic, minced
1 medium shallot, minced
Kosher salt
16 whole cleaned fresh sardines (about 1 1/2 pounds; see Tip)

Prepare a medium-hot grill fire. When hot, wipe down the grill with a paper towel dipped in oil.

Cut 2 of the lemons into 1/4-inch slices and halve the other. Grill the lemon slices and halves until they have nice grill marks, 2 to 3 minutes per side for the slices and 3 minutes total for the halves. Then carefully grill the chiles until lightly charred, about 1 minute (if you have a mesh grill insert, use it to keep the chiles from falling through the grate).

Mince one-quarter of the lemon slices and transfer to a small bowl. Chop the chiles into small pieces (for less heat, remove and discard the seeds first). Add the chiles to the bowl, along with the 1/2 cup olive oil, parsley, garlic, shallot, and 1/2 teaspoon salt. Whisk to blend and set aside.

Season the sardines with 1 teaspoon salt and drizzle with a little olive oil. Grill, turning once, until the fish are just cooked through, about 2 minutes per side.

Arrange the remaining three-quarters of the lemon slices on a platter and top with the grilled sardines. Drizzle the sauce over and around the sardines, reserving any extra to serve on the side. Squeeze the grilled lemon halves over the platter.

Serve warm or at room temperature.

Tip: Sardines are often sold whole (not cleaned), but it's easy to prep them yourself. Starting just below the mouth, use a paring knife to make a shallow slit along the length of the belly, stopping where the visceral cavity ends (about an inch from the tail). Use your fingers to pull out and disconnect the organs, and then rinse under a gentle stream of cold water.

Pescado Veracruzano

SERVES 2

This recipe originated in Mexico (specifically, the namesake town of Veracruz), but the ingredients are Spanish through and through. Using a whole fish is a much better value than buying fillets; plus, once you plate individual portions, it's fun to "graze" on all the bits and pieces that still cling to the bones. (Don't forget the cheeks—they're the best part!)

- 1 whole rock fish (sometimes called Pacific red snapper or rock cod), gutted and cleaned (about 1¼ to 1½ pounds)
- Kosher salt
- 2 tablespoons extra-virgin olive oil, more for drizzling
- 2 large cloves garlic, finely chopped
- 1 medium onion, thinly sliced lengthwise
- 2 bushy sprigs thyme
- 1 bay leaf
- 4 medium tomatoes, coarsely chopped (about 3 cups)
- 1 pickled jalapeño, thinly sliced crosswise (see Note)
- ¼ cup green olives (pitted or not)
- 2 tablespoons capers, rinsed and drained
- 1 teaspoon chopped oregano

Position a rack in the center of the oven and heat to 375°F.

Make 3 cuts on each side of the fish's body, going almost all the way to the bone. Season the fish inside and out with 1 teaspoon salt and place in a baking dish that's big enough to hold the fish comfortably.

In a medium skillet, combine the olive oil and garlic and put the pan over medium heat. When the garlic becomes aromatic and sizzling (about 2 minutes), add the onion, thyme, bay leaf, and ½ teaspoon salt. Raise the heat to medium-high and cook, stirring occasionally, until the onions are softened and slightly browned, 4 to 5 minutes.

Add the tomatoes and jalapeño and continue to cook, stirring occasionally, until the tomatoes have begun to break down into a chunky sauce, adjusting the heat as necessary to maintain a vigorous simmer. Stir in the olives, capers, and oregano and simmer for 2 minutes longer. Taste, season with more salt if necessary, and pour the sauce over the fish.

Cover the dish tightly with foil and bake for 15 minutes. Then remove the foil and continue to bake until the fish is just cooked through and the sauce has reduced a bit, about 10 minutes longer. (To see if the fish is done, use a paring knife to make a small cut at the thickest part of the fish, and peek at the flesh. Cook only until the fish is barely opaque, and no further.)

Drizzle with a little olive oil and let the fish rest for 10 minutes before serving.

Note: Pickled jalapeños are widely available in the Mexican/Hispanic aisle of grocery stores, or at specialty markets. They are sometimes also labeled as "in escabeche."

Seared Saffron Albacore Tuna with Fennel-Olive Tapenade

SERVES 4 TO 6

This entrée can easily be turned into a one-dish meal by serving it atop a bed of young escarole, sliced carrots, and shaved fennel—or any other hearty salad veggies—dressed with a little lemon juice and extra-virgin olive oil. This recipe will work well with other firm fish like swordfish.

TAPENADE

1 large clove garlic
Kosher salt
1 tablespoon capers, coarsely chopped
1 tablespoon champagne vinegar
1 tablespoon freshly squeezed lemon juice
1 medium shallot, minced
1 anchovy fillet, minced
1/4 teaspoon lightly packed saffron threads
1/4 cup extra-virgin olive oil
1/2 teaspoon chopped fresh thyme
2 teaspoons roughly chopped fennel fronds or dill
1/3 cup pitted oil-cured olives, coarsely chopped

TUNA

1/4 cup dry breadcrumbs
1/4 teaspoon lightly packed saffron threads
Kosher salt
1 3/4-pound piece Pacific albacore or tombo tuna, about 4 inches on each side
1 tablespoon extra-virgin olive oil
2 tablespoons unsalted butter

To make the tapenade:

Coarsely chop the garlic, sprinkle with a generous pinch of salt, and use the side of the blade to smash and crush the garlic into a paste. Put in a medium bowl along with the capers, vinegar, lemon juice, shallot, anchovy, and saffron. Whisking constantly, drizzle in the olive oil.

Add the thyme, fennel fronds, and olives and whisk again. Set aside and let the saffron infuse while you prepare the tuna.

To cook the tuna:

Combine the breadcrumbs, saffron, and 1/4 teaspoon salt in a food processor and pulse to blend and chop the saffron a bit (7 or 8 pulses). Pour onto a plate and set aside.

Cut the tuna lengthwise along the grain to make 2 long logs. Trim any connective tissue and season all over with 1/2 teaspoon salt. Roll the logs in the breadcrumbs to coat each broad side lightly.

Heat a large, heavy skillet (ideally cast iron) over medium heat. When hot, add the oil and 1 tablespoon of the butter and let the butter melt. Cut the remaining 1 tablespoon butter into 4 pieces and set aside.

Gently place the tuna logs in the pan and let cook undisturbed for 3 minutes. Use a thin spatula to gently lift the log and check the progress of the browning. Once the first side is golden brown (about 4 minutes), turn to a new side and add a chunk of the butter next to each of the logs. Gently nudge the logs into the newly added butter as it melts. Cook this side until golden and repeat on the remaining sides, adding the 2 remaining chunks of butter after flipping, for a total of 6 to 10 minutes cooking time, depending on size.

Transfer the tuna to a cutting board and let rest for 5 to 10 minutes. Cut the tuna into 1/2-inch-thick slices (a sharp knife with a thin blade works best).

Arrange on a serving platter or individual plates and drizzle the tapenade over the slices.

Rock Cod Chowder in Saffron-Tomato Broth

MAKES ABOUT 9 CUPS

This brothy chowder is loosely inspired by bouillabaisse, the classic Provençal seafood soup, but it's both simpler and easier on the pocketbook. To go all the way with this dish, drizzle the soup with fresh aioli (or mix mayonnaise with minced fresh garlic and thin with lemon juice). Serve with crusty bread.

1/4 teaspoon saffron threads, lightly crushed

1/2 cup boiling water

1 (28-ounce) can whole peeled tomatoes

2 tablespoons extra-virgin olive oil

1 medium leek, white and light green parts only, quartered lengthwise and thinly sliced

1 small fennel bulb, finely diced (if it comes with fronds, chop and reserve 1/4 cup)

1 large sprig thyme (lemon thyme if available)

1 bay leaf

Kosher salt

1 cup dry white wine

3 cups fish, vegetable, or chicken stock (or low-sodium broth)

2 medium Yukon gold potatoes, diced

1 tablespoon freshly squeezed lemon juice, more as needed

1 pound skinless rock cod fillets (or other mild, firm white fish such as ling cod, snapper, or halibut)

Soak the saffron in the boiling water for at least 15 minutes while you prepare the other ingredients.

Working over the can of tomatoes, break open each tomato, scrape the seeds into the can, and put the seeded tomatoes in a bowl. Squeeze the seeded tomatoes in your hand to break them up thoroughly, then strain the juice from the can into the bowl with the tomatoes. Discard the seeds and set the bowl aside.

Heat the olive oil in a large Dutch oven or similar soup pot over medium heat. Add the leek, diced fennel bulb, thyme, bay leaf, and 1/2 teaspoon salt and cook, stirring, until the fennel starts to soften, 4 to 5 minutes. Increase the heat to medium-high and add the wine. Cook until the liquid is reduced by half, 3 to 4 minutes.

Add the stock, tomatoes, potatoes, the saffron and soaking liquid, and 1 teaspoon salt. Bring the liquid to a boil, partially cover the pot, and lower the heat to maintain a bare simmer. Cook, occasionally skimming the scum off the top, until the potatoes and fennel are tender, 20 to 30 minutes.

Meanwhile, cut the fish into 1- to 2-inch pieces and season with 1/2 teaspoon salt.

Add the lemon juice to the soup, then taste and add more lemon juice or salt as needed. Add the fish, along with the fennel fronds if you have them. Cook until the fish is just cooked through and flakes easily, 5 to 10 minutes. If necessary, use a spoon to gently break the fish into smaller chunks.

Serve right away. If you need to reheat, do so gently and briefly to avoid overcooking the fish.

Oven-Seared Shrimp
with Shallots, Chiles, and Thyme

**SERVES 6 AS AN APPETIZER
OR 4 AS A MAIN COURSE**

In this fast and easy recipe, the shrimp release their juices and create a delicious sauce in the pan. Using unpeeled shrimp with heads on does make it a little messier to eat, but the results are finger-licking good. If serving this as a main course, a bed of couscous or steamed rice is a nice accompaniment to help soak up the sauce.

2 pounds large (10/12 count) unpeeled shrimp,
    preferably head-on (see Note)
Kosher salt
6 tablespoons extra-virgin olive oil
2 tablespoons bacon fat (or omit and use
    an additional 2 tablespoons olive oil)
3 small stalks green garlic, chopped (about $^2/_3$ cup),
    or 6 large cloves fresh garlic, minced
I large shallot, minced
2 tablespoons tomato paste
$1^1/_2$ teaspoons coarsely chopped fresh thyme
I teaspoon red chile flakes
I large lemon, zest finely grated and fruit halved
$^1/_2$ cup dry white wine
I tablespoon chopped fresh parsley

Position a rack in the center of the oven and heat to 400°F.

Rinse the shrimp well, pat dry, and season with $^1/_4$ teaspoon salt. Set aside.

Heat 4 tablespoons of the oil and the bacon fat in a large ovenproof skillet (preferably cast iron) or a Spanish cazuela (a rustic clay pan) over medium heat. Add the green garlic, shallot, and 1 tablespoon salt and cook, stirring, until soft and translucent, about 3 minutes. Move the vegetables to one side of the pan and add the tomato paste to the empty side. Cook for 30 seconds, smashing and stirring the tomato paste into the oil, then stir it all together. Add the thyme, chile flakes, and lemon zest and continue to cook for

another 30 seconds. Add the wine and cook for 1 minute longer, stirring and scraping up all the tasty bits as you go.

Add the shrimp to the pan, stir gently to distribute the sauce, and carefully arrange the shrimp in a snug even layer. Pour the remaining 2 tablespoons olive oil evenly over the shrimp and put the skillet in the oven.

Bake for 5 minutes, then stir gently to redistribute the sauce. Continue to bake until the shrimp are just opaque in the center, about 5 minutes longer. Remove from the oven, squeeze the lemon halves over the shrimp, add the parsley, and toss gently.

Transfer the shrimp and sauce to a platter (the shrimp will overcook if they stay in the skillet).

Serve right away or at room temperature, with lots of crusty bread to soak up the delicious sauce!

Note: I don't bother to clean the veins from the shrimp. You can remove them if you prefer, but you will lose a little flavor and the cooking time may vary slightly.

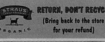

6

THE DAIRY CASE

Our guests are crazy about pastured eggs! It's no exaggeration. People learn our delivery schedules and then call us to have a dozen put aside for them.

I think people get excited about these eggs because they are so simple. The flavor difference between a pastured egg and a commercial egg is huge. And they are a really easy, affordable indulgence. Our most expensive eggs come out to about $0.50 each. That means you can have a really wonderful breakfast for just $1.

— Allison Ball, assistant grocery buyer

THERE'S A LOT OF TRUTH to the saying about happy cows making better milk. In fact, it's true throughout the dairy case. And the best indicators of whether the cows and chickens were happy is to look at their living conditions and their feed. After all, animals that consume the foods that their bodies naturally evolved to process—whether that's grass or flowers, bugs or worms—will thrive and experience fewer health problems than if they were fed grains that their bodies aren't designed to digest. So the more pasture time and the more natural the feed, the happier the animals will be, and the better their milk and eggs will taste.

Dairy and eggs are big business, and just like the meat industry, it's one that has become heavily centralized over the years. Giant factory farms grow ever larger and more powerful: in 2006, fewer than 1 percent of dairy farms (all with two thousand or more head of cattle) produced almost one-quarter of the country's milk. For example, Dean Foods (which owns thirty-seven different brands, including Horizon Organics, Meadow Gold, and Silk) controls 40 percent of the fluid milk, 60 percent of the organic milk, and 90 percent of the soy milk produced in the country.

The price of milk is controlled by a few industry traders at the Chicago Mercantile Exchange, who influence the price by deciding whether to sell or buy futures in Cheddar cheese. Because of this market manipulation, farmers get less and less for their milk as their feed and fuel costs continue to rise. As farmers have spent more to produce milk than they are being paid, many have become victims of foreclosures and desperation sales, which is what made it possible for conglomerate companies to dominate the market. This has made it all but impossible for small, family-run operations to survive, especially those that have eschewed the pharmaceutical-centric approach. It's important to keep these small operations alive; they need all the help they can get. **SO SUPPORT SMALL-SCALE DAIRIES AND EGG PRODUCERS WHENEVER POSSIBLE;** buy directly from them at farmstands or farmers' markets if you can, or from local co-ops or independently owned natural food stores.

MILK

Much of my business can be tied to milk, either directly or indirectly. It's a staple for our customers at the Market, of course, but we also use it extensively at the Creamery & Bakeshop for our ice cream and baked goodies.

How to Buy

Milk is a direct product of whatever inputs the cows are given. Give a cow laboratory-formulated feed, a steady stream of drugs and hormones, and unpleasant living conditions, and you'll get crappy milk. But if you allow a cow to live in its natural setting and to graze on the grasses that its body is designed to thrive on, you'll get flavorful and wholesome milk. **THE CLOSER TO THE NATURAL STATE, THE BETTER**; that also includes how the milk is processed.

PASTURE-RAISED IS BEST. Milk from pasture-raised cows is as unique and evolving as the seasons themselves. The milk is a direct reflection of what's growing in the fields; in the spring when the grass is tender and green, the milk will have slightly verdant notes. In the fall when the grasses are dry, the milk will have a very subtle nuttiness. These changes are not so dramatic as they might sound—it doesn't affect how you'd cook or bake with them—but are a true sign that you're getting milk from cows that are treated well and are eating what nature intended. In addition to better flavor and healthier cows, milk from pastured cows is higher in omega-3s. These are the happy cows I just mentioned, in contrast to the majority of cows, which are raised in high-density feedlots and milked around the clock.

Certification from third-party programs such as American Humane Certified (a program of the American Humane Association) gives you even more assurance that the cows were treated with care and compassion. Look for a seal on the carton or label.

THE ORGANIC LABEL PROVIDES SOME MEANINGFUL ASSURANCES. To qualify for certified organic status, the cows must be fed organic feed, not be given hormones or antibiotics, and—a more recent development—live on pasture for at least 120 days of the grazing season. So by drinking organic milk, you not only avoid pesticides in the feed and pharmaceuticals in the cow, but you can also rest assured that the cows lived on open pasture for at least part of the year. Due to the 2011 approval of GM alfalfa crops, organic milk is the best way to ensure your dairy is GM free.

IF YOU BUY NONORGANIC MILK, MAKE SURE IT'S RBGH- AND RBST-FREE. This guarantees that the cows were raised without the influence of Monsanto's artificial growth hormones, which are widely used to increase milk production. Their use is highly controversial, and their effects on humans have not been adequately studied. The debate even reaches to how dairy products are labeled and is the subject of legislative battles between Monsanto and public health advocacy groups. The good news is that many grocery and food chains (including Kroger and Starbucks) have taken steps to eliminate such dairy products from their product lines.

Straight out of the cow, milk is a miraculously vibrant substance. In addition to the milk solids, water, and fat that make milk what it is, it features a

---

THE PRICE OF MILK, AND MORE . . .

The price of milk has plummeted in recent years, in part because of the subsidy-dependent grains used to feed dairy cows and the consolidation in the industry that has put control into only a few hands. As a result, many dairies are producing as much milk as they can as cheaply as possible—by whatever means necessary. For most commercial dairies, that means feeding the cows cheap grains and a steady stream of growth hormones and antibiotics. The cows are treated more like machines than the animals they really are (in fact, they spend a good part of their lives attached to milking machines).

lively spectrum of enzymes, beneficial microbes, and nutrients—it's just as alive as the blood that's in our own veins! It contains all the essentials needed to help a just-born calf thrive—just as human milk contains all the essentials a human baby needs.

Your typical grocery store milk isn't quite as alive and vibrant, though—for the purposes of stability, safety, and consistency, it has been processed and altered in fairly significant ways:

- **Pasteurization** is the use of high heat to destroy all the living microbes (beneficial as well as illness-causing) present in milk. Pasteurization is a quick and easy way to eliminate the risk of foodborne illness from microbes such as salmonella, *Listeria*, and *E. coli*. There are several different types of pasteurization; all diminish the flavor of the milk somewhat, but it is most pronounced in ultra-high-temperature (UHT or ultra-pasteurized) milk.

- **Homogenization** counteracts milkfat's natural tendency to collect at the top as cream. It's done by forcing milk through very fine filters that break up the fat into smaller molecules that can stay suspended throughout the milk. (It also allows producers to precisely control the fat content of milk and use any surplus to make cream and butter—both of which are more profitable than milk.)

  Some people find that they have a harder time digesting homogenized milk—perhaps because their bodies don't recognize the altered molecules.

RAW MILK: BETTER FOR YOU? Prior to the industrial revolution, raw milk was the norm; however, as dairies became more factory-like and long-distance transportation of milk became possible, milk became less safe to drink. When pasteurization was developed, it was hyped as the solution to what had come to be known as "the milk problem." Although pasteurization does make milk less potentially harmful to drink, it also destroys vitamin C as well as enzymes that help the human body assimilate milk into the system. Aside from the appeal of retained nutrients, some people choose raw milk because they find it easier to digest.

Health benefits aside, I recommend you try raw milk. Unless you have ready access to a cow, it's the closest you can get to unadulterated, straight-from-

---

> ### AT THE VERY LEAST, LOOK FOR MILK THAT IS:
> - **Organic or at least free of growth hormones (rBGH and rBST)**
> - **Minimally pasteurized—if you have the option, avoid UHT or ultra-pasteurized milk**
>
> ### IDEALLY, LOOK FOR:
> - **A small, local dairy that you can support**
> - **Milk from pasture-raised cows**
>
> ### ALSO CONSIDER TRYING:
> - **Raw (unpasteurized) milk**
> - **Cream-top (unhomogenized) milk**

the-source milk. And the flavor difference is pretty incredible.

Raw milk is regulated on the state level, so the availability of raw milk depends on where you live. Its sale is illegal in some states; in others, licensed farmers may sell it, but only on a direct-to-consumer basis. In California, raw milk can be sold in retail stores, as long as it's from a certified dairy (there are currently two in the state). If raw milk isn't legal where you live, ask around. Underground raw milk is available in more places than you might think, and sometimes it's sold as "pet food" (that is, not for human consumption) to circumvent regulations.

. . . .

Many small-scale dairy farmers round out their product line by making cheese or yogurt from the milk they produce. These value-added items enable the farmers to diversify their product lines and extend the shelf life of milk when there's a surplus of it. If your local dairy farmer offers these items, do give them a try!

. . . .

How to Store

The "sell by" date stamped on a carton or bottle of milk does *not* mean you must consume it by that date. In fact, depending on when it was opened, milk should be good for a few days or up to a week *after* the sell-by date, which simply regulates freshness at the store level and ensures that consumers have plenty of time to use the milk after purchase.

Still, you'll get the optimal life out of your milk if you take a few precautions. (Doubly true if you're buying raw milk, which is much more perishable than pasteurized milk.)

- When you're in the store, make milk the last thing you pick up.
- Keep milk as cold as possible. If you have a small cooler, keep it in your trunk and use it to transport the milk (and any other refrigerated items) home.
- Store milk in the coldest part of the refrigerator.
- Sunlight and fluorescent light can destroy the vitamins in milk. If you buy milk in glass bottles, keep it out of the light as much as you can.

How to Use

If you buy nonhomogenized (cream-top) milk what you do with the cream is up to you. Either break it up with a spoon and shake it up to distribute throughout the milk, or spoon it out and enjoy it on its own. Use it just as you would crème fraîche or even very soft butter.

BENEFITS OF GLASS

In an effort to reduce the amount of waste in packaging, some dairy farms have gone back to putting their milk in good old-fashioned glass bottles. You usually pay a deposit on the bottle, which you get back when you return the empty bottle to the store. Transporting, washing, and managing this type of program costs the dairy farm more in the short term, but the landfill savings more than outweigh the monetary costs. If glass-bottled milk isn't available where you shop, ask for it.

ASK YOUR GROCER:

- **Do you know of any producers who use glass bottles? Would you consider stocking their milk?**

BUTTER

At 18 Reasons, our neighborhood education and community center, we're always looking for new and interesting ways to explore food and celebrate the people who make it. Our Butterfest is a gathering devoted entirely to that simple but underappreciated ingredient. The event features a butter-making demonstration, a blind tasting, a potluck, and even an open mic for participants to share their butter stories. The first one was so successful (tickets sold out in just a few days) that it's now an annual event. We look forward to it all year!

How to Buy

Butter in its natural state is made up of three components: butterfat, milk solids, and water. Just as dark chocolate is more intense than semisweet, high-butterfat butters have more oomph than those with less butterfat. High-butterfat or premium butters are particularly good for baking; they yield flakier doughs and a noticeably richer flavor.

All American butters have a minimum 80 percent butterfat content; that's lower than most European butters, which can have as much as 85 percent butterfat. (That's just one reason why Parisian croissants taste better than anything you get at home. Also, being in France makes everything taste better.) **PREMIUM BUTTERS TYPICALLY HAVE HIGHER BUTTERFAT CONTENT THAN YOUR AVERAGE BUTTER;** the percentage is usually printed on the label.

USE UNSALTED (SWEET) BUTTER FOR COOKING. The milk solids in butter make it prone to spoilage. Adding salt lengthens shelf life, so most manufacturers offer their butter in salted and unsalted versions. I think unsalted and lightly salted butter taste creamier and sweeter; you can add salt to suit your own taste.

More critically, though, unsalted butter is better suited for cooking and baking. With salted butter, you never know exactly *how much* salt you're dealing with (it varies from brand to brand), so it's more difficult to control and predict the overall seasoning of a dish. And with baking recipes in particular, the extra salt can really screw things up. Unsalted butter gives you complete control over how much salt you use.

STRAUS FAMILY CREAMERY:
Albert Straus

The rolling, verdant hills where the Straus dairy cows roam are so gorgeous that it's almost cliché. But it's the everyday reality for this family-run business, which in 1994 became the first certified-organic dairy west of the Mississippi. Their milk and cream is especially sweet, which they attribute to the fact that the grass is nourished by the briny coastal fog of nearby Point Reyes National Seashore. It's so good, we use it for every batch of ice cream we make at the Creamery! In addition to creating amazing dairy products, Albert Straus has become a leading voice for organic dairies on the national level, working with the federal government to maintain and improve standards and regulations for organic milk production.

AT THE VERY LEAST, LOOK FOR BUTTER THAT IS:

• Unsalted or lightly salted

• Organic or at least rBGH- and rBST-free

IDEALLY, LOOK FOR:

• Pasture-raised

• High butterfat content, especially for baking

Butter is a byproduct of milk, so the things you look out for in milk also apply to shopping for butter: pasture-raised, or organic, or rBGH- and rBST-free.

How to Store

With unsalted butter you do have a shorter shelf life in the refrigerator, but freezing it will get you lots more storage time (up to a year or more) with absolutely no negative impact on how the butter tastes or behaves in cooking. Just make sure it's well wrapped to keep it from absorbing its neighbors' odors. You can also freeze individual slices for butter-on-the-fly; the smaller pieces thaw quickly and are the perfect size for finishing sauces or melting in a pan.

CULTURED BUTTER

Cultured butter is made from cream that has been allowed to ferment slightly—an inevitability in the days before refrigeration came along. The resulting butter has a tang similar to that of yogurt.

Butter is one of those products that grocery stores regularly put on sale. Stock up and keep it in the freezer. You'll never again have to pay full price for butter!

Compound butters are easy to make and a great way to get a little extra life out of fresh herbs. Finely chop any green leafy herbs you have on hand (parsley, dill, cilantro, tarragon, and thyme all work well) and mix with room-temperature butter, a little lemon zest, and a pinch of salt. Use it as is for spreading, or wrap into a log with plastic wrap, freeze, and then slice into coins. Compound butters are wonderful on steamed veggies or crusty bread, in scrambled eggs or omelets, or as a sauce for fish or meat.

MORE DAIRY

You're also likely to encounter these other dairy products in the dairy case:

- **Buttermilk** is made from milk to which bacterial cultures have been added. There are two types; cultured and Bulgarian; the differentiating factor is the type of acid culture added to the milk. Bulgarian is slightly more acidic, but they are interchangeable for recipes. Buttermilk is generally made from 1 or 2 percent milk, so despite the rich-sounding name, it is actually low in fat.

- **Cream cheese** is a fresh, spreadable cheese that's rich and tangy. Many cream cheeses contain guar or carob gum as thickening and binding agents to keep the fats from separating, thus lengthening the shelf life. Instead of those that employ gum stabilizers, look for cream cheese that has been strained to thicken and bind it.

- **Crème fraîche** is made by combining fresh cream with bacterial cultures. The result is a thick, spoonable product that's a little sweeter than sour cream. It's ideal for finishing soups and sauces or serving with fresh berries. I love to whip it, for a tangier version of whipped cream.

- **Greek yogurt (aka yogurt cheese)** is simply regular yogurt that has been strained to remove much of the liquid. The result is thick and creamy.

- **Kefir** is a fermented (though nonalcoholic) beverage, the product of milk and a bacteria-and-yeast culture. The effect is slightly sour and a little effervescent.

- **Quark** is another fresh cheese with a slightly grainy consistency, similar to ricotta. It is mainly used in baking and cooking.

SAINT BENOÎT YOGURT:
Benoît de Korsak

I'd be hard-pressed to find a more sustainable yogurt producer than Benoît de Korsak. His small operation outside of Petaluma, California, housed in an old milking barn, sources milk from an organic dairy less than a mile down the road. The honey he uses comes from neighboring Marshall's Farm, and the organic fruit purees are made by orchard legend John Lagier. Most impressively, Saint Benoît yogurt is sold exclusively in reusable containers, which speaks to Benoît's deep commitment to minimizing waste in our landfills. The smaller of the two containers is a handsome ceramic crock that's embossed with the company's name and glazed in a gradient of terra-cotta and cream colors. They're so attractive that it's amazing to learn that 80 percent of them (on which consumers pay a deposit) actually get returned to the company for reuse. It's a powerful indicator that deposit-based packaging truly is a viable business model, and it gives me hope for the rest of the dairy community.

YOGURT

Yogurt is one of those foods that, depending on which kind you choose, can be a very healthy snack—or pure junk. The key to good yogurt lies in the ingredients.

- **Pure milk**—This should be the number one ingredient. Go for ones made from organic milk, or at least hormone-free milk.
- **No fillers**—Avoid yogurt that lists thickeners or stabilizers such as carageenan or guar gum. As a rule of thumb, the only unpronounceable ingredients should be the names of the live yogurt cultures (such as *Lactobacillus bulgaricus*).
- **Low or no sugar**—If you buy sweetened yogurt, avoid any containing corn syrup. Otherwise, look for ones that are sweetened with honey, maple syrup, or pure cane sugar—and make sure it's low on the ingredient list.
- **Real fruit**—Enough said.

For the ultimate in flexibility and flavor, buy plain unsweetened yogurt and doctor it yourself. Stir in honey, maple syrup, or a good-quality jam or marmalade. This lets you adjust the flavor and sweetness to your liking and is much more economical. Plus, plain yogurt is great to have on hand for savory cooking.

EGGS

I ate some of the best eggs of my life when I was eleven and visiting my grandmother in Bethlehem. She kept chickens in her backyard, and I remember being so amazed every morning when she would grab the egg from underneath each chicken's warm bottom. The yolks in those eggs were so rich and dark; they made commercial eggs seem dull and flat. I truly think that a good egg is one of the most incredible foodstuffs of nature.

How to Buy

Good eggs don't come only from family backyards (although such flocks are experiencing a renaissance). In fact, it's pretty easy to find them at the grocery store.

Here's the tricky thing, though: **YOU CAN'T ALWAYS GO BY THE TERMINOLOGY** you see on a carton of eggs, because there's virtually no regulation of how terms like "free range" and "range-grown" are used. So producers often put words on their packaging that are technically true but interpreted rather liberally. For instance, "free range" might mean the hens had only occasional access to the outdoors. And some terms, like "natural," are meaningless—there's simply no legal definition for the term when it's applied to eggs.

Some terms *are* meaningful, though, and are more useful indicators of quality, nourishing, flavorful eggs:

- **Cage free**—This guarantees that the hens were not confined to the tiny cages that are typical to the egg industry. It doesn't tell you exactly how much free-roaming space the chickens had, but it does tell you *something*, and that's a positive step.
- **Fertile**—These are eggs from hens that had access to a rooster (without one, hens still produce eggs, but they would never hatch). These eggs are no more nutritious, but it's a good sign as to the kind of life the hens lead.
- **Antibiotic-free**—Chickens are typically fed a steady stream of antibiotics, whether they're sick or not. Over time this makes the chickens, their eggs, and eventually us resistant to the drugs. "No preventive antibiotics" means the chickens were not regularly dosed but may have been treated individually in the case of illness.
- **Vegetarian feed**—Chickens are by nature omnivores, so a vegetarian diet might seem somewhat illogical. However, it's an assurance that the chickens were not fed animal byproducts such as fish meal or other "recycled" chickens that could harbor disease.
- **Non-GMO feed**—Most commercial chickens (whether raised for eggs or for meat) are fed a mix of corn and soy as part or all of their diet, and the vast majority of this feed is genetically modified.
- **Organic**—This means that the chickens fed on certified organic feed, were not given animal byproducts or antibiotics, and had access (though perhaps limited) to the outdoors.

There's one other label to look for and celebrate, and that's **"PASTURE-RAISED" OR "PASTURED EGGS."** It's the magic combination of pure sunlight, open air, plenty of exercise, and natural feed. This means the chickens can run around and peck at the ground and eat bugs and any other tasty things they find. Basically, they live as nature intended. The very best pastured eggs come from farmers who rotate chickens and cows over pasture, resulting in a more dynamic ecosystem and, in turn, tastier eggs. As the season changes and the grasses go from bright green to dry and yellow, the yolks change as well. Keep in mind, though, that "pastured" and "pasture-raised" have no legal definition. The best way to find out what a producer means by this term is to ask: What are the conditions? How much time do the animals spend outdoors? What are they fed in addition to what they forage in pasture?

THE REALLY AMAZING THING IS THAT PASTURED EGGS ARE ACTUALLY HEALTHIER. It's been scientifically proven: compared to conventional eggs, pastured eggs contain less saturated fat and cholesterol and more vitamin A and omega-3 fatty acids (these are the good fats that are recommended in a healthy diet).

Now, if you've ever seen or bought pastured eggs, you may be thinking: "Yeah, yeah. But $6 to $8 for a dozen eggs? You've gotta be kidding me." But when you consider the benefits of pasture-raising—our health, the chickens' health, and the astonishing difference in taste—50 to 60 cents for an egg starts to sound like a bargain. And once you taste them, you'll never want to eat a commercial egg again.

GOOD TO KNOW ABOUT EGG PRODUCTION

There's a lot to dislike about how commercial, mass-market eggs are produced. For starters, chickens are confined to incredibly cramped spaces. The hens are kept indoors in a filthy environment, under lights that simulate three cycles of day and night every twenty-four hours, which tricks the hens' bodies into producing twice as many eggs as they normally would. And worst of all, the hens are fed a calculated mix of feed that usually contains antibiotics (necessary to prevent disease in such unsanitary and cramped conditions), as well as animal byproducts and other things that chickens just aren't meant to eat. In addition to being damaging to the environment and the health of the workers tending them, these unhealthy conditions are to a large extent responsible for egg-related outbreaks of salmonella. In contrast, producers who treat their chickens more humanely by providing them with access to sunlight, outdoor space, and their natural foraged diet, have healthier chickens, which in turn produce safer and more flavorful eggs. Simply put, healthier chickens are better for everyone involved.

AT THE VERY LEAST, LOOK FOR EGGS FROM CHICKENS THAT ARE:

• Cage free

• Fertile

• Antibiotic-free, or no preventive antibiotics

• Fed vegetarian, non-GMO feed

• Certified organic

IDEALLY, LOOK FOR:

• Pasture-raised

EAT GOOD FOOD

How to Store

Keep eggs refrigerated. Eggs are best when consumed within three weeks of when they were laid. A few producers actually stamp the lay date on the carton; if you buy from the farmer, just ask!

How to Use

When you open a carton of pastured eggs, you'll be in awe of how beautiful they are. They come in many colors: blue, green, gray, white, and various shades of brown. Each breed of chicken lays a different-colored egg, and the shades are dependent on the forage that the chicken ate.

You may also be surprised at the variety of sizes represented in that dozen; after all, nature doesn't follow fixed size gradings. (Many factors go into an egg's size, but generally the older the hen, the bigger the egg.) If you're making something like a fritatta or an egg salad, it doesn't matter whether you use six different size eggs or six identical "large" eggs. But in baking cakes and custards and such, success generally relies on exact measurements, so it's best to use whatever size egg the recipe calls for. (All of the recipes in this book were tested using large eggs.)

A kitchen scale is the easiest and most accurate way to determine an egg's size (weighed in the shell, of course):

Jumbo	2^1/$_2$ ounces
Extra Large	2^1/$_4$ ounces
Large	2 ounces
Medium	1^3/$_4$ ounces
Small	1^1/$_2$ ounces
Peewee	1^1/$_4$ ounces

EGG GRADING

Egg cartons are labeled with a USDA-assigned letter grade (AA and A are the ones you're most likely to see). These grades are given based on the quality and cleanliness of the shell, freshness at time of grading, and presence or absence of defects. It is *not*, however, an indicator of the egg's safety.

If you need to separate the whites from the yolks, it's easier to do so when the eggs are still cold. Otherwise, let eggs come to room temperature before using, especially if you're baking with them.

A beautiful egg is pretty much perfect the way it is, which is why my favorite preparation—sunny-side up, with a little salt—is hardly a preparation at all . . . but it's the very best way to showcase a good egg and to taste the rich silky yolk:

Melt a tablespoon or so of butter in a well-seasoned cast-iron or nonstick pan over medium heat. Let the butter cook until it starts to turn brown, and then crack the egg into the pan. Let it cook undisturbed until the white around the yolk is barely set. (You just want the yolk to get warm.) Sprinkle with a little salt—never pepper, which detracts from the egg's flavor. Eat on a piece of crusty toast—no fork—with only your fingers and the bread for soppin' up the yolk.

SOUL FOOD FARM: Alexis and Eric Koefoed

Some of our favorite pasture-raised chickens come from Alexis and Eric Koefoed of Soul Food Farm, just across the bay in Vacaville. After quitting their previous jobs in other industries, the Koefoeds decided to start anew and bought a fifty-five-acre farm, without quite knowing what they'd do on it. They started an egg business, then began selling the chickens directly to us at the Market. The Koefoeds employ the "salad bar" farming methodology (popularized by Joel Salatin of Polyface Farm in Virginia), in which the chickens are periodically rotated through sections of fresh pasture. The chickens graze on the natural flora and fauna of the land and fertilize it at the same time—not only a more natural way of raising chickens but also actively beneficial to the environment. While this book was being written, the Koefoeds decided to focus their efforts on eggs only, due to the challenging logistics and high cost of producing meat birds.

230

Spanish Deviled Eggs
MAKES 12

This recipe is all about the eggs, so use the best you can find; farm-direct pastured eggs are ideal (though even commercial eggs are delicious deviled this way). Deviled eggs tend to disappear the second you serve them, so it's always good to make more than you think you might need. This recipe can easily be doubled.

If you're bringing these to an event, it's best to prepare the components ahead of time and assemble the eggs on site. It's much easier to transport that way.

> 6 large eggs
> $^1/_2$ small clove garlic
> Kosher salt
> 2 tablespoons extra-virgin olive oil
> 2 tablespoons mayonnaise
> 1 tablespoon finely chopped almonds, preferably Marconas
> 1 teaspoon freshly squeezed lemon juice, more as needed
> 1 teaspoon finely chopped parsley, more for sprinkling
> $^1/_4$ teaspoon smoked Spanish paprika (or regular paprika), more for sprinkling

Begin with eggs at room temperature; otherwise, they will need more cooking time. Put the eggs in a medium saucepan and add enough cold water to cover by 1 inch. Put the pan over high heat. As soon as the water boils, turn off the burner and let the eggs sit in the hot water for 10 minutes. Carefully remove from the pan, transfer to a bowl of cold water, and let cool.

Peel the eggs, halve lengthwise, and ease out the yolks into a bowl. Arrange the whites on a serving platter.

Peel and coarsely chop the garlic, sprinkle with a pinch of salt, and use the side of a chef's knife to smash the garlic into a paste. (You should have about $^1/_4$ teaspoon.) Add the garlic to the bowl with the yolks, along with the olive oil, mayonnaise, almonds, lemon juice, parsley, paprika, and $^1/_4$ teaspoon salt. Use a fork to smash the yolks and blend the ingredients. Taste and add more lemon juice or salt as needed,

keeping in mind that you need a flavorful filling to counter the bland egg whites.

Using two teaspoons, divide the yolk mixture among the whites. (For a more refined presentation, you can also pipe the mixture in using a pastry bag.)

Garnish the eggs with a pinch of parsley and paprika. Refrigerate if making ahead, but let them come to room temperature before serving.

Yogurt with Honey, Figs, and Toasted Walnuts
SERVES 1

This is the perfect simple ending to an elaborate meal (or any meal, really). It requires practically no prep and is infinitely modifiable. Figs out of season? Use apples, apricots, or orange segments instead. Don't like walnuts? Use pistachios or hazelnuts. But you will get the richest, most decadent results by sticking with Greek yogurt.

> $^1/_2$ cup plain Greek-style yogurt
> 1 fresh fig, halved or quartered
> 2 tablespoons toasted walnut pieces
> 2 teaspoons honey

Put the yogurt in a small bowl and nestle the fig sections into the yogurt. Top with the walnuts and drizzle with the honey.

Stone Fruit Galette

MAKES ONE 10-INCH GALETTE

This glorious galette, or rustic pie, will accommodate just about any fruit, but its open top makes a particularly pretty frame for the jeweled hues of summer's stone fruits and berries; my favorites are apricot/blueberry for the beginning of summer, and peach/blackberry for the Fourth of July. Fig/raspberry, though not stone fruit, is great in the late summer and early fall.

You could trim the dough into a neat round, but I prefer the rustic look of jaggedy edges—and leaving it untrimmed ensures that not a bit of the buttery dough goes to waste.

Serve with plenty of fresh whipped cream or vanilla ice cream.

DOUGH

11¼ ounces (2½ cups) all-purpose flour, more for rolling
12 tablespoons (6 ounces) cold unsalted butter, cut into ½-inch pieces
1 teaspoon sugar
¼ teaspoon kosher salt
½ cup ice-cold water, more as needed

FILLING

½ cup plus 2 tablespoons sugar
4 teaspoons all-purpose flour
1 teaspoon finely grated lemon zest
Kosher salt
3 cups pitted, sliced peaches, nectarines, or plums, or a mixture (from about 1¼ pounds whole fruit)
1 teaspoon freshly squeezed lemon juice
1 egg white, beaten

To make the dough:

Place the flour, butter, sugar, and salt in the bowl of a stand mixer and freeze for 30 minutes.

Take the bowl from the freezer and put it on the mixer with the paddle attachment. Mix on low speed until it resembles a crumbly meal with the biggest pieces about the size of a pea, about 2 minutes.

With the motor running, drizzle in the water, 1 tablespoon at a time. You may need a little more or less than the ½ cup; use just enough for the mixture to come together into shaggy clumps. Stop mixing as soon as you achieve this consistency.

Dump the dough onto a large piece of plastic wrap and use your hands to press and shape the dough into a 7-inch disk. Wrap in plastic wrap and chill for at least 1 hour or overnight.

Position a rack in the center of the oven and heat to 400°F. Line a large baking sheet with parchment or a nonstick liner.

To make the filling:

Combine the ½ cup sugar, the flour, the zest, and a pinch of salt in a large bowl and whisk to combine. Add the fruit to the bowl, along with the lemon juice. Toss to combine and set aside.

Take the dough from the fridge and put on a lightly floured work surface. Roll the dough into a ⅛-inch-thick round, about 17 inches across. Loosely roll up around the rolling pin and unroll onto the baking sheet.

Put the fruit mixture in the center of the dough, leaving a 3-inch rim all around. Fold the excess dough up and over the fruit, overlapping as necessary. Brush the shaped dough with the egg white and sprinkle with the remaining 2 tablespoons sugar.

Bake until the crust is golden and the fruit is tender, 45 to 55 minutes. Let rest on the baking sheet for 20 minutes before serving.

Note: For variety in color and flavor, you can replace up to 1 cup of the stone fruit with an equal amount of fresh blueberries.

Cardamom Rice Pudding with Golden Raisins

SERVES 8 TO 10

This fabulous pudding has all the flavors of kheer, the Indian rice dessert, but is richer and creamier thanks to the added egg yolks. Many rice pudding recipes are made entirely on the stove top, which requires lots of vigilant stirring (and watching). My version starts on the stove top but is finished in the oven, which leaves your hands free for other things.

Chopped toasted pistachios make a nice garnish for this comforting dessert.

I whole vanilla bean
6 cups whole milk
I cup sugar
³/4 cup uncooked basmati rice (see Note)
¹/2 teaspoon kosher salt
I large egg
2 large egg yolks
³/4 teaspoon ground cardamom
Finely grated zest of I orange
³/4 cup golden raisins (or other dried fruit)

Split the vanilla bean lengthwise and scrape the beans from the pod. Add them both to a large saucepan, along with 4 cups of the milk and the sugar, rice, and salt. Bring just to a boil over medium-high heat (watch carefully—it boils over easily!), partially cover the pan, and lower the heat to a gentle simmer. Cook until the rice is very soft, about 45 minutes, stirring occasionally at first and more frequently as the mixture thickens. Remove the pan from the heat and carefully remove the vanilla bean pods. (You can rinse the pods and store them in a jar of sugar, which will infuse the sugar with vanilla flavor.)

Meanwhile, position a rack in the center of the oven and heat to 350°F.

In a medium bowl, whisk together the remaining 2 cups milk with the egg, yolks, cardamom, and orange zest. Using a heatproof measuring cup, scoop out about 1 cup of the hot rice mixture. Whisking the egg mixture constantly, add the rice mixture to the eggs in a steady stream and whisk to blend. Repeat with another 1 cup of the rice. Then pour the egg mixture back into the saucepan and whisk to blend. Stir in the raisins.

Transfer to an 8 by 12-inch glass or metal baking dish and place the dish in another, larger baking or roasting pan at least as deep as the baking dish. Fill the pan with enough hot water to come halfway up the sides of the baking dish.

Bake uncovered, stirring occasionally, until the pudding is thickened but still fairly fluid, about 40 minutes. (The rice will absorb the remaining liquid as it cools.)

Let cool slightly. Serve while still warm.

Note: You could use jasmine or other long-grain rice instead, but basmati seems to hold up the best under the long cooking time.

Garden of Eden Soup

MAKES ABOUT 5 CUPS

This chilled soup always makes me imagine what summer in Eden must have been like: silky, verdant, bright, and refreshing. My only other need would be a glass of cava or vinho verde to go with it.

The quality of your avocados is key to this recipe. Try to find the Haas or Bacon varieties from a domestic grower—the Fuerte ones from Chile (which are common in supermarkets) are too watery.

1 large English or other thin-skinned cucumber, seeded and coarsely chopped

$^1/_2$ cup plain yogurt, plus more for garnish

$^1/_4$ cup loosely packed cilantro leaves

3 tablespoons champagne vinegar, more as needed

2 tablespoons freshly squeezed lime juice, more as needed

6 large fresh mint leaves

1 medium jalapeño, coarsely chopped (for less heat, remove the seeds first)

1 large scallion, chopped into 1-inch pieces

Kosher salt

$^3/_4$ cup water

2 large avocados (about 1$^1/_4$ pounds), flesh scooped out and coarsely mashed with a fork

$^1/_4$ cup extra-virgin olive oil

Thinly sliced chives, for garnish

Combine the cucumber, yogurt, cilantro, vinegar, lime juice, mint, jalapeño, scallion, 1 teaspoon salt, and the water in a blender. Puree just until smooth. Add the avocados and pulse a few times just to blend. (Don't blend any more than necessary, as it will over-aerate and thicken the soup undesirably.)

Transfer to a bowl and whisk constantly as you slowly drizzle in the olive oil.

Taste and stir in more salt, vinegar, or lime juice as needed. Garnish with a dollop of yogurt and a sprinkle of chives.

7

THE CHEESE DEPARTMENT

I live for "cheese epiphanies": taking people on that journey of starting out being in love with American Monterey Jack, to giving them something that makes them say, "Wow, I didn't know cheese could taste like that!" I really love opening people's eyes to all the styles and flavors represented in the cheeses we offer.

When I recommend a cheese to guests, I always give them a taste, and I always preface it with, "Don't be afraid to tell me that you hate it." That way, they know they won't hurt my feelings. It's best if they can tell me specifically what they don't like about it, whether it's too soft, or they want something stronger, or whatever it is— so I can help find a cheese that better suits their tastes. I want our guests to feel confident and be happy with their decision.

— Anthea Stolz,
cheesemonger

LIKE SO MANY OF MY GENERATION, I grew up in a household where Velveeta was bought by the boxload. The 1970s were a bleak time for cheese in general, but Velveeta and Kraft Singles (products whose categorization as "cheese" is generous at best) were the gold standard for most households. It was all I knew as a kid.

That all changed with a single meal at Paul Bocuse's restaurant near Lyon, France, when I was twenty years old. Its three Michelin stars should tell you something about the extravagance of the experience, but even so, I was truly unprepared for the cheese course. We were six courses into the meal already when a literal caravan of cheese carts came rolling toward us. Each of the four carts represented a different category of cheeses, effectively breaking this one course into four subcourses.

Choosing from all those cheeses was pretty overwhelming, so we simply asked the waiter what his favorites were. He carefully cut six or eight selections from the whole wheels and told us that if we wanted more of any of them we were more than welcome to it.

There was so much care and attention devoted to the course—almost as if it were more important than all the other courses that had preceded it.

After that meal, I became more and more interested in cheeses. As I learned how much time and effort cheese-making required, I understood why the staff at Paul Bocuse treated it with such reverence. Since then, I've tried to show the same reverence for it at my own table.

CHEESE 101

Knowing how cheese is made helps demystify the endless types and categories of cheeses that are out there. I'm about to offer a bare-bones description of the process; the variations on techniques and ingredients are nearly infinite. (If you want to go deeper, there are lots of great cheese books out there—see page 285 for some of my favorites.)

But all cheese starts with milk or cream from a cow, goat, sheep, or buffalo, or a combination thereof. You don't have to be a dairy expert to know that milk is liquid and cheese is solid, so one of the first steps in cheesemaking is to start that shapeshifting process. The cheesemaker does that by mixing the milk or cream with bacterial cultures, a coagulant, and salt. The cultures help lower the pH of the milk, which in turn helps the coagulant curdle the milk. (These ingredients are sometimes added in different phases, depending on the type of cheese desired.) This process produces the proverbial curds (solids) and whey (runoff liquid) that Little Miss Muffet so enjoyed.

Most of the time the cheesemaker will strain off the liquid whey to isolate the solid curds. For some cheeses, the process stops here and you end up with what's called a **FRESH CHEESE**. This category includes farmer cheese, cottage cheese, fromage blanc, and quark—just to name a few. (The unique attributes of each come from variations in milk, coagulants, and technique.) Fresh mozzarella is another fresh cheese; to make it, the curds are pulled and stretched under hot water to produce the stringy texture.

Fresh cheeses are still fairly perishable—we've all discovered a container of moldy cottage cheese in the back of the fridge at some point. To boost shelf life (and to make a different and more interesting product), a cheesemaker may choose to further manipulate the curds in order to make an **AGED CHEESE**.

To do this, the cheesemaker drains the curds again using heat and/or pressure and forms the curds into the desired shape. Once formed and molded, the cheese is ready for aging. Time is not the only factor in

---

RICOTTA is a fresh cheese that came about as a byproduct of cheesemaking. It is traditionally made from cooked-down whey, and its name literally means "recooked." Most commercially made ricotta, however, is made from whole milk.

MASCARPONE and **CRÈME FRAÎCHE** are often stocked in the cheese section, but technically they are not cheese but forms of cream thickened by addition of an acid.

COAGULANTS AND WHY THEY MATTER

The type of coagulant has a big effect on the texture of the resulting cheese. Acids like lemon juice and vinegar produce delicate curds, whereas the enzyme rennin produces more robust ones. And bacterial coagulants not only solidify the curds but also contribute to the overall flavor of the cheese.

The vast majority of cheeses are coagulated at least in part with rennet, which produces a desirable consistency and can be used in conjunction with flavor-contributing bacteria. It is most often derived from the stomachs of young calves, so some consumers, especially vegetarians, avoid cheeses made with animal rennin. There are vegetarian alternatives out there; good cheesemongers will note the coagulant type on their signage or be able to tell you if you inquire.

---

aging cheese; the temperature, humidity, and ambient mold in the aging room, as well as any mold added to the cheese itself, will also influence the type and quality of the final cheese.

Aging cheese is not just a matter of putting it in a room and letting it rest until it's "ready"; the cheese must be actively cared for during this time. At a bare minimum, the cheese must be monitored and turned so that it ages evenly, but there are other techniques that produce specific characteristics in the end product. These are most often described in terms of what kind of rind they produce, but in fact they affect every morsel of the entire wheel.

- **Natural rinds** are created by perhaps the simplest aging technique: the wheels rest in a controlled environment over a period of time. Sometimes the wheels are wrapped in cloth, stacked in a particular way, or rubbed with salt or other dry ingredients to encourage further compression and drying of the cheese. There might be a little mold on the surface of the cheese, but it is not a defining characteristic as such.

  EXAMPLES: *Clothbound and English Cheddars, Stilton, Manchego, Parmigiano-Reggiano*

- **Bloomy rinds** are those with a flexible, snowy outside and a soft, creamy interior. The rinds are formed thanks to the growth of friendly mold such as *Penicillium candida* or *Penicillium camemberti*, which is introduced in the coagulation process or in the aging room (or both).

  EXAMPLES: *Brie, Camembert, Boucheron*

- **Washed rinds** are made by periodically curing the cheese with saltwater (aka brine), beer, wine, spirits, or other liquids. This helps keep the cheese and rind from drying out, and the washing liquid itself imparts flavor to the cheese. It also encourages the growth of moisture-loving bacteria called *B. linens*, which create a somewhat sticky, often reddish surface. These cheeses tend to be decidedly pungent and complex in flavor.

  EXAMPLES: *Taleggio, Epoisses, Livarot, Morbier, Raclette*

Cheese is a living thing; it contains and relies on an entire microcosm of bacteria and mold to make its transformation from liquid to solid. As a result, aging cheese is not easy, and to do it successfully many variables must be accounted for: not just temperature and

---

BLUE CHEESE comes about when a specific mold (such as the familiar-sounding *Penicillium roqueforti*) is introduced to the cheese. The mold is most often added to the milk; once shaped into a wheel, the cheese is pierced to create air channels where the mold can thrive. The cheese wheels are then allowed to age naturally in a controlled environment where the mold can do its thing. Blue cheese can be aged in a variety of ways.

In cheeses labeled **DOUBLE AND TRIPLE CREAM**, the original milk mixture is enriched with a dose of cream. (Double cream cheese has a minimum of 60 percent butterfat, and triple cream a 70 percent minimum.) As you can imagine, this makes for a richer, more decadent cheese; you usually see this in soft, bloomy cheeses such as Brie and Brillat Savarin.

AFFINEURS

Because the aging of cheese (*affinage* in French) is such a complicated art, it is its own profession in many traditions of cheesemaking. Interestingly, in these cultures there's absolutely no shame in a cheesemaker's handing cheese over to an *affineur* (aging expert). In fact, some of the world's very best cheesemakers rely on independent affineurs, who often enjoy just as much recognition as the cheesemakers themselves. Some well-regarded affineurs include Neals Yard Dairy in the UK, Guffanti in Italy, and Hervé Mons and Marcel Petite in France.

---

humidity, but also ambient microbes, seasonal variations in the milk, and other factors. Even two cheeses made from the same batch of milk and aged in the same room might turn out very differently. Cheesemakers must constantly adjust for these variations by handling, cleaning, and monitoring each wheel individually. That requires a great deal of attention as well as a deep understanding of how cheese evolves in different environments. Great cheesemakers treat each wheel like a child, recognizing that each is unique and special in its own way.

The price of cheese can sometimes be (ahem) difficult to swallow. In many, many cases, cheeses are expensive for good reason. To take a simple example, many of the recipes in this book call for Parmigiano-Reggiano cheese, which comes from a designated area in the Emilia-Romagna region of Italy. As a DOC product, the name and entire production process is controlled and regulated by the Italian government: the milk must be raw and come from grass-fed cows; the cheese must be aged for a minimum of twelve months; and it must pass inspection by a master grader, who relies on a hammer and his or her ear to determine whether a wheel is worthy. Those requirements take time and labor, and although they could be automated or sped up through technology, outsourcing, or simply making the cheese somewhere else, the cheese wouldn't taste the same.

Cracking open an 80-pound wheel of Parmigiano-Reggiano

So although true Parmigiano-Reggiano is made in great quantity, its price will—and should—always reflect the higher cost of traditional techniques. (The Italian government recognizes the cultural importance of this traditional product by subsidizing production, thus making the retail price of Parmigiano-Reggiano lower than the true production cost.) Besides, no factory-made, waxy-textured "Parmesan" can ever compare in flavor to the real thing. Even at $20 per pound, true Parmigiano-Reggiano is a deal.

If you still don't believe that handcrafted cheese is worth it, take the simplest example: fresh mozzarella. Put your average mass-produced fresh mozzarella up against a freshly made cow or buffalo milk mozzarella. You'll be astounded by the creamy, sweet milk flavor of the freshly made one; it will make the factory version seem flavorless.

Technique and location are not the only things that make a cheese extra-special. Just like wine, a very carefully made cheese can be a pure expression of where it comes from, thanks to the soil, the climate, and the type of grasses that the animals graze on. And just like wine, cheese has a short ingredient list, so the quality of those ingredients matters. Any cheesemaker will tell you that well-treated cows produce the best milk, and without good milk, you cannot make good cheese.

ORGANIC MILK IS A GOOD STARTING POINT—BUT IT'S NOT THE BE-ALL AND END-ALL. Buying organic cheese ensures that the milk came from animals fed organic feed or pastured and not given hormones

or preventive antibiotics. However, remember that some dairy farmers choose not to be certified organic, whether because of the cost, out of philosophical opposition to the system as a whole, or simply because they're going above and beyond the standards set forth by the USDA. I found this to be true even in England, where a well-known cheese authority told me that "a good cheesemaker is going to want to use the best milk they can find, no matter what. Whether it's organic is beside the point." So don't dismiss non-organic cheeses offhand. Instead, take the opportunity to probe and learn about the cheesemaker's philosophy on milk, including where they source it.

To get the best milk possible, many artisanal cheesemakers have a very close relationship with dairy farmers. Their cheesemaking facilities are often physically close to the dairy farms as well, allowing regular visits. This gives them the utmost insight into how the animals are treated, what they're eating, and what the milk is like throughout the year. Why does the time of year matter? Artisan cheesemakers tend to prefer milk from animals that are **PASTURE-RAISED**, and as we discussed in The Dairy Case chapter, raising animals on pasture yields milk whose flavors, fat content, and even color vary over the course of the year.

Because of this, artisanal cheese is seasonal. The best cheese is often made with summer milk because the cows have so much fresh pasture to graze on, enriching the milk with lots of flavor and fat. In many cultures, the cheese made from summer milk is highly prized

COWGIRL CREAMERY: Maureen Cunnie and Eric Patterson

Founded by Peggy Smith and Sue Conley, "the Cowgirls" make some pretty amazing—even legendary—cow's milk cheeses. There's the Mt. Tam, with its snow-white, velvety bloom; the Red Hawk, robust with its terra-cotta-tinged washed rind; and the St. Pat, enveloped in stinging nettle leaves. Their cheese is a true expression of the Northern California land where the cows live and produce milk. But Cowgirl Creamery's importance goes far beyond the products they make. Because they believe so strongly in supporting the American artisan cheese movement, they are also distributors and retailers, carrying other producers' cheeses as well as their own. This diversified business model has found great success, and the Cowgirls' products are now available throughout the country. I'm impressed that they've managed to scale up their operation to a nationwide level without compromising the integrity of their product. The Cowgirls' commitment to handcrafted cheese and artisan producers is a driving force behind the cheese renaissance in this country. They deserve every bit of the recognition and success that comes their way.

and often cause for celebration. It's fun to taste the difference in batches depending on when they were made. Commercially produced cheeses don't have these fluctuations in flavor because the milk comes from cows that are confined and fed a consistent diet of grain supplemented with silage (fermented hay), which yields milk that does not vary from season to season.

THE BREED OF THE ANIMAL ALSO PLAYS AN IMPORTANT ROLE IN THE QUALITY OF THE MILK AND THE FLAVOR OF THE FINISHED CHEESE. Holstein cows (the classic black-and-white variety) are prolific producers of milk; consequently, most American cheeses are made from Holstein milk. Other breeds such as the Jersey cow produce about one-third less milk than Holsteins, but their milk is very rich (about 40 percent more butterfat), and the resulting cheese is simply otherwordly. This kind of variation holds true for different breeds of sheep, goat, and buffalo as well. Whatever the animal, the best cheesemakers value quality over quantity in the milk they use, which translates into the final product as well.

SOME CHEESEMAKERS RAISE ANIMALS AND PRODUCE THE MILK THEMSELVES; THEIR PRODUCTS ARE CALLED "FARMSTEAD CHEESES." Not only do these cheesemakers have the ultimate control over the quality of the animals and milk, but they also eliminate transport from dairy farm to cheesemaker: milk simply does not get any fresher.

RAW MILK IS AT THE CENTER OF GREAT DEBATE IN THE CHEESE WORLD. Many artisan cheesemakers prefer to use raw milk because it's an unadulterated, more elemental ingredient; heating milk, especially heating it enough to pasteurize it, unavoidably changes the way it tastes when it is made into cheese. It's a simple matter of kitchen chemistry: extreme heat alters the shape of protein chains. It's true for eggs and just as true for milk. Cheese made from raw milk is more complex and a purer expression of where the

REDWOOD HILL FARM: Jennifer and Scott Bice

Goats come first at Redwood Hill Farm—literally. It started with a few pet goats for the Bice family, as part of a 4-H project. That eventually led to a goat milk dairy in 1968; ten years later, Jennifer and her late husband Steven Schack took over the business and diversified

the product line to include cheeses, yogurt, and kefir. Their delicious products are now distributed nationwide, but Redwood Hill Farm maintains an artisanal approach: four of the ten Bice siblings contribute to the business, the cheeses are all made by hand, and all their goats have names. (And very happy goats they are.)

Jennifer manages the dairy while her brother Scott tends to the herd of goats.

milk came from compared to one made from pasteurized milk.

Our government, however, is unfairly risk-averse; it requires that any raw milk cheese be aged for at least sixty days (currently under debate to be extended to ninety days) before it can be sold. This regulation is primarily designed to reduce the risk of *Listeria* infection and other foodborne illnesses associated with unpasteurized milk.

That means that most young cheeses—domestic or imported—are made with pasteurized milk, and it means that some of the world's truly great, iconic cheeses cannot be imported to the United States. Because raw milk cheeses are the exception rather than the norm, they are usually labeled as such as a selling point. Unfortunately, for the time being at least, you won't find that label on any fresh or lightly aged cheeses. These raw milk cheeses are the ones to seek out when traveling abroad.

How to Buy

It's not just the affineur's job to care for cheese. Because cheese is a living, natural product, it's also up to the retailer to continue to keep it in optimal condition. Finding a conscientious cheesemonger—whether in a supermarket or a stand-alone cheese shop—can make all the difference in the quality of cheese that you get.

I CAN TAKE ONE LOOK AT THE CHEESE SECTION OF A MARKET AND, WITHOUT READING LABELS OR SIGNAGE, KNOW IF IT'S WORTH SHOPPING AT. How? By looking at how the cheeses are wrapped. If the cheeses are in those shrink-wrapped, heat-sealed packages, it means that the store is not cutting the cheese themselves; instead, they're getting cut and wrapped at a distribution center or at the factory itself. So not only is the cheese likely to be mass-produced, but also the retailer is doing as little as possible to care for the cheese. **LOOK FOR CHEESES THAT ARE HAND-WRAPPED, WHETHER IN PAPER OR PLASTIC.**

And for any given type of cheese, **THE FEWER PIECES ON DISPLAY, THE BETTER**; cheeses start to change and degrade as soon as a wheel is cut into, so a careful cheesemonger will cut only as many wedges as they can sell in a few days. This not only ensures the maximum freshness of the cut wedges but also helps preserve the remaining uncut wheel. It's a rare cheese shop that only cuts cheese to order; the economies of staffing such an outlet make these few and far between. If such a shop exists in your town, please support them as much as you can.

There's another reason to shop at stores that cut and wrap their own wedges: **BOTH YOU (AND THE RETAILER) GET TO TASTE.** There's no better way to find out whether you like a certain food than to put it in your mouth. But don't limit yourself to pre-cut samples; if a cheese catches your eye, go ahead and ask for a taste. Any good cheesemonger will be happy to do this for you anyway, but some cheeses (especially very soft ones) simply do not lend themselves to self-service sampling.

I try to support locally made products whenever I can, but when it comes to cheeses, this is a challenge. After all, cheese is rich in history and tradition, and those traditions often have inextricable ties with the place of origin. Take Vlaskaas, a Dutch cow's milk cheese; traditionally, it was made only during the flax-harvesting season as a means to feed harvest workers. As flax production waned over the years, the cheese

---

AT THE VERY LEAST, LOOK FOR CHEESES THAT ARE:

- Well cared for (cut in the store, and in small quantities)
- From a cheesemonger who will give you a taste before you buy

IDEALLY, LOOK FOR:

- Made from organic or high-quality, breed-specific milk
- Farmstead cheeses
- Artisanally made and/or aged

---

eventually disappeared and was forgotten. In 2004, though, the Dutch government rediscovered the recipe and enlisted the help of the Beemster cheese-making cooperative to revive its production. Not only is it a wonderful cheese, but also I think it's worth supporting culturally important cheeses with a story of this kind.

I SUPPOSE THAT'S MY GUIDING FORCE WITH CHEESE: IT DOESN'T NECESSARILY HAVE TO BE LOCAL, BUT IT SHOULD HAVE A STORY. (And, of course, it should taste good.) One "indicator of story" is AOC or DOC (designation of origin) certification, which tells you that the cheese is backed by tradition. These certifications are usually identifiable by a stamp, seal, or other marking, often stamped right onto the cheese itself.

Until fairly recently, American cheesemakers spent most of their energy trying to emulate traditional European cheeses: to replicate Gruyère or Brie or Stilton as faithfully as possible. However, a new generation of American cheesemakers are instead developing and establishing their own unique styles. As these artisans explore new and interesting ways to express American *terroir*, many of their cheeses will become just as classic and unique as the European ones. These guidelines will help you enjoy cheese more:

- **Buy cheese in smaller quantities**—Buying less cheese and using it up quickly not only encourages you to enjoy the cheese at its peak but also makes it less likely to be forgotten in the back of the fridge. Also, when you buy and consume cheese in smaller increments, you'll find yourself buying cheese more frequently, which brings me to my next point . . .
- **Try a variety of cheeses**—Be adventurous! There's something to be said for favorite cheeses you come back to time and time again, but there's nothing like discovering a new cheese and learning the story behind it.

EAT GOOD FOOD

LAST, AND MOST IMPORTANT: LOOK FOR AND SUPPORT ARTISANAL PRODUCERS, wherever they happen to be. Cheesemaking is a labor of love, and it's difficult to do well. I'm always happy to support people who are passionate about what they do, because the product is usually out of this world. As the price of fluid milk has plummeted below the cost of production for many farmers, cheese is a great way to add value (and shelf life) to the milk that these farmers produce, helping ensure viability for our dairy farmers and their land.

Just because a store has their wedges already wrapped doesn't mean you can't have a smaller piece. If the store is weighing and wrapping their own cheese, it's no big deal for them to cut the perfect size for you. Just ask!

As you taste and become acquainted with an artisanally made cheese, don't be alarmed if it tastes slightly different each time you buy it. These nuances are the product of not just the seasonal changes in the milk itself, but other variables as well: everything from weather patterns to the ever-shifting cloud of microbial fauna where the cheese is made and aged, to the age of the cheese when it's eaten, to the simple fact that the cheese is made by a human being. These slight variations make each cheese a reflection of a specific time and place, and they are worthy of celebration.

Cheeses labeled pecorino are made from sheep's milk (*pecora* is Italian for ewe). They can be used young for eating or aged for grating.

How to Store

Providing the right combination of cool air and humidity is the key to helping your cheese last longer. Here are a few tricks I like to use:

- **Wrap cheese in cheese paper, if you can find it**—This specially made two-ply paper provides just the right amount of moisture and ventilation for cheese. Ask for it at your local cheese shop or order it online (see page 285). As an alternative, try waxed paper topped with a layer of plastic wrap. Plastic alone is impermeable and thus not ideal for storage; if you buy a cheese that's wrapped in plastic, swap in cheese paper or plastic-topped waxed paper as soon as you get it home.

- **The vegetable drawer is the perfect spot** for cheese in your refrigerator, especially if you have some moisture-providing veggies in there as well. (And don't even think of freezing cheese—it destroys the character, flavor, and texture.)

- **Don't worry if a little mold develops** on the rind or cut surface of a cheese. Chances are that it's neither harmful nor detrimental to the interior. Just cut off and discard the moldy parts before using. (If there's significant molding that seems to have taken on a life of its own, though, you'd probably better say goodbye to that particular wedge.)

- **Trust your instincts**—If it looks awful or smells ammoniated, it probably needs to be tossed.

TIPS FOR CHEESE SUCCESS:

- Buy smaller amounts.
- Use it up.
- Try new kinds.
- Ask for a sample.
- Store it properly (in cheese paper or waxed paper topped with plastic, and kept in the produce drawer of your refrigerator).
- Grate and crumble your own cheese.
- Find ways to use up scraps.
- Let cheese warm up before serving.
- Try a plated cheese course at your next dinner party.

A selection of Northern California cheeses, arranged from mildest to most pungent (and the order in which they should be tasted):

1 **Cowgirl Mt. Tam—** triple cream cow's milk

2 **Andante Acapella—** young goat's milk

3 **Redwood Hill Crottin—** aged goat's milk

4 **Bellwether San Andreas—** sheep's milk with membrillo (quince paste) as an accompaniment

5 **Point Reyes Blue—** cow's milk with local honey drizzled over

A PLATED CHEESE COURSE

How to Use

You don't need me to tell you to grate cheese over pasta or serve a wedge of it with crackers and grapes. But I do want to share some tips that might help you enjoy it in new ways.

When food, especially cheese, is cold, the molecules just sit inertly on your taste buds. Sure, it'll taste like something, but if you let it come to room temperature, it will be completely different. Room temperature cheese not only tastes better but also tastes *more like what it is*. So be sure to **GIVE YOUR CHEESE A CHANCE TO WARM UP.** It takes longer than you might think, and the bigger the piece the longer it will take. For an eight-ounce piece of cheese, count on at least one hour out of the fridge before serving it.

SMELL AND FEEL ARE JUST AS IMPORTANT AS TASTE IN EXPERIENCING A CHEESE. Once the cheese is at room temperature, pick it up, feel it, and smell it. Then, if possible, break it in half and smell it again on the broken edges. You'll pick up on nuances that you might not have if you relied on taste alone.

ARE YOU SUPPOSED TO EAT THE RIND? Unless the cheese is cloaked in wax and/or cloth, the rind is technically edible. But there is no right or wrong answer; I've seen some cheese experts carefully taste every part except the rind, and I've seen others eat the whole thing. It's up to you. As a simple rule of thumb, the rind on soft cheeses, especially bloomy rinds, is edible and quite interesting. The rind on hard cheeses is not always as tasty. But if you're serving yourself from a cheese board, cut and take the rind with your piece whether you want to eat it or not. It's poor form to dig out the inside of a soft cheese, leaving a hollow shell of rind behind. Not only is it unsightly, but it makes things difficult for the next person.

YOU CAN ACTUALLY TASTE THE RIPENING PROCESS IN SOME BLOOMY CHEESES. An example is the Andante Acapella shown opposite; the softer, runny area near the rind is more mature than the chalky, crumbly part near the center. On cheeses like these, try tasting each area separately, starting with the least aged (the chalky center). It's a wonderful illustration of how the flavors and textures of a cheese evolve through the aging process.

Cooking with Cheese

There is nothing like a gorgeous, creamy buffalo mozzarella melted onto a crisp, crackery pizza. Or folding light, fluffy sheep's milk ricotta into the Apricot and Arugula Salad on page 250. However, a gorgeous, cave-aged Gruyère in your favorite mac 'n' cheese is probably not the best way to enjoy the cheese itself.

What's the difference? In the first two examples, the cheeses are combined with other ingredients in a way that keeps the cheeses relatively distinct and intact. **BUT MELTING A VERY SPECIAL ARTISANAL CHEESE INTO SAUCE DILUTES THE NUANCES** of the cheese among the other ingredients (and empties your wallet while you're at it).

Don't get me wrong: I'm not recommending using generic, giant-brick cheese for cooking, but it's worth finding a good middle-ground cheese for those kinds of uses. For instance, an organic (or rGBH-free) sharp Cheddar or a less-expensive Emmentaler would be a perfectly good choice.

DO NOT BUY PRESHREDDED OR PRECRUMBLED CHEESE UNLESS THE CHEESEMONGER DOES THE SHREDDING. For a long time, we at the store bought bags of preshredded Parmigiano and then packaged it into individual containers for our shelves. But a few years ago, we did a taste test comparing this preshredded Parm with some we had shredded ourselves. The results were astounding; nobody could deny that the freshly shredded was significantly more flavorful. Then and there we decided to shred Parmigiano in-house. It takes a lot more labor and production space to pull this off, but it's worth it.

We are fairly unique in doing so. The vast majority of markets do not take the time or effort to shred or crumble their own cheese, so unless you know for sure, I encourage you to take matters into your own hands and shred or crumble your own cheese—whatever kind it is. You'll get much more flavor for your money, and

---

IF MAKING THIS . . . TRY A GOOD-QUALITY VERSION OF THIS:

Mac 'n' cheese—Farmhouse Cheddar or a block Gouda. However, this is one dish where almost any cheese, including a mixture of cheeses, can work wonderfully.

Lasagna—Ricotta (strain if it's high-moisture), mozzarella (not fresh—it gets rubbery), or sheep's milk cheeses such as pecorino (hard-aged or younger).

Pizza—Fresh ricotta, fresh mozzarella, Taleggio, fresh goat cheese, or crumbled blue.

Grilled cheese—Use the best farmhouse Cheddar or Gruyère you can find! I never skimp on cheese or the bread for grilled cheese—they're the main ingredients, so pick ones that will shine!

Risotto—Parmigiano-Reggiano is the classic for a good reason. Just remember that in risotto, the rice should be the star of the show. Use cheese in moderation.

Gratins—Gruyère or other mountain cheeses, or Parmigiano-Reggiano (or both).

Quiche and fritattas—Gruyère, Parmigiano-Reggiano, fresh goat cheese, fresh mozzarella, or farmhouse Cheddar.

the sensory pleasure of grating a chunk of Parmigiano-Reggiano at the table . . . watching the freshly grated flakes wriggle as they come into contact with the warm food . . . drinking in that seductive scent that wafts in the air. Think about that the next time you're tempted by a tub of grated Parmesan!

Italians have long added leftover Parmigiano rinds to soups; they add extra body and flavor. You too can save any little scraps you have and look for ways to add them to your cooking.

That life-changing cheese course at Paul Bocuse's restaurant opened my eyes to the delights of giving cheese center stage. You can serve cheese in a couple of different ways. One is to **BUILD A CHEESE BOARD** by arranging a couple of different cheeses on a platter and letting people help themselves. The other approach is just as easy, but surprisingly less common, and that's to **SERVE INDIVIDUAL PORTIONS** of cheese on a plate for each guest. There's a lot to be said for the cheese board, especially for larger, stand-up parties, but I actually prefer to serve individual portions whenever I can. Not only is it easier to predict how much cheese you'll need, but the more structured serving mode encourages guests to really taste, enjoy, and talk about the cheeses.

The question of what cheeses to serve is entirely up to you. It's always nice to have a variety, but that can mean a lot of different things. You could select cheeses from a single country, type of milk, or aging technique, or simply serve a few of your favorite cheeses.

It does help if the cheeses are different enough in flavor and texture to make easy comparisons and contrasts. If they're too similar, it can be frustrating to try to tell them apart.

Always arrange and taste cheeses in order from mildest to most pungent—it helps prevent palate fatigue.

BASIC STEPS TO TASTING CHEESE Tasting cheese is all about paying attention to your senses and asking questions as you go along. This will help you pick up on subtle flavors and textures and notice differences from one cheese to the next.

- **Look at the cheese**—Does it look soft and runny or hard? Is it solid, or does it have holes or cracks? Is there evidence of mold, either on the surface or inside? What color is the mold?

- **Pick it up and smell it**—Does it smell like the sweet grass that the cow grazed on? Is it funky and barnyard, or sweet and intense? Break a piece in half and smell it again. Does it smell different now?

- **Taste it methodically**—Start in the center, moving toward the rind in small successive bites. Note the evolution of taste as you go; the flavor usually gets stronger and more intense as you get closer to the rind.

- **Share your thoughts** with whomever you are tasting. Jot down a few notes so you can refer to them the next time you taste the same cheese.

Grilled Peaches with Blue Cheese and Hazelnuts

SERVES 4 TO 8

These grilled peaches are infinitely versatile: you can eat them by themselves as a light first course; for a more substantial salad, serve them on a bed of lightly dressed arugula. They are even lovely as dessert. The best part is that you can grill the peaches a few hours ahead of time and then assemble them just before serving.

For best results, use peaches that are ripe but still relatively firm; the extra sturdiness makes them easier to manipulate on the grill. And freestone varieties (ones where the pit separates cleanly from the flesh) are by far easier to work with here than clingstones. If you can't find hazelnuts, almonds or walnuts will work nicely, too.

> 4 ripe peaches
> Extra-virgin olive oil, for brushing and drizzling
> 6 tablespoons balsamic vinegar (see Note)
> 1/2 cup crumbled blue cheese
> 1/4 cup toasted skinned hazelnuts, coarsely chopped (see Tip)
> 20 tiny basil leaves (or 3 or 4 large basil leaves, torn into pieces)

Prepare a medium-hot fire in a gas or charcoal grill or a grill pan over medium-high heat. Meanwhile, halve and pit the peaches, and brush a little oil over the cut sides.

When the grill is hot, put the peaches cut side down on the grill. Let cook undisturbed for at least 2 minutes; then peek at one and check the browning (if it sticks, it means it hasn't browned enough). Cook until the peaches have nice dark grill marks, 1 to 2 minutes longer. Then flip them over and cook just until heated through and softened slightly, about 4 minutes longer. Remove the peaches from the grill and set aside.

Put the vinegar in a small saucepan over medium-high heat and bring to a rapid simmer. Cook until it has reduced to about half its original volume and has become noticeably thicker, 3 to 5 minutes. Remove from the heat and let cool slightly.

Divide the cheese among the peaches, mounding it slightly in the cavity where the pit was. Sprinkle the hazelnuts and basil over the cheese. To finish, drizzle with the reduced vinegar and a bit more of the olive oil.

Tip: To toast hazelnuts, spread them evenly on a rimmed baking sheet and broil, shaking the pan frequently, until toasted and fragrant, about 5 minutes. (They toast from the inside out, so let your nose guide you rather than your eyes.) Remove the skins by putting the nuts on a clean kitchen towel, gathering the corners to make a bundle, and rubbing the bundle against the palm of your hand.

Note: Though it can be hard to find, Pedro Ximinez sherry vinegar would be spectacular here. It has a lovely fruity quality that's a little brighter than balsamic but reduces to the same lovely syrupy consistency.

Grated Summer Squash with Truffle Pecorino

SERVES 4

This salad is a wonderful way to venture into the world of raw squash. Using the truffle version of pecorino isn't absolutely critical, but its earthiness is a fantastic counterpoint to the brighter flavors of squash and lemon juice. For best results, use the smallest, firmest, freshest squash you can find—they're easier to grate and taste better than the more mature ones. And because this salad is so simple (almost minimalist), the quality of your olive oil really counts.

4 small summer squash (green or yellow or a mix—about 1 pound total)
2-inch chunk truffle pecorino cheese
2 teaspoons freshly squeezed lemon juice, more as needed
2 teaspoons extra-virgin olive oil, plus more for drizzling
Kosher salt

Trim the squash, grate on the large holes of a box grater, and transfer to a medium bowl. Finely grate enough of the cheese to make $1/4$ cup and add to the bowl. Use a vegetable peeler on the remaining chunk of cheese to make a small pile of cheese shards, and set them aside.

Drizzle the lemon juice and olive oil over the squash, add a few large pinches of salt, and mix well. Taste and add more lemon juice or salt as needed. Transfer to a serving bowl, drizzle with a little more olive oil, and sprinkle the cheese shards over the top of the salad.

Tip: Because squash has so much water, it starts to wilt and release liquid as soon as it comes into contact with salt. So for best results, serve this salad within minutes of making it.

Apricot and Arugula Salad with Fresh Ricotta

SERVES 4

This salad is a delightful interplay of sweet, creamy, tangy, and peppery flavors. If you prefer, you can swap in ricotta salata or a mild feta for the ricotta; both are saltier than fresh ricotta, so skip the seasoning with zest, salt, and pepper.

Apricots have but a brief appearance even at the peak of their season. If you miss them, you can substitute with any other stone fruit. White nectarines, peaches, pluots, or plums would be particularly nice. In the fall, sliced fuyu persimmons are perfect. Whatever fruit you use, just make sure it's ripe and flavorful.

$1/4$ cup fresh ricotta
$1/2$ teaspoon finely grated lemon zest
Kosher salt and freshly ground black pepper
1 tablespoon cider vinegar, more as needed
$1/4$ teaspoon Dijon mustard
4 teaspoons extra-virgin olive oil
3 cups lightly packed baby arugula (about $2 1/2$ ounces)
3 medium apricots, cut into $1/4$-inch wedges

In a small bowl, combine the ricotta, zest, $1/4$ teaspoon salt, and a pinch of black pepper. Set aside.

Combine the vinegar, mustard, and $1/4$ teaspoon salt in a small bowl. Whisk to blend, and continue to whisk as you drizzle in the olive oil.

Put the arugula and apricots in a large bowl, drizzle about two-thirds of the dressing over, and toss gently but thoroughly with your hands. Toss and taste the salad. Add more dressing or vinegar, salt, and pepper as needed. Spread on a serving platter, or divide among 4 salad plates.

Scatter teaspoonfuls of the ricotta mixture over the salad.

Tip: Make extra of the ricotta mixture and spread it on bruschetta or toast.

Roasted Beet Salad with Pickled Onions and Feta

SERVES 4 TO 6

This hearty salad is a near-constant in our deli case and a favorite among guests and staff. Although the beets are the star of the show, the pickled onions play an important supporting role, adding textural interest and a vinegary punch.

At the store, we cook the beets by baking them whole, in a deep roasting pan with 1 inch of water. For a small, at-home quantity I suggest steaming. It's faster because steam gets hotter than boiling water (which maxes out at 212°F) and uses less energy than turning on the oven. However, if you prefer to roast or boil your beets, feel free—the results will be just as tasty.

$^1/_4$ small red onion, thinly sliced lengthwise
3 tablespoons champagne vinegar
Kosher salt
$1^1/_2$ pounds (about 5 medium) beets
1 tablespoon extra-virgin olive oil
$^1/_4$ teaspoon Dijon mustard
$^1/_4$ teaspoon honey
2 tablespoons chopped fresh parsley
2 ounces feta cheese, crumbled ($^1/_2$ cup)

Combine the onion, vinegar, and a couple of pinches of salt in a small bowl and set aside.

If using baby beets, leave the skin on but halve or quarter them as needed so that they're all about 1 inch thick. If using medium or large beets, peel and cut into 1-inch chunks.

Fit a steamer basket in a large pot, add water just to the bottom of the basket, and arrange the beets in a snug single layer. Bring the water to a boil over medium-high heat, cover the pot, and reduce the heat to maintain a vigorous simmer. Cook until the beets are completely tender when pierced with a skewer, about 30 minutes. (Keep an eye on the water level during cooking, and add more if it threatens to dry up.) Remove from the heat and let cool. If you're using

baby beets, slip the skins off as soon as they're cool enough to handle.

Reserving the liquid, remove the onion from the vinegar and add to the beets. In another bowl, whisk together the oil, mustard, honey, 1 tablespoon of the reserved vinegar, and a few big pinches of salt.

Add the dressing, the parsley, and all but 2 tablespoons of the feta to the beets. Toss well and taste; season with more salt or vinegar as needed. Garnish with a sprinkling of the remaining feta on top.

Note: The beautiful hue of beets will stain your hands and clothes. Wear gloves and an apron if pink isn't your color!

Tip: Use any color beets you have available; if you choose to use both golden and red beets, toss them with the dressing separately to keep the red beets from staining the yellow ones.

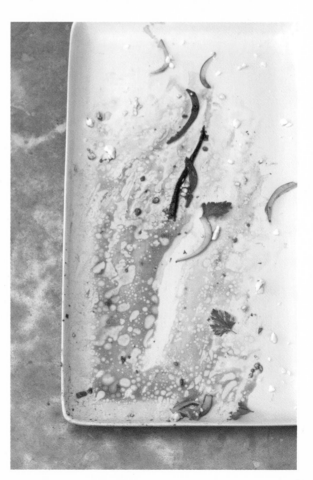

8

THE BAKERY:
BREAD AND BAKED GOODS

We make our baked goods in small batches using the best ingredients we can get. It gives us more control over the quality, because we don't want to make so much that they sit on the shelf for too long. Freshness is key! With mass-produced baked goods, you never really know when they were made. We control our production so that our baked goods are up to our own standards, and those of our guests.

— Kris Hoogerhyde, partner, Bi-Rite Creamery

Our training as pastry chefs taught us that seasonal fruits and simple ingredients always make a superior product. Our ingredient lists are minimal—we don't include anything extraneous, and we don't use artificial colors, flavors, or preservatives. We want to give our guests the perfect, simple dessert—to complete and balance their meal experience. We hope that our simple, nostalgic recipes evoke a memory from childhood.

— Anne Walker, partner, Bi-Rite Creamery

THE BEST BREAD I've ever had comes from just down the street at Tartine Bakery. Chad Robertson, partner and bread baker there, works magic with his dough. The dark and almost glistening crust forms a robust, protective shell around the crumb within; you need real conviction to tear off a hunk. The interior is home to holes and pockets of varying sizes, and although completely baked through, it retains just enough moisture to make it feel a tiny bit tacky. The result is a symphony of flavor, texture, aroma, and even sound that plays out as you eat it (see the photo on page 265).

As good as it is, Tartine's bread is not easy to come by—even when you're as nearby as I am. The loaves don't come out of the oven until 5 p.m., and you'd better be there when they do, because they usually sell out within thirty minutes. People traverse the city just to get their hands on this bread, but I would drive fifty miles if I had to. It's that good.

BREAD

Bread is a pretty magical product. In its most basic form, it is made of flour, water, salt, time, and heat. Combined in the right way, you can start with a gloppy, sticky mess and end up with a beautiful bronze boule of deliciousness. Combined in the wrong way, you still start with a gloppy, sticky mess . . . and end up with an inedible brick!

How to Buy

Among food professionals, there are invisible but undeniable lines that divide cooks, pastry folks, and bread bakers. Cooks, as a lot, approach their trade with a certain free-wheeling, improvisational methodology, whereas pastry chefs thrive on precision and exactitude—so much so that they rely on "formulas" rather than recipes. Bread bakers, on the other hand, are in their own little category that manages to straddle these otherwise-opposing philosophies. Bread bakers start with measured quantities of flour and water, but nature itself—in the form of temperature, humidity, and the ever-changing, yeast-laden microbial fog that we live in—is an equally important and omnipresent ingredient; it causes the dough to behave very differently from day to day, and bread bakers must adjust their recipes and techniques accordingly. It's an interactive process, and a very skilled bread baker relies on instinct, touch, and experience just as much as on measurements.

All this is true even if you're using a packaged bread mix. But true artisan breads—ones made by hand and in small batches—are often made with techniques that make the dough even more unpredictable. Artisan bakers face even greater challenges to produce great bread—or produce it consistently—but the ones who pull it off exhibit an incredible amount of desire, passion, and skill. Not only that, but the product is unquestionably superior.

Many (but not all) masters of artisan bread embrace techniques such as these:

- **Natural leavening**—Instead of relying solely on commercial yeast, naturally leavened breads are made from doughs that rise (at least in part) from a naturally cultured "starter." This gives the bread depth of flavor and a unique tanginess (which can vary widely depending on the starter and how it's used). Some examples of naturally leavened breads include levain, sourdough, and pain de campagne.
- **A wet dough and slow rise time**—If you've ever made bread at home, you know that a very wet dough can be difficult to work with. Some artisan bakers (particularly ones using natural leavening) strive for moisture-rich dough because it requires a long, leisurely rising period; the resulting bread has a deeper, more distinct flavor. And the extra moisture lengthens shelf life.
- **A wood-fired oven**—Very few bakers attempt baking with actual fire; it's so specialized that it requires its own skill set. Whereas gas or electric ovens provide a predictable, consistent level of heat with the flick of a switch, wood fires must be nurtured and tended. The baker must have an extremely close relationship with the oven—to find

the hot spots just by putting a hand in the oven, to understand the life of a fire as it blazes and eventually dwindles, and to innately gauge the baking time from batch to batch. As for the end product, the ultra-high radiant heat of a wood oven gives you a super-golden exterior while maintaining moisture in the crumb.

All this is sort of the gold standard for artisanal bread. However, there are also many fantastic breads that are made with commercial yeast and baked in electric ovens. Regardless of the ingredients, equipment, or technique, a great loaf of bread will exhibit one or more of these hallmark traits:

- **Unabashedly dark and blistery crust**—A brown exterior is an important contributor to the bread's overall flavor. It pains me to see the pale baguettes and boules in some grocery stores; bread should look like antique mahogany furniture, not the blonde birch you see at IKEA! Also, unevenly sized blisters on the crust are a sign that the bread has some natural leavening in it.
- **A combination of flours**—Using rye and/or whole wheat in addition to white flour gives the bread a more interesting flavor.
- **A healthy mid-split rise**—Once the dough has been portioned and shaped, it's often slashed with a razor before going into the oven. (The slashes on a baguette are a classic example.) Any dough will expand as it bakes, and a particularly wide split shows that the dough rose significantly during baking. It's a sign of a light crumb and good texture.
- **A moist crumb**—This not only provides a more pleasant mouthfeel but also means it won't burn quite as readily as a drier loaf would when toasted.

There's so much to love about artisan bread . . . crackly crust, a resilient chew, crumb with personality. But, I realize that your kid may resist that beautiful whole wheat–walnut levain for her PB&J. Sometimes sliced sandwich bread is called for. In that case, look for a simple ingredient list: ideally, organic flour, yeast, and salt.

Sliced bread often contains some sweetener, as well, which is added to feed the yeast and ensure a rapid rise. **LOOK FOR THOSE SWEETENED WITH REGULAR SUGAR, ORGANIC CANE JUICE, AGAVE, OR HONEY.** Avoid loaves that contain high-fructose corn syrup, which is often added to mask the unpleasant chemical taste of dough conditioners and preservatives that keep breads soft and free of mold for weeks. Also avoid bread with partially hydrogenated oils and fats, another common but unsavory way to prolong a loaf's shelf life.

LOOK FOR BREADS MADE WITH 100 PERCENT WHOLE WHEAT, WHOLE GRAINS, AND AS FEW INGREDIENTS AS POSSIBLE. White flour is refined using a process that strips many nutrients from the flour. To compensate for this, the USDA requires white flour to be "enriched" with nutrients. Whole wheat and other whole grain flours still contain their naturally occurring nutrients—another reason to go for breads made with these flours.

Typical supermarket sliced bread has anywhere from fifteen to forty ingredients, whereas a good loaf of bread will have five to ten, most of which are easily recognizable to the consumer. These tie in to the fundamental difference between a well-made loaf and a mass-produced, commercial loaf: time. Because large-scale commercial bakeries do everything possible to speed up the rising and baking process, they end up using additives to compensate for the resulting flavor and texture deficiencies.

PRESERVATIVES AND "DOUGH CONDITIONERS" ARE ALL TOO COMMON IN SLICED BREAD. You'll know them because their names look like the chemicals they are: potassium bromate, sodium stearoyl lactylate, monocalcium phosphate, calcium sulfate, and calcium propionate are just a few.

How to Store

Good artisan bread is usually fine at room temperature for a few days when stored in a tightly rolled paper bag. For longer storage, wrap well in plastic and refrigerate (this compromises the quality of the crust, but slows the drying-out process and buys you a few more days). Just be sure to toast it or revive it in a 400°F oven.

If you know you have more bread than you can eat in a few days, try freezing half for later. (Don't wait for it to go stale—freeze it in anticipation.) This keeps the bread relatively fresh and has very little detrimental effects. Either keep the bread in a single chunk and wrap well in plastic wrap and then foil, or slice it and seal in a zip-top bag (later you can put frozen slices straight into the toaster).

And if your bread does begin to go past its prime, try some of the tricks listed in the box on page 258.

How to Use

GRILLING BREAD is one of my favorite ways to make toast. Brush it with a little olive oil and grill until well marked on both sides. Sprinkle with salt as soon as it comes off the grill (the salt sticks better when the bread is hot). This is also a great way to revive day-old bread; the combination of olive oil and high heat gives it new life.

BRUSCHETTA AND CROSTINI are not only crowd-pleasing appetizers but also economical. Out of one baguette you can get twenty or so thick bruschetta slices, or forty or so thin slices for crostini. Brush with oil, sprinkle with salt, and bake in a 400°F oven until golden. Once cooled, you can top them with just about anything; they're the perfect vehicle for leftover veggies, meats, or cheeses in almost any combination.

PAR-BAKED BREAD

Most grocery stores that feature bakeries are indeed baking bread, but, technically speaking, they are not truly *making* it. They're actually selling par-baked bread, which is produced en masse at a central bakery and baked only just enough to set the crumb; the loaves are then frozen and shipped to grocery stores, where they are "finished off" in the store's ovens as needed. Although this is hardly what you'd call artisan bread (despite grocery stores' liberal use of the term), some of it is actually of decent quality. Still, be sure to read the labels and buy only the ones with short, sweet, and pronounceable ingredient lists; despite being baked fresh daily, many are nonetheless loaded with preservatives.

FIREBRAND ARTISAN BREADS: Matt Kreutz

Matt Kreutz, co-owner of Firebrand Artisan Breads, claims that time and temperature are the most important elements that go into his bread. But after visiting his workshop in Oakland, California, which he operates with his wife Mary, it's safe to say that care and attention have a lot to do with it, too. Matt hand-tends every loaf he makes (anywhere from 350 to 550 a day), at multiple stages: punching down the dough as it rises in large plastic tubs; shaping and slashing the loaves; rotating them as they bake in the wood-fired brick oven, using a peel to move two or three loaves at a time; and checking each one—top, bottom, and sides—for color before pulling it out. Matt nurtures and coddles each baguette, brioche, and boule into a crusty dark state of perfection. Firebrand's breads are unlike any that I've had, and they're some of my favorites.

THINGS ARE GETTING STALE

The shelf life of an artisan loaf is admittedly fleeting (one to four days depending on the loaf), but luckily there are many techniques for using every bit of it! To start with, always toast or grill less-than-fresh bread before using to help liven it up.

Breadcrumbs and croutons are a great way to use bread (stale is actually preferable over fresh because it's a little more robust). Kept in a sealed container, toasted croutons will keep for a few days, and breadcrumbs freeze fabulously.

Bread in soup; *pappa al pomodoro*, the classic Italian version, combines tomatoes and bread into a pureed soup. But you can also stir chunks or cubes of bread into soup and leave them as is. One of my favorite soups is a simple but beautiful arrangement: a slice of grilled bread piled with cooked chard, topped with a poached egg, and drenched with a rich, garlicky chicken broth. It's heaven.

Bread salad (also known as *panzanella*) gives leftover bread new life as a salad when toasted or grilled and combined with tomatoes, balsamic vinaigrette, and fresh basil. In fact, day-old bread is ideal in this instance, as fresh bread is too delicate and falls apart once it comes in contact with the dressing. Try the Grilled Bread Salad with Tomatoes and Parmigiano on page 263.

To make **toad in the hole**, cut an egg-size hole in a large slice of bread. Melt some butter and olive oil in a hot pan, add the bread (both the slice and the torn-out piece), and crack an egg into the hole. Drizzle with a little more olive oil, season with salt and pepper, and cook, flipping halfway through.

French toast is wonderful with less-than-fresh bread, as it has a nice bit of chew to it.

BUTTERED BREADCRUMBS make any dish seem luxurious and extravagant. In fact, they're dead easy and cheap, and can be made ahead of time. Just melt several tablespoons of butter in a skillet over medium heat. Add breadcrumbs and cook, stirring constantly, until golden and crunchy. Sprinkle over pasta, gratins, soups, or even plain ol' mac 'n' cheese. To make fabulous croutons, use the same technique on small cubes of bread.

BAKERY AND SWEETS

My wife, Anne, is a pastry chef; she's sweet and I'm salty—go figure! But as a result of her talents, I am pretty spoiled when it comes to baked goods. I'm not the only one, though; our customers at the Market are just as spoiled. In addition to running the Creamery, Anne, our business partner Kris Hoogerhyde, and their team of talented pastry chefs make all the baked goods and desserts we sell at the Market. Anne and Kris's baked goods are executed precisely and with great skill, but what really differentiates their treats is the balance of homey, familiar flavors and contemporary, seasonally driven sensibility. For evi-

dence, look no further than the dessert recipes herein—Anne and Kris created them all!

How to Buy

It is rare to find a grocery store that truly makes their cakes and cookies from scratch. Rather than hiring skilled bakers to produce high-quality products in-house, most supermarket bakeries rely on ingredients and procedures that require practically no skill or training to execute. That means prefabricated mixes, frozen doughs, and commercially made frosting; filling a cake order becomes a matter of assembly, and nearly identical to what you yourself would get from a "dump and stir" cake mix and a couple of tubs of storebought frosting. (Like supermarket bread, sometimes the baked goods come in frozen and already assembled. They need only to be defrosted before they go into the case.)

IF YOU BUY BAKED GOODS, AVOID THE ARTIFICIAL—IN ALL ITS FORMS. This trend toward prefabrication wouldn't be quite so deplorable if the baked goods actually tasted good or were made from pure, "clean" ingredients. Unfortunately, most fail on both counts. Because traditional baked goods are high in fat and dairy products (which are not only perish-

Bi-Rite Creamery partner Kris Hoogerhyde and other bakers putting on the finishing touches

able but also expensive) and fragile in general, commercial baked goods are particularly prone to containing trans fats, laboratory-made sweeteners, artificial colors, and preservatives. The more you replace familiar, flavor-loaded ingredients like butter and honey with shortening and corn syrup, the less it's going to taste like something Mom used to make. Read the labels, and avoid artificial colors, flavors, preservatives, emulsifiers, stabilizers, or artificial sweeteners or fats: things such as vanillin, milk protein concentrate, modified cornstarch, guar gum, xanthan gum, sodium stearoyl lactylate—you get the picture. If you can't find an ingredient list, ask. And remember: if it doesn't look natural, it probably isn't.

• •

If you're not sure, check the fruits. If you see cherry pie being sold in December, you can be sure that the bakery is using canned or frozen fruit. Seek and support bakeries that not only highlight the seasons but also respect their limitations. If you're not sure what's in season, flip back to The Produce Department chapter, or walk over to the produce section of the store and ask someone.

• •

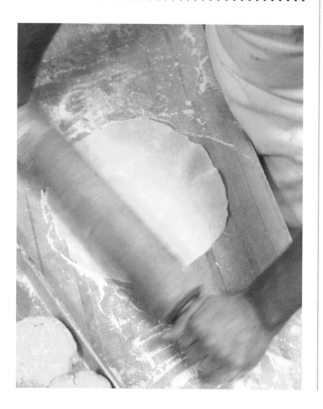

Here are some other clues you can look for when judging quality:

- **Slight irregularities in shape and size**—Baked goods should be fairly uniform, but a little variation is a sign you're looking at the product of human hands.
- **Subdued colors**—Although it's not a guarantee, subtler colors suggest the use of natural rather than artificial colors.
- **Deep color in cookies and especially crusts**—Every good baker knows that deeper color means more flavor. (For a great example of deep color, look no further than the photo of pie crusts opposite.)

How to Store

In general, baked goods are not meant to be stored for very long. So eat them up! Cookies should be stored in an airtight container at room temperature. Pies and cakes can be left out for a day or two at cool room temperature. But anything with a crust won't hold up for very long. And you have my permission to eat them for breakfast while they're still good!

Frosting acts as a layer of protection for cakes; the minute you break that seal by cutting the cake, it starts to dry out. Minimize this by laying a piece of plastic wrap directly on the exposed faces of the cake.

How to Eat

Unless specified otherwise, baked goods should be served at room temperature.

WHY NOT DIY? I'd like to close this chapter by veering away from the professional bakery to extol the virtues of baking at home. Although I am a cook at heart, I still think there's something special about the hands-on techniques, enticing smells, and dramatic transformations that happen in baking. It's so satisfying to create something that is not only beautiful and decadent but also so well suited to sharing. Everything about baking elicits a warm, fuzzy, and loving experience, not only for you, the baker, but also for everyone who gets a taste. So whether it's a special occasion or just a rainy afternoon, I encourage you to explore (or revisit) the magic of baking in your own kitchen.

Grilled Bread Salad with Tomatoes and Parmigiano

SERVES 6

This salad is a traditional way to use up day-old bread; the dressing softens the bread and makes it a little more palatable. You can use fresh bread, but stale bread will hold up better under the dressing (super-fresh bread has a tendency to fall apart).

4 (1-inch-thick) slices rustic bread (about half of a 1-pound loaf)
1/4 cup extra-virgin olive oil, more as needed
1 clove garlic, cut in half
Kosher salt and freshly ground black pepper
2 tablespoons balsamic vinegar, more as needed
1 small shallot, minced
5 medium tomatoes, cut into chunks (about 1 3/4 pounds)
8 large basil leaves, torn into pieces
1 1/2-inch chunk Parmigiano-Reggiano (about 1 ounce)
1 cup lightly packed baby arugula

Prepare a medium-hot gas or charcoal grill. Brush the bread with 2 tablespoons of the olive oil and grill until golden on both sides, about 4 minutes total. Rub the cut side of the garlic lightly across both sides of the bread and sprinkle lightly with salt. Let cool slightly, then tear into bite-size chunks.

Combine the vinegar, shallot, remaining 2 tablespoons olive oil, a few good pinches of salt, and a few grinds of black pepper in a medium bowl. Add the tomatoes and basil leaves and toss gently to coat. Add the bread, toss gently again (use your hands for best results), and set aside for at least 10 minutes.

Meanwhile, use a vegetable peeler to make shards out of the Parmigiano.

When you're ready to serve, toss in the arugula and about two-thirds of the Parmigiano. Taste the salad and add more salt, vinegar, or olive oil as needed.

Garnish with the remaining Parmigiano and lots of black pepper.

Apricot-Ginger Scones

MAKES 8 SCONES

These scones appear atop our deli case every morning, although not for long—we always sell out within a couple of hours. Unlike many scones, they're not too sweet. Pair with a cup of coffee and the newspaper and you have the formula for a perfect Sunday morning. If you're serving a crowd, this recipe can be doubled. You'll need an extra-large bowl for your mixer, or you can make them by hand.

1/2 cup plus 1 tablespoon heavy cream
1 large egg
1 1/3 cups (6 ounces) all-purpose flour, more for rolling
1 cup rolled oats
1 cup dried apricots, chopped (see Note)
3 tablespoons finely grated ginger
3 tablespoons granulated sugar
2 1/4 teaspoons baking powder
1/2 teaspoon kosher salt
Finely grated zest of 1 large orange
4 tablespoons (2 ounces) cold unsalted butter, cut into 1/2-inch pieces
1 1/2 tablespoons turbinado sugar, for sprinkling

Position a rack in the center of the oven and heat to 400°F. Line a large rimmed baking sheet with parchment or a nonstick liner.

In a small bowl, whisk together 1/2 cup of the cream and the egg and set aside.

In the bowl of a stand mixer fitted with a paddle attachment, combine the flour, oats, apricots, ginger, granulated sugar, baking powder, salt, and orange zest. Mix just to blend.

Add the butter and mix on medium-low speed until the butter is the size of small peas, about 1 minute. Add the cream mixture and mix on low speed just until it comes together in a ball, about 15 seconds. (To make by hand, whisk together the dry ingredients in a large bowl, use a pastry blender or two knives to cut in the butter, and stir in the cream.)

continued on page 264

Grilled Bread Salad with Tomatoes and Parmigiano, *continued*

Turn the dough out onto a lightly floured surface (it will be fairly sticky) and shape into a disk about 7 inches across. Cut the disk into 8 wedges (for the cleanest cuts, wipe off your knife between cuts), brush with the remaining 1 tablespoon cream, and sprinkle with the turbinado sugar. Transfer to the baking sheet, keeping the scones at least 1 inch apart.

Bake for 15 minutes, then lower the heat to 350°F. Bake until the scones are just set and golden brown, 10 to 15 minutes longer.

Cool on a rack until warm or room temperature. Scones are best eaten the day they're made.

Note: California dried apricots produce the best results, as they are more intensely flavored and a bit more acidic than the Turkish variety.

Tip: Once you make and shape the dough, you can keep it for a couple of weeks in the refrigerator as long as it's well wrapped.

Cornmeal Biscotti with Cranberries and Pistachios
MAKES ABOUT 18 BISCOTTI

These green-and-red-studded biscotti look vaguely Christmassy but are good any time of year. Feel free to swap in other nuts or dried fruit—this combo is particularly pretty but you could use golden raisins, almonds, or hazelnuts as well. To make the biscotti even more decadent, dip in melted chocolate.

2²/₃ cups (12 ounces) all-purpose flour, more for rolling
1¹/₂ teaspoons baking powder
¹/₂ teaspoon kosher salt
1¹/₄ cups granulated sugar
8 tablespoons (4 ounces) unsalted butter, at room temperature
2 large eggs, plus 1 lightly beaten egg for brushing

³/₄ cup shelled pistachios, lightly toasted
¹/₂ cup dried cranberries
Finely grated zest of 2 large oranges
3 tablespoons medium-grind cornmeal
2 tablespoons turbinado sugar, for sprinkling

Position a rack in the center of the oven and heat to 350°F. Line a large rimmed baking sheet with parchment or a nonstick liner.

In a medium bowl, whisk together the flour, baking powder, and salt and set aside.

In the bowl of a stand mixer fitted with a paddle attachment, combine the granulated sugar and butter. Mix on medium-high speed until light and fluffy, about 2 minutes. With the motor running, add the 2 whole eggs one at a time, blending thoroughly after each addition.

Scrape down the sides of the bowl, add the pistachios, cranberries, and orange zest, and mix on low speed until blended. Add the cornmeal and mix again to blend. Add the reserved flour mixture and mix on low speed just until the dough comes together in a ball, about 20 seconds.

Turn the dough out onto a lightly floured surface and roll into a log about 12 inches long. Transfer to the baking sheet and press to flatten the log to a 1-inch thickness. Brush with the beaten egg and sprinkle with the turbinado sugar.

Bake until the log is just firm to the touch, about 50 minutes. Let cool for 20 minutes, then use a serrated knife to slice the log diagonally at ³/₄-inch intervals. (The slices may look a little underdone at the center, which is okay.)

Arrange the slices on the baking sheet and bake for 10 minutes. Carefully flip the biscotti over, return to the oven, and bake until lightly toasted, about 10 minutes longer. They will still be somewhat soft but will harden as they cool.

Cool on a rack. Stored in an airtight container, these biscotti will keep for at least a week.

Bread and Butter and Salt

SERVES YOU WELL

You'd think that a recipe for bread and butter and salt would be unnecessary. But I truly believe that one of life's greatest eating pleasures consists of a loaf of wonderful crusty bread, sweet butter or olive oil, and salt. Those three components, eaten with your hands and shared among friends, truly is a sustaining combination. The country loaf from Tartine is pictured below.

A loaf of good crusty bread
Unsalted butter from pasture-raised cows, barely cool or at room temperature
Plain ol' kosher or a fancy kind of salt

Rip a hunk of bread off the loaf (use a knife if you must, but I swear it tastes better if you tear it). Smear the bread with some butter—be generous—and sprinkle with salt. Eat recklessly, and pay no attention to the inevitable crumbs (unless you want to eat them, which is even better).

If you like, gild the lily with boquerones (marinated Spanish anchovies) or thin-sliced dry-cured ham.

Challah

MAKES TWO 1-POUND BRAIDS

———

This challah has so many things going for it: the dough is very easy to work with, the braids are gorgeous, and the fine-crumbed texture is to die for. There's just a little sugar in this egg-rich dough, which means it works just as well for sandwiches as well as for bread pudding. My favorite use is in French toast!

You might want to save this recipe for a weekend, because the first step requires an overnight rest in the refrigerator—it takes a little longer but gives the bread a more complex flavor.

SPONGE
3/4 cup warm water (about 100°F)
1/4 ounce (2 1/4 teaspoons) active dry yeast
3/4 cup plus 2 tablespoons (4 ounces) all-purpose flour
1/2 teaspoon sugar

DOUGH
4 cups (1 pound 2 ounces) all-purpose flour, more as needed
1/4 cup plus 1 tablespoon sugar
3 tablespoons grapeseed or other neutral oil, plus more for the bowl
2 1/4 teaspoons kosher salt
3 large whole eggs
2 large egg yolks (save the whites for the garnish)

GARNISH
1 or 2 egg whites, lightly beaten
1/4 cup poppy or sesame seeds (optional)

Day 1, make the sponge:

In a medium bowl, whisk together the water and yeast. Add the flour and sugar and mix until just combined. Cover the bowl loosely with plastic wrap and refrigerate overnight; the next day, the sponge should be bubbly and doubled in size.

Day 2, make the dough:

Put the sponge in the bowl of a stand mixer fitted with a dough hook. Add the remaining dough ingredients and mix on low speed until smooth and elastic, about 10 minutes. (The dough should clean the sides of the bowl after a couple of minutes; if it clings to the sides, add a tablespoon or two of flour.)

Coat the inside of a large bowl with oil. Shape the dough into a ball and transfer to the bowl, turning it a couple of times to coat. Cover with plastic wrap and put the bowl in a warm, draft-free place. Let rise until doubled in size, about 1 1/2 hours.

To make the braids and garnish:

Punch down the dough and turn out onto a lightly floured surface. Divide the dough into 8 equal pieces (about 4 1/2 ounces each) and using a light touch, roll each piece into a very loose ball. Cover the balls with plastic wrap to keep them from drying out. Take out one ball and roll into a 9-inch-long rope, tapering the ends slightly. Re-cover with plastic wrap and roll out the remaining balls in the same way.

Line a large rimmed baking sheet with parchment or a nonstick liner. Braid the ropes as follows. As you reposition each rope, pull very gently to elongate it slightly.

1. Take out 4 of the ropes and press them together at one end.
2. Take the first (far left) rope, cross over the middle, and put down between the third and fourth ropes.
3. Take the fourth (far right) rope, cross over the middle two, and put down between what are now the first and second ropes.
4. Then cross the middle two ropes over each other, right over left.
5. Repeat the process and continue until you reach the end. Pinch each end to seal and tuck under.

Repeat with the remaining 4 ropes. Place the braids on the lined baking sheet and cover loosely with plastic wrap. Let rise in a warm place until doubled in size, at least 1 hour.

Meanwhile, position a rack in the center of the oven and heat to 375°F.

When the braids have finished rising, brush with the reserved egg whites and sprinkle with the poppy or sesame seeds.

Bake the braids for 10 minutes, then lower the heat to 350°F. Continue to bake until the crust is dark golden brown and it sounds hollow when you tap the bottom of the loaf, 15 to 17 minutes longer. (Rotate the pan if the browning seems uneven.)

Let cool completely on a rack.

The Bakery: Bread and Baked Goods

9

WINE AND BEER

When I'm considering whether to add a particular wine to our assortment, I first taste it (standard practice for any good wine buyer). I then look for how the wine is made and cared for. I look at the vineyard, because that's where the wine starts. If you're not taking care of the vineyards, you're not making good wine. I also look at the winemaker: their philosophy of making wine, whether they're using native yeasts, and whether they have their own unique style.

With guests, the question I ask most often is, "What are you making for dinner?" And then I'll literally look in their shopping basket to see what they're buying. The answers really help me make solid, relevant recommendations.

—Trac Le, wine buyer

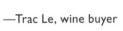

"Food without wine is a corpse; wine without food is a ghost; united and well matched they are as body and soul, living partners."

—André Simon (1877–1970)

SIMON'S QUOTATION HANGS ABOVE our wine section, and I think it sums up all that's important about wine. To me, wine and food are each wonderful on their own, but together they add up to so much more than the sum of their parts. And wine and cuisine are both powerful expressions of place. Every bottle tells a story about the person making it, the soil it was grown in, the weather during the growing season and harvest, and the food and culture that it evolved alongside.

I didn't realize how important culture was to wine until I took a wine tasting trip through Italy. When we arrived at the Azienda Agricola San Quirico in the historic Tuscan town of San Gimigniano, our noses were greeted by terra-cotta pots filled with the most fragrant basil I had ever encountered. After a tour of the property and family stories, we were invited to a classic Tuscan meal: linguine with garlic, tomatoes, scampi, and that fragrant basil, carefully dressed in the estate's own olive oil. As I alternated sips of the local wine with bites of pasta, a light went off in my head: food and wine evolve together. People make wine to go with their food and vice versa.

Up to that point, I was constantly trying to come up with dishes that matched a specific wine, or to find a wine that would work with a particular dish. But with this one meal, I realized that all I had to do was trace a wine back to the region it came from. Voilà! Pairing practically took care of itself.

When I came back to the Market, I found myself talking about wine in a new way. I wanted our guests to see wine as an inexpensive way to visit a foreign land, right at the dinner table. It's cheaper than a plane ticket.

WHERE TO GO FOR WINE

There is a *lot* of wine in the world. Some of it is terrible, some of it is incredible, and most falls somewhere in between. There's no shortage of choices as you shop for wine, which can be good, but it easily becomes overwhelming.

Rather than get bogged down by decoding labels and memorizing vintages or relying on subjective point systems, I propose a much simpler and much more rewarding approach. The key is to build a relationship with a top-notch wine retailer you trust who will help you bypass the dreck and home in on wine that you will enjoy.

This is an iterative process. It takes a little research and trial and error to find such a shop, but it's an investment of time that will pay off in the long run. The more often you go, the more the staff there will learn about your tastes. They'll start to make informed suggestions for you, and before long it'll be as if you have your very own personal wine shopper.

You are probably not going to find this person in a grocery store.

This may not even be an option, depending on where you live; in some states or areas, you may have no choice but to buy from a state-run operation or from a supermarket. No matter where you go, a well-curated selection and helpful staff are what you should be looking for. **THE IDEAL IS SHOPPING AT AN INDEPENDENTLY OWNED STORE THAT SPECIALIZES IN WINE AND SPIRITS** or a supermarket with an in-house buyer who makes decisions based on their guests' desires rather than a corporate schematic. It's your best bet for getting a great selection and personalized service. Start by Googling "wine shop" for your city or town, maybe read a few Yelp reviews, and then go check a few of them out. Keep trying until you find one you like, as you may not find "the one" right away. Think of it as interviewing candidates for a job—the job, of course, being to get your business.

Sometimes the shops that are frequented by wine collectors or known for their "cult" wines are not the best for those just starting to explore—nor are they always budget-friendly. I prefer shops that cater to more than just wine geeks, but nonetheless offer well-curated selections and an intimate environment.

Start your "interview" by taking a look around the shop, asking yourself these questions:

- **Is there someone to talk to?** A good wine shop will have plenty of staff people eager to help you. Even better if they approach you first and ask if you need help finding anything.
- **What's the signage like?** The more signage on individual wines, the better. It shows that the shop is trying to make the wines accessible, and it makes the shopping process less intimidating. A closer look will tell you even more: are the signs copied and pasted from the winery's website, or are they written by the shop's staff? Look for handmade signs that not only tell you what the wine tastes like but also convey some emotion or excitement about the wine.

EAT GOOD FOOD

If you see lots of Parker (or other reviewer) ratings, dig deeper. Although the points mean *something*, it's still a highly subjective system that favors a single "ideal" wine profile—not the only factor to consider.

- **See anything you recognize?** If the shop has giant displays of Yellow Tail front and center, there's still a chance they have some good wines back there. But it is a sign that they're emphasizing mass-produced, low-cost wines and may not be so interested in unique wines from smaller producers—the kind that tell a story. (The mass-produced wines are adulterated, acidified, and manipulated to taste the same year after year. The only story they tell is of the science lab they're crafted in.)
- **How is the wine stored and cared for?** People who take care of their stores also take care of their wine. Dusty bottles or bottles displayed in direct sunlight do not bode well. Clean bottles and shelves protected from light are good signs; even better if some of the bottles are stored on their sides (especially important for older wines, as this helps keep the corks from drying out).

NEXT, FIND A STAFF PERSON AND STRIKE UP A CONVERSATION. This is your chance to gauge the knowledge and passion of the people working there. It's also your first opportunity to start building that rapport. You can start the conversation in one of two ways:

IF YOU'RE SHOPPING FOR A SPECIFIC TYPE OF WINE OR OCCASION, DESCRIBE THE PARAMETERS. Something as simple as "I'm going to a dinner party and I offered to bring a bottle" will do. A good salesperson will probe you for these details before showing you a single bottle:

- **What kind of wines do you like?** This shows a sincere desire to match a wine to you, and not the opposite. If you don't know what you like, or if you have a hard time describing it, just do the best you can. Remember: it's the salesperson's job to listen and guide you through the process.
- **How much are you looking to spend?** $15 will buy you a great bottle of wine. But so will $50 or

$500. There's good wine in every price range, so let your budget be the starting point, and don't be shy about it. Great salespeople won't hesitate to tell you about a great $18 bottle even if you're willing to spend $30. Why? It shows that they're most interested in finding a wine you'll like, rather than selling you the most expensive wine they can.

Certain types of wine are always more expensive because of the time and materials required to make them (oak-aged California Cabernets are a great example). But if you're on a budget, consider offbeat varietals or wines from undervalued regions, which offer comparable characteristics at a much friendlier price point. See the table on page 275 for suggestions.

- **Will you serve this with food? What kind?** If you know what's being served, great—the clerk should find something that will pair well with the food. But if you don't know, the clerk should still be able to find a flexible, food-friendly wine or two.

IF YOU'RE GAME FOR ANYTHING, TURN THE TABLES. Ask the clerk what *her* favorite wine is at the moment, and pay attention to the enthusiasm with which she responds. If she's really into wine, she'll probably say she can't narrow it down to just one! This is a great way to discover unique and interesting wines that you might not otherwise consider.

ONCE YOU'VE NARROWED THE OPTIONS DOWN TO A FEW BOTTLES, LISTEN TO THE WAY THE STAFF PERSON DESCRIBES EACH OF THEM. Does he sound excited? Is he speaking in plain English or throwing around a bunch of wine lingo just to sound smart? This gives you clues about the store's (and the staff's) passion for wine, their knowledge about it, and their ability to communicate. Don't put up with snobbishness, attitude, or pressure; it has to feel right if you are going to have fun in the process.

DON'T FORGET TO ASK THE OBVIOUS: "HAVE YOU TASTED IT?" It might sound silly, but this is actually one of the most important questions to ask. It not only gets you closer to understanding what a wine is really like, but it can also be telling about the store itself. A good wine shop encourages—even requires—their staff to taste new wines as they come in: not just to know the product better and exercise their palates, but also to make sure the wines taste good and fit the profile of what their guests like. (If you get the impression that the clerk has tried only a few of the store's holdings, you might want to go elsewhere.)

Another great reason to ask if the clerk has tasted it? Her description might be based on something she read, or she may simply be describing general characteristics (things that would be true for *all* Oregon Pinots, for instance). There's no substitute for a firsthand tasting experience; if you just wanted tasting notes, you could look them up on the Internet.

Many of these pointers will help guide you through a restaurant's wine list as well.

Take notes, especially for wines you really like or dislike, so you can use that information the next time you shop. Write down the importer's name if there is one, the region the wine came from, the grapes or blend used—whatever you feel it was about the wine that you enjoyed (or didn't enjoy). Be sure to take note of wines you try at restaurants as well. With this basic information, you can ask your retailer if they have it or can get it. Plus, the more you taste and the more conscious you are when tasting, the better your palate will get and the more fun drinking wine will be.

WHAT TO BUY

Once you have your "go-to" wine source picked out, the rest is easy—you have folks ready and willing to help you find appropriate wines for any occasion. Of course, there's more to wine than what it costs and what it tastes like; where it came from, how it was made, and who made it are also important considerations.

NEAR AND FAR: HOW DIFFERENT THEY ARE. You could take cuttings from a single grape vine, plant them in opposite ends of the world, and get two completely different wines. Even if the winemaking methods were exactly the same, the simple fact that *place has a taste* makes the two otherwise identically made wines notably and inarguably different from one another. That, friends, is *terroir,* and is one of the things that makes wine so special.

PASSION, AND A GOOD STORY, COUNT FOR A LOT. As with cheese, the *terroir* of wine poses a challenge when you're trying to support local producers. As passionate as I am about local foods and local wines, there is something magical and very special about traditional wines made in Europe.

But whether you decide to stick with local wine or go farther afield, seek out wine that has a story behind it. The wine might be produced by a four-hundred-year-old, family-run winery; it might be a renegade winemaker who studied with the biggest producer in France and later struck out to make unique, niche wines in small batches; or it might be your neighbor who quietly makes wine in a nondescript warehouse on the edge of the city. They're all making the wine because they love it, and they're doing it in their own way. That's worth supporting.

TECHNIQUE AND INGREDIENTS ALSO MATTER. Even though the overall process of making wine is more or less universal (crush grapes, ferment, filter, and bottle), a winemaker still has quite a bit of latitude as far as specific techniques and philosophies, each of which influences the character of the wine. Here are some to look out for:

- **Sulfites** are a natural byproduct of fermentation, and therefore exist in very small amounts in any wine. Sulfites have preservative properties, so most winemakers choose to add sulfites to further the wine's shelf life and to stabilize the wine's flavors. Some people experience adverse reactions to sulfites, such as headaches; wines labeled "No Added Sulfites" may produce fewer (or no) such side effects.
- **Organic** wines are not only made from organic grapes but also must be made without added sulfites. (This is true only for 100-percent certified-organic wines. A wine labeled "Made with Organic Grapes" may have added sulfites.)
- **Vegan/vegetarian** wines are labeled as such not because of the bottle's contents, but because of the materials used in processing. (Most wines are fined through animal byproducts such as egg whites or gelatin.) "Vegan" or "vegetarian" wines use alternative materials that are not derived from animals.
- **Wild (or "native") yeast** wines are the wine equivalent of sourdough bread. The vast majority of winemakers—both large and small—rely on commercially produced yeast for fermenting the grape juice. This provides consistency in strength, quantity, and strains of yeast used, which in turn results

in a more consistent product. However, a small but passionate constituency of winemakers relies solely on yeasts that occur naturally in the air. These wines are more difficult to pull off successfully, but the wild yeast produces wine that tastes more directly of the time and place where it was made.

- **Natural wines** are made with as little manipulation (technological or otherwise) as possible. That generally means relying on wild yeast, adding sulfites only when absolutely necessary, and not filtering or fining the wine. This approach requires a great deal more skill—and luck—on the part of the winemaker, and the resulting wines are undeniably more interesting than any commercially made wine. The wines may also be more volatile and can have a shorter shelf life as a result. Buy them and drink them right away, unless you know they are ageworthy!
- **Biodynamic** refers to a farming philosophy that emphasizes farmland as a living ecosystem. It makes use of prescribed homeopathic techniques

and incorporates cosmic rhythms (such as the phase of the moon) into its approach. Biodynamic wines are often also organic and/or made with native yeast. Although biodynamic certification is offered through the Demeter organization, the use of the term itself is not regulated.

- **Kosher** wines are made under the strict supervision of a rabbi and are typically flash-pasteurized (either as juice or in the finished product). Kosher wines have come a long way from Manischevitz; nowadays there are lots of good seder options out there.

• •

Take advantage of tastings. Many wine shops regularly conduct tasting events for the public. They're often free, and because they're usually organized around a specific grape or region, it's a good way to explore within a category. And if you're new to wine or have a hard time describing the wines you like, it's an easy way to get more experience and learn the lingo.

• •

Follow the importers. Wine importers tend to specialize not just in specific regions but also in wines that fit within a specific profile of flavor and body. So when you find a non-American wine you really like, take note of the importer (it's usually listed on the back label). The next time you go wine shopping, ask the clerk what else they have from the same importer. In this way, you'll discover other wines that you'll probably enjoy. Here are a few of the importers I trust implicitly: Kermit Lynch, Louis/Dressner, Rosenthal Wine Merchants, Robert Chatterdon, and Terry Theise.

• •

AT THE VERY LEAST, LOOK FOR WINES THAT ARE:

- **Local or have a good story (or both)**
- **Made by passionate people**
- **A reflection of where they came from**

IDEALLY, LOOK FOR WINES WITH:

- **Other unique characteristics (like natural or biodynamic)**

HOW TO ENJOY WINE

Although I taste wine three or four times a week at the store, I still don't consider myself a wine expert. Whenever I go to a tasting or meet a winemaker, I realize that there's so much more to learn; besides, great wines start in the vineyard and every year's harvest produces different results. Wine is a constantly moving target.

RESIST THE TEMPTATION TO TRY TO "CONQUER" WINE. It's an impossible task, and this unachievable goal actually makes drinking wine *less* rewarding. So liberate yourself from any overachiever tendencies. Remember that pleasure is the objective. And anybody, from novices to supertasters to winemakers themselves, is perfectly qualified for that.

THE FIVE STEPS OF TASTING. Drinking wine and tasting wine are two different endeavors. Everyone knows how to drink; you lift your glass, take a sip, and swallow. But *tasting* wine is more studied and conscious. It's a rewarding process, because it uncovers subtleties that might not be obvious with a regular "drinking" sip. Here's how:

1. **Swirl**—This aerates the wine's volatile compounds and fills the glass so you can smell them. For best results, fill your glass no more than one-quarter to one-third full; it prevents spills and ensures plenty of room for the wine vapor to collect.
2. **Sniff**—Put your nose right into the glass and take a few short whiffs. "Listen" to your nose. What do you notice? How would you describe it? Sniff some more. (Remember, much of what you taste is through your nose.)
3. **Sip**—Take a bit of wine into your mouth and slurp some air in at the same time. Don't worry about being gauche; this is what the pros do. It aerates flavor molecules and sends them to the back of your nose, where your brain picks up and processes them. (Don't swallow yet!)
4. **Swish**—Move the wine around in your mouth. This not only gives all of your taste buds an equal chance to taste the wine, but also alerts you to the wine's viscosity or "body." Then either swallow the wine or spit it out if you prefer.

THE UNDERDOGS:
GRAPES AND REGIONS YOU SHOULD KNOW

The world of wine is a bit of a popularity contest: the best-known grapes and regions are also the most expensive. Whether you're limited by your wallet or just want to drink something new, consider trying one of these underappreciated wines.

GRAPE VARIETALS

White

- **Chenin Blanc**—One of the signature grapes of France's Loire region, Chenin Blanc is also the key to many excellent South African wines. It can be made into dry or sweet wines and is an exceptionally food-friendly grape.

- **Grüner Veltliner**—Its crisp minerality and good acidity make this Austrian standard one of the most versatile food wines there is, especially for Asian and spicy foods.

- **Kerner, Müller-Thurgau, and other grapes of northeast Italy**—These wines can be incredibly complex and aromatic and are amazing food companions. These and many other wines from indigenous grapes from the Alto Adige are often great values.

Red

- **Gamay**—Most famous as the grape of Beaujoulais Nouveau, but don't hold that against Gamay. These wines, although unabashedly fruity, can still be complex and intriguing. Look for wines from Morgon, Fleurie, Beaujolais, and Moulin-à-Vent.

- **Cabernet Franc**—This underappreciated grape can exhibit a range of personalities, from light, soft, and herbal to big-bodied and robust. Cabernet Franc from the Loire regions of Chinon and Bourgueil are some of my favorites.

- **Nebbiolo**—Considered a noble grape in Italy, Nebbiolos don't get much play Stateside. Versatile enough to make delicate or muscular wines, they have robust tannins that give them substantial aging power. Nebbiolos need food and are especially wonderful with salumi. The Barolo region of Piedmont is the most famous site for these wines.

REGIONS

- **Loire**—This region, although one of the most famous in France, is more or less ignored by the American wine press. The Loire is a leader in making biodynamic and organic wines and has a longstanding tradition of light- and medium-bodied, food-friendly wines.

- **Sicily**—Sicily's volcanic soil produces many high-quality wines in a wide array of styles. Nero d'Avola, the region's most famous grape, makes a very versatile, easy-drinking wine.

- **Portugal**—Like its neighbor Spain, Portugal gives you a lot of bang for your wine-buying buck. It was formerly known solely for its fortified (port) wines, but importers are starting to recognize the values to be had here.

- **Central Europe**—There are some fun and very interesting wines coming out of this area, particularly Slovenia, Hungary, Bulgaria, and Greece. They tend toward the light- and medium-body profile and are often good values and very food-friendly.

- **Lebanon**—It's perhaps the most unexpected country in this lineup, but Lebanon produces some extraordinary wines at extraordinarily low prices for the quality.

- **Southern Hemisphere**—There are tremendous values to be found in wines from New Zealand (especially Riesling and Pinot Noir), Australia (Shiraz), Argentina (Malbec), Chile (Carmenere), and South Africa (Chenin Blanc and Pinotage).

- **American wine regions**—In California, look for wines from Mendocino, the Central Coast, and Sonoma. Oregon, New York, and Washington wines can also be a great value, with many varietals and styles to choose from.

5. Stop—It's only after the wine leaves your mouth that many of the flavors surface, so pay attention! Pause for a few seconds and take it all in. Notice how the flavors evolve on your palate, and how long they last (this is known as the wine's "finish.") Then, and only then, should you go for another taste, following the same steps.

WHAT TO DRINK WITH WHAT. People talk about pairing wine and food as if there are hard and fast rules that should be followed. In fact, wine and food can be paired together in many more ways than most people imagine. (Believe it or not, some lighter reds *do* go nicely with fish!) There is no right or wrong choice. Be less concerned about pairing your wine with food; concentrate on enjoying, experimenting, and exploring new wines. This is the only way you will learn to make wine part of your daily life.

Instead of strict rules, I prefer to work within a few guidelines that leave room to be creative and have fun. They're all oriented around a single premise:

Trac tasting with Eric Cohen of Shoe Shine Wine

THE WINE AND FOOD SHOULD COMPLEMENT EACH OTHER WITHOUT ONE DOMINATING. If you consider the following six components of any wine, you'll have no problem making good matches:

- **Acid**—High-acidity wines are more food-friendly because they stand up to food and cut through rich flavors. Conversely, low-acid wines tend to become diminished in flavor or fall flat with food. High acidity can be the product of less-ripe (lower-sugar) grapes, a cooler climate, or a specific grape varietal.

- **Oak**—After fermentation and before bottling, most wines are aged, which allows the flavors to mellow and meld. Some wines are aged in brand-new oak barrels and will take on flavors of the wood itself (often described as vanilla, butterscotch, or buttery). These oak-heavy wines tend to overshadow many foods. The most food-friendly wines are ones in which oak is used minimally (either with a short aging time or using previously used barrels) or not at all, such as those aged in stainless steel or cement tanks.

- **Tannins**—If you've ever had one of those "big" California Cabernet Sauvignons that makes the inside of your mouth feel like a sweater, you've experienced tannins. These chemical compounds act as a natural preservative and can come from grape skins themselves or as a result of extended aging in oak. Tannins give wine a certain robust flavor and mouthfeel that can be overwhelming when you taste the wine on its own. However, fatty foods and tannic wines are made for one another; the tannins cut through the richness, and the fat smoothes out tannins' bracing qualities. (Try eating some salami next time you are tasting a tannic wine and see what a bit of fat in your mouth will do to the experience.) Tannins also give wines structure for aging, as they mellow out over time.

- **Sweetness**—Spicy foods tend to accentuate the alcohol in wine, making the wines taste "hot" or harsh. A slightly sweet (or "off-dry") wine mitigates this effect. German Rieslings and Loire Chenin Blancs are good examples of grapes that can maintain great acidity while providing a touch of sweetness. Just make sure you are not buying a dessert wine (unless that's what you're after).

- **Alcohol**—For the last few decades, American winemakers have produced wines with higher and higher alcohol levels—from 14.5 percent to 16 percent alcohol by volume. These high-octane wines not only overpower most foods but also get you drunk and leave you with a screaming headache in the morning. Thankfully, more and more producers are going back to making wines with lower alcohol (around 12 to 13.5 percent), which are much more food-friendly.

- **Body**—Also referred to as a wine's "weight" or "mouthfeel," this is another component of a wine's overall intensity. Lighter-bodied wines are usually better paired with delicately flavored foods, which is why fish and white wine are so often an amiable match. Conversely, richer foods are better able to stand up to fuller-bodied wines and are typically good pairings.

How to Store

Careless storage can ruin a bottle of wine, but it takes only a few simple tricks to keep wine in optimal condition. Store bottles on their side, which keeps the cork moist and ensures a good seal. You don't need to invest

COOKING WITH WINE

If you have a recipe that calls for wine, do not feel bad about using an everyday-caliber wine. You could dip into your special-occasion stash, but the nuances will be lost in the final product, so you're pretty much wasting your money. On the other hand, swill will taste like swill whether you cook with it or not! Just use something that's good enough to drink on its own and is within the parameters of the recipe (a "light-bodied red," or whatever it is). Think of Julia Child: a glass of wine in one hand, a knife in the other, and the open bottle handy to add to a dish as needed.

For extra credit, buy a second bottle of a wine you intend to cook with, and serve the wine alongside the meal. It'll be a match made in heaven.

PUT A CORK IN IT

As you buy and enjoy wine, it's inevitable that you'll eventually encounter a bottle with the dreaded cork taint. This happens when the cork becomes contaminated by a harmless but unsavory chemical, which in turn makes the wine taste (actually, smell) like a wet dog or moldy cardboard. It's unfortunate, and can be disappointing, but it does happen. (It's nobody's fault—how and when it happens is still somewhat of a mystery.)

If you think your wine is "corked," you should absolutely return it to the shop where you bought it. Any good shop will exchange the bottle for another one. Don't drink it all (more than likely, you won't want to anyway); give the shop a chance to taste it for themselves.

in a specialized wine cooler, but do keep your wine in a cool place and away from light. Basements naturally feature both qualities, and by storing your wine there you're automatically qualified to call it a "wine cellar." If you want to store wine in the kitchen, try to find the coolest spot. Above the refrigerator is usually the worst place because it tends to be quite warm and is likely to cook the wine.

If you have unfinished bottles, simply recork and store in the fridge for up to a day or so. Beyond that, the wine will have lost most of its unique flavor.

Break out of your habits. The wine world is so vast that you could drink a different wine every day for the rest of your life and never have the same wine twice. And though it's great to have a reliable, go-to everyday wine, life's too short to drink the same wine over and over. Seize every opportunity to try something new. Still, there's something to be said for buying several bottles of the same wine and drinking them over a long period of time, because you can taste the evolution of the wine's characteristics from year to year. Keep a journal and record your tasting notes. It's a great way to learn and get even more excited about drinking wine. Besides, most wine shops offer discounts for purchases of six or twelve bottles, so take advantage of it.

BEER

No matter where you live, you're likely to have at least one small-scale brewery nearby. Even in its earliest days, the United States boasted a plethora of local and regional beer producers, making the beverage landscape incredibly diverse. In the years following Prohibition, however, a handful of monolithic breweries began to dominate the market; not only did most small producers go out of business, but the variety of beers available became extremely limited, as well. The big breweries takeover was so successful that by the 1960s, Anchor Brewing in San Francisco was the only craft brewery left in the United States.

Thankfully, a lot has changed since then! Americans have developed a renewed interest in unique, small-batch beers, and there are now more than 1,600 craft breweries in the United States, making many times that number in individual varieties and styles of beer.

How to Buy

What is "craft" beer, exactly? The Brewers Association, an industry group, considers any brewery producing fewer than two million barrels of beer annually to be a craft brewery. That might sound like a lot, until you consider that Anheuser-Busch produces about 150 million barrels a year.

IT'S ALWAYS GREAT TO SUPPORT SMALLER PRODUCERS, BUT THERE'S AN EVEN BETTER REASON TO DRINK CRAFT BEER: INTERESTING, UNIQUE, AND OFTEN AMAZING TASTE. Craft brewers, as a group, are incredibly passionate and creative people. They get excited about recreating ancient beer recipes, perfecting the classics, and coming up with new styles altogether. Craft brewers have been known to put cardamom and cloudberries in their brews, age them in barrels made of exotic wood, and rely on wild yeasts for their fermentation.

Craft beers are often made with significantly more grain and hops than industrial beers—one reason why they are more expensive. In fact, some ultra-desirable beers fetch prices as high as fine wines! Still, most craft beers remain well within most folks' everyday budgets.

Knowing how beer is made helps demystify and differentiate the main categories of beer. Most beers, from Bud to monk-made Belgian beers, are made using the same basic steps and ingredients:

1. **Malt** (barley that has been sprouted and dried) or other grains are mixed with hot water to make a sort of tea called "wort." The malt (or other grains) is what gives the beer its underlying flavor and body.
2. **Hops,** which act as a natural preservative and lend aroma and bitterness to the beer, are added to the wort. The mixture is boiled for a period, and then brewer's yeast is added to kick off the fermentation process.
3. **When fermentation is complete**, the beer rests to fully develop the flavors, undergoes recarbonation, and gets bottled (but not always in that order).

Fresh hops are a highly perishable ingredient—so much so that they must be brewed immediately upon picking—which is why most beer is made from dried hops. Dried hops certainly get the job done, but they're undeniably different from fresh ones; think of the flavor difference between fresh sage and dried in a soup or roast, and you get the idea. A handful of breweries have taken on the challenge of using fresh hops, which requires them to grow the hops themselves or develop very close relationships with hops farmers.

Bottle conditioned beers are those that undergo their final stages of fermentation in the bottle, rather than in the tank. This technique gives the beer a boost of natural carbonation, as well as a full body and rich flavor.

Beers fall into two main categories: lagers and ales.

LAGERS are made from a class of yeasts that have adapted to cold temperatures. Most mass-market beers are lagers: they're light in body and color and relatively low in alcohol. PILSNERS are the most famous of lagers, hailing from the Czech Republic. They're mild, smooth, and crisp.

ALES encompass a diverse and sweeping array of styles. Compared to lagers, they tend to be fuller-bodied, more intensely flavored, and higher in alcohol (sometimes significantly so). **WITBIERS (OR WHITE BEERS)** originated in Belgium and northern France. They are made with unmalted wheat along with aromatics and spices; the resulting beer is whitish and cloudy and has a unique, light bitterness. **HEFEWEIZENS (OR WHEAT BEERS)** are a German-style beer featuring a hefty dose of malted wheat. The medium-bodied, cloudy beers often feature citrusy notes. **BELGIAN ALES**, a whole category in themselves, are usually medium-bodied and incredibly fruity and floral in flavor. Most notable is **SAISON**, a style that traditionally uses wild yeasts for its fermentation. **BROWN ALES** are an English style made from toasted or roasted malts, giving them their characteristic nutty flavor. **PORTERS AND STOUTS** take brown ales a step further, with even darker color, richer flavor, and fuller body. Guinness is the world's most recognized stout. **PALE ALES (OR INDIA PALE ALES OR IPAS)** are characterized by their predominant hoppy bitter flavor. Originally developed for their extended shelf life (thanks to the preservative effect of the extra hops), they've become a favorite among craft beer aficionados. IPAs vary greatly in their degrees of bitterness.

· ·

Many beer labels, especially on IPAs, list a rating for International Bittering Units score. This score measures the alpha acid in a beer (which comes from hops) and indicates the beer's hoppiness. Beers with IBUs of less than 20 have very little (or no) hoppy bitterness. Most beers fall into the next range or 20 to 45 IBUs and have mild to pronounced hoppiness. Beers with an IBU of 45 or higher have a great deal of bitter hoppiness. Interestingly, *perception* of hoppiness is subjective and influenced by the sweetness contributed by the beer's malt, so the IBU rating doesn't always map directly to how bitter a beer will taste to you.

· ·

FINALLY, A WORD ON PACKAGING: DON'T SHUN A BEER JUST BECAUSE IT COMES IN A CAN. Once relegated to the cheapest of swills, cans are now embraced by a handful of artisan brewers. The benefits are many—not only are the cans more durable and cheaper to ship, but they also protect the beer from damaging light—making canned beer a solid choice for the environment as well as for your palate. Just recycle the cans!

How to Store

Although extreme temperature fluctuations aren't ideal for beer, light is actually the bigger threat, so **STORE BEER AWAY FROM DIRECT SUNLIGHT**. (It's for this reason that many beers are bottled in brown glass, which provides much better protection than green or clear glass does.)

How to Use

The most devoted of beer aficionados will tell you that each beer is uniquely suited to a particular shape glass and serving temperature. Although they have a point, **DRINKING IT OUT OF A FRIENDLY PINT GLASS IS HARDLY GOING TO DIMINISH YOUR ENJOYMENT** of a good-quality beer. Still, I find that many beers benefit from being served in a tulip-shaped stemmed glass (such as the kind often used for Chimay, a Belgian ale) or even a wine glass.

· ·

Although I'm a fan of craft beer that comes in a can, I'm not big on drinking it straight out of the can. The taste of the metal comes through too much and dominates over the beer's own flavors. For best results, pour canned beer into a glass before enjoying.

· ·

DO AVOID SERVING BEERS ICE-COLD, though, as this causes a brew's flavors and aromatics to become muted. Many beers, especially darker ones, benefit from slightly warmer than refrigerator temperatures. Some beers have their ideal serving temperature listed on the label; otherwise, experimentation is the way to go. All you have to do is start with a cold one and notice how the flavors evolve as it approaches room temperature.

SAY YES TO

GOOD

FOOD

THREE TIME

A DAY

ONWARD

IT WOULD HAVE BEEN very easy to write a book solely about all the great food available in Northern California. However, the resulting book would have verged on "preaching to the choir," and it probably wouldn't have had much appeal outside of the Bay Area.

I wanted to go beyond that. In my fourteen years of owning Bi-Rite Market, I have learned so much about food, our environment, and our food system (much of it thanks to our enthusiastic and inquisitive guests), that I wanted to share this knowledge with the rest of the country. And so I challenged myself to write a book that would be relevant, interesting, and useful to eaters all across the country. It's my sincere hope that this book will resonate with readers, cooks, and eaters in Peoria, Illinois (where my sister lives), just as much as it will in New York City.

To accomplish this, I took frequent forays outside of my gourmet utopia to consider the realities of how most Americans do their grocery shopping. I visited grocery stores, farmers' markets, and other food retail establishments everywhere I traveled, every chance I got.

Over the eighteen months I spent writing this book, I found myself in the odd position of chasing a moving target, for I discovered that our food landscape is rapidly evolving and—yes!—improving in many ways. More and more grocery stores are carrying pasture eggs. Our farmer population is finally growing again instead of plummeting. CSAs are popping up in the smallest of communities. I discovered independently owned stores throughout the country selling great products, supporting their local economies, and with similar missions to ours: of building communities through food. The more I learned, and the more I wrote, the more hopeful I became about the future of food in America.

However, we cannot simply wait for more change to happen. We cannot rely on retailers or the government to lead the charge in this movement, nor can it be limited to the products we buy and put on our plates. To be truly successful and sustainable, it must be part of a bigger evolution in understanding, appreciating, and celebrating food. It's about nurturing our communities just as much as it is about sustaining ourselves. It's about having a say in how our food system operates, knowing exactly where our food comes from, and caring about how food was produced and by whom. It's about appreciating the hard work that farmers and ranchers put into the food that nourishes us. It's about slowing down, giving thought, and respecting and acknowledging that a person with a face grew this food to share with us. We still don't value food as much as it deserves.

After all, sharing food is one of the most intimate acts we can engage in, and is one of the best means for bringing people together in a meaningful manner. Each of us can make a difference every time we sit down to eat, not just in what we choose to eat, but in how we consume it as well.

Eating responsibly is everyone's responsibility. I hope this book inspires you to:

- Realize how valuable and important food is to sustaining our communities
- Eat less and waste less
- Cook more often and share meals with your family and friends
- Take your kids to a farm so they understand how food is grown
- Ask more questions and demand better products
- Get your hands dirty and experience the joy of growing your own food
- Celebrate food, the people who produce it, and the land it comes from

Most of all . . .
Be spontaneous. Have fun. Share. Give thanks.

RECOMMENDED READING AND RESOURCES

GENERAL GOOD READING

Publications, Blogs, and Radio

Civil Eats: civileats.com

Diner Journal: dinerjournal.com

Edible Communities: ediblecommunities.com

Free Range Studios: freerangestudios.com

Grist: grist.org

Livable Future Blog: livablefutureblog.com

Public Radio Kitchen: publicradiokitchen.org

The Story of Stuff: thestoryofstuff.com

The True Cost of Food Video: sierraclub.org/
truecostoffood/movie.asp

Organizations

ALBA, The Agriculture and Land-Based Training
Association: albafarmers.org

Craft Brew: craftbrew.org

Eat Local Challenge: eatlocalchallenge.com

Food Alliance: foodalliance.org

Food and Water Watch: foodandwaterwatch.org

Organic Consumers: organicconsumers.org

Slow Food USA: slowfoodusa.com

Southern Foodways Alliance: southernfoodways.com

Stone Barns Center: stonebarnscenter.org

SPECIFIC TOPICS

The Food System

Bringing It to the Table: On Farming and Food by Wendell
Berry

Cheap by Ellen Ruppel Shell

*Diet for a Hot Planet: The Climate Crisis at the End of
Your Fork and What You Can Do about It* by Anna
Lappé and Bill McKibben

Ethics of What We Eat: Why Our Food Choices Matter by
Peter Singer and Jim Mason

Fast Food Nation by Eric Schlosser

Food Rules by Michael Pollan

Grub: Ideas for an Urban Organic Kitchen by Anna Lappé
and Bryant Terry

The Omnivore's Dilemma by Michael Pollan

The Rough Guide to Food, UK edition

The Unprejudiced Palate by Angelo Pellegrini

Shopping, Ingredients, and Cooking

GENERAL/MULTIPLE TOPICS

Eating Between the Lines by Kimberly Lord Stewart

Food Lover's Companion by Sharon Taylor Herbst

Food Matters by Mark Bittman

Grub by Anna Lappé and Bryant Terry

How to Cook Everything by Mark Bittman

On Food and Cooking by Harold McGee

What to Eat by Marion Nestle

Zingerman's Guide to Good Eating by Ari Weinzweig

PANTRY

California Olive Oil Council: cooc.com

The New American Olive Oil by Fran Gage

PRODUCE

The Complete Vegetable Book by Clare Connery

Environmental Working Group, publisher of the
"Dirty Dozen" list of most heavily sprayed produce
crops: ewg.org, including the Dirty Dozen list and
app: foodnews.org/walletguide.php

Field Guide to Produce by Aliza Green

The Greenhorns, an organization for and by young
farmers: greenhorns.net

Melissa's Great Book of Produce by Cathy Thomas

BUTCHER AND SEAFOOD

American Grass Fed: www.americangrassfed.org

Animal Welfare Approved: animalwelfareapproved.org

Blue Ocean Institute: blueocean.org

Certified Humane: certifiedhumane.org

Environmental Defense Fund, information on contaminants in fish: edf.org

Environmental Defense Fund's Seafood Selector: oceansalive.org

Ethics of What We Eat: Why Our Food Choices Matter by Peter Singer and Jim Mason

Field Guide to Meat by Aliza Green

Fish Forever by Paul Johnson

FishWise (retail labeling program): sustainablefishery.org

Good Meat by Deborah Krasner

Marine Stewardship Council: msc.org

Monterey Bay Aquarium Seafood Guide: seafoodwatch.org

New England Aquarium: neaq.org

Primal Cuts: Cooking with America's Best Butchers by Marissa Guggiana

Righteous Porkchop by Nicolette Hahn Niman

The River Cottage Meat Book by Hugh Fearnley-Whittingstall

DAIRY AND CHEESE

American Farmstead Cheese by Paul Kindstedt

Atlas of American Artisan Cheese by Jeffrey Roberts

The Cheese Companion by Judy Ridgeway

Cheese Lover's Companion by Sharon Tyler Herbst and Ron Herbst

The Cheese Primer by Steve Jenkins

The New American Cheese by Laura Werlin

The Untold Story of Milk by Ron Schmid

WINE

The Oxford Companion to Wine by Jancis Robinson

Wine Lover's Companion by Ron Herbst

The Natural Process Alliance, an industry organization that sets standards for natural winemaking: naturalprocessalliance.us

WHERE TO BUY

Helpful Resources to Find Local, Sustainable Food

Localharvest, an online resource for finding farms, ranches, farmers' markets, CSAs, and artisan food producers near you: localharvest.org

Eat Well Guide, another resource that also includes restaurants, wholesale vendors, stores, and personal chefs: eatwellguide.org

Eatwild, a nationwide directory of farms that raise their animals on pasture: eatwild.com/products

The Green Guide, which provides information on making green choices in what you eat (and the rest of your life, too): thegreenguide.com

Sustainable Table rBGH-free list, provides information on rBGH-free dairy brands sold in your area: sustainabletable.org/shop/dairymap

Some Favorite Mail-Order Sources

Cowgirl Creamery, for their own as well as other artisanal cheeses: cowgirlcreamery.com

Dean & Deluca, especially good for high-quality olive oils, vinegars, and spices: deandeluca.com

Di Bruno Brothers, purveyors of cured meats, cheeses, oils, and other specialty items: dibruno.com

Foodzie, an online resource for small-batch, artisanal food products: foodzie.com

Formaticum, source for cheese paper: formaticum.com

Heritage Foods USA, mail-order heritage meats, including turkeys and also a great source of information on heirloom ingredients: heritagefoodsusa.com

Kalustyan's, a New York institution known particularly for their spices; they also have a huge array of beans and grains, condiments, pickles, candies, snacks, and other specialty items from near and far: kalustyans.com

Market Hall Foods, where I got my start in specialty food! They are a great resource for just about everything, but especially for olive oils and vinegars, cured and tinned fish, salts, honeys, and unique baking ingredients: markethallfoods.com

Murray's Cheese, one of New York's finest cheese shops, with many cheeses available online: murrayscheese.com

Zingerman's, known far and wide for their high-quality, hard-to-find specialty ingredients: zingermans.com

The Bi-Rite family having fun

THANKS

To **OUR GUESTS**, and all those we "feed," who have been so supportive as we continue to learn how best to serve you. Keep asking questions and keep digging deeper. It's the only way our food systems will change.

For the entire team at Bi-Rite, current, past, and future. You know who you are. All of you who have worked so hard, shared your passions, served our guests so endearingly. You have always believed in the mission, even before we could articulate it. Thank you for being part of our family; Bi-Rite would not be possible without you. Special thanks to Allison Ball, Kirsten Bourne, Kris Hoogerhyde, Trac Le, John Lee, Morgan Maki, Eduardo Martinez, Sergio Martinez, Raphael Mogannam, Chili Montes, Simon Richard, Anthea Stolz, and Anne Walker for their input and help with this book.

To all of our amazing suppliers: without you, we would be selling Twinkies. You all are such great teachers, and so inspiring with your commitments to doing the right thing. We wish we could have included all of you in the book, but then it would have been bigger than the Bible.

Thanks especially to the many producers and businesses who generously spent time with us and allowed us to share their stories:

ALBA farmers
Apple Hill Ranch
Blue Moon Organic Farm
Catalán Farm
Cowgirl Creamery
Devil's Gulch Ranch
Drakes Bay Family Farms
Firebrand Artisan Breads
Full Belly Farm
Gabriel Farm
Katz & Company

Marin Roots Farm
Mariquita Farm
Martin's Farm
McEvoy Ranch Olive Oil
Monterey Fish Market
Napa Valley Lamb
Neil's Yard Dairy
Nielsen-Massey Vanillas
Redwood Hill Farm
Saint Benoît Yogurt
Shoe Shine Wine
Soul Food Farm
Straus Family Creamery
Two Dog Farm

Katherine Cowles, our agent, who guided us, advised us, and most importantly, pushed us to write a book that's far more than just a collection of recipes.

France Ruffenach, for making everything (and everyone) look so good, for capturing the essence of our community and life, for having so much fun during the whole process, and for being so engaged with us. We will never forget you, suited up in a beekeeper's outfit, screaming, but still able to capture our first rooftop honey harvest. Thanks also to George Dolese for your impeccable taste, your brilliant styling ideas, and your endless supply of Q-tips.

The staff of Ten Speed Press, especially Aaron Wehner, Melissa Moore, and Nancy Austin, not just for your faith, but also for entertaining our crazy ideas. Also thanks to Kristin Casemore, Michele Crim, Jenny Fernandez, Kristi Hein, and Karen Levy.

Our fearless recipe testers, whose eager mouths and critical eyes made our recipes ready for the "real world": David Kover, Bruce Cole, Kenneth Berger, Kevin Hogan, Susan Kim, Blake Engel, Deborah Kamali, Elizabeth Gough-Gordon, Erin Kuka, Jacky Hayward, Jean Lider, Julie Kahn, Margaret Shear,

Martha Cheng, Mary Thompson, Matt King, Steve Rich, Susan Reale, and Terril Neely. Also thanks to Chad Robertson at Tartine Bakery, who gave us guidance in this area.

Tiana Kahakauwila, Karen Solomon, and Naomi Starkman for their insight.

Craig Stoll, for sharing his coveted spaghetti recipe, which our testers clamored to try out.

Special thanks to Julie Brothers, Paige Green, and Blair Sneddon for permission to include some of their wonderful images.

To Heather and Becky Chan for designing a timeless logo and their never ending commitment to produce graphic materials that resonate with our mission.

From Sam

My wife, Anne, and my daughters, Zoe and Olive, for always being so supportive and loving, and for putting up with me when I get a wacky idea stuck in my head. I am nothing without you.

My mother, for always inspiring me, for teaching me how to love, and for teaching me that a recipe is whatever you want it to be, that it's something you learn, not follow, and that you just feel your way through it.

My father, who always challenged me to excel and was relentless in turning me into a grocer by the time I was six. You were right; I finally learned to appreciate your wisdom.

My uncle Jack, my dad's partner, for being a teacher and mentor without even realizing it. I learned so much from you and Dad. Thank you.

My brother Sal and sister Freida, my partners in our restaurant, who believed in me and let me run wild, even though I always drove them crazy. Freida, I'll never forget you chasing me up Bush Street, and Sal, I hope you appreciate how important it is not to bruise your lettuce.

My brother Raph, founding partner with me at Bi-Rite, for trusting me and keeping me on point. So glad you are still with me.

I love you all.

Dabney, for pushing me to do this, believing it was a good project, and patiently listening to me go off on tangents, always keeping your focus and eye on what would best serve our reader. This would not have been possible without you and definitely would not have been as fun and fulfilling.

My deepest gratitude also goes to the service team at Bi-Rite for affording me the time to work on this project: Ron De Leon, Chris Fry, Liz Martinez, Patrick Mills, Steffan Morin, and Calvin Tsay.

From Dabney

Thanks first and foremost to Sam, for your willingness to do this project and your instant, unquestioning faith that I was capable of helping you pull it off. Your wisdom, integrity, and generosity come through in everything you do, and you are a constant inspiration to me.

Eternal thanks to Tyler: for being a good eater, for indulging my obsessions, and for convincing me that I could do this.

And of course, to the people who started it all: Mom, for instilling in me an appreciation for the written word, and Dad, for passing on generations of Gough farming knowledge. Thank you.

INDEX

Some of the recipes in this book include raw eggs, meat, or fish. When these foods are consumed raw, there is always the risk that bacteria, which is killed by proper cooking, may be present. For this reason, when serving these foods raw, always buy certified salmonella-free eggs and the freshest meat and fish available from a reliable grocer, storing them in the refrigerator until they are served. Because of the health risks associated with the consumption of bacteria that can be present in raw eggs, meat, and fish, these foods should not be consumed by infants, small children, pregnant women, the elderly, or any persons who may be immuno-compromised.

Published in the United States by Ten Speed Press, an imprint of the Crown Publishing Group, a division of Random House, Inc., New York.
www.crownpublishing.com
www.tenspeed.com

Ten Speed Press and the Ten Speed Press colophon are registered trademarks of Random House, Inc.

All photographs by France Ruffenach with the exception of the following:
Photograph bottom of page 3 courtesy of Julie Brothers
Photograph page 59 courtesy Anne Walker
Photographs pages 4, 67, 255 courtesy Paige Green
Photographs pages 17, 69, 83, 143, 167, 169, 221, 237, 269 courtesy Blair Sneddon

Library of Congress Cataloging-in-Publication Data is on file with the publisher

ISBN 978-1-58008-303-4

Printed in China

Design by Nancy Austin
Food and prop styling by George Dolese

10 9 8 7 6 5 4 3

First Edition

DIG DEEPER.
GOOD FOOD IS EVERYWHERE.